A to Z of

AMERICAN

WOMEN

IN THE

PERFORMING

ARTS

LIZ SONNEBORN

Facts On File, Inc.

A to Z of American Women in the Performing Arts

Copyright © 2002 by Liz Sonneborn

Facts On File, Inc.
132 West 31st Street
New York, NY 10001-2006

Library of Congress Cataloging-in-Publication Data

Sonneborn, Liz.
   A to Z of American women in the performing arts / Liz Sonneborn.
     p. cm.
   Includes bibliographical references and index.
   ISBN 0-8160-4398-1 (hardcover)
   1. Women entertainers—United States—Biography—Dictionaries. I. Title.

PN2286.8 .S66   2001
791′.082′0973—dc21 [B]   2001023580

Facts On File books are available at special discounts when purchased in bulk quantities for businesses, associations, institutions or sales promotions. Please call our Special Sales Department in New York at (212) 967-8800 or (800) 322-8755.

You can find Facts On File on the World Wide Web at http://www.factsonfile.com

Text design by Cathy Rincon
Cover design by Joan M. Toro

Printed and bound in the United States

VB Hermitage 10 9 8 7 6 5 4 3 2 1

This book is printed on acid-free paper.

CONTENTS

INTRODUCTION

In American society, female performers have always played a unique role. By definition, they have had to live public lives, even during periods when women were expected to be devoted to home and hearth. Through the very act of demanding a spot in the limelight, female entertainers have presented a defiant challenge to cultural norms. Consciously or unconsciously, they have helped create new visions of what a woman is and could be.

Since the 19th century, Americans have looked to performers to help them define the characteristics of a modern woman. In the 1830s, stage star Fanny Kemble inspired a cultlike following of young women, who slavishly studied her clothes and manners for clues about how they should look and live. From Ethel Barrymore to Mary Tyler Moore to Madonna, many performers have likewise been idolized by admirers as the feminine ideals of their time.

Other female performers have made an impact by choosing to be provocateurs. Eva Tanguay became one of the greatest stars of vaudeville, less through her talent, than by her total disinterest in propriety. Tanguay excited audiences by her provocative dress and behavior, which also prompted them to question outmoded Victorian ideas about a woman's place in society. Similarly, Mae West became a star in the 1920s and 1930s largely because of her willingness to talk about sex with a frankness then unacceptable in general discourse. Like many later comedians, West used humor to blunt the blow of her words. Comics such as Roseanne, Joan Rivers, and Lily Tomlin have followed in her stead, using humor to unleash their anger about what they see as the second-class status of women without inciting the anger of their audience. More recently, a keen sense of humor—combined with a knack for self-reinvention and unerring sense of the zeitgeist—has made the singer Madonna one of the most famous and perhaps one of the most influential women in the world.

For many fans, the lives of female performers have been at least as exciting, if not more so, than their performances. Often the fascination lay in the mere fact that as successful professionals, these women could earn money and spend it as they wished. One such performer was Gay Nineties actress Lillian Russell, who became a fantasy figure for many women awed by her lavish lifestyle.

Another enviable aspect of the performers' lives was the independence that they enjoyed. With hefty incomes, they were more able to live free of men's control than was the average woman. And with fame, they were often permitted more latitude to explore nontraditional lifestyles and romantic arrangements. In a time when divorce was uncommon, movie fans relished titillating stories of the multiple marriages of stars such as Lana Turner and Judy Garland. The public occasionally condemned an especially obvious disregard for social dictates, as in the case of Elizabeth Taylor's and Ingrid Bergman's highly publicized extramarital affairs. Tellingly, after an almost ceremonial display of disdain, both of these actresses were later taken back into the hearts of their admirers, where they were held perhaps even closer because of their transgressions.

Many female performers have used their fame and wealth less to mock society mores than to change them. Particularly important has been the role of African-American performers in breaking down racial barriers. Among the most emotional moments of the civil rights movement was classical singer Marian Anderson's 1969 concert held at the Lincoln Memorial after she was denied the right to sing at Constitution Hall because of her race. Though perhaps less dramatic, the contributions of many other popular stars, such as Diana Ross and Diahann Carroll, were equally important. As the lead singer of the Supremes, Ross became a popular-culture icon beloved equally by African Americans and whites, while Carroll as the star of the television series *Julia* (1968–70) was welcomed each week into the homes of millions of American families of all races.

As among the most famous, most loved, and most powerful women in the nation, female performers have played an instrumental role in the history of the United States. Taken together, the biographical essays in this volume seek to tell their story, revealing the myriad of ways they have helped shape American culture. In addition to offering a discussion of each subject's life and career, the profiles attempt to explain these performers' importance in their day and continuing significance in our own.

It should be mentioned, though, that this reference is not intended to discuss every notable female entertainer. Certainly, anyone familiar with American popular culture could easily list dozens of other performers who might have been included. A completely comprehensive biographical dictionary on this subject would certainly require many more pages, if not volumes, than are available here. Instead, this book aims to provide an introduction

to 150 performers, selected as representatives of the wide range of experience women have had in the American entertainment industry.

Although personal taste certainly played a role in the selection process, certain criteria guided the decisions about which subjects to include. The women profiled were chosen represent as many different time periods and many different fields of endeavor as possible. For instance, circus performer Lillian Leitzel, violinist Maud Powell, and actress Charlotte Cushman are largely unknown today, but their popularity in their time earned them a spot in this discussion. An effort has also been made to include women from a variety of racial and ethic backgrounds. The struggles of Bessie Smith, Carmen Miranda, and Anna May Wong, for instance, help give a sense of the unique challenges of minority performers trying to establish themselves within the American mainstream.

Due to space constraints, this book defines "women in the performing arts" fairly narrowly, focusing on performers rather than talents working behind the scenes. Many performers included, however, had important second careers offstage or offscreen. For instance, the profile on singer Buffy Sainte-Marie discusses her work as a songwriter, and the essay on actress Ida Lupino explores her importance as a film and television director.

The definition of "American" for the purposes of this volume is slightly less stringent. Many foreign-born figures—such as Elizabeth Taylor, Claudette Colbert, and Ingrid Bergman—are included because the book could hardly be considered complete without them. A few important foreign performers were excluded on the somewhat subjective grounds that their most significant work was done outside the United States. For example, by this criteria, Sophia Loren was seen as more an Italian than an American performer and consequently was left out of the book.

Many younger performers were also excluded, because their talents are too new and untested to determine whether their work will ultimately stand the test of time. However, a few performers in mid-career were considered important enough to deserve a profile. Jodie Foster and Julia Roberts, for instance, were included on the justification that if neither made another film, she would still be remembered as having made a unique and important impact on Hollywood.

Finally, particularly seminal performers—such as Mary Pickford, Lucille Ball, and Judy Garland—were deemed worthy of lengthy profiles so that their contributions could be more fully discussed. In most cases, however, the length of an essay should not be construed as a commentary on the subject's importance. More often, the profiles followed the common-sense rule that figures with lengthy careers demanded longer essays than those who held the public's attention for relatively little time.

A

❖ ALLEN, GRACIE (Grace Ethel Cecile Rosalie Allen)
(1895–1964)   *Comic, Actress*

One of the most popular comedians of radio and television, Grace Ethel Cecile Rosalie Allen was born on July 16, 1895, in San Francisco. As a child, she learned traditional Irish dancing from her father, and at 14 she made her vaudeville debut. With her three sisters in an act called "The Four Colleens," she was soon touring the vaudeville circuit throughout the United States. By the time they reached New York City, all the "colleens" but Grace had dropped out. As an emerging star, she asked for better billing and quit when her demands were ignored.

Unable to find good bookings on her own, Allen contemplated quitting show business and enrolled in secretarial school. But she changed her mind in 1923 after meeting George Burns, then an unsuccessful vaudevillian. The two decided to perform as a comedy team in an act crafted by Burns. Initially, Allen was the "straight man," but after seeing audiences respond to her comic timing, Burns reversed their roles. As they refined the act, the character of Gracie emerged as a genial scatterbrain, whose non sequiturs and malapropisms tested the patience of her reasonable boyfriend, George. Although other female comics played it dumb, Allen's Gracie was unique. The act eschewed outrageous costumes and pratfalls, instead relying almost exclusively on verbal humor. The laughs also were prompted less by Gracie's stupidity than by her bizarre perspective on the world. As Burns once explained, the humor in her "logical illogic" grew out of that fact that "Grace played her as if she were totally sane, as if her answers actually made sense."

Soon after marrying in 1926, Allen and Burns became one of vaudeville's hottest acts. In addition to headlining at the United States's best vaudeville theaters, they became stars in England during 1928 and 1929. There they made their radio debut on the BBC, an engagement that was extended for 20 weeks. Despite their success abroad, Allen's high voice was deemed too squeaky for American radio until fellow vaudeville star Eddie Cantor invited her to be a guest on his radio show. As a team, Allen and Burns became the regular comedy act on bandleader Guy Lombardo's program. In 1932, they received their own show, *The Adventures of Gracie* (later renamed *The George Burns and Gracie Allen Show*), which became a favorite with listeners throughout the 1930s.

Although their radio work was more popular, Allen and Burns also appeared in 15 short films and features during this period. Allen starred in three other films, including *The Gracie Allen Murder Case* (1939), which made her the first American actress to have her name appear in a movie title.

Throughout Allen's life, Burns was the driving force behind her career. Working with a team of writers, he produced their radio scripts, giving them to Allen on the day of the show. The system allowed her to maintain a fresh take on their material, giving her performance an improvisational feel that contributed to her appeal. Still, for all his work behind-the-scenes, Burns always attributed their popularity to Allen's comic talents. "Gracie was the whole show," he once bluntly explained.

Alarmed by a dip in ratings, Burns retooled the show in 1945, abandoning his and Allen's old routines and reworking the program into a situation comedy. In 1950 he also insisted that they adapt the show to the new medium of television despite Allen's discomfort performing before a camera. Their show was a hit and was later credited with many innovations, including having the characters break the "fourth wall" by talking directly to the camera.

For Allen, however, the show became increasingly taxing. She was plagued by migraine headaches and other health problems, which Burns felt were the result of the "chronic strain of making like someone [she wasn't]." At her insistence, the show ended in 1958 after 299 episodes. Allen spent her remaining years entertaining and spending time with her and Burns's two adopted children and their grandchildren. An often reluctant performer who nevertheless conquered vaudeville, radio, and television, Allen died of a heart attack in Hollywood on August 26, 1964. In 1997 American Women in Radio and Television acknowledged her trailblazing contribution to American popular culture by naming its highest honor the Gracie Allen Award.

Further Reading

Blythe, Cheryl, and Susan Sackett. *Say Good Night, Gracie!: The Story of Burns and Allen.* New York: Dutton, 1986.

Burns, George. *Gracie: A Love Story.* New York: Putnam, 1988.

Clements, Cynthia, and Sandra Weber. *George Burns and Gracie Allen: A Bio-Bibliography.* Westport, Conn.: Greenwood Press, 1996.

Recommended Recorded and Videotaped Performances

The Burns and Allen Show (1950). Columbia/Tristar, VHS, 1996.

❖ ANDERSON, LAURIE
(1947–   )   *Performance Artist*

The first performance artist to find a mainstream audience, Laurie Anderson was born on June 5, 1947, in Glen Ellyn, Illinois, an affluent suburb of Chicago. After studying violin in high school, Anderson attended Barnard College in New York City, majoring in art history. She continued her education at Columbia University, where she earned a master's degree in fine arts.

As part of New York's conceptual art scene, Anderson began producing performance pieces in the early 1970s. In *Duets on Ice* (1974), she played the violin, accompanied by a taped instrumental track hidden inside the violin. While playing, she wore ice skates encased in ice. When the ice melted, the performance was over. In other early works, including *Songs and Stories for the Insomniac* (1975) and *Refried Beans for Instants* (1976). Anderson combined music, sound, and the spoken word. Using references to popular culture to produce social and political satire, the stories she told in performance were anthologized in two collections, *Airwaves* (1977) and *Music for Electronic and Recorded Material* (1977).

In 1980, Anderson began performing *United States II*. A section of the piece called "O Superman" featured Anderson's voice electronically distorted by a Vocoder. Released as a single in England, "O Superman" became a surprise popular hit, reaching number two on the British charts. In addition to marking Anderson's first financial success, the single led to a long-term record deal in the United States with Warner Brothers.

In 1982, her label released *Big Science*, which included excerpts of an expanded performance piece titled *United States I–IV*. Premiering at the Brooklyn Academy of Music in February 1983, *United States* was a multimedia concert that ran for eight hours over two evenings. Anderson described the piece as a "big portrait of the country" and divided it into four sections on transportation, politics, money, and love. The extravaganza brought together monologues, music, sounds, light shows, and photographs to create a witty commentary on modern American life. As Anderson attracted sold-out crowds while touring with the piece through the United States and Europe, *Time* magazine declared that *United States* was "the biggest, most ambitious and most successful example to date of the avant-garde hybrid known as performance art."

Anderson brought *United States* to an even larger audience in 1984, when a live album and book chronicling the performance were released. The same year, she brought out *Mister Heartbreak*. The album included a piece titled "Sharkey's Day" that featured the voice of novelist William Burroughs. Two years later, Anderson released the album *Home of the Brave* and a concert film with the same title.

On the heels of *Natural History*—a 1986 greatest hits tour—Anderson moved in a new direction. Of this period, she later explained, "I was tired of being Laurie Anderson. I wanted to start over." Responding to criticism that her performances were becoming overproduced, she began creating simpler pieces, such as *Empty Places* (1989) and *Voices from Beyond* (1991). She also performed excerpts of *Stories from the Nerve Bible*, a collection of writings and pictures published in 1994. In Anderson's solo show, *The Speed of Darkness* (1996), she returned to familiar themes of art and technology while approaching them through her own personal stories.

After taking voice lessons, Anderson sang for the first time on the album *Strange Angels* (1990). Her other recordings included *Bright Red* (1994), an album produced by Brian Eno and featuring a duet with rock star Lou Reed, with whom Anderson has been romantically linked. Anderson also experimented with an interactive CD-ROM titled *Puppet Motel* (1995).

In 1999, Anderson returned to the stage with the ambitious *Songs and Stories from Moby Dick*. A postmodern reworking of Herman Melville's classic novel, the performance piece marked the first time Anderson performed with a sizable cast. In *Moby Dick*, Anderson also employed the "talking stick," an inventive instrument that translates movement into sound. Calling the piece "10% Melville, 90% Laurie," Anderson in *Moby Dick* grappled with larger, eternal themes, such as the search for the meaning of life, suggesting a new direction for her future work.

In 2001, Anderson wrote an impressionistic essay on New York City for *Encyclopedia Britannica*, to be included next to the scholarly entry.

Further Reading

Anderson, Laurie. *Stories from the Nerve Bible: 1972–1992, A Retrospective*. New York: HarperPerennial, 1991.

Goldberg, Roselee. *Laurie Anderson*. New York: Abrams, 2000.

Recommended Recorded and Videotaped Performances

Talk Normal: The Anthology. . . . Rhino, CD, 2000.

United States Live (1984). Warner Brothers, CD, 1991.

❖ ANDERSON, MARIAN
(1897–1993) *Singer*

Celebrated as one of the greatest singers of her time, Marian Anderson used her prodigious talents to break racial barriers in American art and culture. In Philadelphia, Pennsylvania, she was born on February 17, 1897, the first of three daughters. Her father, a deliveryman, died of a brain tumor when Marian was 12. Five years later, her mother became seriously ill, leaving Marian with the burden of her family's financial support.

Anderson's musical talents emerged early. As a child, she taught herself to play the family piano and did odd jobs to buy a violin from a pawnshop. At six, she joined the choir at the Union Baptist Church, and at eight, she performed her first solo. She awed the congregation with both her rich voice and extraordinary range.

As a teenager, Anderson tried to attend a local music school, but was turned away because she was African American. The members of her church then raised funds to pay for the services of Giuseppe Boghetti, a professional vocal coach. Boghetti introduced her to classical music and became the most important of Anderson's many teachers.

Well-established on the African-American church circuit, Anderson made her New York debut at Town Hall in 1924. The recital was a profound disappointment: The turnout was modest, and the reviews were unenthusiastic. Anderson was so devastated that she considered giving up her singing career. The next year, however, she triumphed at a National Music League competition, beating out more than 300 other aspiring classical singers. As her prize, Anderson performed a solo at the New York Philharmonic. Her success, however, did little to advance her career. Anderson's race continued to keep her from finding bookings in theaters catering to white audiences.

In 1931, Anderson was awarded a grant from the Julius Rosenwald Fund to study in Europe. There, she found whites much more receptive to her singing. From 1933 to 1935, Anderson toured widely, visiting Scandinavia, France, England, Italy, Austria, and Spain. Her enormous repertoire included 200 songs in nine languages. In each performance, she combined classical works with spirituals she had first learned in church. Anderson soon emerged as a star, earning accolades wherever she performed. Most memorably, composer Arturo Toscanini, on hearing Anderson sing in Austria, told her that "Yours is a voice such as one hears once in a hundred years."

Equally impressed was American impresario Sol Hurok. After seeing Anderson in concert in Paris, he asked to manage her on a tour through the United States. Although so far her talents had been given their due only in Europe, Anderson welcomed the chance to return home.

In 1935, Anderson again performed at New York's Town Hall, this time to great acclaim. Her extensive tours were equally successful. Booked two years in advance, her concerts were sold out across the United States. In 1936, she became the first African American to perform at the White House.

Two years later, Hurok attempted to book a concert at Washington, D.C.'s Constitution Hall, which was owned by the Daughters of the American Revolution (DAR). The organization told Hurok the dates he wanted were not available. However, the real reason for DAR's refusal was clear: It did not want to allow an African American to perform in the hall. Expressing the outrage of many, First Lady Eleanor Roosevelt resigned from the DAR in protest.

Secretary of the Interior Harold Ickes offered Anderson an alternate location for her Washington concert: the steps of the Lincoln Memorial. On April 9, 1939, Anderson performed for a crowd of 75,000, while another 2 million listened to the concert on the radio. The performance finally made Anderson a star in her native country. It also made her into icon in the fight against racism. A mural commemorating the event was unveiled at Department of the Interior headquarters in 1943.

Now a celebrity, Anderson was more in demand than ever as a concert singer. A year after marrying Orpheus H. Fisher, an architect, she broke the attendance record at Los Angeles's Hollywood Bowl in 1944. In 1952, she made her television debut on *The Ed Sullivan Show*.

Fulfilling a lifelong dream, Anderson became the first African American to sing at New York's Metropolitan Opera House in 1949. Although, at 52, Anderson was past her prime, the performance inspired eight curtain calls. Her foray into opera would open doors for LEONTYNE PRICE and many other young African-American opera singers.

Anderson sang at the inaugurations of presidents Dwight D. Eisenhower and John F. Kennedy before her retirement in 1965. Throughout her long career, she was given an array of honors. In addition to 24 honorary doctorates, Anderson was presented with the Presidential Medal of Freedom in 1963 and a Kennedy Center Honor in 1978.

She also received a Grammy Award for lifetime achievement in 1991. Respected both for her prodigious talent and her grace under pressure, Marian Anderson died two years later, on April 8, at the age of 97.

Further Reading

Anderson, Marian. *My Lord, What a Morning.* New York: Viking, 1956.

Keiler, Allan. *Marian Anderson: A Singer's Journey.* New York: Scribner, 2000.

Recommended Recorded and Videotaped Performances

Marian Anderson: Bach, Brahms, Schubert. RCA, CD, 1989.

Schubert and Schumann Lieder. RCA, CD, 2000.

Spirituals. RCA, CD, 1999.

❖ **ARDEN, EVE (Eunice Quendens)**
(ca. 1908–1990) *Actress*

Best known for playing caustic, worldly wise career women, Eve Arden was a popular actress of stage, film, radio, and television for nearly 50 years. She was born Eunice Quendens in Mill Valley, California, on April 30 in either 1908 or 1912 (sources vary on her birth year). Her mother, Lucille, who divorced her husband when Eunice was two, made her living as a milliner, the source of Arden's later taste for extravagant hats.

A grammar school recital made Eunice desperate for a career in show business. With the support of her mother, she started working in local theatrical companies at age 16. After being discovered by producer Lee Schubert, she was invited to join the Ziegfeld Follies as a chorus girl in 1934. While at the Follies, Quendens was asked to adopt a shorter, simpler stage name. She later claimed she took the name "Eve Arden" as a tribute to her favorite perfume (Evening in Paris) and favorite cosmetics brand (Elizabeth Arden).

By the mid-1930s, Arden was appearing regularly in small film roles, while periodically returning to her first love, the theater. She was a standout as a wisecracking starlet in *Stage Door* (1937), but her greatest movie role came in 1945's *Mildred Pierce,* in which she played the quick-witted best friend of the long-suffering title character. For her work, Arden earned an Academy Award nomination. The part also helped establish her most enduring screen persona. Throughout the late 1940s, wise and witty female characters were regarded as "Eve Arden roles."

Arden also began working in radio in 1947. The following year, she enjoyed tremendous success with *Our Miss Brooks,* a radio comedy about a high school English teacher. A favorite with audiences, the show was brought to television in 1951, where it ran for three years. In 1953 Arden won an Emmy for performance. She later returned to television in two short-lived series, *The Eve Arden Show* (1957–58) and *The Mothers-in-Law* (1967–69).

Arden continued to make occasional appearances in film and on stage until 1983, when her husband, actor Brooks West, fell ill and died. After a brief marriage to an insurance agent in the late 1940s, Arden had wed West in 1951 and together they had raised four children, three of whom were adopted. She greatly valued family life and her long, successful marriage. To a reporter she once confessed that she sometimes envied more glamorous actresses, but added that she knew "if they only had what I've had—a family, real love, and an anchor—they would have been happier." After West's death in 1983, Arden retired from public life. She herself died of cancer on November 12, 1990, in Beverly Hills.

Further Reading

Arden, Eve. *Three Phases of Eve: An Autobiography.* New York: St. Martin's Press, 1985.

Van Dyck Card, James. "Arden, Eve." In *American National Biography,* edited by John Arthur Garraty and Mark C. Carnes, vol. 1, pp. 580–581. New York: Oxford University Press, 1999.

Recommended Recorded and Videotaped Performances

Mildred Pierce (1945). Warner Home Video, VHS, 2000.

Our Miss Brooks (1956). Warner Home Video, VHS, 1995.

❖ **ARTHUR, JEAN (Gladys Georgianna Greene)**
(1900–1991) *Actress*

Specializing in playing offbeat, vivacious career women, Jean Arthur was one of Hollywood's best-loved comedians during the golden age of American film. She was born Gladys Georgianna Greene in 1900 in Plattsville, New York, though she was raised in Manhattan. At 15, she left school to become a model. After a talent scout spotted one of her photographs, she signed a film contract and moved to Los Angeles.

Taking the stage name Jean Arthur, she appeared in about 20 low-budget comedies and westerns during the 1920s. She worked regularly, yet the breakthrough role she craved eluded her. In 1931, Paramount Studios dropped Arthur from its roster of ingenues. Without a contract, she headed back to

Jean Arthur in *Only Angels Have Wings* (1939)
(Museum of Modern Art Film Stills Archive)

New York to make a stab at a stage career. Arthur appeared in a variety of Broadway and off-Broadway plays, in which she honed her comedic style. Favoring theater over film work, she later remembered this period as "the happiest years of my life."

Arthur was lured back to Hollywood with a five-year contract with Columbia Pictures in 1934. The same year, she married producer Frank Ross, whom she divorced in 1949. Arthur had had a previous marriage to photographer Julian Anker, which lasted only a day.

In 1935, Arthur finally got the film vehicle she had been looking for—the leading female role in John Ford's comedy *The Whole Town's Talking* (1935). Arthur played a working girl with a hard facade but a soft heart underneath. Moviegoers so embraced her character that she would be called upon to play a variation on it in a string of romantic comedies. Arthur worked with many of the film industry's top directors, including George Stevens and Howard Hawks, but she is most remembered for three films she made with Frank Capra—*Mr. Deeds Goes to Town* (1936), *You Can't Take It With You* (1938), and *Mr. Smith Goes to Washington* (1939).

Arthur was famed for her distinctive voice, which was simultaneously husky and whispery. Film critic Pauline Kael once fittingly described it as "one of the best sounds in romantic comedies of the 30s and 40s." Another of her trademarks was the air of confidence projected by her characters, who always seemed well equipped to take care of themselves no matter what came their way. Offscreen, however, Arthur was overwhelmed by insecurity. She was so terrified of performing that after a take she would often race to her dressing room to weep and vomit. Capra said that he directed Arthur by literally pushing her in front of the camera, but that once there "that whining mop would magically bloom into a warm, lovely, poised, and confident actress."

Arthur was also in constant battle with Columbia head Harry Cohn. Over and over, she infuriated Cohn by rejecting roles she considered inappropriate for her talents. In part to soothe the tensions between them, screenwriter Garson Kanin tailored a lead specifically for her in *The More the Merrier* (1943). Playing a woman forced to live with two men because of the wartime housing shortage, Arthur won her only Oscar nomination for the film.

In 1944, Columbia finally released Arthur from her contract. Though she was now free to make the films she wanted, her crippling fear of the camera made doing so nearly impossible. She appeared in only two more movies—*A Foreign Affair* (1948) and *Shane* (1953). Arthur also made an ill-fated attempt to revive her stage career. She starred in a successful revival of *Peter Pan* in 1950, but otherwise stage fright and psychosomatic illness foiled her efforts. In one notorious instance, Arthur was set in 1967 to star on Broadway in *The Freaking Out of Stephanie Blake*. At an out-of-town tryout, she came onstage and immediately went out of character. After introducing the cast, she graciously told the audience she would not be able to perform. The play's producer, shouting from the back of the theater, cowed her into going ahead with the performance, but Arthur quit the play as soon as the curtain fell.

After brief stints teaching acting at Vassar College and the North Carolina School of the Arts, Arthur retired to Carmel, California. There, Hollywood's most reluctant star died on June 19, 1991, at the age of 91.

Further Reading

Oller, John. *Jean Arthur: The Actress Nobody Knew.* New York: Limelight Editions, 1997.

Pierce, Arthur, and Douglas Swarthout. *Jean Arthur: A Bio-Bibliography.* New York: Greenwood Press, 1990.

Recommended Recorded and Videotaped Performances

Mr. Deeds Goes to Town (1936). Columbia/Tristar, DVD/VHS, 2000/1997.

Mr. Smith Goes to Washington (1939). Columbia/Tristar, DVD/VHS, 2000.

The More the Merrier (1943). Columbia/Tristar, VHS, 1993.

Only Angels Have Wings (1939). Columbia/Tristar, DVD. VHS, 1999/1992.

B

❖ BACALL, LAUREN (Betty Joan Perske)
(1924–) *Actress*

Best remembered for her film collaborations with her husband Humphrey Bogart, Lauren Bacall was born Betty Joan Perske in New York City on September 16, 1924. While still in high school, Perske began taking classes at the New York School of the Theater. Through her uncle, Perske was introduced to her screen idol, BETTE DAVIS. Davis told her that she had to be certain she wanted to act because "it's hard work and it's lonely." Ever the realist, Perske continued pursue her goal despite Davis's warning.

After a year of study at the American Academy of Dramatic Arts, Perske turned to modeling. Her lean figure and sharp features caught the attention of magazine editor Diana Vreeland, who put her on the cover of the March 1943 issue of *Harper's Bazaar*. Several Hollywood luminaries, including David O. Selznick and Howard Hughes, tried to sign Perske to a film contract. Renamed Lauren Bacall, she accepted an offer from director Howard Hawks. In his film *To Have and Have Not* (1945), he cast her as Bogart's love interest, though she was 25 years his junior.

Hawks carefully orchestrated Bacall's film debut. He told her how to move, speak, and behave, using his stylish wife, Slim, as a guide. Bacall herself, however, originated the most distinctive aspect of her character. When acting with Bogart, she was so frightened that she held her chin close to her neck to keep her head from trembling and looked at him through upturned eyes. Dubbed "the Look," the posture became a new symbol of confident female sexuality.

To Have and Have Not was an enormous success and won Bacall enthusiastic reviews. During the filming, she also began a romance with Bogart, though he was still involved in a turbulent marriage. They kept their affair quiet until he could obtain a divorce. On May 21, 1945, Bacall and Bogart were married. They eventually had two children, Stephen and Leslie.

Conceding to Bogart's wishes, Bacall made home and family her first priority, though she continued to appear in films. Her second movie. *Confidential Agent* (1945), was a failure, prompting many critics who had earlier praised her work to question whether she could act at all. Realizing that her reception depended heavily on the quality of her material, she began fighting for better roles. Bacall soon revived her career with several onscreen pairings with Bogart, including *The Big Sleep* (1946) and *Key Largo* (1948). She also proved herself a deft comedian in *How to Marry a Millionaire* (1953), which costarred MARILYN MONROE and BETTY GRABLE.

In 1956 Bogart was diagnosed with cancer of the esophagus. Bacall devoted herself to nursing her husband until his death the following year. The loss of Bogart devastated Bacall. Self-described as "desperate for companionship," she was briefly engaged to Frank Sinatra. He later ended their romance. Bacall then fled Hollywood for Broadway, where she starred in the unsuccessful comedy *Goodbye, Charlie* (1959). In New York, she met actor Jason Robards Jr. whom she married in 1961. They had one son, actor Sam Robards.

Bacall devoted much of her time during their eight-year marriage to their family life. She did, however, appear in three films, including *Sex and the Single Girl* (1964) and *Harper* (1966), and starred in the Broadway hit *Cactus Flower* (1965). After divorcing Robards, Bacall returned to work full time and had one of the greatest successes of her career. In 1969, she played the lead in *Applause!*, a musical based on the classic Bette Davis film *All About Eve* (1950). Her performance won Bacall a Tony Award.

After an eight-year hiatus, Bacall returned to film in *Murder on the Orient Express* (1974). Throughout the rest of the decade, she took on occasional roles in such movies as *The Shootist* (1976) and *H.E.A.L.T.H.* (1979). Bacall also wrote *By Myself* (1979), an autobiography that focused on her relationship with her mother and with Bogart. As the title implied, she wrote the book without the assistance of a ghostwriter. For her effort, she won the National Book Award in 1980. In the 1980s, Bacall triumphantly returned to the stage in *Woman of the Year* (1980), for which she won her second Tony. In London, she also starred in a production of Tennessee Williams's *Sweet Bird of Youth* (1985) directed by playwright Harold Pinter. The film industry, however, seemed to find little place for Bacall. Although she publicly proclaimed her desire to work in movies, she insisted that there were very few roles available to women her age. In most of

her later film appearances, she has been relegated to small roles in which she is asked to play a witty, urbane woman much like herself. The best of these parts came in *The Mirror Has Two Faces* (1997), a romantic comedy costarring and directed by BARBRA STREISAND. Bacall's insightful performance as Streisand's vain and lonely mother earned her her first Oscar nomination. Though Bacall remains best loved as a film star, she has since acted most often in commercials and on the stage, including a production of Noel Coward's *Waiting in the Wings* in 2000.

Further Reading

Bacall, Lauren. *By Myself.* New York: Knopf, 1979.
———. *Now.* New York: Knopf, 1994.
Royce, Brenda Scott. *Lauren Bacall: A Bio-Bibliography.* Westport, Conn.: Greenwood, 1992.

Recommended Recorded and Videotaped Performances

The Big Sleep (1946). Warner Home Video, DVD/VHS, 2000.
Intimate Portrait: Lauren Bacall. Unapix, VHS, 1999.
The Mirror Has Two Faces (1996). Columbia/Tristar, DVD/VHS, 2001.
To Have and Have Not (1945). Warner Home Video, VHS, 2000.

❖ BAEZ, JOAN
(1941–)   *Singer, Songwriter, Musician*

The queen of 1960s folk music, Joan Baez is as well known for her political activism as for her pure soprano. She was born on January 9, 1941, in Staten Island, New York but her family moved frequently in her youth. Her father, a physicist of Mexican heritage, was an academic researcher who had eschewed more lucrative defense work on moral grounds. Joan's parents, both Quakers, nurtured her social conscience. Her mistreatment by schoolmates because of her dark skin also contributed to her sympathy with the less fortunate.

While attending high school in Palo Alto, California, Baez began playing the guitar. After graduating in 1958, she enrolled at Boston University but soon became caught up in the renaissance of folk music pioneered by Pete Seeger and the Kingston Trio. Playing coffeehouses in Boston and Cambridge, Baez developed a reputation as a keen interpreter of classic folk. In the summer of 1959, she was invited to perform at the first Newport Folk Festival. Her performance made her an overnight star of the folk scene.

Baez refused better-paying offers to sign with Vanguard Records, then the premier folk label. In 1960, Vanguard released *Joan Baez,* an album of traditional folk songs, including "House of the Rising Sun." The first of Baez's eight gold records, it reached number three on the charts.

Baez continued to tour concert halls and campuses to growing crowds. In 1963, she played to an audience of more than 20,000 at Los Angeles's Hollywood Bowl. Baez constantly broadened her repertoire, singing spirituals, hymns, and country and western tunes. She also sang songs by contemporary folk and rock artists, including Phil Ochs, Leonard Cohen, the Beatles, and most notably Bob Dylan. In addition to touring frequently together, Baez and Dylan became linked romantically.

By the mid-1960s, Baez was using her celebrity status to bring attention to political and social causes she held dear. In 1964, she refused to pay 60 percent of her income tax as a protest against the United States's military arms buildup. A vehement opponent of the Vietnam War, Baez was arrested two years later for blocking the doors of an armed forces induction center. She married draft resister David Harris in 1968. Soon after she became pregnant with their son Gabriel, Harris was arrested and sent to federal prison for 20 months.

Baez's antiwar stance won her both supporters and detractors. She was scheduled in 1967 to perform at Constitution Hall in Washington, D.C., a venue controlled by the conservative Daughters of the American Revolution (DAR). When the DAR refused to allow her to play the hall, Baez gave an outdoor concert at the Washington Monument that attracted a crowd of more 30,000. Baez was also well-received when she performed at the legendary Woodstock concert in 1969.

In the 1970s, Baez developed her talents as a songwriter with such albums as *Blessed Are . . .* (1971) and *Diamonds & Ruse* (1975). The decade also brought her her greatest commercial success—a cover of The Band's "The Night They Drove Old Dixie Down," one of the biggest singles of 1972. The same year, Baez began a long-term association with the human rights watchdog group Amnesty International and took a controversial tour of North Vietnam. In 1979, she helped found Humanitas International Human Rights Committee, an organization devoted to promoting human rights and nuclear disarmament through educational seminars.

In her autobiography *And a Voice to Sing With* (1987), Baez wrote of "the ashes and silence of the 1980s"—a decade that largely ignored both her music and politics. Nevertheless, she performed to acclaim at the Live Aid concert of 1985 and garnered a Grammy nomination for "Asimbonanga," a song from *Recently* (1987), her first studio album in eight years.

Baez devoted much of the early 1990s on what she called "inner work," including therapy to help her overcome stage fright and other phobias that had plagued her for years. At the same time, she discovered a new generation of singer-songwriters playing, in Baez's words, "this folk/rock kind of music that still suits me best." Baez's own work was revitalized as she began touring with younger artists such as Dar Williams, Indigo Girls, and Sinead Lohan. Heading into her sixth decade in music, Baez maintained that she could now perform "a freer concert than I ever thought I could give." As she told the *New York Times* in 2000, in recent years she has succeeded in "get[ting] past the myth of being Joan Baez and learn[ing] to enjoy my life."

Further Reading

Baez, Joan. *And a Voice to Sing With: A Memoir.* New York: Summit Books, 1987.

Fuss, Charles. *Joan Baez: A Bio-Bibliography.* Westport, Conn.: Greenwood, 1996.

Recommended Recorded and Videotaped Performances

Rare, Live and Classic. Vanguard, CD set, 1993.

❖ **BAILEY, PEARL (Pearl Mae Bailey)**
   (1918–1990)   *Singer, Actress*

Pearl Bailey's sultry voice and personal warmth combined to make her a star of cabaret, Broadway, and musical film. She was born Pearl Mae Bailey in March 29, 1918, in Newport News, Virginia, where her father was a minister. She first performed in his church, singing and dancing for the congregation. When she was four, Pearl's parents divorced. With her mother and three older siblings, she moved first to Washington, D.C., then to Philadelphia, Pennsylvania.

Bailey considered becoming a teacher before being drawn into show business at 15, after she won $5 in a talent contest at a Washington, D.C. club. Bailey paid her dues as a chorus girl in Philadelphia and a singer and dancer on the vaudeville circuit in central Pennsylvania. Gradually, she moved into playing African-American nightclubs, before becoming a vocalist for big bands led by Cootie Williams and Edgar Hayes. By 1944, Bailey was headlining at New York's most popular clubs. In between delivering growling renditions of such standards as "Toot-Toot Tootsie" and "Bill Bailey, Won't You Please Come Home," Bailey took to talking with the audience. Her folksy bantering became central to her casual performing style.

Bailey made her Broadway debut in the all-black revue *St. Louis Woman* (1946). Her two songs were the highlight of the show and helped earn her a Donaldson Award for Broadway's best newcomer. Over the next decade, she appeared in many musicals, including *Arms and the Girl, Bless You All,* and *House of Flowers* (1954). Bailey also carved out a career in film. Her most notable performances were the African-American musical dramas *Carmen Jones* (1954) and *Porgy and Bess* (1959). In the early 1960s, Bailey returned to cabaret, often with her fourth husband, jazz drummer Louis Bellson, in her band. Bailey and Bellson adopted two children, Tony and Dee Dee.

The pinnacle of Bailey's career was her performance in the lead role of a revival of *Hello, Dolly!* in 1967. Theater critic Clive Barnes wrote that she "took the whole musical in her hands and swung it around her neck as easily as if it were a feather boa." The show ran for two years and earned Bailey a special Tony Award.

In the 1970s, Bailey appeared regularly on television, particularly on talk shows, which proved a particularly good forum for her charmingly straightforward repartee. She also had her own syndicated cooking show, *Pearl's Kitchen.* In addition to a collection of her recipes, Bailey wrote five books, including three autobiographies. Although she never finished high school, she enrolled at Georgetown University in the late 1970s. In 1985, she graduated with a degree in theology at the age of 67.

Bailey also had a distinguished career as a goodwill ambassador for the United Nations (UN). During the Ford, Reagan, and Bush (Sr.) administrations, she was named a special delegate to the UN and toured throughout Africa and the Middle East to promote racial harmony. In the 1980s, Bailey also became a dedicated advocate for AIDS research.

After decades of heart trouble, Pearl Bailey died of a heart attack on August 17, 1990, while recovering from knee surgery. More than 2,000 people attended her funeral in Philadelphia. Speaking for the many who respected Bailey as both a performer and a humanitarian, bandleader Cab Calloway, a longtime friend, told the press, "Pearl was love, pure and simple love."

Further Reading

Bailey, Pearl. *Between You and Me.* New York: Doubleday, 1989.

———. *The Raw Pearl.* New York: Harcourt, Brace & World, 1968.

———. *Talking to Myself.* New York: Harcourt Brace Javonovich, 1971.

Recommended Recorded and Videotaped Performances

Carmen Jones (1954). Twentieth Century-Fox, VHS, 1994.
16 Most Requested Songs. Sony/Columbia, CD, 1991.

❖ BAKER, JOSEPHINE (Josephine Carson)
(1906–1975)   *Dancer, Singer*

Throughout her flamboyant life, African-American performer Josephine Baker was as much known for her celebrity as for the dancing talent that first made her famous. Born Josephine Carson on June 3, 1906, she was raised in poverty by her unmarried mother in St. Louis, Missouri. Otherwise, little is known for certain about her early years. She is said, however, to have witnessed the St. Louis riots of 1917, during which 39 African Americans were killed. The incident helped inspire her lifelong interest in the fight for civil rights.

At 14, Josephine left home. By 18, she had already been married twice and had taken the name of her second husband, William Baker. During these years, she began her show business career, performing mostly in tent shows, traveling acts that toured African-American venues in the South. Known for her comic dancing, she made her debut on Broadway in *The Chocolate Dandies* (1924).

The next year, Baker headed off for Paris to appear in an all-black show titled *La Revue Nègre*. Although she was not initially the star, from the start she was the revue's main attraction. Baker was a sensation dancing the Charleston, a dance that excited Parisians' newfound enthusiasm for American jazz. But she stunned her sophisticated audiences even more by performing one number in the nude. The show, specifically Baker's appearance in it, had a great effect on Paris's theater and art worlds. Artists such as Man Ray and Alexander Calder asked Baker to model for them. One of her greatest admirers was Pablo Picasso, who saw her as a living embodiment of the African sculpture that had inspired his Cubist period. Comparing her to an ancient Egyptian queen, Picasso declared that Baker was "the Nefertiti of now."

Josephine Baker in about 1938
(© Hulton-Deutsch Collection/CORBIS)

After taking the *Revue* to Berlin, Baker returned to Paris to even greater acclaim as the star of the Folies Bergère. There she developed one of her signature acts: singing "Yes, We Have No Bananas" wearing a skirt made from bananas and little else. Now the toast of Paris, she became equally notorious for her impulsive behavior and many passionate love affairs.

During the late 1920s, Baker frequently toured Europe. She also opened Chez Josephine, her own Paris nightclub, which was frequented by artists and writers, including Ernest Hemingway and Gertrude Stein. In her performances, she began taking her singing more seriously. By the early 1930s, she was well known for the song "J'ai Deux Amours," whose chorus explained, "I have two loves: my country and Paris." In 1937 Baker formally became a French citizen with her marriage to her third husband, Jean Lion, a handsome French millionaire. The couple separated only 14 months later and were divorced in 1941.

As war broke out in Europe in 1939, Baker showed her patriotism by entertaining French troops and working for the Red Cross. After France fell to the Nazis, she moved to North Africa. There, she was asked to join the French Resistance because, as an entertainer, she could easily travel through Europe and gain access to the highest circles of society. In gratitude for her work as a Resistance courier and spy, the French government awarded her the Croix de Guerre after the war.

In the late 1940s, Baker resumed her performing career, appearing largely in Europe. In 1951, however, she made a controversial tour of the United States. Baker drew headlines as she refused to work in any theater that would not admit blacks. She was also involved in a well-publicized incident at the Stork Club, one of New York City's leading nightspots. When the club personnel refused to serve her, she became angry and lashed out at fellow patron and newspaper columnist Walter Winchell for not coming to her defense. A regular at the Stork Club, Winchell retaliated by denouncing her in his popular column, calling her a communist and, even more outrageously, a Nazi sympathizer. However preposterous, his charges left a taint on her reputation in America. Nevertheless, Baker continued to speak out against segregation. In addition to performing at benefits for civil rights groups, she delivered a notable speech at the Lincoln Memorial alongside Martin Luther King Jr. during the 1963 March on Washington.

Baker also launched a more personal mission to promote racial harmony. With her fourth husband, Jo Bouillon (whom she married in 1947), she began adopting children of different racial and religious backgrounds and bringing them to live in her French chateau Les Milandes. Between 1954 and 1965, Baker took in 10 boys and two girls, whom she called collectively the "rainbow tribe." Originally, she planned to turn Les Milandes into a tourist attraction, devoted to demonstrating that people of different race could live in peace. Baker, however, grossly underestimated the enormous costs of renovating Les Milandes to her standards and of raising her large family. Despite her efforts to bring in more money through touring, her debts continued to rise. In 1969 Les Milandes was sold at a public auction. Now homeless, Baker and her children were given refuge by Princess Grace (formerly GRACE KELLY), who provided them with a small villa outside of Monaco.

Baker's financial difficulties deepened as her failing health began to interfere with her work. Nevertheless, by the mid-1970s, she was able to stage a comeback. Baker had a successful engagement at New York's Carnegie Hall in 1973. The next year, she triumphed in *Josephine*, a retrospective of her career that debuted in Monte Carlo. Baker brought the show to Paris, where it premiered on April 8, 1975. Two days later she suffered a cerebral hemorrhage, which took her life on April 14. With her death, Josephine Baker—the raw beauty who had helped to define Parisian culture during the Jazz Age—became the first American woman to receive a state funeral in France.

Further Reading

Baker, Jean-Claude, and Chris Chase. *Josephine: The Hungry Heart*. New York: Random House, 1993.

Hammond, Bryan, comp. *Josephine Baker*. Boston: Little Brown, 1988.

Rose, Phyllis. *Jazz Cleopatra: Josephine Baker in Her Time*. New York: Doubleday, 1989.

Recommended Recorded and Videotaped Performances

Intimate Portrait: Josephine Baker (1998). Unapix, VHS, 1999.

The Josephine Baker Story (1991). HBO Studios, VHS, 1999.

Princess Tam Tam (1935). Kino Video, VHS, 1999.

Zou Zou (1934). Kino Video, VHS, 1999.

❖ **BALL, LUCILLE** (Lucille Désirée Ball)
(1911–1989) *Actress*

The most influential woman in the history of television, Lucille Ball remains among the medium's best-loved performers. She appeared on weekly series almost continually for 23 years, always playing a variation on "Lucy," the wacky, red-headed scatterbrain who, unlike Ball, had ambitions that far outstripped her talents.

Born on August 8, 1911, Lucille Désirée Ball overcame a desperately unhappy childhood. She spent her early years in Jamestown, New York, where her father died when she was three. Her mother remarried and left Ball in the care of her stepgrandparents, stern disciplinarians who tried to stifle Lucille's natural bent toward theatricality.

With her mother's support, Ball left home at 15 to attend John Murray Anderson/Robert Milton School of the Theater and Dance in New York City. Doubtful of her own talent and intimidated by her fellow students (who included the future film star BETTE DAVIS), Ball quit the school and returned to Jamestown after only a month. She quickly recovered from her bout of insecurity and started visiting New York to find work as an actress. A striking beauty, she had more initial success as a model. Her image in an ad for Chesterfield cigarettes attracted an agent and won her a role in *Roman Scandals* (1933), an extravaganza directed by Busby Berkeley and starring Eddie Cantor. With characteristic focus, Ball used the opportunity to watch and listen, hoping to learn everything possible about working in films. Show business legend holds that when, for a comic bit, the filmmaker needed a beauty to have her face sprayed with mud, Ball volunteered. Impressed with her pluck, Berkeley supposedly said, "Get that girl's name. That's the one who will make it."

Ball began appearing in small film roles and was placed under contract first by Columbia and then by RKO. Although she received regular work, the film industry had difficulty using Ball well: With the looks of an ingenue and the spirit of a comic, she defied attempts to type her in conventional roles. Her best early role was in *Stage Door* (1937), where as a smart-mouthed aspiring actress she stood out in a cast that also included KATHARINE HEPBURN, GINGER ROGERS, and EVE ARDEN.

In 1940 Ball was cast in the film version of the Broadway musical *Too Many Girls*. One of the performers recruited from the Broadway cast was Desi Arnaz, a young Cuban musician who was five years her junior. Immediately, Ball and Arnaz were attracted to each other, even though early in their romance, it was obvious their personalities clashed. Despite their tendency toward frequent and ferocious arguments, the practical Ball and reckless Arnaz were married within months.

Ball thought she had found her breakthrough role as a bitter nightclub singer in *The Big Street* (1942). But, instead, soon after it appeared, RKO chose not to renew her contract. Ball, then 33, signed up with another studio, Metro-Goldwyn-Mayer (MGM). Seeing her years as an ingenue warning, she welcomed the studio's attempts to remake her image. As part of her MGM makeover, her brown hair was dyed a fiery red designed to make her stand out in Technicolor films. Although her red hair would become her trademark, Ball's stint working for MGM was a disappointment. A studio that specialized in musicals, it produced few vehicles that could showcase the nonsinging Ball. After several years of being cast in ever smaller parts, MGM released her from her contract in 1946.

From 1947 to 1951, Ball starred in the radio program *My Favorite Husband*, a role that brought her to the attention of the early television industry. When CBS approached Ball with the idea of featuring her in a television version of her show, she was hesitant at first. At the time, movie industry leaders so looked down on the new medium of television that starring in a television series would essentially end any chance she would ever have at movie stardom. The offer, however, was still intriguing to Ball for personal reasons. She had been looking for a project on which she and Arnaz could work together, believing that might help save their rocky marriage. A bandleader, Arnaz was often on tour. His infidelities while away had

15

already led Ball to file for divorce in 1944, but the couple soon reconciled.

Ball proposed that Arnaz be cast as the male lead in *My Favorite Husband,* but CBS balked. A Cuban American with a strong accent, Arnaz did not strike the network executives as right for the part of a midwestern banker. They were also not convinced that America would embrace Ball and Arnaz as a couple because of their mixed ethnicity. To change their minds, Ball and Arnaz set out on a touring act, blending music and comedy. Hailed by *Variety* as "a socko new act," the show was such a success that CBS became interested in designing a program for the couple. The enterprise, though, was still considered so risky that CBS insisted Ball and Arnaz take a cut in salary. They agreed in exchange for CBS's grant of ownership of the show to Desilu, a production company the couple borrowed $5,000 to form.

Six months pregnant with her first child, Lucie Désirée Arnaz, Ball filmed a pilot for *I Love Lucy* in early 1951. On October 15, the program premiered and quickly became the most popular show on television. At its height, as many as two-thirds of American families with television sets were faithful viewers. One of the most successful shows in the history of the medium, it was rated the number-one show for four years of its six-year run.

I Love Lucy featured the adventures of Lucy and Ricky Ricardo, played by Ball and Arnaz, and their friends and landlords Ethel and Fred Mertz (played by Vivian Vance and William Frawley). The show often focused on the mayhem set in motion by Lucy's desire for a performing career against Ricky's wishes. At the core of its success was Ball's flair for slapstick, a talent her film career had never exploited well. Using Ball's comic skill and innate appeal to their best advantage, *I Love Lucy* struck a chord with the public almost immediately. Recognizing the effect, Ball once recalled, "I never found a place of my own, never became truly confident, until, in the Lucy character, I began to create something that was truly mine. The potential was there. Lucy released it."

I Love Lucy was also an innovator in the television industry. At Ball and Arnaz's insistence, it was filmed before a live audience using three cameras, a technique then rare but now almost universally used for situation comedies. It also explored new subject matter when Ball became pregnant with her second child during the show's second season. She persuaded CBS to allow her character also to become pregnant, leading to one of the most successful ratings stunts in television history. On January 9, 1953, Lucille Ball gave birth to Desi Arnaz Jr. by a cesarean section scheduled for the day that Lucy Ricardo gave birth to "Little Ricky" on *I Love Lucy.* A record-making 44 million viewers tuned in to see Little Ricky's arrival.

While still America's number-one show, *I Love Lucy* went off the air in 1957. Although Ball and Arnaz reprised their characters in a series of specials, their offscreen marriage had completely unraveled, owing largely to Arnaz's drinking and philandering. They finally divorced in 1960. The next year, Ball married a young comedian, Gary Morton, who remained her husband until her death.

In 1962 Ball also severed professional ties with Arnaz by buying out his share in Desilu. Because of their television work, the production company had become so successful that it was able to buy RKO, the movie studio that years ago had unceremoniously declined to renew Ball's contract. From 1962 through 1967, Ball served as Desilu's president and CEO, giving her more power in the television industry than any woman had held before. Although Desilu began to struggle financially, during Ball's tenure it produced two enduring television classics—*Star Trek* and *Mission Impossible.* Ball finally sold the company to Paramount for $18 million, when she decided she could no longer perform both the role of executive and of television star.

After *I Love Lucy,* Ball returned to television in *The Lucy Show,* which was later renamed *Here's Lucy.* From 1962 to 1974, she played a widow and working mother whose constant scheming exhausted her boss Mr. Moody (Gale Gordon). Initially, *The Lucy Show* reunited Ball with Vivian

Vance, and on *Here's Lucy* she eventually costarred with her two teenage children.

Even after she left episodic television, Ball still appeared regularly on specials and occasionally in films. She also made a splash on Broadway in *Mame* in 1974 and was recognized for her dramatic range in *Stone Pillow* (1983), a television movie in which she played a bag lady. A late effort to return to television in a situation comedy, however, proved a disaster. The much-hyped *Life with Lucy* (1986) drew few viewers and was yanked from the air after only eight episodes. The debacle did little to tarnish Ball's reputation as the queen of television comedy. Three weeks after the last *Life with Lucy* program aired, she was in Washington, D.C., to receive from President Ronald Reagan a Kennedy Center Award, the United States's highest honor for a performer. Following her death on April 26, 1989, the many glowing tributes from her peers and fans gave further testament to her enduring appeal and influence.

Further Reading

Ball, Lucille, with Betty Hannah Hoffman. *Love, Lucy.* New York: Putnam, 1996.

Brady, Kathleen. *Lucille: The Life of Lucille Ball.* New York: Hyperion, 1994.

Recommended Recorded and Videotaped Performances

CBS Salutes Lucy: The First 25 Years (1976). Image Entertainment, DVD/VHS, 2001.

Collectors Choice Double Feature: The Lucy Show (1951). Madacy Entertainment, DVD, 1999.

Lucy and Desi: A Home Movie. White Star, VHS, 1994.

❖ BANKHEAD, TALLULAH
(1902–1968) *Actress*

In her lifetime, Tallulah Bankhead's name became synonymous with outrageous theatricality—a characteristic she displayed onstage and off. Born on January 31, 1902, Bankhead was a member of one of the most distinguished families in Huntsville, Alabama. (Both her father and grandfather had been U.S. congressmen.) Several weeks after her birth, Bankhead's mother died, and she and her older sister were sent to live with relatives in the town of Jasper. She spent much of her youth, however, in boarding schools, where at an early age she showed her flair for the dramatic.

Her show business career began in 1917 after she won a contest held by *Picture Play* magazine. As her prize, she traveled to New York City to appear in a bit movie part. She stayed on in the city, taking up residence at the Algonquin Hotel, a haunt for literary wits of the era. The flamboyant Bankhead became a favorite of Dorothy Parker, Robert Benchley, and others of the famed "Algonquin Round Table" in the hotel bar.

At 21, Bankhead decided to try her luck on the English stage. She was an immediate sensation, although few of the plays in which she performed were memorable. The attraction instead was Bankhead herself. Her larger-than-life persona—witty, urbane, and dressed to the hilt—was especially popular with young women. To them, Bankhead represented a new breed, an independent woman who felt no compunction to obey society's constraints.

Bankhead spent eight years in London, but in 1931 the money of Hollywood lured her home. She signed a five-picture contract with Paramount, which misused her by trying to promote her as a femme fatale. By 1934, she had returned to the stage, this time in New York.

Bankhead's acting style was highly mannered, guided far more by natural instinct than studied technique. Her lack of formal training was never more evident than when she appeared in *Antony and Cleopatra* with John Emery, an actor she married in 1937. Emery's performance was highly praised, while Bankhead's suffered in the comparison. In 1941, the marriage ended in divorce.

Bankhead, however, did earn great acclaim for two classic roles she originated: Regina in Lillian Hellman's *The Little Foxes* (1939) and Sabina in Thornton Wilder's *The Skin of Our Teeth* (1942). For both roles, she received the award for the best acting of the year from the New York Drama Critics Circle.

In 1944, she was also recognized by the New York Film Critics Circle for her performance in her one great film, Alfred Hitchcock's *Lifeboat* (1944).

Bankhead retired from the stage in 1950, but found a second career as a star of radio. As the host of the popular *Big Show* (1950–52), she interviewed celebrities and entertained her listeners with references to an exaggerated rivalry between her and BETTE DAVIS, who performed several of her signature stage roles on screen. During the 1950s, she also hosted NBC's *All-Star Revue* (1952–53) and frequently had guest appearances on other television programs.

Bankhead made her final stage appearance in 1964 in Tennessee Williams's *The Milk Train Doesn't Stop Here Anymore.* Her return, however, was hardly a triumph. Many years of hard living had taken their toll. Cast as an aging actress destroyed by drugs and liquor, Bankhead was more living her part than playing it. She made only two more professional appearances on television—one on *Batman,* the other on *The Tonight Show*—before her death from emphysema on December 12, 1968.

Further Reading

Bret, David. *Tallulah Bankhead: A Scandalous Life.* New York: Robson Books/Parkwest, 1996.

Brian, Denis. *Tallulah, Darling.* New York: Pyramid Books, 1972.

Carrier, Jeffrey L. *Tallulah Bankhead: A Bio-Bibliography.* New York: Greenwood, 1991.

Gill, Brendan. *Tallulah.* New York: Holt, Rinehart & Winston, 1972.

Recommended Recorded and Videotaped Performances

Give My Regards to Broadway. Aei, CD, 2000.

Lifeboat (1944). Twentieth Century-Fox, VHS, 1999.

❖ BARA, THEDA (Theodosia Goodman, Theodosia de Coppet)
(1890–1955) *Actress*

Hollywood's first femme fatale, Theda Bara was born Theodosia Goodman in Cincinnati, Ohio, on July 20, 1890. The daughter of a prosperous garment factory owner, she spent two years at the University of Cincinnati before her family moved to New York City in 1905. There, she began pursuing an acting career with limited success. In addition to working as a film extra, she made her Broadway debut in *The Devil* (1908), billed (using her mother's maiden name) as Theodosia de Coppet.

Though undistinguished, her early work brought her to the attention of film director Frank Powell, who cast her as the lead in *A Fool There Was* (1915). Based on a play inspired by Rudyard Kipling's poem *The Vampire,* the silent movie told the story of a seductress's destruction of an upstanding married man who falls under her spell.

Fool was an enormous success, and Goodman, now acting under the stage name Theda Bara, became an instant star. Her new acclaim was largely due to a publicity campaign orchestrated by the Fox Film Company. With her name, Bara was given a new personality and history by studio's publicity machine. The press was told that she was born in an oasis in the Sahara Desert, the product of an illicit relationship between a French artist and his Egyptian mistress. "Theda Bara" was said to be an anagram for "Arab Death," a claim seemingly supported by publicity stills that showed a heavily made-up Bara dressed in exotic costumes and surrounded by skulls and skeletons.

As overblown as Bara's public persona was, it struck a chord with her mostly female audience. Some female moviegoers were so appalled by Bara's man-destroying "vamp" that they destroyed posters bearing her image and spearheaded church-sponsored campaigns to ban her films. More, however, found a guilty pleasure in Bara's screen image, which offered an exciting alternative to the pure and virtuous female characters that then dominated films. Her more adventurous female fans copied her dark makeup and made a catchphrase of her famous line, "Kiss me, my fool." Others sought her advice about love and sex in the hundreds of fan letters she received each week.

Signed to a contract with Fox, Bara made some 40 more films. In most, she played a variation of the

Theda Bara in about 1915
(Museum of Modern Art Film Stills Archive)

"vamp" while playing well-known characters such as Cleopatra, Salome, and Mata Hari. A quiet, refined woman, Bara sought to broaden her range in less sensational roles, such as the female lead in an early film adaptation of *Romeo and Juliet* (1916). Her public, however, was only interested in seeing Bara as an evil woman, and their enthusiasm for even that persona was short-lived. By 1919, when her Fox contract expired, Bara had become a frequent subject of parody. Although her over-the-top screen image seemed liberating at first, film audiences came to see its inherent ridiculousness. While changing popular tastes following the horror of World War I probably contributed to the public's rejection of Bara, she herself believed that filmgoers had merely become more sophisticated. She once explained that early in her career her fans "thought that the stars of the screen were the way they saw them. Now they know it is all make-believe."

Bara tried to revive her vamp character on Broadway in *The Blue Flame* (1920) but was laughed off the stage. She made a few more attempts at a comeback before retiring in 1926. Her last film was *Madame Mystery* (1926), a comedy short directed by Stan Laurel, in which Bara herself lampooned the roles that had made her famous. She spent the rest of her life out of the limelight, sharing a Beverly Hills home with one of her film directors, Charles J. Brabin, whom she married in 1921. On April 7, 1955, Bara died of cancer at the age of 69.

With the exception of *A Fool There Was,* Bara's films are all now lost. Still, the screen's original vamp has had a long-lasting influence. Through her phenomenal success, she was the first to show Hollywood the popular appeal of the "bad girl"—a lesson the film world has well remembered ever since.

Further Reading

Bodeen, DeWitt. *From Hollywood: The Careers of 15 Great American Stars.* South Brunswick, N.J.: A. S. Barnes, 1976.

Genini, Ronald. *Theda Bara.* Jefferson, N.C.: McFarland & Company, 1996.

Golden, Eve. *Vamp: The Rise and Fall of Theda Bara.* Vestal, N.Y.: Emprise, 1996.

❖ BARRYMORE, ETHEL (Ethel May Barrymore)
(1879–1959)   *Actress*

Hailing from America's most distinguished acting family, Ethel May Barrymore was born in Philadelphia on August 16, 1879. Her parents, Maurice Barrymore and Georgiana Drew, spent much of her childhood on tour, so she and her two brothers, Lionel and John, were cared for by their maternal grandmother, Louisa Lane Drew. One of the leading stage comedians of the 19th century, Drew was also the manager of Philadelphia's Arch Street Theater for 30 years.

At six, Ethel was sent the Academy of Notre Dame, the convent boarding school her mother had attended. In 1893, however, her mother removed her from the academy so that the girl could accompany her to California. Ill with tuberculosis, Georgiana Drew hoped the warm climate would restore her health, but instead she died after several months. Ethel, only 13, was left to arrange for her return to the East and the shipment of her mother's casket.

In Philadelphia, Ethel went back to school, but soon her education came to an end. As her grandmother left her post at Arch Street and her father remarried, she was told that she would have to go to work to earn her own livelihood. The situation put an end to her childhood dream of becoming a concert pianist. Instead, she practically turned to the family business. "Acting was, after all, the only thing I could do best," she later remarked.

Barrymore made her stage debut in 1894, appearing in a touring production of *The Rivals* starring her grandmother. She was then taken under the wing of her uncle, John Drew, one of Broadway's greatest stars. He arranged for her to appear in a series of small stage roles while serving as the understudy for more substantial parts. Her early appearances earned her an invitation to appear in *Secret Service* (1897) in London. The arrival of the American beauty not only excited theatergoers—it also thrilled English high society, who quickly embraced the sophisticated, yet fresh Barrymore. When she returned to New York City, she left behind a number of rejected suitors, including the future prime minister Winston Churchill.

To Barrymore's surprise, she found that her London success had made her a celebrity in her native land. She was soon being offered leading roles and in 1901 became an established star in *Captain Jinks of the Horse Marines.* Widely admired for her regal manner, Barrymore was particularly popular with young women, who took to emulating the clothing and hairstyles she wore on stage.

Cast increasingly in ingenue roles, Barrymore longed for more serious, substantial parts. She was particularly eager to show off her acting in order to combat rumors that was just a beautiful clotheshorse with little real talent. In 1910, she

Ethel Barrymore in about 1900
(Library of Congress, neg. no. USZ62-97334)

finally earned the respect she craved playing a woman trapped in an unhappy marriage in *Mid-Channel.* The success came on the heels of her own marriage to Russell Griswold Colt, the wealthy son of the president of the United States Rubber Company, in 1909. The couple had three children— Samuel, Ethel, and John.

In 1918 Barrymore had another success with *Déclassée,* which ran for more than 200 performances. Her triumph, though, ushered in a period of professional and personal turmoil. She appeared in a series of lightweight, badly-received plays and had a brief, disastrous run as Shakespeare's Juliet, a part she was deemed too old to play. At the same time, her marriage to Colt fell apart. The two were divorced in 1923.

Barrymore's fortunes reversed in 1926, when she was cast in the lead in W. Somerset Maugham's *The Constant Wife.* She appeared in the play for three years in New York and on tour. Now recognized as the grande dame of the American theater, she received a permanent monument to her achievements when the Shubert brothers named their new theater after her in 1928.

Despite Barrymore's fame, she continued to have difficulty finding good vehicles for her talents as she grew older. Adding to her frustration over the lack of good roles, she also faced a battle with the Internal Revenue Service, which held that she owed a fortune in back taxes. Her desperation led her to set aside her disdain for the film industry and accept a high-paying offer to appear in *Rasputin and the Empress* (1932). The film also starred her brothers Lionel and John, both of whom had earned their own substantial reputations as actors. The movie marked the only time the three Barrymore siblings performed together. To further dispel her financial crisis, Ethel Barrymore also performed in her own radio program on NBC, in which she played many of the roles she had made famous on the stage.

By the late 1930s, Barrymore had returned to the theater but did not find a solid role until 1940, when she starred in *The Corn Is Green*. In her greatest stage success, she played Miss Moffitt, a Welsh schoolteacher determined to educate a young coal miner. Receiving the best reviews of her career, she gave 461 performances on Broadway. While touring with the show, she appeared in the film *None But the Lonely Heart* opposite Cary Grant. Her performance won her an Oscar as best supporting actress in 1944.

Soon afterward, Barrymore suffered a near-fatal bout of pneumonia. Concerned about her health, she decided to move to California. In demand ever since her Academy Award win, Barrymore made 20 films between 1946 and 1957, appearing mostly in supporting roles. Her late film work brought her three more Oscar nominations for *The Spiral Staircase* (1946), *The Paradine Case* (1947), and *Pinky* (1949). She also briefly hosted her own television program, *The Ethel Barrymore Theatre*. After more than 60 years of acclaim, Barrymore died on June 18, 1959, and was buried next to her brothers in a Beverly Hills cemetery, reuniting in death the most celebrated siblings in American theater and film.

Further Reading

Barrymore, Ethel. *Memories: An Autobiography.* New York: Harper, 1955.
Peters, Margot. *The House of Barrymore.* New York: Knopf, 1990.

Recommended Recorded and Videotaped Performances

None But the Lonely Heart (1944). Turner Home Video, VHS, 1998.
Rasputin and the Empress (1932). Warner Home Video, VHS, 1993.
The Spiral Staircase (1946). Anchor Bay Entertainment, DVD/VHS, 2000.

❖ **BERG, GERTRUDE** (Gertrude Edelstein)
(1899–1966) *Actress*

The creator and star of radio's *The Goldbergs*, Gertrude Berg was born Gertrude Edelstein in New York City on October 3, 1899. When she was seven, her father bought a resort in the Catskills. There, Gertrude made her show business debut, performing skits she wrote and depicting characters based on relatives from the Jewish community in which she was raised.

In 1918, she married Lewis Berg, a chemical engineer, with whom she had two children. While raising her family, Gertrude Berg took playwriting courses at Columbia University and started writing radio plays. In 1929 she made her first sale to NBC, but her show, a soap opera titled *Effie and Laura*, was canceled after one episode. The same year she had far better luck with *The Rise of the Goldbergs*. Later renamed *The Goldbergs,* the show ran for 20 years and became one of the most popular programs in the history of radio.

In addition to writing most of the episodes, Berg starred as Molly Goldberg, the matriarch of a Jewish family from the Bronx. A self-sacrificing fount of common sense, the character was largely responsible for introducing the type of the "Jewish mother" to American popular culture. Although Berg's characters were sometimes faulted as stereo-typical portrayals of Jewish immigrants, her gentle humor sketched the Goldbergs with such warmth and affection that they were embraced by a weekly audience of millions.

Berg proved to be a skillful businesswoman, maintaining control over the show she created and negotiating advantageous contracts for herself. She also made the most of *The Goldbergs'* success by taking her characters into other media. In 1948, her play *Molly and Me,* was a hit on Broadway, and in 1951 she brought the Goldbergs to the screen in *Molly.* In addition, Berg published Goldberg short stories and even authored *The Molly Goldberg Cookbook* (1955).

Gertrude Berg also oversaw in 1949 *The Gold-bergs'* transition from radio to television, becoming in the process one of the few women to write for television in its early days. Although *The Goldbergs* on television never equaled the success it had had on radio, the show ran for six seasons. In the early 1950s, the show was almost canceled when Berg refused to buckle under to a sponsor's pressure to fire her costar Philip Loeb, who was accused of having communist sympathies. The show was saved only after Loeb decided to resign. To combat a fall in ratings, Berg moved the Goldbergs from the Bronx to the suburbs in 1955. Nevertheless, the program was canceled the following year.

In the late 1950s and early 1960s, Berg trans-formed herself into a Broadway star. Among the plays in which she performed were *The Solid Gold Cadillac* (1956), *The Matchmaker* (1957), and *Dear Me, the Sky Is Falling* (1967). Her most memorable work, however, was in *The Majority of One* (1959), a drama that tackled such difficult issues as racial prej-udice and the loneliness of her widowed character. Berg's sensitive performance won her a Tony Award. While preparing to open in a new play, she died of natural causes on September 15, 1966.

Further Reading

Berg, Gertrude, with Cherney Berg. *Molly and Me.* New York: McGraw-Hill, 1961.

Marc, David. "Berg, Gertrude." In *American National Biography,* edited by John Arthur Garraty and Mark C. Carnes, vol. 3, pp. 629–630. New York: Oxford University Press, 1999.

❖ BERGEN, CANDICE
(1946–) *Actress, Talk Show Host*

After an early career in film, Candice Bergen cre-ated one of television's most intriguing characters in *Murphy Brown.* Born May 6, 1946, Bergen is the daughter of radio and film comedian Edgar Bergen. At her birth, the press announced that Charlie McCarthy—the dummy Edgar used in his famed ventriloquist act—now had a sister. Can-dice indeed had an intense case of sibling rivalry with the wooden puppet. In her autobiography, *Knock Wood* (1984), she recalled the haunting memory of her father placing her on one knee and Charlie on the other, using his voice to speak for both of them.

Candice was raised in Beverly Hills, California, where most of her playmates were the children of Hollywood stars. Disturbed by the effect this pam-pered environment was having on their daughter, the Bergens sent Candice to a finishing school in Switzerland when she was 14. After a few months, Candice greeted her visiting parents, offering them one of her cigarettes and a drink. The Bergens immediately took her back to Beverly Hills for the rest of her high school education.

In 1963, Candice Bergen enrolled at the Uni-versity of Pennsylvania to study art history. How-ever, she was more interested in her burgeoning modeling career than in her studies. After flunking out, Bergen moved to New York City, where she attracted the attention of the director Sidney Lumet. He cast her in *The Group* (1966), in the daring role of Lakey, a young lesbian. Now in demand for ingenue parts, Bergen appeared in a string of undistinguished films, including *The Sand Pebbles* (1966), *T. R. Baskin* (1971), and *The Wind and the Lion* (1975). Critics inevitably were awed by her beauty, though most shared Bergen's own sense that her acting was stiff and stilted.

Reviews were far kinder to her layered performance in *Carnal Knowledge* (1971), a black comedy in which she played a Smith College student romanced by two roommates played by Jack Nicholson and Art Garfunkel.

In the 1970s, Bergen also developed an accomplished career as a photojournalist. With her Hollywood pedigree, she was able to interview top stars, such as Paul Newman and Lee Marvin. In addition, she won coveted international assignments, including the job of reporting on Kenya's Masai tribe for *National Geographic. Esquire, Life,* and *Playboy* were among the other national magazines that published Bergen's work.

As an actress, Bergen had a breakthrough in *Starting Over* (1979), in which she had a small role as Burt Reynolds's self-indulgent ex-wife. Not wanting to compete with her father, she had previously shied away from comedy. The film's showcase of her comedic flair, however, won her some of her best reviews as well as an Oscar nomination for best supporting actress. She returned to comedy in 1981 in the critically disparaged *Rich and Famous.*

In 1979 Bergen met French film director Louis Malle, whom she married the next year. The couple split their time between homes in Los Angeles, New York, and the countryside of France. Bergen gave birth to their daughter, Chloe, in 1985.

Bergen set off on still another career path in 1988, when she lobbied for the lead role on *Murphy Brown,* a television situation comedy about a straight-talking journalist working on a television news magazine. Contrasting Murphy's professional success with her personal loneliness, the show's creator, Diane English, called it "a sort of cautionary tale about getting what you wished for." From the outset, the series was a hit, and earned Bergen five Emmy Awards. It also placed her at the center of a national controversy when Vice President Dan Quayle denounced as immoral a story line that had the pregnant and unmarried Murphy deciding to have her baby and raise him on her own.

During the 10-year run of *Murphy Brown,* Malle fell ill. He died of cancer in 1995. Five years later, Bergen married real estate mogul Marshall Rose, a longtime friend. Also in 2000, Bergen began hosting *Exhale,* an hour-long talk show for the cable channel Oxygen. A fitting showcase for Bergen's intelligence and charm, the show has featured such high-profile guests as JODIE FOSTER, Hillary Clinton, and Madeleine Albright. Bergen also returned to film acting in 2001 with a supporting role in the comedy *Miss Congeniality.*

Further Reading

Bergen, Candice. *Knock Wood.* New York: Linden Press, 1984.

Ehrman, Mark. "The US Interview: Candice Bergen." *US Weekly.* April 24, 2000, pp. 54–61.

Stoddard, Maynard. "Candice Bergen: Sweet Success." *Saturday Evening Post.* May/June 1992, pp. 38+.

Recommended Recorded and Videotaped Performances

Carnal Knowledge (1971). MGM/UA, DVD/VHS, 1999.
The Group (1966). MGM/UA, VHS, 1996.
Starting Over (1979). Paramount, VHS, 1993.

❖ BERGMAN, INGRID
(1915–1982) *Actress*

During her rocky career, screen idol Ingrid Bergman was beloved, then reviled, then beloved again by American moviegoers. Born on August 29, 1915, in Stockholm, Sweden, she was raised by her father, Justus, after her mother died when Ingrid was three. Justus Bergman nurtured Ingrid's interest in the arts. Their trips to the theater inspired her to crave a career as an actress. After Justus's death, 13-year-old Ingrid went to live with her uncle and aunt, who were far less sympathetic to her ambitions. While attending a private girls' school, she began working as a movie extra against their wishes.

In 1933, Bergman won a scholarship to the school of the prestigious Royal Dramatic Theater, the alma mater of film star GRETA GARBO. The next year, she won her first movie part and was subsequently offered a contract by Svensk Filmindustri. After a series of small roles, she was given the lead in her sixth film, *Intermezzo* (1937). Bergman played a young pianist who has an affair with married violinist, but in the end sacrifices her love so that he can return to his family. The romance made her one of the most sought-after actresses in Sweden. In the year of its release, she also married dentist and medical student Peter Lindstrom. She gave birth to their child, Pia, in 1938.

After several more films in Sweden and one in Germany, Bergman was called to Hollywood by producer David O. Selznick. He was so impressed by her work in *Intermezzo* that he wanted to produce an American remake. The second time around, the film again made her star to watch, this time in Hollywood. Selznick signed his new ingenue to a seven-year contract. Her new studio began promoting Bergman as a natural beauty, pointing out that, unlike most starlets, she had not been transformed by the makeup department to seem more glamorous.

Even so, Hollywood created its own image of Bergman, casting her often as an innocent. Bergman resented the mold and lobbied for meatier roles. When Selznick lent her to another studio for *Dr. Jekyll and Mr. Hyde* (1942), she convinced the director, Victor Fleming, to allow her and LANA TURNER to swap roles so that she could play a prostitute instead of Jekyll's dutiful fiancée.

In 1942, Selznick again loaned Bergman out for *Casablanca,* the film that would make her a legend. As Ilsa Laszlo, Bergman effectively played a woman torn between love and doing what was right, as she had earlier in *Intermezzo.* With the movie's success, she became one of America's hottest stars. Bergman followed *Casablanca* with a string of popular films. In 1944, she earned her first Academy Award for *Gaslight* (1946), in which she portrayed a wife driven mad by her husband. Bergman also made two memorable movies with director Alfred Hitchcock—*Spellbound* (1945) and *Notorious* (1946).

When her contract with Selznick expired in 1946, she took advantage of her newfound freedom to appear as Joan of Arc on Broadway in *Joan of Lorraine.* The play broke box-office records and

Ingrid Bergman with Charles Boyer in *Gaslight* (1944)
(Museum of Modern Art Film Stills Archive)

won Bergman a Tony Award. However, her next three films—*Arch of Triumph* (1948), *Joan of Arc* (1948), and *Under Capricorn* (1949)—failed to strike a chord with moviegoers or critics.

Hoping to reinvigorate her movie career, Bergman wrote to Italian director Roberto Rossellini, expressing her desire to work with him. When he agreed to write a part for her, she traveled to Rome to meet him. Their film collaboration quickly turned into a love affair. Bergman, whose marriage was already crumbling, had had several secret extramarital relationships. But her affair with Rossellini was discovered by the press and widely reported, especially after Bergman became pregnant with Rossellini's child. Once embraced by the American public for her seeming purity, Bergman was suddenly the target of savage attacks on her morality. Colorado Senator Edwin C. Johnson even denounced her on the senate floor as "a powerful influence for evil." As Bergman's daughter Pia once observed, she went "from being a saint to a tramp in a few days."

Freshly divorced from Lindstrom, Bergman married Rossellini in 1950 soon after giving birth to their son, Robertino. Two years later, they had twin girls, Isotta and Isabella, the latter of whom would become a noted model and actress. For the next seven years, Bergman acted exclusively in Rossellini's films, including *Stromboli* (1950) and *Viaggio in Italia* (1953), but none were successful. Their relationship grew equally troubled. In 1958, their marriage was annulled, and Bergman married theatrical producer Lars Schmidt. She and Schmidt were divorced in 1975.

After seven years of exile, Bergman made a triumphant return to Hollywood, playing the title role in *Anastasia* (1956). She won her second Oscar for best actress for the movie, a gesture widely interpreted as a symbol of forgiveness of her past indiscretions. Two years later, Cary Grant, her costar in *Notorious,* introduced her as a presenter at the Academy Awards, pointedly calling her "a great actress and a great lady" to thunderous applause.

Though clearly back in the Hollywood fold, Bergman found fewer good film and stage roles. Her later films were relatively light fare, such as *Indiscreet* (1958), *Cactus Flower* (1969), and *Murder on the Orient Express* (1974), which earned her a third Oscar, this time for best supporting actress. After being diagnosed with breast cancer, she made one last great film, *Autumn Sonata* (1978). Directed by Ingmar Bergman (the two are unrelated), the movie brought together the two giants of the Swedish cinema to tell the story of a renowned pianist confronting her failure as a mother. Capping her occasional work in television, Bergman found her final role in *A Woman Called Golda* (1982), a biography of Golda Meir, for which she won an Emmy Award.

On August 29, 1982—Bergman's 67th birthday—she finally succumbed to cancer. In a late interview, she looked back on her often tumultuous life and career without regrets. Bergman said, "When I was very young in Sweden, I used to pray 'God, please don't let me have a dull life.' And He obviously heard me."

Further Reading

Bergman, Ingrid, and Alan Burgess. *Ingrid Bergman: My Story.* New York: Delacorte, 1980.

Leamer, Laurence. *As Time Goes By: The Life of Ingrid Bergman.* New York: Harper & Row, 1986.

Spoto, Donald. *Notorious: The Life of Ingrid Bergman.* New York: HarperCollins, 1997.

Recommended Recorded and Videotaped Performances

Autumn Sonata (1978). Home Vision Cinema, DVD/VHS, 2000/1999.

Casablanca (1943). Warner Home Video, DVD/VHS, 2000.

Intermezzo (1939). Anchor Bay Entertainment, VHS, 1999.

Notorious (1946). Anchor Bay Entertainment, DVD/VHS, 1999/1998.

❖ BOW, CLARA
(1905–1965)   *Actress*

Called by F. Scott Fitzgerald the "quintessence of what the term 'flapper' signifies," Clara Bow was American film's greatest sex symbol during the 1920s. Born in Brooklyn, New York, on July 29, 1905, she survived a brutal childhood, marred by poverty and her mother's severe mental illness. Bow found comfort in the movies and dreams of stardom, especially after winning a beauty contest that gave her a small movie part as a prize. After several years in Hollywood, she secured a contract with independent producer B. P. Schulberg that initially paid her $50 a week.

Embued with a strong work ethic, Bow made 55 films between 1923 and 1930. In most, she portrayed a young working girl who asserted her independence by smoking, drinking, wearing short skirts, and dancing all night. Although other stars also adopted the pose of the flapper, Bow, with her pixyish face and fiery, bobbed hair, was by far the most popular, receiving at her height more than 40,000 fan letters a week. She was known by the public as the "It Girl" after appearing in the 1927 film adaptation of popular author Elinor Glyn's novel *It*. "It" became a euphemism for the earthy, highly energized sex appeal of Bow—a distinct departure from the exotic allure of earlier film sirens such as THEDA BARA.

Bow's life was sensational offscreen as well. The lover of many of Hollywood's leading men and a cohort of gangsters and bootleggers, Bow was dubbed "crisis-a-day Clara" by her producer. Her unconventional love life prompted a major public scandal when her former secretary Daisy Defoe wrote a tell-all book in retaliation for Bow's accusations of embezzlement. Defoe's disloyalty lead to one of several nervous breakdowns Bow suffered during her film career. It also encouraged her studio, Paramount, to fire her in 1931. Paramount, however, had already seen evidence that Bow's film popularity was waning. With the advent of sound movies and stationary microphones, the frantic movements of Bow's signature acting style had to be reined in, eliminating much of her screen appeal.

Within six months, Bow married cowboy film star Rex Bell and retired to his ranch in Nevada. She made several attempts at returning to film, but her efforts were defeated by bad reviews. By the mid-1930s, Bow had given up on Hollywood and devoted herself to raising her and Bell's two sons. Yet, even in the relative quiet of her later life, she continued to be plagued by insomnia and a growing fear that she had inherited her mother's mental problems. By the early 1950s, Bow had moved permanently to Los Angeles in order to be closer to her psychiatrists and to a mental hospital in which she was periodically institutionalized. Largely removed from the public eye, the former "It Girl" died of a heart attack in her home on September 26, 1965.

Further Reading

Morella, Joe and Edward Z. Epstein. *The "It" Girl: The Incredible Story of Clara Bow.* New York: Delacorte, 1976.

Stenn, David. *Clara Bow: Runnin' Wild.* Expanded edition. New York: Cooper Square, 2000.

Recommended Recorded and Videotaped Performances

Clara Bow: Discovering the "It" Girl (1999). Kino Video, VHS, 1999.

It (1927). Kino Video, VHS, 1999.

Wings (1927). Paramount, VHS, 1996.

❖   BRICE, FANNY (Fanny Borach)
     (1891–1951)   *Comic, Actress*

On the stage and on the radio, Fanny Brice was one of America's favorite comics for more than four decades. Born Fanny Borach on October 29, 1891, she grew up in Newark, New Jersey, where her parents owned seven saloons. She had an early taste of show business while performing impromptu song and dance numbers on tables at the Borachs' establishments.

Fed up with her husband's gambling, Brice's mother, Rose, left him and moved her children to Brooklyn, New York. There, at 14, Brice made her performing debut at Keeney's Theater, where she won first prize in a talent contest. She made the rounds at other amateur night competitions before landing parts in several burlesque shows. Afraid that her skinny frame would keep her out of chorus lines, Brice found a better outlet for her talent while appearing in a show titled *The College Girls* (1909–10). Performing "Sadie Salome," a comic song by Irving Berlin, she sang in the character of a Jewish girl whose family was appalled by her pursuit of a stage career. The act established Brice as a comedian and introduced audiences to her comically exaggerated Jewish accent, which would become one of her trademarks.

While touring in *The College Girls,* Brice met and married Frank White, a barber. The couple stayed together for a mere three days. They were not officially divorced until 1913.

Having established herself in burlesque, Brice was hired in 1910 to perform in the Ziegfeld Follies. She would remain associated with the vaudeville extravaganza on and off for 14 years, eventually becoming the Follies' biggest star. Brice became well-known for her comic singing routines. Particularly popular was her performance of "Second Hand Rose," a song about the hapless daughter of a secondhand goods dealer, and her parodies of celebrities such as screen vamp THEDA BARA.

Brice was also renowned for the emotional singing style she reserved for serious ballads. One of her signature songs was *My Man,* in which she sang of being loyal to her lover despite the pain he caused her. The lyrics were generally thought to refer to her romance with con man Nick Arnstein, whom she married in 1919 after a lengthy love affair. They had two children before Arnstein was sent to jail on a fraud charge in 1924. Although she never fell entirely out of love with him, Brice divorced Arnstein in 1927 for adultery.

After leaving the Follies in 1924, Brice made appearances in several films, including *My Man* (1927) and *The Great Ziegfeld* (1936). She also appeared regularly in Broadway shows. Among the most notable were *Sweet and Low* (1930) and *Crazy Quilt* (1931), both produced by songwriter Billy Rose, whom Brice married in 1929. In *Sweet and Low,* Brice developed the character of "Babykins," a wisecracking baby who proved wildly popular with her fans. Renamed "Baby Snooks," the character made her radio debut in 1936 and became a regular on the program *Good Times* the following year. In 1944, Baby Snooks received her own show, and on it continued to delight audiences until Brice's death on May 29, 1951, of a cerebral hemorrhage.

For the next generation, Brice was reborn in the popular stage musical *Funny Girl* (1964), which made BARBRA STREISAND a star. It and the subsequent film adaptation told of Brice's career with the Follies and her ill-fated romance with Arnstein, while a film sequel, *Funny Lady* (1975), focused on her marriage to Rose. Both films presented Brice as a confident, charming woman with a genius for parody. Her influence both as a verbal and physical comedian continues to be felt today.

Further Reading

Goldman, Herbert G. *Fanny Brice: The Original Funny Girl.* New York: Oxford University Press, 1992.
Grossman, Barbara Wallace. *Funny Woman: The Life and Times of Fanny Brice.* Bloomington: Indiana University Press, 1991.

Recommended Recorded and Videotaped Performances

Everybody Sing (1938). MGM/UA, VHS, 1992.
Funny Girl (1968). Columbia/Tristar, VHS, 1997.
Funny Lady (1974). Columbia/Tristar, VHS, 1997.
Ziegfeld Follies (1946). Warner Home Video, VHS, 1994.

❖ BROOKS, LOUISE (Mary Louise Brooks)
(1906–1985)   *Actress*

Described as "the most seductive, sexual image of Woman ever committed to celluloid" by her biographer Kenneth Tynan, Louise Brooks inspired a cult following largely based on a single film—German filmmaker G. W. Pabst's *Pandora's Box* (1928). On November 14, 1906, she was born Mary Louise Brooks in Cherryvale, Kansas. Her interest in dance led her parents to enroll her in the Wichita College of Music, which expelled her at 15 for bad behavior.

To further her career, Brooks moved to New York, where she joined RUTH ST. DENIS's Denishawn dance troupe. A petite beauty, she attracted many wealthy suitors and began living extravagantly on her boyfriends' incomes. Dismissed from Denishawn for her poor work habits, Brooks performed as a chorus girl on Broadway and a nightclub performer in London before making her screen debut in 1925.

Under contract to Paramount, she began acting in a series of American films, including Howard Hawks's *A Girl in Every Port* (1928) and William Wellman's *Beggars of Life* (1928). During this period, she briefly married director Edward Sutherland but resumed her flamboyant lifestyle after their divorce in 1928.

Unhappy with the Hollywood system, Brooks asked for a raise from Paramount. When her

Louise Brooks in *Pandora's Box* (1928)
(Museum of Modern Art Film Stills Archive)

request was refused, she impulsively headed off for Germany to work with director G. W. Pabst. Pabst desperately wanted Brooks to play the lead in *Pandora's Box* (1928), a silent film adaptation of two plays by German writer Frank Wedekind. Brooks's character, Lulu, was a new type of femme fatale— one who radiated an unbridled and unapologetic sexuality that brought ruin to those attracted to her and to herself. Condemned as decadent, both *Pandora's Box* and *Diary of a Lost Girl* (1929), Brooks's second movie with Pabst, were box office failures. After making *Prix de Beauté* (1930), a French film, she returned to Hollywood in 1930.

Assuming she could pick up her American film career where she had left it, Brooks was shocked to find that no one was willing to hire her. Paramount may have blackballed her in the industry in retaliation for Brooks's breaking of her contract. But Brooks's outspoken scorn for Hollywood no doubt

also contributed to her situation. Although her friends continued to find her occasional bit parts, a discouraged Brooks retired from films in 1938.

Brooks tried running a dance studio in Wichita in the 1940s but soon moved back to New York City. Aside from a six-month stint on a radio soap opera, she found few acting jobs. Reduced to working as salesclerk at Saks Fifth Avenue, Brooks moved to Rochester, New York, in 1956. Exceedingly well-read and intelligent, she began a second career as a writer. Her witty articles about the silent film era and her own experiences in Hollywood appeared in numerous serious film magazines, including *Film Culture* and *Sight and Sound.*

Brooks's writings found a ready audience among film enthusiasts, who were just beginning to rediscover the films she made with Pabst. Particularly influential to the reevaluation of Brooks's work was the 1955 "Sixty Years of Cinema" show at Paris's Musée National d'Art Moderne. In the exhibit, film archivist Henri Langlois memorably declared, "There is no GARBO! There is no DIETRICH! There is only Louise Brooks!"

Her legend was furthered by critic Kenneth Tynan with the publication of his evaluation of Brooks in the *New Yorker* magazine in 1979. Titled "The Girl in the Black Helmet"—a reference to Brooks' bobbed flapper haircut—the piece was largely written with her cooperation, though Brooks and Tynan later had a falling-out. In 1982, Brooks chose to tell her own story in *Lulu in Hollywood,* a compilation of her magazine articles augmented with some new material. With the image of the exuberant, pleasure-seeking Lulu permanently etched into the American imagination, Brooks died of a heart attack at her home on August 8, 1985.

Further Reading

Brooks, Louise. *Lulu in Hollywood.* Expanded Edition. Minneapolis: University of Minnesota Press, 2000.

Paris, Barry. *Louise Brooks: A Biography.* Minneapolis: University of Minnesota Press, 2000.

Tynan, Kenneth. *Show People: Profiles in Entertainment.* New York: Simon & Schuster, 1980.

Recommended Recorded and Videotaped Performances

Louise Brooks: Looking for Lulu (1998). Image Entertainment, VHS, 1999.

Pandora's Box (1928). Home Vision Cinema, VHS, 1993.

❖ BURNETT, CAROL
(1933–) *Actress, Singer*

Best loved for her long-running variety series, Carol Burnett is a remarkably versatile performer, accomplished in comedy, drama, and musical theater. She was born on April 16, 1933, in San Antonio, Texas, where her alcoholic parents left her in the care of her maternal grandmother. While still in grade school, Carol moved with her grandmother to Los Angeles, where they lived in a one-room apartment with Carol's mother, relying on welfare payments to make ends meet. Carol often escaped from her desperate home life by going to the movies, often five or six times a week.

After graduating from Hollywood High School, Burnett received a scholarship to the University of Southern California. She intended to study journalism but was soon drawn to the theater department. At a school-sponsored workshop, she and fellow student Don Saroyan performed a musical number from *Annie Get Your Gun.* An audience member was so impressed he offered to loan the team $1,000 each so that they could move to New York to break into Broadway theater.

On December 17, 1955, Burnett married Saroyan in New York. On the same day, she made her television debut on *The Winchell-Mahoney Show,* a national children's program on which she played the girlfriend of a ventriloquist's dummy. As a secret "hello" to her grandmother, Burnett tugged on her earlobe during the program. The gesture became her trademark.

After appearing in *Stanley,* a failed situation comedy with Buddy Hackett, Burnett began making guest appearances on *The Garry Moore Show* (1958–67). At the same time, she was making a name for herself on the New York nightclub scene,

singing "I Made a Fool of Myself over John Foster Dulles." She was invited to perform the novelty song on *The Tonight Show* and *Toast of the Town.* In 1959 Burnett also won acclaim on Broadway in *Once Upon a Mattress,* a musical based on the fairy tale "The Princess and the Pea."

In 1962, Burnett won an Emmy for her work on *The Garry Moore Show.* The same year, she signed a 10-year contract with CBS. While her career was thriving, her marriage was suffering. She divorced Saroyan and in 1963 married Joe Hamilton, the producer of *Garry Moore.* Burnett and Hamilton would have three daughters.

With Hamilton as the producer, Burnett began starring in her own television variety series, *The Carol Burnett Show,* in 1967. The format proved a perfect venue for showcasing her comic and musical talents. Building a warm rapport with viewers, Burnett began each show by answering questions from the audience. The rest of the program featured musical numbers and comedy sketches performed with guest stars and a company of supporting players that included Harvey Korman and Tim Conway. Among the most memorable sketches were elaborate spoofs of classic films such as *Gone With the Wind* (1939) and *Sunset Boulevard* (1950).

After an 11-year run, Burnett opted to end the series. She explained, "My view is leave before they ask you to." Burnett spent the late 1970s and 1980s performing in theatrical films and movies for television. Among her films were *A Wedding* (1978), *The Four Seasons* (1981), and *Annie* (1982). She also showed herself to be an adept dramatic actress in *Friendly Fire* (1979) and *Hostage* (1988), in which she starred with her daughter Carrie Hamilton.

In the 1980s, Burnett experienced a series of personal difficulties. She divorced Joe Hamilton in 1984 and was forced to deal with Carrie's drug problems. Burnett also became involved in a landmark lawsuit after the *National Enquirer* published a story saying she had been seen drunk and unruly in a Washington, D.C. restaurant. Burnett won her slander suit and was eventually awarded

29

$800,000, which she used to establish scholarships for the study of journalistic ethics.

Burnett returned to both series television and the theater in the 1990s. She frequently guested on *Mama's Family* (1983–90), a situation comedy based on characters in a series of sketches from her show. Burnett also starred in two variety programs, *Carol & Company* (1990) and *The Carol Burnett Show* (1991), but both were soon canceled. She found greater success onstage, appearing in *Moon Over Buffalo* (1995) and *Putting It Together* (1998), in which she performed songs written by Stephen Sondheim. Burnett, however, is still best remembered for her classic television series. In 2001, 30 episodes were collected into a videotape series introduced by Burnett, Korman, and Conway.

Further Reading

Burnett, Carol. *One More Time.* New York: Random House, 1986.
Newsmakers 2000. Detroit, Mich.: Gale Group, 2000.
Norwich, William. "Carol Burnett." *Interview.* October 1994, pp. 174+.

Recommended Recorded and Videotaped Performances

Annie (1982). Columbia Tristar, VHS, 1997.
Let Me Entertain You: Carol Burnett Sings. Polygram Records, CD, 2000.

CALLAS, MARIA (Cecilia Sophia Anna Kalogeropoulos)
(1923–1977) *Singer*

Few performers have ever inspired as passionate a following as did opera diva Maria Callas. Born Cecilia Sophia Anna Kalogeropoulos on December 2, 1923, she was the second daughter of a prosperous family that emigrated to New York City from Greece several months earlier. After her pharmacist father lost his business following the 1929 stock market crash, her mother, Evangelia, became less interested in her marriage and more in the dream of making one of her daughters into a celebrated performer.

Leaving her husband behind, Evangelia and her girls moved back to Greece in 1937. Soon, the 13-year-old Callas lied about her age to secure an audition at the National Conservatory at Athens. Recognizing her precocious singing talents, Maria Trivella and, later, Elvira de Hidalgo took her on as pupil. De Hidalgo proved an especially strong influence. Herself a celebrated soprano, she helped shape the awkward teenager into a skilled stage performer. She also taught Callas to sing in the bel canto style, which emphasized tonal purity and precise vocal technique.

Callas made an impressive debut in 1940 at Athens's National Lyric Theater, but had difficulty advancing her career amidst the chaos of World War II. With Europe in shambles, after the war she moved back to the United States, where she hoped to establish her reputation. The Metropolitan Opera in New York was willing to sign her to a contract, but unhappy with the parts she was offered, she declined. She was then hired by the United States Opera Company, a new institution that went bankrupt before she had a chance to perform.

On the advice of friends and colleagues, the frustrated Callas decided to try her luck in Italy. In Verona in 1947, she had a successful turn in Amilcare Ponchielli's *La Gioconda* that would reshape both her professional and personal life. Impressed by the young talent, her conductor Tullio Serafin began promoting her in Italian opera circles. During the engagement, she also met Giovanni Battista Meneghini, a businessman who was immediately taken with Callas. Wealthy and solicitous enough to pamper her as she saw fit, Meneghini married Callas in 1949 and abandoned his business enterprises to manage her career.

Under Serafin's guidance, Callas took up an ambitious bel canto repertoire. She startled opera fans with her range in 1949 by performing

Wagner's *Die Walküre* and Bellini's *I Puritani*—operas that required very different styles—in the course of two weeks. Critics hailed her as the first soprano in almost 100 years with the capacity to sing the bel canto works of the romantic period, some of which had not been performed in decades. Some audience members complained that her voice lacked purity, but many more marveled at her dramatic onstage power. She earned a reputation as one of the greatest singing actresses in opera history. Film director Luchino Visconti was so thrilled by her work that he put aside his cinematic career temporarily in 1955 to stage a production of *La Traviata,* her performance in which is often cited as the height of her career.

In 1954 Callas at long last made her singing debut in the United States, starring in Vincenzo Bellini's *Norma* at the Lyric Opera in Chicago. She then joined the Metropolitan for two seasons (1956 and 1958), an event that landed her face on the cover of *Time* magazine. Her fame in the United States and abroad was furthered by a series of enormously successful recordings she made for EMI's Angel Records during this period.

Callas's association with the Metropolitan ended with a violent disagreement with its director. Such fallings-out were common in her dealings with conductors, company managers, and even other singers. Although the highly self-critical Callas was rarely more demanding of others than she was of herself, the press loved to report stories of her arguments and feuds. Opera fans, too, were excited by her larger-than-life personality. Some developed an almost cultish affection for Callas, while others were equally devoted to her rivals. During some performances, her detractors could be heard booing and hissing the star—a distraction that Callas once dismissed as "a part of the scene . . . a hazard of the battlefield. Opera is a battlefield and it must be accepted."

Callas set off a new round of criticism when in 1959 she became involved in an international scandal by falling into an affair with shipping magnate Aristotle Onassis. The romance ended both of their marriages and threatened her career as she began to ignore her voice while embracing Onas-

Maria Callas
(© Hulton-Deutsch Collection/CORBIS)

sis's high-society lifestyle. Callas was involved with Onassis for eight years before her hopes for marriage were dashed by his 1968 wedding to former first lady Jacqueline Kennedy.

Personally devastated, Callas also found her career in ruins. Slammed by ungracious reviews, she had retired from performing in 1965 following her appearance in Giacomo Puccini's *Tosca* at the Royal Opera House in London. One of the few bright spots of her late career was a series of classes she taught at New York's Julliard School of Music between October 1971 and March 1972. (Her instruction there later became the subject of Terrence McNally's Tony Award–winning 1996 play *Master Class.*)

In 1973 and 1974, Callas embarked on an ill-advised comeback in several tours through Europe, North America, and the Far East. Even some of her most ardent fans regarded the tours as a regrettable spectacle of a once-great artist refusing to accept that her voice had lost its power. Despite the critical drubbing she received, Callas continued to perform until 1976. In that year, while she was rehearsing in a Paris theater, a journalist sneaked in to listen and snapped some photographs of her. Although much of the resulting article was sympathetic to Callas, one photo that accompanied it showed the star sitting with her head in her hands, a posture the caption incorrectly attributed to sorrow over her failing voice. (In fact, Callas was suffering from a headache.) Humiliated by the piece, Callas sued the paper and won, although she did not live to see the verdict. On September 16, 1977, she died of a heart attack in her Paris home, but the legend of her tumultuous life and passionate art has only continued to grow.

Further Reading

Gage, Nicholas. *Greek Fire: The Story of Maria Callas and Aristotle Onassis.* New York: Knopf, 2000.

Lowe, David A., ed. *Callas: As They Saw Her.* New York: Ungar, 1986.

Scott, Michael. *Maria Meneghini Callas.* Boston: Northeastern University Press, 1991.

Recommended Recorded and Videotaped Performances

Maria Callas at Juilliard: The Masterclasses. Angel Classics, CD, 1995.

Maria Callas, La Divina: A Portrait (1987). Image Entertainment, DVD, 2000.

Maria Callas: The Legend. Angel Classics, CD, 2000.

Maria Callas: Life and Art (1987). EMD/EMI Classics, DVD, 1999.

Maria Callas: The Paris Debut (1958). EMD/EMI Classics, VHS, 1992.

❖ CARPENTER, KAREN
(1950–1983) *Singer, Musician*

Half of one of the most successful pop acts of the 1970s, Karen Anne Carpenter was born on March 2, 1950, in New Haven, Connecticut. When she was 13, her family moved to Downey, California, a suburb of Los Angeles. Karen and her older brother Richard grew up listening to her father's extensive collection of jazz and big band records, inspiring both to become accomplished musicians. Richard studied piano, while Karen took up the drums.

In 1965, Karen's ambitious brother formed the Richard Carpenter Trio, a jazz instrumental group featuring her, Richard, and their friend Wes Jacobs. The trio played at local clubs and weddings. Often, at Richard's urgings, Karen sang at their engagements, though she continued to think of herself as a drummer first. After winning the 1966 Hollywood Battle of the Bands, the group signed a record contract with RCA. The Carpenters and Jacobs recorded two unreleased albums before RCA decided that a jazz group had little commercial viability. As a solo performer, Karen also recorded a single for Magic Lamp, but the small record label went out of business soon after its release.

In 1967, Richard formed a new group, Spectrum, with Karen and four other musicians. Featuring more of a pop sound, Spectrum was booked at Disneyland and several local clubs but disbanded when it could not secure a record deal. Karen briefly studied music at California State University, but her performing career always came before her schoolwork.

Now performing as a duo called the Carpenters, in 1968 Karen and Richard put together a demo, using a friend's garage as their recording studio. Their new music showcased their vocal harmonies in imitation of the Beach Boys—one of the three B's (along with the Beatles and Burt Bacharach) that they cited as their greatest influences. For months, the Carpenters shopped their demo to Los Angeles record companies. Eventually, it fell into the hands of trumpeter Herb Alpert, the cofounder of A&M Records. Particularly impressed by Karen's contralto singing voice, Alpert signed them to a contract on April 22, 1969.

The Carpenters first album, *Offerings* (1969, later retitled *Ticket to Ride*), was a modest success, but their second, *Close to You* (1970), made them instant stars. Featuring the singles "Close to You" and "We've Only Just Begun," it became the first of their seven gold albums and earned them a Grammy for best new artist. Throughout the early 1970s, the Carpenters dominated the charts, selling more than 80 million records. Despite their huge popular following, critics often complained that their sound was too soft and their songs were too saccharine. Many professionals in the music industry, however, admired Richard's clean arrangements and Karen's unusual voice. The natural expressiveness of her singing was particularly well-served by melancholy songs, such as their hits "Superstar" and "Rainy Days and Mondays."

Years of touring and recording began to take its toll on the Carpenters by the mid-1970s. Richard became addicted to prescription drugs, while Karen, disturbed by references to her weight in the press, began dieting excessively and eventually developed anorexia. By 1975, her weight had dropped to 80 pounds, though her voice remained unaffected by her disease. That year, the Carpenters had to cancel two tours because Karen was too ill to perform.

In part to free herself from her brother's influence, Karen began working on a solo album with producer Phil Ramone in 1979. Its raw sound convinced her record company that it would alienate the Carpenters' fans. The album was not released until 1996.

Karen suffered another disappointment in 1981, when her one-year marriage to real estate developer Thomas J. Burris fell apart. Unhappy and no longer able to deny her disease, she moved to New York to enter therapy with anorexia expert Steven Levenkron. Over the next year, she gained 30 pounds. Convinced she was cured, she returned to California to record another album with Richard in December 1982. Three months later, she collapsed at her parents' home. On February 4, 1983, Karen Carpenter at 33 died of heart failure as a result of the stress her anorexia had placed on her body. Her early death put a public face on her disease, leading to increased awareness of the dangers of anorexia worldwide.

Further Reading

Coleman, Ray. *The Carpenters: The Untold Story.* New York: HarperCollins, 1994.

Schmidt, Randy, ed. *Yesterday Once More: Memories of the Carpenters and Their Music.* Cranberry Township, Pa.: Tiny Ripple Books, 2000.

Recommended Recorded and Videotaped Performances

Carpenters, The Interpretations: A 25th Anniversary Celebration. Uni/Polygram Video, VHS, 1995.

Close to You: Remembering the Carpenters (1997). MPI Media Group, VHS, 1998.

From the Top. Uni/A&M, CD set, 1992.

Karen Carpenter. Uni/A&M, CD, 1996.

❖ CARROLL, DIAHANN (Carol Diahann Johnson)
(1935–) *Actress, Singer*

Already a star of stage and film, Diahann Carroll made history in 1968 by becoming the first African-American woman to star on her own television show. Born Carol Diahann Johnson on July 17, 1935, she grew up in Harlem. Her mother nurtured Carol's interest in becoming a performer, though Carol's own fierce ambition was even more important to building her career. Seeking out contests and competitions, she won a scholarship to study voice and enrolled in New York City's High School of Music and Art. While there, she sent a photograph of herself to *Ebony* magazine, which hired her to appear in a fashion spread. Carroll later credited her modeling experience with teaching her how to carry herself with poise. Using the stage name Diahann Carroll, at 16 she made her national television debut as the winning contestant on *Arthur Godfrey's Talent Scouts.*

To please her parents, Carroll enrolled in New York University while pursuing her singing career. After winning $3,000 on another televised talent contest, she found work in New York clubs and was signed by an agent. After a year of college, Carroll quit school to devote herself to performing full time.

In 1954, Carroll won her first movie role, playing a sidekick in the musical *Carmen Jones,* which starred DOROTHY DANDRIDGE and PEARL BAILEY. The next year, Carroll made her Broadway debut in *House of Flowers,* for which she earned a Tony Award nomination. During its run, she met casting director Monte Kay, whom she married in 1956. They had one daughter, Suzanne, before divorcing.

Carroll returned to the screen in *Porgy and Bess* (1959), in which she costarred with Sidney Poitier. During the filming, she and Poitier began a tumultuous on-again-off-again romance that lasted for eight years. She also appeared in *Paris Blues* (1961) and *Goodbye Again* (1962), before heading back to the stage in *No Strings* (1961–62). This musical was written by Broadway legend Richard Rodgers with Carroll in mind for the lead role of Barbara Woodruff, a sophisticated fashion model. Carroll won a Tony for her performance and toured with show after its Broadway run.

Carroll returned to the nightclub circuit before being cast as the lead in *Julia,* a television situation comedy about a widowed nurse raising her son alone. Premiering in September 1968, *Julia* was America's highest-rated show within a month. Carroll was hailed for breaking a color barrier by playing a middle-class professional at a time when African-American women seldom appeared on television unless they were portraying a maid. Some African Americans, however, complained that *Julia,* with its relatively bland and uncontroversial scripts, created an unrealistic portrayal of black life in America. Carroll was shaken by the criticism and exhausted by the rigorous schedule in producing the show. By 1970, she asked to be released from her contract.

As she struggled to find better roles, Carroll experienced renewed turmoil in her private life. She became romantically linked with television host David Frost, but called off their marriage at the last minute. A week later, she married Freddie Glusman, a store owner. Within months, they were divorced.

In 1975, Carroll found perhaps her best role in *Claudine,* a comedic drama in which she played a single mother of six children in Harlem. Though known as a fashion plate, she embraced the unglamorous role. She explained, "I couldn't wait to put aside the couture gowns. . . . I wanted to let my talent out, to expose it, to test it." Her performance won her an Academy Award nomination for best actress. While publicizing *Claudine,* Carroll met Robert DeLeon, the 26-year-old managing editor of *Jet* magazine. They were married for two years, until DeLeon's death in an auto accident in 1977.

Carroll soon returned to work, acting onstage in *Same Time, Next Year* (1978) and *Agnes of God* (1983). She also appeared frequently on television, most notably joining the cast of the popular prime-time soap opera *Dynasty* in 1984 as the impeccably dressed and perfectly coiffed Dominique Deveraux. The same year, she started dating singer Vic Damone. From 1987 to 1996, they were married and frequently performed together.

Carroll has complained that, as an older African-American woman, there are few roles open to her. Yet, she has continued to work steadily, often finding meaty roles in respected projects. In 1997 she won rave reviews playing a voodoo priestess in *Eve's Bayou.* Now a staple of television movies, she has also been praised for her work in *The Sweetest Gift* (1998), *Having Our Say* (1999), *Sally Hemings: An American Scandal* (2000), and *Livin' for Love: The Natalie Cole Story* (2000).

Further Reading

Carroll, Diahann, and Ross Firestone. *Diahann! An Autobiography.* Boston: Little, Brown, 1986.
"Diahann Carroll." In *Contemporary Black Biography.* Vol. 9. Detroit: Gale Research, 1995.

Recommended Recorded and Videotaped Performances

Carmen Jones (1954). Twentieth Century-Fox, VHS, 1994.
Eve's Bayou (1997), Vidmark/Trimark, DVD/VSH, 2001/1998.
The Time of My Life. Sterling-Koch, CD, 1997.

❖ CARTER, MAYBELLE
(1909–1978) *Musician*

Considered the mother of country music, Maybelle Carter was born Maybelle Addington on May 10, 1909. She grew up in rural Virginia near the town of Nickelsville, where her father operated a general store. Like many mountain families, the Addingtons played music for their entertainment. By the time Maybelle was 12, she was a talented musician, proficient on the guitar, autoharp, and banjo.

In 1926, Addington married Ezra Carter, with whom she had three daughters, Helen, June, and Anita. Maybelle Carter also began performing with Ezra's brother Alvin Pleasant (known as A. P.) and his wife Sara, playing at parties and other local social gatherings. The Carters perfected intricate arrangements of vocals and instruments. A. P. sang bass and Sara sang lead as well as playing the guitar and autoharp. But Maybelle perhaps most shaped the Carter Family sound by her unique guitar work.

When Maybelle was pregnant with her first child, the Carter Family traveled down a dirt road for a record company tryout in Bristol, Tennessee. Their performance so impressed talent scout Ralph Peer that he asked them to record six songs that day. The session is regarded as one of the first efforts to record country music.

In 1928, the Carter Family had its first hit with the upbeat "Keep on the Sunny Side." Their other popular songs included "Wabash Cannonball" and "Will the Circle Be Unbroken." Maybelle Carter's greatest contribution to popular music was arguably her guitar playing on "Wildwood Flower." On this song, she created a new way of using the guitar, by playing the melody on the bass strings and the rhythm on the treble strings. Her inventive guitar work has influenced nearly every popular and rock guitarist who followed her. Jerry Garcia of the Grateful Dead once said that there was a bit of the Carter Family in every song he wrote.

Between 1927 and 1941, the Carter Family recorded about 270 songs. They also broadened their audience by appearing frequently on high-powered Mexican radio stations, often featuring their children as singers in on-air performances. When A. P. and Sara divorced in 1943, Maybelle continued to perform with a new Carter Family—a foursome that included her and her three daughters. By 1950, they were appearing regularly on the Grand Ole Opry, the premier show for country music artists. Maybelle Carter and her daughters also toured with Chet Atkins and Elvis Presley and were frequent guests on *The Johnny Cash Show* (1969–71), whose host is married to Maybelle's daughter June.

By the 1960s, Maybelle Carter had achieved the status of legend. Her musicianship was revered by folk artists such as Bob Dylan who had come to prominence in the popular music scene. She appeared to much acclaim at the Newport Folk Festival in 1963 and 1967 and recorded a three-album set titled *Will the Circle Be Unbroken* (1972) with the Nitty Gritty Dirt Band.

In 1970, Maybelle Carter attended a ceremony inducting the original Carter Family into the Country Music Hall of Fame. She continued to perform until a year before her death on October 23, 1978.

Further Reading

Bufwack, Mary A., and Robert K. Oermann. *Finding Her Voice: The Saga of Women in Country Music.* New York: Crown Publishers. 1993.

Wolfe, Charles K. "Carter, Maybelle." In *American National Biography,* edited by John Arthur Garraty and Mark C. Carnes, vol. 4, pp. 492–493. New York: Oxford University Press, 1999.

Recommended Recorded and Videotaped Performances

The Best of the Best of the Carter Family. King, CD, 1997.
Wildwood Pickin'. Vanguard, CD, 1997.

❖ CASTLE, IRENE (Irene Foote)
(1893–1969) *Dancer*

With her husband, Vernon, Irene Castle was the leading popularizer of ballroom dance in the early 20th century. Born Irene Foote on April 7, 1893, she was the daughter of a prominent physician in New Rochelle, New York. Irene studied dancing and performed in several amateur theatricals before meeting Vernon Castle in 1910. With his help, she was hired for her first professional job, a small dancing part in *The Summer Widowers*. The next year, over her father's objections, the two were married.

The English-born Vernon had already established himself as a dancer in comedic roles. His specialty was playing a gentleman drunk, who elegantly fell about the stage while trying to hide his condition. After their marriage, Irene joined Vernon in *The Hen-Pecks* (1911), a production in which he was a featured player. The two then traveled together to Paris to perform in a dance revue. The show closed quickly, but the couple was then hired as a dance act by the Café de Paris. Performing the latest American dances, the Castles were soon the rage of Parisian society. Their success was widely reported in the United States, preparing their way for a triumphant return to New York in 1912.

The Castles were hired to stage dance exhibitions at Louis Martin's, a Broadway cabaret. Their routine presented a series of popular dances, such as the one-step, tango, fox-trot, and the Castle Walk, their signature dance. The dance floor was then turned over the couples in the audience, who did their best to imitate the Castles' footwork. In addition to cabaret, the Castles also became staples of Broadway. Among their shows were *The Sunshine Girl* (1913) and *Watch Your Step* (1914), which boasted a score written by Irving Berlin with them in mind.

Emerging as America's premier dance team, the Castles were trendsetters in a number of arenas. Their infectious enthusiasm for dance encouraged admirers to try new forms of social dance. Considered paragons of respectability and class, the Castles specifically helped remove the stigma of vulgarity from close dancing. The Castles' performances, often set to ragtime and jazz rhythms, also popularized African-American music among well-heeled whites. Irene's fashion sense, too, started national trends. Her elegant, yet simple, flowing gowns were often featured in fashion magazines. She is also credited with introducing American women to the bob—the short hairstyle favored by flappers in the 1920s.

With the assistance of literary agent Elizabeth Marbury, the Castles became enormously adept at capitalizing on their fame. In New York, they established their own supper club and a dance school named Castle House, where they instructed the children of high-society families. For their middle-class fans, they published *Modern Dancing* (1914), one of the first instructional books on ballroom dance. They also starred in *Whirl of Life* (1915), their first film biography, and licensed their name to a variety of products, including Castle Corsets.

With the onset of World War I, Vernon joined the British Royal Flying Corps, while Irene attempted to establish a solo career, appearing on Broadway and in film serials. In 1917, the Castles' performance career came to a tragic end when Vernon, assigned to instruct pilots in Fort Worth, Texas, was killed in a crash during a routine flight. In the early 1920s, Irene tried to recreate the magic she had with Vernon with a new dance partner, William Reardon, but their pairing never caught on with the public.

Irene Castle continued to perform periodically on Broadway, but by the late 1920s was much more engrossed in her work with the antivivisection movement. In 1928, she established an animal shelter called Orphans of the Storm, which she held society balls to support. After Vernon's death, she married three more times and had two children, Barbara and William. Suffering from emphysema, she died on January 25, 1969. Though largely forgotten today, the Castles' career and performance style were immortalized on screen in *The Story of Vernon and Irene Castle* (1939), the last of nine films starring dance greats GINGER ROGERS and Fred Astaire.

Further Reading

Castle, Irene, as told to Bob and Wanda Duncan. *Castles in the Air*. Garden City, N.Y.: Doubleday, 1958.

Fanger, Iris M. "Castle, Irene and Vernon." *International Encyclopedia of Dance*, edited by Selma Jeanne Cohen, vol. 1, pp. 78–80. New York: Oxford University Press, 1998.

Recommended Recorded and
Videotaped Performances

The Story of Vernon and Irene Castle (1939), Turner Home
Video, VHS, 2000.

❖ **CHARISSE, CYD (Tula Ellice Finklea,
Natacha Tulaelis, Felia Siderova, Lily
Norwood)**
(1921–) *Dancer, Actress*

Arguably the greatest female dancer in Hollywood
history, Cyd Charisse was born Tula Ellice Finklea
in Amarillo, Texas, on March 8, 1921. As a girl,
she became known as Sid, her brother's mispro-
nunciation of "sis." At eight, she began taking ballet lessons. Five years later, she started training
with the dancer Nico Charisse in Los Angeles. She
was asked to join the prestigious Ballet Russe in
1937. Following company custom, she was billed
under the Russian-sounding names Natacha
Tulaelis and Felia Siderova. While on a tour of
Europe, Finklea married Charisse in 1939. Before
their divorce in 1947, the couple had one son. In
1948 she married singer Tony Martin, with whom
she had another child, also a boy.

Leaving Europe after the outbreak of World
War II, Charisse returned to Hollywood and
started appearing in films under the name Lily
Norwood. After performing small dance roles in
such films as *Something to Shout About* (1943) and
Thousands Cheer (1943), she was signed by Metro-
Goldwyn-Mayer (MGM) in 1946. Now billed as
Cyd Charisse, she paid her dues as a background
dancer in several films. Among the films in which
she was featured more prominently were *Till the
Clouds Roll By* (1946), in which she danced with
Gower Champion, and *Unfinished Dance* (1947).
Charisse was also called upon to play ethnic roles
in such films as *Fiesta* (1947) and *Sombrero* (1953).

Charisse's break came in 1952, when she
appeared in the classic musical *Singin' in the Rain.*
In the film's "Broadway Melody" sequence, she
memorably portrayed a femme fatale in a dance
with Gene Kelly. In 1953, she was paired with

Cyd Charisse with Fred Astaire
in *The Band Wagon* (1953)
(Museum of Modern Art Film Stills Archive)

MGM's other great male dancer, Fred Astaire, in
The Band Wagon (1953). Common to many of her
films, the script cast her a sophisticated, elegant
woman who had be persuaded to abandon her pre-
tensions before she could be loved. The movie featured one of her most famous dances recorded on
film—the "Dancing in the Dark" ballet choreographed by Astaire. He once aptly described his
dance partner as "beautiful dynamite."

During the golden age of the MGM musical,
Charisse also found choice roles in *Brigadoon*
(1954), *It's Always Fair Weather* (1955), and *Silk
Stockings* (1957), which reunited her with Astaire.
Although a far better dancer than actress, she also
appeared in nonmusical dramas, among them *Party
Girl* (1958) and *Two Weeks in Another Town* (1962).

As Charisse's film career faded, she started
appearing in nightclubs with her husband. She also

performed on stage in regional theater and summer stock. Charisse, however, did not make her Broadway debut until 1992, when she was invited to join the cast of the two-year-old musical hit *Grand Hotel*. At 71, she told *People* magazine that dancing on Broadway "was one goal I hadn't achieved, and it's exciting to do it now." The same year, Charisse won the Gypsy Lifetime Achievement Award from the Professional Dancer's Society.

Further Reading

Billman, Larry. "Charisse, Cyd." *International Encyclopedia of Dance,* edited by Selma Jeanne Cohen, vol. 1, pp. 108–109. New York: Oxford University Press, 1998.
Martin, Tony, and Cyd Charisse. *The Two of Us.* New York: Mason/Charter, 1976.

Recommended Recorded and Videotaped Performances

The Band Wagon (1953). Warner Studios, VHS, 2000.
Brigadoon (1954). Warner Studios, DVD/VHS, 2000.

❖ CHER (Cherilyn Sarkisian, Cher Bono)
(1946–   ) *Singer, Actress*

Throughout her up-and-down career, Cher has continually emerged as one of America's most durable performers. Born Cherilyn Sarkisian on May 20, 1946, she survived a difficult childhood in El Centro, California. Her mother, Georgia, a part-time fashion model and country singer, was married eight times, including twice to Cher's father, John Sarkisian. Helping to bring up her half-sister Georgeanne, Cher later remembered being so poor that she "went to school with rubber bands wrapped around my shoes to keep the soles on."

At 16, Cher moved out of her mother's house and dropped out of high school, intending to pursue an acting career. Her plans changed after meeting 27-year-old record promoter Sonny Bono at a coffee shop. Finding her work as backup singer, Bono became her professional mentor and lover. On October 27, 1964, they were married in Tijuana, Mexico.

Bono developed a nightclub act for himself and Cher, billed first as "Caesar and Cleo," then as "Sonny and Cher." After recording two modestly successful singles, they struck gold in June 1965 with their recording of Bono's song, "I Got You Babe." A number-one hit, the single eventually sold 4 million copies. Sonny and Cher recorded six albums, although they became as well known for their hippie-style clothing—most memorably bell-bottom pants and furry vests—as for their music. Sonny and Cher also tried, with less success, to break into movies. They both appeared as themselves in *Good Times* (1967), and Cher starred as a runaway in *Chastity* (1969), which Bono wrote and produced. Their only child, born in 1969, was named after the latter film.

As their pop music career began to fade, Bono, against Cher's wishes, revived their nightclub act. To help shed their hippie image, Cher wore slinky, low-cut evening gowns and perfected a joking banter with Bono between songs. An appearance on *The Merv Griffin Show* caught the attention of CBS, which signed them to star in a six-week variety series. Premiering on August 1, 1971, *The Sonny and Cher Comedy Hour* was an instant hit, making television stars out of Sonny and Cher overnight. Cher also launched a new career as a solo recording artist. Her singles included "Gypsies, Tramps, and Thieves" and "Half Breed," a reference to her part-Cherokee heritage.

Sonny and Cher's series ran for three years. At its height in 1974, Cher shocked their fans by filing for divorce, maintaining that Bono had kept her in "involuntary servitude." Soon after the divorce was granted, Cher married rock musician Gregg Allman, but she left her new husband after nine days. Cher and Allman had one son, Elijah Blue.

After the failure of their marriage, both Cher and Bono launched unsuccessful solo series before trying to revive their variety show in 1976. For the public, however, their divorce had destroyed the magic of the Sonny and Cher duo. The show was swiftly canceled.

With the encouragement of her boyfriend, record executive David Geffen, Cher returned to nightclubs, becoming a Las Vegas headliner. Creatively, however, this bored her and she quickly abandoned her $350,000-a-week paycheck to fulfill her childhood dream of becoming a serious actress. In New York, she was hired to star in the Broadway production of *Come Back to the Five and Dime, Jimmy Dean, Jimmy Dean* in 1982. The same year, she appeared in the film adaptation, which brought her to the attention of director Mike Nichols. He hired Cher for a supporting role in *Silkwood* (1983), for which she was nominated for an Academy Award. Now an acclaimed actress, she starred in *Mask* (1985), *Suspect* (1987), and *Mermaids* (1990). The pinnacle of her film career came with her performance as a frumpy widow transformed by love in the romantic comedy *Moonstruck* (1987). The role won her the Oscar for best actress.

In the 1990s, Cher fell victim to Epstein-Barr disease, leaving her too exhausted to sustain her music and film careers. She did, however, appear in a series of cosmetics infomercials, which led many in entertainment industry to declare she was a has-been. "I became a joke on *Letterman* and *Saturday Night Live*," she recalled of this period. "It was just a huge, devastating misjudgment of what people would accept from me."

Even as her work was being dismissed, Cher's personal life kept her in the public eye. In 1994, her daughter, Chastity, publicly announced that she was a lesbian, detailing for the press Cher's initial difficulty in coming to terms with the fact. Four years later, Sonny Bono, now a congressman from California, died in a skiing accident. Cher delivered an emotional eulogy, which without her knowledge the major television networks broadcast live. To her fellow mourners, she described her moving tribute to Bono as "the most important thing I've ever done in my life."

The loss of Bono ironically ushered in another career upswing for Cher. In 1999, she released a new album, featuring the surprise hit "Believe." The dance song became the number-one single in 23 countries, making it her greatest success as a recording artist. Just one in a series of many dramatic comebacks, this rebirth of Cher's career

inspired a joke often repeated in entertainment circles: After a nuclear war, the only creatures sure to survive are roaches and Cher.

Further Reading

Cher, and Jeff Coplon. *The First Time*. New York: Simon & Schuster, 1998.

Taraborrelli, J. Randy. *Cher: A Biography*. New York: St. Martin's Press, 1986.

Recommended Recorded and Videotaped Performances

Cher: Live in Concert (1999). HBO Studios, DVD/VHS, 1999.

Moonstruck (1988). MGM/UA Studios, DVD/V, 2000/2001.

Sonny and Cher: Nitty Gritty Hour (1970). View Video, VHS, 1992.

The Way of Love: The Cher Collection. Uni/MCA, CD set, 2000.

❖ **CLINE, PATSY (Virginia Patterson Hensley)**
(1932–1963)   *Singer*

With her infectious blend of hillbilly and pop, Patsy Cline became one of the first female stars of country music. Born Virginia Patterson Hensley on September 8, 1932, she began her performing career at four, when she won an amateur talent contest in her hometown of Winchester, Virginia. By eight, she was learning to play the piano and singing in her church choir.

While working as a drugstore clerk to support her family, Hensley began performing in local clubs in 1948. She was spotted by Wally Fowler of the Grand Ole Opry radio show, who encouraged her to pursue her singing career in Nashville. Hensley took his advice but quickly ran out of money while trying to break into the music industry. Back in Winchester, in 1953 she married Gerald Cline, who disapproved of her singing professionally. They divorced three years later.

Slowly, Patsy Cline continued to build her career. After touring with Opry stars Faron Young and Ferlin Husky, she was signed to a recording contract with Four Star Sales. Her first record, "A Church, a Courtroom and Then Good-Bye," was released in 1955. Her recordings with Four Star were largely undistinguished, with the notable exception of "Walkin' After Midnight." She performed the song on the nationally televised show *Arthur Godfrey's Talent Scout* on November 8, 1956. The audience response was enormous, and Four Star quickly released "Walkin'" as a single. The record rose to number three on the country chart and number 12 on the pop chart.

For the next three years, Cline's career stagnated as Four Star struggled to produce a follow-up hit. During this period, she married Charlie Dick, with whom she had two children, Julia and Randy. In 1959, Cline signed a new contract with Decca, which began promoting her heavily. The following year, she became a regular performer on the Grand Ole Opry.

Cline sealed her stardom in 1961 with the release of two chart-toppers, "I Fall to Pieces" and "Crazy." These were followed over the next two years by a string of hits, including "When I Get Through with You, You'll Love Me," "Faded Love," and "Leavin' on Your Mind." On these recordings, Cline was paired with producer Owen Bradley, who backed her strong, emotional vocals with lush orchestrations. The records were instrumental in developing a pop-influenced style of country that helped widen country's commercial appeal.

While returning home from a benefit concert in Kansas City, Cline died in a plane crash on March 5, 1963, near Camden, Tennessee. Though her recording career lasted only eight years, Cline's records continue to be enormously popular and influential. LORETTA LYNN, Linda Ronstadt, and k. d. lang are among the hundreds of singers who owe a debt to Cline. Her greatest-hits album is the best selling of any by a female artist, and her version of "Crazy" was certified in 2000 as the number-one jukebox hit of all time by the Amusement and Music Operators of America. In 1973, 10 years after her death, Cline became the first woman inducted into the Country Music Hall of Fame as a solo act.

Further Reading

Hazen, Cindy, and Mike Freeman, eds. *Love Always, Patsy: Patsy Cline's Letters to a Friend.* New York: Berkley Books, 1999.
Nassour, Ellis. *Honky Tonk Angel: The Intimate Story of Patsy Cline.* New York: St. Martin's Press, 1993.

Recommended Recorded and Videotaped Performances

The Patsy Cline Collection. Uni/MCA, CD set, 1991.
Sweet Dreams (1985). HBO Home Video, DVD/VHS, 2000/1998.

❖ COLBERT, CLAUDETTE (Lily Claudette Chauchoin)
(1903–1996)   *Actress*

Known best for her romantic comedies, Claudette Colbert was one of film's greatest leading ladies of the 1930s. On September 13, 1903, she was born Lily Claudette Chauchoin in Paris. When she was six, her family moved to New York City, where she dreamed of becoming a fashion designer. With the encouragement of playwright Anne Morrison, she instead reluctantly opted for a stage career, beginning in 1923 with a three-line part in *The Wild Westcotts.* Professionally, she called herself Claudette Colbert, taking her paternal great-grandmother's maiden name as her surname.

Colbert spent several years in small stage roles before finding her breakout role in *The Barker* (1927), in which she played a carnival snake charmer. During its extended New York run, she married her costar, actor Norman Foster, whom she divorced six years later. Colbert also made her first film, *For the Love of Mike* (1927), a silent campus comedy directed by Frank Capra. The experience convinced Colbert that film acting was not for her. Performing in silents did not give her a chance to use what she considered one of her best assets—her low, mellow voice.

With the onset of the Great Depression, funding for Broadway shows dried up. Colbert realized that if she wanted to work, she had no choice but to become a film actress—a prospect made more

Claudette Colbert with Clark Gable in *It Happened One Night* (1934)
(Museum of Modern Art Film Stills Archive)

attractive by the advent of talking pictures. She moved to Los Angeles and was quickly typecast in virtuous ingenue roles. Eager to show her range, she played the wicked Empress Poppaea in *The Sign of the Cross* (1932), Cecil B. DeMille's extravaganza set in Nero's Rome. A scene in which she took a bath in asses' milk made her a sex symbol and a star.

After appearing in several undistinguished films, Colbert found her best part in Frank Capra's *It Happened One Night* (1934). She was unimpressed by the script, but jumped at the chance to act opposite *Night*'s male star, Clark Gable. Though dismissed by all as a routine comedy during its filming, it became one of the great sleeper hits in Hollywood history. It won five

Academy Awards, including one for Colbert for best actress. She became forever associated with one of its most famous scenes, in which she taught Gable a lesson in hitchhiking by lifting her skirt to display her shapely leg and bringing a car to a screeching halt.

The business-savvy Colbert parlayed the success of *Night* into a long-term contract with Paramount, which made her one of the highest-paid actresses of the 1930s and 1940s. Colbert took on a variety of films, from the campy *Cleopatra* (1934) to the tearjerker *Imitation of Life* (1934) to the dramas *Private Worlds* (1935) and *Since You Went Away* (1944). For these last two films, she received her second and third Oscar nominations. Colbert, however, made her most indelible mark in comedies, including *Bluebeard's Eighth Wife* (1938), *Midnight* (1939), *The Palm Beach Story* (1942), and *The Egg and I* (1947).

Among her peers, Colbert earned a reputation as the most levelheaded of all Hollywood stars. She exuded a natural sense of style and confidence onscreen and offscreen. As she once noted, "I don't need that awful artificial glamour that Hollywood devises for people who don't have any personalities." Colbert was well-known for insisting on being photographed from the left to hide a small bump on her nose—a habit inspired by "professionalism, not vanity." What might have seemed narcissistic was actually just another example of her practical approach to doing her job.

For a star of her stature, Colbert also had a remarkably uneventful personal life. In 1935 she married her doctor, Joel Pressman, whom she called her best friend. Their successful marriage ended with Pressman's death in 1968. When asked to write an autobiography, she refused, explaining "The trouble is I've been happy, and that's no story."

Colbert continued to work in films through the 1950s, although good roles were increasingly hard to find. One of her greatest disappointments was losing, as a result of a skiing accident, the role of the sharp-tongued Margo Channing in *All About Eve* (1950), which won BETTE DAVIS an Oscar. Colbert later bemoaned that she "just never had the luck to play bitches. Those are the only parts that ever register, really."

After appearing in more than 60 films, Colbert left Hollywood to return to Broadway in 1961. Aided by her timeless beauty and ever-slender figure, she was cast in many hit plays, including *The Marriage-Go-Round* (1956), *The Irregular Verb to Love* (1963), and *The Kingfisher* (1978). She also appeared frequently on television. Her last role in the 1986 miniseries *The Two Mrs. Grenvilles* earned her an Emmy nomination. Colbert then retired to her plantation in Barbados, where she was known as a gracious host to her many guests. After suffering a stroke in 1993, she died at her home on July 30, 1996, at the age of 92.

Further Reading

Everson, William K. *Claudette Colbert*. New York: Pyramid, 1976.

"Hollywood Legend Claudette Colbert Dies." *The Los Angeles Times,* July 31, 1996, p. 1.

Quirk, Lawrence J. *Claudette Colbert: An Illustrated Biography.* New York: Crown Publishers, 1985.

Recommended Recorded and Videotaped Performances

Cleopatra (1934). Universal, VHS, 2000.

It Happened One Night (1934). Columbia Tristar, DVD/VHS, 1999/1998.

The Palm Beach Story (1942). Universal, VHS, 1998.

❖   **CRAWFORD, JOAN** (Lucille Fay LeSueur)
(1904–1977)   *Actress*

One of the most successful products of the Hollywood star system, Joan Crawford was born Lucille Fay LeSueur in San Antonio, Texas, on March 23, 1904. Her working-class family was rocked by the desertions of first her father and later her stepfather. Once a celebrity, she remembered her early years with bitterness. As Crawford told a reporter, "We can skip my childhood. I didn't have any. Everything I have in life, Hollywood gave me."

After finishing high school, Lucille LeSueur left home to attend Stephens College in Missouri but dropped out after only a few months. She then worked as a telephone operator and a salesclerk before landing a job as a chorus girl. Performances in Detroit and Chicago led to a stint on Broadway and a Hollywood screen test.

In 1925 LeSueur arrived in Los Angeles with a contract from Metro-Goldwyn-Mayer (MGM). Studio head Louis Mayer declared that the starlet's surname sounded uncomfortably close to "sewer" and, as a publicity stunt, announced a nationwide contest to find her a new name. Soon, Lucille Fay LeSueur was appearing in bit parts as Joan Crawford. A diligent on-the-job student of the filmmaking process, she had her breakthrough role as a flapper in the silent feature *Our Darling Daughters* (1928).

The following year, Crawford eloped with Douglas Fairbanks Jr. the son of film great Douglas Fairbanks Sr. Although she was already a rising star, the elder Fairbanks and his wife, screen legend MARY PICKFORD, viewed her as an upstart. With characteristic determination, Crawford launched a campaign to win them over, presenting herself as a homebody and replacing her flapper costumes with chic, sophisticated fashions. Her inability to gain their acceptance helped bring on her divorce from Fairbanks in 1933.

Crawford found more success in her career as, unlike many film personalities, she easily made the transition from silents to talkies. Although she sang and danced in some of her early movies, she became well-known for playing upwardly mobile young women in rags-to-riches stories such as *Possessed* (1931) and *Mannequin* (1937). Crawford also delivered standout performances in small parts in *Grand Hotel* (1932) and *The Women* (1939).

While at MGM, Crawford embraced the studio's legendary star treatment like no other actress. She welcomed MGM's efforts to transform her from a scrappy young woman to a glamorous screen goddess. Her new image came to dominate her personal as well as her professional life. Crawford once said that whenever she appeared in public, she was "ready and well-dressed as I possibly can be. When somebody says, 'There's Joan Crawford,' I say, 'It sure the hell is.'" To ensure her continued popularity, she was active in her fan clubs, readily signed autographs, and often answered fan mail herself.

Also a staple of fan and gossip magazines were stories of Crawford's personal life. During the course of two more failed marriages (Franchot Tone, 1935–39; Philip Terry, 1942–46), she adopted four children and set about creating a domestic haven to stand as a testament to her success at home as well as on screen. However, according to her eldest daughter, Christine, in her savage tell-all biography *Mommie Dearest* (1978), her children's home life was scarred by Crawford's capricious physical and emotional abuse.

By the early 1940s, Crawford was facing professional turmoil as well. After 18 years at MGM, the studio began to regard her as a has-been and made little effort to find films to suit her. Crawford asked to be released from her contract and subsequently signed on to work for Warner Brothers. There, her career was revived as she was cast as powerful, determined, and sometimes ruthless women in a string of successful melodramas and film noir features. Her best-known and arguably her greatest role was in *Mildred Pierce* (1945), in which she played a woman willing to make any sacrifice to give her daughter the finer things in life. For her performance, she won an Academy Award for Best Actress. She was later nominated for Best Actress Oscars for *Possessed* (1947) and *Sudden Fear* (1952).

In 1955 Crawford married for a fourth time to Alfred N. Steele, an executive of Pepsi-Cola. She and Steele made their home in a Manhattan townhouse, which Crawford spared no expense in decorating. The couple's highly public, lavish lifestyle came to an end with Steele's sudden death from a heart attack in 1959. For a time, Crawford took over his spot on Pepsi-Cola's board of directors, making her the first woman to hold such a position within the company.

Having spent much of former husband's fortune, Crawford returned to Hollywood but had difficulty finding roles. She was finally teamed with BETTE DAVIS in the unlikely success *What Ever Happened to Baby Jane?* (1962). A ghoulish thriller about a deadly rivalry between two elderly sisters, the film earned Davis an Oscar nomination, but Crawford, much to her chagrin, was overlooked—a situation that did nothing to soothe the widely reported animosity between the two stars. On Oscar night, when Davis lost to newcomer Anne Bancroft, Crawford could barely contain her delight as she bounded onstage to accept the award on the absent Bancroft's behalf.

After *Baby Jane,* Crawford acted mostly in lesser genre films, delivering her final movie performance in the undistinguished *Trog* (1970). She also made occasional television appearances, most notably replacing her daughter Christine in several episodes of the soap opera *Silent Storm* and playing a blind woman in an installment of the horror series *Night Gallery.* Crawford's *Night Gallery* marked the directoral debut of Steven Spielberg, and in her later years, she often took credit for discovering him.

Crawford spent her final years as a recluse, discomforted that as an older woman she could no longer maintain her glamorous image. Suffering from stomach cancer, she died on May 10, 1977, at her home in New York City.

Although her acting ability was never as celebrated as those of her contemporaries such as Bette Davis and KATHARINE HEPBURN, Crawford enjoyed astounding longevity in a business that often seemed all too ready to cast her aside. She remained a star not because of her unquestionable talent but because of her sheer, unflagging determination to stay on top. Crawford's journey from working girl to glamour girl informed her best roles and earned her the affection of millions of fans who loved to cheer her on.

Further Reading

Crawford, Christina. *Mommie Dearest.* New York: William Morrow, 1978.

Crawford, Joan, with Jane Kesner Ardmore. *A Portrait of Joan: The Autobiography of Joan Crawford.* Garden City, N.Y.: Doubleday, 1962.

Guiles, Fred Lawrence. *Joan Crawford: The Last Word.* Secaucus, N.J.: Carol Publishing Group, 1995.

Walker, Alexander. *Joan Crawford: The Ultimate Star.* New York: Harper & Row, 1983.

Recommended Recorded and Videotaped Performances

Mildred Pierce (1945). Warner Home Video, VHS, 2000.

Possessed (1947). Warner Home Video, VHS, 1991.

Rain (1932). VCI Home Video, VHS, 2000.

What Ever Happened to Baby Jane? (1962). Warner Home Video, VHS, 2000.

❖ **CUSHMAN, CHARLOTTE**
(1816–1876) *Actress*

The first American actress to achieve international acclaim, Charlotte Cushman was born in Boston, Massachusetts, on July 23, 1816. Descended from the original Plymouth colonists, Cushman's family suffered financial disaster in 1829 when her father, a merchant, declared bankruptcy and disappeared. Only 13 at the time, Charlotte was forced to quit school and take work as a domestic to help support her mother and her sister Susan.

With characteristic single-mindedness, Charlotte became determined to find better work at higher pay. Blessed with a strong voice, she began taking singing lessons, which she paid for herself from her meager wages. In 1835 she made her professional opera debut in Boston. Encouraged by generous reviews, Cushman secured an apprenticeship at the St. Charles Theater in New Orleans. In her first performance, she strained to reach notes too high for her range, causing a New Orleans critic to dismiss Cushman's singing as "squalling." Humbled by the experience, Cushman took the advice of the theater's manager, who suggested that, with her natural theatricality, she might find more success as a dramatic actress.

In the late 1830s, Cushman was hired to play a wide variety of roles in theaters in Albany, Philadelphia, and New York City. Unlike most young actresses, she generally shied away from ingenue roles. Tall and plain, she felt physically uncomfortable playing a romantic lead. Temperamentally, she also preferred strong, independent characters. Her early successes included roles as an old gypsy in the stage adaptation of Sir Walter Scott's *Guy Mannering* and as the prostitute Nancy in a version of Charles Dickens's *Oliver Twist.* For the role of Nancy, Cushman spent five days touring New York's slums to watch the movements and behavior of the city's poor streetwalkers. Although her audiences appreciated the authenticity of her performance, Cushman soon dropped Nancy from her repertoire for fear that playing such an unsavory character would slow her rise in high society. She turned, instead, to powerful female roles from Shakespeare, especially Lady Macbeth and *Henry VIII*'s Queen Katherine.

Despite her growing fame, Cushman was dissatisfied with her career. While one of the United States's leading actresses, she longed to prove herself on the English stage, then considered far more sophisticated and professional than the American theater. Her

Charlotte Cushman in *Guy Mannering* in about 1855
(Library of Congress, neg. no. USZ62-55591)

desire to perform in London was also guided by more practical concerns. As the sole breadwinner of her family, Cushman wanted the impressive income only an performer with experience in England could command. For example, for a two-week stint at a Boston theater, Cushman was paid a mere $100 while her costar, William Macready, a well-known English actor, received $2,900.

Carrying letters of introduction from her many well-connected friends, Cushman set off for England in the fall of 1844. The following February, she made her London debut in *Fazio,* a popular melodrama about a woman who, in a fit of jealousy, reveals her husband's embezzlement to the authorities. The audience seemed indifferent to Cushman's performance until the play's climax, when her character, hearing her husband sentenced to death, begs

him for forgiveness. Her passion thrilled the audience, who rose to their feet and cheered Cushman at the play's end. Overnight, she became one of London's biggest stars.

During her triumphant English tour, Cushman also earned accolades for her depiction of Romeo, often in productions featuring her sister Susan as Juliet. At the time, actresses often played male characters, usually because it allowed them to wear pants or tights that displayed their legs. Sex appeal, however, seemed to play little role in the audience's appreciation of Cushman's Romeo. Instead, playgoers seemed to respect the credibility her height, mannish features, and low voice gave her in the part.

Cushman remained a fixture of the American and English theater for the next three decades. Yet, she remained ambivalent toward acting. Repeatedly, she declared herself retired, only later to change her mind and announce her return to the stage. With each comeback, she demanded a higher and higher salary. Her money funded lavish homes in Rome and Newport, Rhode Island, where she entertained an ever-growing circle of female friends. She developed a romantic attachment with several of these women, most notably the American sculptor Emma Stebbins. Cushman's companion for 20 years, she published a collection of Cushman's letters two years after Cushman's death from cancer on February 18, 1876.

Following her final performance in 1874, a teary-eyed Cushman told her audience the "secret of my success in life": "To be thoroughly *in earnest,* intensely in earnest in all my thoughts and in all my actions, whether in my profession or out of it, became my one single idea." It was just this intensity and focus that made Cushman the most respected American actress of the 19th century.

Further Reading

Dudden, Faye E. *Women in the American Theater: Actresses and Audiences, 1790–1870.* New Haven, Conn.: Yale University Press, 1994.

Leach, Joseph. *Bright Particular Star: The Life and Times of Charlotte Cushman.* New Haven, Conn.: Yale University Press, 1970.

D

❖ **DANDRIDGE, DOROTHY (Dorothy Jean Dandridge)**
(1922–1965) *Actress, Singer*

The first African-American leading lady to be nominated for a best actress Oscar, Dorothy Jean Dandridge was born in Cleveland, Ohio, on November 9, 1922. She made her show business debut at four, encouraged by her ambitious mother, Ruby. Ruby concocted a song-and-skit show featuring Dorothy and her older sister Vivian. Billed as the "Wonder Kids," the Dandridge sisters toured throughout the South for five years.

To advance her daughters' careers, Ruby relocated the family to Los Angeles in the early 1930s. There, she made a living playing bit parts on radio and in films, generally playing a domestic—then one of the few roles open to African-American actresses. Rudy also recruited a third singer, Etta Jones, and reshaped the Wonder Kids into the Dandridge Sisters. The new act had its greatest success in 1936, when the group began appearing regularly at Harlem's famed Cotton Club. The trio also appeared in several films—most notably the Marx Brothers' classic *A Day at the Races* (1937)—before parting ways in the early 1940s.

Dorothy Dandridge's solo career was interrupted by her 1942 marriage to Harold Nicholas, one half of the tap-dancing duo the Nicholas Brothers. The union was already strained by Nicholas's infidelities, when Dandridge in 1945 gave birth to a severely brain-damaged girl, whom the couple named Harolyn. Dandridge suffered enormous guilt after the birth and throughout her life blamed herself for Harolyn's condition. Unwilling to deal with the difficult situation, Nicholas deserted his family, and Dandridge returned to show business to pay for Harolyn's placement in a private institution.

Though hobbled by insecurities, Dandridge quickly found fame performing as a nightclub singer. Elegant, sultry, and astoundingly beautiful, she was sought after by the most exclusive venues, many of which had never before featured an African-American performer. Dandridge routinely insisted that the clubs she played reserved a table for members of the local chapter of the National Association for the Advancement of Colored People (NAACP), thereby, at least for a night, integrating formerly segregated establishments.

Dandridge also sought work in Hollywood. After appearing in several undistinguished films, she won her signature role, the title character in *Carmen*

Dorothy Dandridge in 1954
(Library of Congress, neg. no. USZ62-109664)

Jones (1954). A recasting of Georges Bizet's opera *Carmen* with new lyrics written by Oscar Hammerstein II, the film featured an all-black cast and told the story of a sensual woman whose infidelity leads to the ruin of her lover, played by Harry Belafonte. As the sashaying Carmen, Dandridge made a spectacular femme fatale, and her performance was hailed by critics and the public alike. In addition to becoming the first African American nominated for a best actress Oscar, she was the first black performer to present an award during an Academy Awards telecast. In November 1954, Dandridge also became the first African American to appear on the cover of *Life* magazine.

Despite her fabulous success in *Carmen Jones,* Dandridge was soon disappointed by the lack of serious roles open to her. Her beauty and glamour made her a natural to be cast in romances, but at the time African-American couples were a rarity on screen and interracial romances were all but unheard of.

Dandridge did make history in the controversial and unsuccessful *Islands in the Sun* (1957), in which her character was the first black leading lady to be held in the arms of a white actor. Her only other notable film role was in *Porgy and Bess* (1959), in which she played Bess opposite Sidney Poitier.

As Dandridge watched her film career fade, her personal life also began to unravel. After her longtime affair with *Carmen Jones*'s director, Otto Preminger, fell apart, she married restaurateur Jack Dennison in 1959. Dennison flooded Dandridge's money into his own restaurants and persuaded her to invest in risky oil deals. By the time the couple divorced in 1962, Dandridge was so debt-ridden that, much to her dismay, she had to place Harolyn in a public institution. Despite her desperate circumstances, Dandridge had begun to launch a successful comeback in the nightclub circuit, when on September 8, 1965, she was found dead in her Hollywood home at the age of 42. Dandridge had overdosed on an antidepressant, but it remains unclear whether her death was intentional or accidental.

Even though her career was short, Dandridge was never forgotten by her fans, especially African Americans who were inspired by her success at breaking Hollywood's color barriers. In 1977, she was inducted into the Black Film Hall of Fame, and in 1983, with the lobbying of costars Sidney Poitier and Harry Belafonte, she was given a star on the Hollywood Walk of Fame. By the mid-1990s, leading young African-American actresses, including WHITNEY HOUSTON and Vanessa Williams, were vying to portray Dandridge on screen. The first to succeed was Halle Berry, who starred in the acclaimed HBO television movie *Introducing Dorothy Dandridge* in 1999.

Further Reading

Bogle, Donald. *Dorothy Dandridge.* New York: Amistad Press, 1997.

Dandridge, Dorothy, and Earl Conrad. *Everything and Nothing: The Dorothy Dandridge Tragedy.* New York: Abelard-Schuman, 1970. Reprint: New York: Harper-Perennial, 2000.

Recommended Recorded and Videotaped Performances

Carmen Jones (1954). Twentieth Century-Fox, VHS, 1994.
Introducing Dorothy Dandridge (1999). HBO Home Video, DVD/VHS, 2000.

❖ **DAVIS, BETTE (Ruth Elizabeth Davis)**
   (1908–1989) *Actress*

One of Hollywood's most influential personalities, Bette Davis, in her films of the 1940s, defined a new breed of strong, independent women, while redefining the film industry's standards of beauty with her unconventional looks. On April 5, 1908, Ruth Elizabeth Davis (known as Betty to her family) was born in Lowell, Massachusetts. When she was 10, her parents divorced, leaving her mother, Ruth, to raise Betty and her sister, Barbara. Davis later credited Ruth's example with inspiring the confidence and determination that would guide Davis throughout her life.

Encouraged by her mother, Betty developed an early fascination with the theater. Having changed the spelling of her name after reading Honoré de Balzac's *La Cousine Bette,* she applied to Eva Le Gallienne's famed acting school in New York City but was rejected. Davis dismissed Le Gallienne's advice that she pursue another profession and instead enrolled in John Murray Anderson's rival drama school. She performed in director George Cukor's stock company in Rochester, New York, before winning her first major off-Broadway role in *The Earth Between* (1928). The next year, she had her first Broadway triumph in a small role in *Broken Dishes,* which ran six months.

Based on her theater work, Davis was given a screen test for Metro-Goldwyn-Mayer (MGM), but the studio rejected her out of hand. Physically, she lacked the glamour-girl beauty favored by Hollywood, although her large, expressive eyes played well to the camera. Her highly mannered acting style and exaggerated diction also seemed too stagy to translate well to the screen.

Despite this setback, the persistent Davis was given a second screen test in 1930, which won her

a six-month contract with Universal. Her movie debut in *The Bad Sister* (1931) and her other early films, however, were not encouraging. As Hollywood insiders had suspected, audiences were initially put off by Davis's unique looks, voice, and mannerisms. Her film career was all but over when actor George Arliss insisted that she be loaned out to Warner Brothers for *The Man Who Played God* (1932). The film was a hit and earned Davis a contract with Warner Brothers, the studio for which she would work for the next 18 years.

Almost from the start, Davis butted heads with studio head Jack Warner over the roles she was given. She complained repeatedly about the quality of her films and, two years into her contract, convinced Warner to loan her to RKO so she could appear in the film adaptation of W. Somerset Maugham's *Of Human Bondage* (1934). Her energetic performance as Mildred, a vulgar waitress who inspires a odd infatuation in the film's sensitive hero (played by Leslie Howard), won near universal praise. Her fans were outraged when she was not nominated for an Oscar for her performance. The next year, however, Davis won the award for a much lesser film, *Dangerous*—an honor even Davis recognized as a "consolation prize" for the previous snub.

Davis was now seen as one of Hollywood's brightest stars, but with the exception of *The Petrified Forest* (1936), she continued to be disappointed with the films Warner Brothers offered her. Her irritation came to a head when in 1937, she refused to follow Jack Warner's orders and headed to England to appear in British films. The action was unprecedented in Hollywood. At the time, common wisdom held that contracted players had no choice but to do as the studio told them, like it or not. Warner sued Davis and won, but the highly publicized court battle changed Hollywood forever. Although the contract system would largely stay in place for decades, Davis introduced the film industry to the idea of actors working as free agents and choosing their own parts, the system that rules Hollywood today.

Ironically, Davis reaped enormous benefits from her unsuccessful rebellion. Embarrassed by

Bette Davis with Henry Fonda in *Jezebel* (1938)
(Museum of Modern Art Film Stills Archive)

the lawsuit, Warner took her demands more seriously than before, and as a result, the legal action ushered in the best period of her career. In 1938 she won a second Academy Award for *Jezebel* (1938), in which she played a conniving Southern belle during the Civil War. (According to Davis, she had been offered the role of the era's most famous Southern femme fatale—Scarlett O'Hara in *Gone With the Wind* (1939)—but rejected the role because they wanted to pair her with Errol Flynn, whom she felt was wrong for the role of Rhett Butler.) The next four years, she received four of her 10 best-actress nominations for performances in several of her best pictures: *Dark Vic-*

tory (1939), *The Letter* (1940), *The Little Foxes* (1941), and *Now, Voyager* (1942). In these and other films of the 1940s, Davis generally played fiercely independent women, though some were decent and long-suffering, while others were cruel and scheming.

Toward the end of the decade, Davis's stormy relationship with Jack Warner again began to deteriorate. The two had their final showdown in 1949 when she demanded the firing of King Vidor, her director on *Beyond the Forest* (1949). She declared that she wanted out of her contract if he were not replaced. A frustrated Warner this time refused to back down. By the time Davis finished the film, her professional ties with Warner Brothers were severed.

Free from studio control at last, Davis was approached by Twentieth Century-Fox to replace an injured CLAUDETTE COLBERT in *All About Eve* (1950), a sophisticated comedy about the theater world. The movie gave Davis her greatest role—the aging theater diva Margo Channing, who is determined to ward off the attempts of newcomer Eve Harrington to steal her spot in the limelight. Announcing to her intention to do battle with Eve, Margo says, "Fasten your seatbelts—it's going to be a bumpy ride"—a now famous line with which Davis will forever be associated.

In her later years, Davis grew increasingly frustrated trying to find roles that were equal to her talent. Desperate for work, in 1962 she took a part opposite her longtime rival JOAN CRAWFORD in a horror film, *What Ever Happened to Baby Jane?* The movie was an unexpected hit and inspired the follow-up *Hush, Hush, Sweet Charlotte* (1964) in which Davis was paired with Olivia De Havilland. Though Davis continued acting, often in television movies, during the 1970s and 1980s, her films were largely unmemorable. An exception was the role as a blind woman in *The Whales of August* (1987), in which she shared the screen with another legend, LILLIAN GISH.

By her own admission, Davis's work always took precedence over her private life. Married and divorced four times, she wrote in her autobiography *The Lonely Life* (1962), "No man could ever share my drive or vision. No man has ever understood the sweetness of my joy at the end of a good day's work." She found more satisfaction with her daughter Barbara (known as B. D.) and two adopted children, Margot and Michael. But in her late years, she felt betrayed by B. D., whose book *My Mother's Keeper* (1985) portrayed her as a bad mother. Davis wrote her own book, *This 'n That* (1987) as a challenge to B. D.'s representation of her.

Long in ill health, Davis died on October 6, 1989, in Paris after attending a Spanish film festival. She is remembered for her strong will—on screen and off—and credited with broadening the range of film roles available to women by showing the appeal of heroines with minds of their own.

Further Reading

Davis, Bette. *The Lonely Life: An Autobiography.* New York: Putnam, 1962.

Davis, Bette, with Michael Herskowitz. *This 'n That.* New York: Putnam, 1987.

Higham, Charles. *Bette: The Life of Bette Davis.* New York: Macmillan, 1981.

Quirk, Lawrence J. *Fasten Your Seat Belts: The Passionate Life of Bette Davis.* New York: William Morrow, 1990.

Recommended Recorded and Videotaped Performances

All About Eve (1950). Twentieth Century-Fox, DVD/VHS, 1990.

Dark Victory (1939). Warner Home Video, DVD/VHS, 2000.

Jezebel (1938). Warner Home Video, DVD/VHS, 2000.

The Little Foxes (1941). MGM/UA, VHS, 2000.

Of Human Bondage (1934). Monterey Home Video, VHS, 1996.

❖ DAY, DORIS (Doris Mary Anne von Kappelhoff)
(1924–) *Singer, Actress*

Radiating an open-hearted optimism, Doris Day become one of America's favorite big band singers of the 1940s and film stars in the 1950s and 1960s. Born Doris Mary Anne von Kappelhoff on April 3, 1924, she grew up in a suburb of Cincinnati, Ohio. As a girl, she studied tap dancing and ballet with an eye toward becoming a professional dancer. She had already joined the Fanchon and Marco stage show when her career was cut short by a car accident, which shattered her right leg. Giving up her dream of dancing, Doris started studying voice. By 1938, she was singing on local radio and performing in Cincinnati clubs. At about this time, Doris took the stage name "Day," inspired by "Day by Day," one of her most requested tunes.

Doris Day worked with Bob Crosby's orchestra in Chicago before being hired by bandleader Les Brown in 1939. While singing with Brown's band, she married trombonist Al Jorden, who beat and terrorized her during their brief relationship. They had a son, Terry, in 1942, and divorced the following year.

In 1943, Day returned to Les Brown's "Band of Renown," with whom she recorded 12 hit records. Among them were "My Dreams Are Getting Better All the Time" (1943) and "Sentimental Journey" (1943). With excellent vocal control, she was known for communicating deep emotions without being overly theatrical. Day left Brown's band in 1946, the same year she married saxophonist George Weidler. She was devastated when, eight months into the marriage, he suddenly asked for a divorce. Day married a third time in 1951 to agent Marty Melcher.

Day began her career in Hollywood in 1948, when she played a nightclub singer in *Romance on the High Seas*. Establishing a pattern in her early years in film, she had a hit single with "It's Magic," one of the songs she performed in the movie. Other popular songs she introduced in her films included "Secret Love" (from *Calamity Jane,* 1953) and "Que Sera Sera" (from *The Man Who Knew Too Much,* 1956).

In the 1950s, Day displayed a remarkable versatility as an actress. She excelled in such light musicals as *April in Paris* (1952) and *The Pajama Game* (1957). But she proved equally adept in dramas, including *Young at Heart* (1954) and *Love Me or Leave Me* (1955). Day, however, found her greatest film success in the 1960s. Well into her thirties, she reestablished herself as the most popular female star of romantic comedy. She was paired successfully with many leading men, including Clark Gable (*Teacher's Pet,* 1958), James Garner (*Move Over, Darling,* 1963; *The Thrill of It All,* 1963), and Cary Grant (*That Touch of Mink,* 1962). Yet her most fondly remembered onscreen relationship was with Rock Hudson. Day and Hudson starred in three comedies—*Pillow Talk* (1959), *Lover Come Back* (1961), and *Send Me No Flowers* (1964). In the first

two, Day portrayed happy career women, a rarity at the time. Wearing stylish clothes and frequenting sophisticated New York nightspots, these heroines were successful and secure professionals, excited primarily by their work. Day's characters, however, were inevitably tamed by romance, and in the process accepted the roles of wife and mother as the mores of the era required.

Day had her last film role in the family comedy *With Six You Get Eggroll* (1968). In the year of its release, her husband Marty Melcher died. She soon discovered that he had committed her to a television series without her consent. Day also found out not only that the money she had earned over her career had disappeared because of bad investments but also that she was more than $500,000 in debt. Hesitantly, Day accepted her new role as a television star, appearing in a situation comedy titled *The Doris Day Show* (1968–73). In her caustic autobiography, she wrote that the unexpected obligation was "doubly repulsive" to her because of the sitcom's hackneyed premise: "A farm. A widow with a couple of little kids living on a farm. With Grandpa, naturally." After the show, Day largely retired from show business. Except during a brief fourth marriage to Barry Comden (1976–81), Day has since devoted herself to campaigning for her literal pet cause—animal welfare—from her home in Carmel, California.

Further Reading

Freedland, Michael. *Doris Day: The Illustrated Biography.* London: Andre Deutsch, 2000.
Hotchner, A. E. *Doris Day: Her Own Story.* New York: William Morrow & Co., 1976.

Recommended Recorded and Videotaped Performances

Love Me or Leave Me (1955). Turner Home Entertainment, VHS, 2000.
The Pajama Game (1957). Warner Home Video, DVD/VHS, 1999.
Pillow Talk (1959). Universal, DVD/VHS, 1999/2000.
16 Most Requested Songs: Doris Day. Sony/Columbia, CD, 1992.

❖ DEGENERES, ELLEN
(1958–   ) *Actress, Comic*

In 1997, television star Ellen DeGeneres made history by announcing that both she and the character she played were gay. Born on January 26, 1958, DeGeneres was raised by Christian Scientist parents in New Orleans, Louisiana. After her parents divorced in 1971, she moved with her mother to Atlanta, Texas. By her early twenties, DeGeneres had returned to New Orleans and began performing in comedy clubs. Her stand-up routines soon won her a following on the comedy circuit. In 1982, the Showtime cable channel named her the "Funniest Person in America."

DeGeneres appeared regularly on television throughout the rest of the 1980s. She made her debut on *The Tonight Show* in 1986 and became the first female comic invited to talk with host Johnny Carson on her initial appearance. In addition to performing on talk shows such as *The Late Show with David Letterman, Larry King Live,* and *Good Morning, America,* DeGeneres made several forays into series television. On *Open House* (1989), she played a wacky office worker, and on *Laurie Hill* (1992), she had a recurring role as a nurse. DeGeneres also appeared on several HBO comedy specials, including a one-woman show for which she was nominated for a Cable Ace Award.

In 1994, DeGeneres was cast in *These Friends of Mine,* an ensemble situation comedy on ABC dealing with the relationship among four friends. After repeated retoolings, the show, eventually retitled *Ellen,* became more focused on DeGeneres's character. Even with the reworking of the show, critics agreed that the sitcom failed to provide an adequate showcase for the charm DeGeneres displayed in her standup act.

During *Ellen*'s fourth season, DeGeneres and the show's staff decided to reveal that her character was a lesbian. At the same time, DeGeneres herself chose to declare on the cover of the April 14, 1997 issue of *Time* magazine, "Yep, I'm gay." The announcement initiated a national debate. Gay rights groups hailed DeGeneres as a hero, while right-wing leader Jerry Falwell dubbed her "Ellen DeGenerate." As the controversy grew, major sponsors, including Chrysler and Wendy's, pulled their advertisements from her show.

On April 30, 1997, DeGeneres's character came out of the closet on an hour-long episode of *Ellen,* which featured cameo appearances by Laura Dern, OPRAH WINFREY, Melissa Etheridge, and k. d. lang. The show was titled "The Puppy Episode," a joking reference to a network executive's suggestion that the series writers give DeGeneres's character a dog to help boost ratings. The episode did in fact bring *Ellen* its best ratings ever; it was the most-watched television program for the week it aired.

DeGeneres continued to generate headlines, especially after she made public her romantic relationship with actress Anne Heche. The publicity, however, did little to help draw viewers to DeGeneres's show. ABC canceled *Ellen* in 1998. Some fans accused the network of refusing to promote the show because of its gay content.

As *Ellen* was drawing to a close, DeGeneres tried to make the move into films. Vehicles such as *Mr. Wrong* (1996) and *Edtv* (1999), however, failed at the box-office. She had more success with the *If These Walls Could Talk 2* (2000), an HBO anthology of three stories about lesbianism. DeGeneres starred with Sharon Stone in a comedic segment, written and directed by Heche, about a lesbian couple's efforts to have a child.

Following a well-publicized breakup from Heche in 2000, DeGeneres set off on a 36-city tour with a new stand-up routine. With a return to the gentle style of humor that made her famous, she hoped to remind her audience she was more than just "the lesbian comedian." As she told *Time* in 2000, she wanted her old fans to "realize they can come and see me and they won't feel left out."

Further Reading

DeGeneres, Ellen. *My Point . . . and I Do Have One.* New York: Bantam Books, 1995.

Handy, Bruce. "Roll Over, Ward Cleaver." *Time*. April 17, 1997, p. 78.

Wieder, Judy. "Ellen: Born Again." *The Advocate*. March 14, 2000, p. 28.

Recommended Recorded and Videotaped Performances

Ellen DeGeneres: The Beginning. Warner Home Video, DVD/VHS, 2001.

If These Walls Could Talk 2. Warner Home Video, VHS, 2000.

❖ DE MILLE, AGNES

(1905–1993)   *Dancer, Choreographer, Director*

On Broadway and at the ballet, Agnes de Mille was a pioneer who introduced distinctly American themes and movements into the world of dance. Born in New York City on September 18, 1905, she was raised in one of the most prominent U.S. show business families. Her father, William, was a playwright and theater director, and her uncle Cecil was perhaps the country's best-known film director.

When Agnes was nine, her family moved to Los Angeles so that her father could find work in the growing movie industry. Agnes soon knew her way around a movie set and frequently took jobs as an extra. However, she was far more impressed by the dance performances she attended. Admiring the work of RUTH ST. DENIS, ISADORA DUNCAN, and Anna Pavlova, she grew determined to become a dancer herself, despite her parents' disapproval of her plans. She finally convinced them to pay for ballet lessons when she was 13, far older than most professional dancers begin their formal training. Bowing to family pressure, she gave up her dream in 1921 and entered college at the University of California, Los Angeles. Four years later, she graduated *cum laude* with a degree in English.

Now 20 years old, de Mille moved back to New York and renewed her commitment to a dance career. She soon found her body ill-suited for work as either a ballerina or a Broadway chorus girl. She later wrote, "I was built like a mustang, stocky, mettlesome and sturdy"—a distinct contrast from the lithe and leggy bodies of most professional dancers. With characteristic pluck, de Mille decided that if no one would hire her to perform their dances, she would create her own with her body type in mind. In 1928, she began a decade-long period of staging concerts of her own dance compositions in the United States and Europe. Highly dramatic, they were unique in telling the stories of frontierswomen and other ordinary Americans and in integrating movements de Mille borrowed from folk dances. Already seen as an innovator in modern dance, de Mille in 1931 staged some of her works at the Dance Repertory Theater, which also showcased early dances by MARTHA GRAHAM and DORIS HUMPHREY.

The next year, de Mille set off for England, where she studied ballet with Anthony Tudor. While living in London, she made a substantial impact on English dance by introducing her associates to new currents in American modern dance, particularly the technical innovations of Graham. As World War II broke out in Europe, de Mille returned home and took a post as a choreographer for the Ballet Theater (later renamed the American Ballet Theater). There, she created her first major work, the controversial *Black Ritual* (1939), which featured an all-black cast. She found greater popular success with *Three Virgins and a Devil* (1941), a comic dance piece that Graham called "a little masterpiece."

Based on the strength of her work with the Ballet Theater, the director of Ballet Russe de Monte Carlo hired de Mille to choreograph an "all-American" ballet. The result was her most famous ballet, *Rodeo* (1941). Danced to the music of Aaron Copland, *Rodeo* told the story of a cowgirl looking for a man. De Mille found hiring dancers for the work taxing since classical ballet instruction did little to prepare them for the vigorous movements her dance demanded. Of her cowboy dancers, she later wrote, "Alas, though big boys, they had been trained to move like wind-blown petals. 'Raise your arms,' I begged them. 'You have men's arms, . . . they can control a heavy, moving rope, or the brute furies of an eight-hundred-pound animal.'" Despite the challenges of bringing *Rodeo* to the stage, its premiere was an enormous success. With de Mille dancing the role of the cowgirl, the ballet's performers received 22 curtain calls.

The success of *Rodeo* made de Mille the natural choice to choreograph *Oklahoma!* (1943), a musical by Richard Rodgers and Oscar Hammerstein about cowboys and ranchers at the beginning of the 20th century. *Oklahoma!* is now seen as a hallmark in American theater because it was the first musical to fully integrate music and dance into the dramatic action. In addition, de Mille's choreography changed Broadway dance by blending ballet and modern dance. It also introduced the device of the "dream dance." At the end of the first act, the lead female character, Laurie, has a dream that reveals her subconscious fears and desires, which are acted out by dancers in an extended ballet sequence. The "dream dance" immediately became a staple in American musical theater.

Soon after *Oklahoma!*'s premiere, de Mille married Walter Foy Prude. The couple remained together until Prude's death in 1988. They had one son, who was born in 1946.

Oklahoma!'s phenomenal five-year run made de Mille Broadway's most sought-after choreographer. She created dances for many classic musicals including *Carousel* (1945), *Brigadoon* (1947), *Gentlemen Prefer Blondes* (1949), and *Paint Your Wagon* (1951). With the production of *Allegro* (1947), De Mille also became the first woman to direct and choreograph a Broadway show. While working on Broadway, de Mille continued her association with the Ballet Theater. Her most important ballet of this period was *Fall River Legend* (1948), which was based on the Lizzie Borden ax-murder case.

In the 1950s, de Mille became one of the foremost promoters of modern dance. On tours in 1953 and 1954, she managed the Agnes de Mille Dance Theater, which helped popularize her choreography by staging excerpts from her Broadway works and selections from her early concerts. In two television documentaries, *The Art of Ballet* and *The Art of Choreography* (both 1956), she sought to explain two of her greatest loves to a mass audience. Also to interest the public in dance, de Mille launched side careers as a writer and a lecturer. The author of many books, some autobiographical, de Mille is among the most eloquent writers on American modern dance.

To preserve her works for future generations, de Mille helped establish the Agnes de Mille Heritage Dance Theater at the North Carolina School of the Arts in 1973. The venture floundered, however, when de Mille suffered a stroke two years later. In spite of her deteriorating health, she was determined to fight her limitations so she could continue to work. She even taught herself to write with her left hand in order to record her recovery in her book *Reprieve* (1976). Examples of her late choreography include *Texas Fourth* (1976), *The Informer* (1988), and *The Other* (1992), a dance dealing with the theme of death that was to be her final work. De Mille died on October 6, 1993, leaving an incomparable legacy as a dancer, choreographer, writer, and champion of American dance.

Further Reading

De Mille, Agnes. Dance to the Piper *and* And Promenade Home: *A Two-Part Autobiography.* New York: Da Capo Press, 1979.

Easton, Carol. *No Intermissions: The Life of Agnes de Mille.* Boston: Little Brown, 1996.

Recommended Recorded and Videotaped Performances

Brigadoon (1954). Warner Home Video, DVD/VHS, 2000.

Oklahoma! (1955). Twentieth Century-Fox, DVD/VHS, 1999.

❖ **DEL RIO, DOLORES (Lolita Dolores Martinez Asunsolo y Lopez Negrette)** (1905–1983) *Actress*

A star of both American and Mexican cinema, Dolores Del Rio was born Lolita Dolores Martinez Asunsolo y Lopez Negrette on August 3, 1905.

She grew up in a wealthy family in Durango, Mexico. After being educated in a convent school, at 16 she married writer Jaime Del Rio.

A member of Mexico City's high society, Dolores Del Rio met director Edwin Carewe at a tea party in 1925. Struck by her beauty, Carewe persuaded her to return to Hollywood with him. Del Rio appeared in Carewe's *Joanna* (1925), the first of a dozen silent features she would make in the United States. Because of her dark features, she was most often cast as an ethnic or European beauty. She was a French girl in *What Price Glory* (1926), a Russian peasant in *Resurrection* (1927), and an American Indian maiden in *Ramona* (1928).

Del Rio was well established as a leading lady when the advent of sound pictures threatened her career. She knew little English and spoke with a heavy accent. Despite these obstacles, however, Del Rio remained a box-office draw. She made her first talkie, *The Bad One,* in 1930, the same year she married art director Cedric Gibbons. She and Gibbons lived extravagantly and were one of Hollywood's most glamorous couples until their divorce in 1941.

Del Rio worked steadily throughout the 1930s, although she was typecast as the exotic love interest. Only her dignity helped her overcome the silliness of many of these roles. For instance, in director King Vidor's *Bird of Paradise* (1932), she played a Polynesian princess who, as punishment for her love of a white man, threw herself into a volcano. Among Del Rio's better roles was that of a Brazilian heiress in *Flying Down to Rio* (1933), in which she danced with a young Fred Astaire.

In 1942, Del Rio appeared in *Journey Into Fear,* directed by Orson Welles, with whom she had an intense romance. Unsatisfied with the parts she was offered, she then left Hollywood to carve out a new career in the growing Mexican movie industry. Del Rio quickly became Mexico's leading actress, largely on the basis of two classic films— *Maria Candelaria* (1943) and *Flor Silvestre* (1943)—which paired her with director Emilio Fernandez. Throughout the 1940s and 1950s, Del

Rio remained a star in Mexican film, while occasionally performing on stage in productions of classics such as Oscar Wilde's *Lady Windermere's Fan* and Henrik Ibsen's *Ghosts*. In 1960, she married theater producer and director Lewis Riley.

Periodically, Del Rio appeared in American movies. Most notable were *The Fugitive* (1947) and *Cheyenne Autumn* (1964), both directed by John Ford. She also played Elvis Presley's Kiowa Indian mother in *Flaming Star* (1961). By the 1970s, Del Rio had largely left film behind, devoting herself instead to charity work. She made her last appearance in *The Children of Sanchez* in 1978. Five years later, she died on April 11, 1983, of hepatitis. Del Rio today seems remarkable for working more than 50 years in an industry traditionally unwelcoming to Hispanic women.

Further Reading

Hershfield, Joanne. *The Invention of Dolores Del Rio*. Minneapolis: University of Minnesota Press, 2000.

Woll, Allen L. *The Films of Dolores Del Rio*. New York: Gordon Press, 1978.

Recommended Recorded and Videotaped Performances

Cheyenne Autumn (1964). Warner Home Video, VHS, 1990.

Flying Down to Rio (1933). Turner Home Video, VHS, 2000.

Maria Candelaria (1943). Cobra Prodocciones, VHS, 1993.

❖ **DIETRICH, MARLENE (Maria Magdalena Dietrich)**
(1901–1992) *Actress, Singer*

Mysterious and alluring, Marlene Dietrich brought to Hollywood a European sophistication that made her an icon. She was born in Berlin on December 27, 1901, as Maria Magdalena Dietrich. Nicknamed Leni, she trained to become a concert violinist but decided to become an actress instead after injuring her hand.

Marlene Dietrich in *The Blue Angel* (1930)
(Museum of Modern Art Film Stills Archive)

Sporting bobbed hair and often men's suits, Dietrich embraced the freewheeling atmosphere of post–World War I Berlin. While studying at Max Reinhardt's acting school, she sang in cabarets and played small roles in films. Professionally, she called herself Marlene (pronounced Mar-LAY-na), a conflation of her first and middle names. While on the set of *Tragedy of Love* (1923), she met Rudolf Sieber, a casting assistant. She and Sieber married and had one child, Maria. They soon separated but never divorced, though Dietrich had many affairs with lovers of both sexes during their marriage.

By the 1930s, Dietrich had established herself in German film and theater. On the strength of one of her performances, director Josef von Sternberg invited her to star in his film version of *Professor Unrath,* a novel by Heinrich Mann. The film, *Der Blaue Engel* (1930), told the story of an amoral nightclub singer, Lola Lola, who uncaringly destroys a pompous professor who has fallen in love with her. As Lola Lola, Dietrich sang her trademark song, "Falling in Love Again," and created an indelible femme fatale that made film an enormous hit with German audiences. During the filming, Mann predicted, "The success of this film will be found in the naked thighs of Miss Dietrich."

The film's English-language version, titled *The Blue Angel* (1930), became Dietrich's ticket to Hollywood. With von Sternberg, she was courted by Paramount, which hoped they could have the same success with Dietrich as Metro-Goldwyn-Mayer had with its exotic European beauty, GRETA GARBO. The studio set about giving Dietrich a glamorous new image. She lost 30 pounds, had cosmetic surgery to slim her nose, and possibly had molars removed to make her sunken cheeks even more dramatic.

For Paramount, Dietrich made six more films with von Sternberg at the helm. They included *Morocco* (1930), *Dishonored* (1931), and *Shanghai Express* (1932). In these Dietrich–von Sternberg collaborations, Dietrich played variations on the same character, a world-weary woman with no illusions about romance who nevertheless in the end sacrifices all for love. The formula was embraced by American moviegoers, who made Dietrich one of the highest paid stars of the early 1930s.

Dietrich and von Sternberg's last film, *The Devil Is a Woman* (1935), failed at the box office. Feeling defeated by the American film industry, von Sternberg returned to Germany. Dietrich stayed on but found her popularity slipping away. After making the disappointing *Angel* (1937) with director Ernst Lubitsch, Dietrich was labeled by film distributors as "box-office poison." Paramount dropped her contract, and she considered permanently returning to Europe to try to revive her career there.

Instead, Dietrich took a chance, playing a saloon girl named Frenchy in satire of Westerns titled *Destry Rides Again* (1939). She approached the role with enthusiasm, drawing on her cabaret experience to give a first-rate comedy performance. Her old fans enjoyed this new Dietrich, and once again she was considered a major star.

Her comeback, however, was soon interrupted by World War II. Dietrich was invited by Joseph Goebbels to come back to Germany to star in Nazi propaganda films. She refused, instead renouncing the Nazi regime and her German citizenship. During the war, she traveled widely, performing in more than 500 shows for the USO. For her efforts to build troop morale, she was awarded the Medal of Freedom.

After the war, Dietrich returned to Hollywood and acted in films by many of the world's greatest directors, including Billy Wilder (*A Foreign Affair,* 1948; *Witness for the Prosecution,* 1957), Fritz Lang (*Rancho Notorious,* 1952); and Orson Welles (*A*

Touch of Evil, 1958). Few were profitable, however. By the late 1950s, Dietrich tried to branch out. After two failed attempts of radio shows, she developed a nightclub act, following the example of JUDY GARLAND. Dietrich's show was a great success and had runs in Las Vegas, New York, and London. She even briefly appeared in Berlin, although many Germans still considered her a traitor for her anti-Nazi stance. Dietrich recast the act as a full-scale musical revue, which ran on Broadway for six weeks in 1967.

Dietrich moved to Paris in 1972. She gave her final live performance in 1975 and appeared in her last film—*Just a Gigolo,* opposite David Bowie—in 1978. Dietrich also lent her voice, though not her face, to *Marlene* (1979), a documentary made by her friend, actor Maximilian Schell. She refused to appear on camera, explaining to Schell in the film, "I've been photographed to death and I don't want any more." On May 6, 1992, Marlene Dietrich died at 90, leaving behind a wealth of celluloid images showing her as wished to be remembered— intriguing, seductive, and always beautiful.

Further Reading

Dietrich, Marlene. *Marlene.* New York: Grove Press, 1989.

Spoto, Donald. *Blue Angel: The Life of Marlene Dietrich.* New York: Doubleday, 1992.

Recommended Recorded and Videotaped Performances

The Blue Angel (1930). Madacy Entertainment, VHS, 1997.

Destry Rides Again (1939). Universal, VHS, 1993.

An Evening with Marlene Dietrich (1973). MPI Home Video, VHS, 1999.

A Touch of Evil (1958). Universal, DVD/VHS, 2000.

❖ **DILLER, PHYLLIS (Phyllis Ada Driver)**
 (1917–)   *Comic, Actress*

The first woman to become a star of standup comedy, Phyllis Diller was born Phyllis Ada Driver in Lima, Ohio, on July 17, 1917. Hoping to become a professional musician, she attended the Sherwood Music Conservatory and Bluffton College. While at Bluffton, she met and married Sherwood Diller. Phyllis dropped out of school and had the first of their five children in 1940.

Sherwood proved to be terrible provider. He moved the family to northern California, in search of work, but was unable to keep any job for long. The Dillers relied on a small inheritance from Phyllis's parents to make ends meet. When the money ran out, she had no choice but to find a job herself. She began working in advertising and eventually became a publicist for a San Francisco radio station. Still hoping for a career in show business, she began using her free time to develop a comedy act. With encouragement from her husband, Diller began performing for social clubs and church groups and hired a drama coach to help hone her timing.

In 1955, after more than a year of working on her act, Diller had her first professional job, a two-week engagement at the San Francisco club the Purple Onion. At the time, the field of stand-up comedy was completely dominated by men. Initially, her audiences were unsure what to make of Diller. As she later said, "Being a woman, right away you walk out to almost total rejection." Diller found, however, that as long as she could make them laugh, audiences would slowly warm to her. Her two-week stint was so successful that she played the Purple Onion for 87 more.

Onstage, Diller wore outrageously gaudy dresses, false eyelashes, and wild wigs. Her other trademarks were her foot-long cigarette holder and her raucous laugh, which she invented to fill uncomfortable silences when jokes failed to get a laugh. She was given the nickname "Killer Diller" because of her rapid-fire delivery. Diller often told as many as 12 jokes a minute. The jokes themselves focused on the things she knew best—housekeeping and family. She took a special satisfaction in ridiculing her fictitious one-toothed husband, whom she called "Fang." Her husband jokes were to her a sweet revenge for the wife jokes that then made up much stand-up repertoire.

After several years of touring clubs with her act, Diller had her first national exposure as a guest of

The Tonight Show in 1959. She immediately became a fixture of television variety and comedy shows, which led to bigger audiences at her club dates. By the mid-1960s, Diller was one of the most famous and successful comics in the United States. At the height of her success, she divorced Sherwood Diller and married singer Warde Donovan. They, too, were later divorced.

During this period, Diller also appeared in a string of weak comedy films, including *Boy, Did I Get a Wrong Number* (1966) and *Did You Hear the One About the Traveling Saleslady* (1968). She had another side career as an author of advice manual parodies. Among her popular books were *Phyllis Diller's Housekeeping Hints* (1966) and *Phyllis Diller's Marriage Manual* (1967). She had less success as the star of two failed television series, *The Pruitts of Southhampton* (1966) and *The Beautiful Phyllis Diller Show* (1968).

Diller continued to perform comedy on stage and on television, though in the 1970s she also started to play piano concerts with symphony orchestras. More recently, she has renewed her film career with small movie roles, most notably providing the voice of Queen in the animated feature *A Bug's Life* (1998).

Further Reading

Collier, Denise, and Kathleen Beckett. *Spare Ribs: Women in the Humor Biz.* New York: St. Martin's Press, 1980.
Horowitz, Susan. *Queens of Comedy.* Newark, N.J.: Gordon & Breach, 1997.

Recommended Recorded and Videotaped Performances

Biography: Phyllis Diller. A&E Home Video, VHS, 2000.
Boy, Did I Get a Wrong Number (1966). MGM/UA, VHS, 1993.

❖ DUNCAN, ISADORA (Dora Angela Duncan)
(1877–1927) *Dancer*

The mother of American modern dance, Isadora Duncan transformed not only the arts but society itself by her intense celebration of the female creative spirit. On May 27, 1877, she was born Dora Angela Duncan in San Francisco. Her father was a banker whose involvement in a scandal depleted the family fortune soon after Dora was born. As a result, her parents divorced, and her mother took the four Duncan children to nearby Oakland, moving from house to house, trying to keep a step ahead of the bill collectors. With few financial resources available, Dora and her siblings were taught to scorn material possessions but to love literature, music, and dance. Often left with no adult supervision, they also learned to be independent, even as small children.

Dora showed an early talent for social dancing, which she learned from her older sister Elizabeth. By the time Dora was 10, she had quit school to supplement the family income by teaching dance lessons. Soon she was regularly performing dance recitals for San Francisco's elite.

To further her career, Duncan and her family moved first to Chicago and then to New York City, where in 1896 she was hired by a theatrical company as a dancer and an actress. She spent two unhappy years in the job, all the while resenting the company director's authority over her and her work. Duncan had a more satisfying experience giving private performances in the homes of New York's upper class. Although she studied ballet while living in the city, her performances were far more influenced by the Delsarte system of movement that was then in vogue. Developed by acting and singing teacher François Delsarte, it taught series of gestures as a means toward expressing emotions. Drawing from Delsarte, Duncan, dressed in classical Grecian garb, translated poetry and music into movement, often striking poses reminiscent of ancient Greek statues.

Duncan's success as a dancer continued after she moved to Europe in 1899. Despite her limited formal education, she took the opportunity to steep herself in European culture and art. She read voraciously, studied museum collections, and cultivated friendships with noted scholars and artists. Whether scrutinizing works at the British Museum or contemplating the philosophies of Friedrich Nietzsche and Arthur Schopenhauer, the goal of her self-education was to learn more about the body and its movements.

Through her experiences in Europe, Duncan refined her performance style. In a radical departure from most dance performances of the day, she eschewed scenery, narratives, and large ensembles. Duncan instead danced solos against a stark curtain, usually wearing only a simple, flowing tunic or robe. The bare setting gave the audience nothing to watch but Duncan's fluid movements, which were inspired by her emotional response to her musical accompaniment. Rather than dancing the prescribed steps of the ballet tradition, she sought to discover movements that were natural to the body and that observed gravity's pull rather than trying to defy it.

Her attitude toward dance was also revolutionary. In a time when popular dance performance was considered somewhat unseemly, she insisted on playing only in the most respectable venues, such as opera houses and concert halls. Duncan also dismissed standard dance music, instead setting her movements to classical compositions. Some critics considered this approach scandalous. But in eyes of most audience members, her dances did not debase the music. The music instead helped to elevate her dances to the status of high art.

Duncan's dancing was hailed throughout Europe and Russia. But in the United States, the reception to her work was decidedly chilly. On a 1908 tour, she was frustrated by the contempt she inspired in many of her countrypeople. Much of their reaction, however, had less to do with her performances than with her insistence on publicly flaunting convention. She had numerous love affairs and unapologetically gave birth out of wedlock to two children by different fathers.

In her always volatile personal life, Duncan suffered a nearly unendurable tragedy in 1913 when her two children drowned in the Seine after a traffic accident. She tried to cure her misery by impulsively getting pregnant, but her third child died soon after birth. These emotional trials, combined with the outbreak of World War I, seemed to inspire Duncan's art to move in a new direction.

Her dancing became more static and dramatic, focusing increasingly on strong, bold gestures rather than the more lilting movements she had favored in her youth.

After the war, Duncan became determined to start a school of dance. She had previously created one in Germany and one in France, but both had been short-lived. For years she scoured for funds. Finally in 1921 the Soviet Union promised to provide the money she needed. In Moscow she set out to create her school, envisioning it not as a training ground for professional dancers, but as a means of promoting dance as a vital component of modern life.

To her disappointment, the Soviet government reneged on its offer. Desperate to raise the funds for her school on her own, Duncan returned to the United States for a tour. She brought with her Sergei Essenin, a young Soviet poet whom she married in 1922.

The U.S. tour was a disaster from the start. Her association with the Soviet Union left her open to accusations of being a communist. Characteristic of the American response, the famed evangelist Billy Sunday condemned her as a "Bolshevik hussy." Adding to her soiled reputation was the erratic behavior of Essenin, whose mental illness contributed to his suicide in 1925.

The bad press eventually lead to Duncan's deportation. She spent her last years in Russia, Germany, and France. Although her freewheeling lifestyle had taken its toll on her body, she still had enough of a commanding presence to give a celebrated final performance at the Théâtre Mogador in Paris in 1927.

In the same year, on September 14, Duncan crawled into her car, ending a visit in Nice by saying, "Goodbye, my friends, I'm off to glory"— words that would become famous for their irony. Seconds later, Isadora Duncan was dead. Her long scarf had become caught in the spokes of one of the car's wheels. As the vehicle moved forward, the scarf snapped her neck, killing her instantly.

Today, Duncan's dances are seldom performed, yet her contribution to dance still looms large. She gave the world the idea that a single dancer on a bare stage could create a work of art, a notion that is at the foundation of all modern dance. She also liberated dancers from the confines of constricting costumes and programmed steps, freeing them to express personal emotion through movements of their own invention. The immense value Duncan placed on independence, on stage and off, also provided a powerful example to young women of the early 20th century seeking their own liberation from social conventions. Her admirers saw that Duncan's life may have been undisciplined and reckless, but it was also always her own.

Further Reading

Blair, Fredrika. *Isadora: Portrait of the Artist as a Woman.* New York: McGraw-Hill, 1986.

Daly, Ann. *Done into Dance: Isadora Duncan in America.* Bloomington: Indiana University Press, 1995.

Duncan, Isadora. *My Life.* 1927. Reprint, New York: Liveright, 1972.

Macdougall, Allan Ross. *Isadora: A Revolutionary in Art and Love.* New York: T. Nelson, 1960.

Recommended Recorded and Videotaped Performances

Isadora (1968). MCA Home Video, VHS, 1992.

Isadora Duncan: Technique and Repertory Dance. Princeton Book Company, VHS, 1995.

❖ DUNHAM, KATHERINE
(1909–)   *Dancer, Choreographer*

Drawing on her study of anthropology, Katherine Dunham introduced movements from African and Caribbean ritual traditions into American modern dance. Born on June 22, 1909, to an African-American father and a white mother, she spent her early years in Glen Ellyn, Illinois. After her mother's death when she was five, Katherine and her older brother Albert were sent to live with her paternal aunt in a family full of musical performers. Though they were desperately poor, Dunham remembered fondly this early introduction to music and the theater.

After remarrying, her father moved the children to Joliet, Illinois. His abusive behavior drove Albert out of the household. After winning a scholarship to the University of Chicago, he helped Katherine leave as well. She worked at the Chicago Public Library while taking dance lessons before she also enrolled in the university when she turned 18.

Dunham began formally studying anthropology, but her interest in dance remained strong. With several other students, she founded the short-lived Ballet Negre. At about this time, she also married a fellow dancer, Jordis McCoo.

In 1934 Dunham founded the Negro Dance Group, which eventually grew into the Katherine Dunham Dance Company. The company was invited to perform at the Chicago World's Fair that year. The success of this performance helped Dunham win a research grant from the Rosenwald Foundation. After several months of study with the head of African studies at Northwestern University, Dunham headed for Jamaica, Martinique, Trinidad, and Haiti to learn firsthand about their indigenous dance traditions. For 18 months, she toured remote villages, slowly winning the confidence of the inhabitants, who were unaccustomed to visitors. They allowed her to watch and perform in their ritual dances. In Haiti, she was also initiated into a voodoo cult. Dunham later wrote three books about her experiences in the Caribbean—*Journey to Accompong* (1946), *The Dances of Haiti* (1947), and *Island Possessed* (1969).

After returning to the United States in 1936, she was awarded a bachelor's degree from the University of Chicago. Though Dunham also earned a master's degree from Chicago and a doctorate from Northwestern, she began increasingly to see her future in dance. Sponsored by the Federal Works Theater Project, her first major work was *L'Ag'Ya* (1938), a dance that told of a love triangle through movements based on a Martinique fighting dance. In addition to working from her anthropological research, Dunham drew on the instruction of her Russian dance teacher Ludmilla Speranzeva, who emphasized dance's ability to tell a story.

During the production of *L'Ag'Ya,* Dunham met costume and set designer John Pratt. After her divorce from her first husband, they married in 1941. The couple had one child, Marie Christine, whom they adopted in 1951.

In 1940 Dunham reached out to a larger audience by taking her company to New York City, where they performed in *Tropics, Le Jazz Hot,* and several other dance revues she created. Audiences were enthusiastic, and Dunham and her dancers were soon hired to perform in the all-black Broadway musical *Cabin in the Sky.* In the show, Dunham was cast as the temptress Georgia Brown, a part that allowed her to act and sing as well as dance. Members of Dunham's company also appeared in several films, including *Star-Spangled Rhythm* (1942) and *Stormy Weather* (1943).

In New York, Dunham established her own dance school in 1945. There, she taught a combination of classical ballet and African, Caribbean dance, and African-American folk dance that became known as the Dunham Technique. In addition to formal dance instruction, lessons explored acting, voice, and the ethnography of dance. This interdisciplinary approach attracted to the school a diverse of group of performers, including Marlon Brando, Eartha Kitt, and Chita Rivera.

Following successful tours in the United States, the Dunham Company started performing abroad in the late 1940s. Proving especially popular in Europe, the company went on to tour 57 countries in six continents over the next two decades. These travels took Dunham back to Haiti, where she and her husband bought a villa, Habitation Le Clerc, in 1949.

Dunham's dancers had their last major show in 1962 with *Bamboche,* a revue based on the dances of Haiti. Two years later, Dunham provided daring choreography for a production of Giuseppe Verdi's *Aïda* at New York's Metropolitan Opera. Plagued by arthritis, Dunham then decided to disband her company and went into semiretirement in 1965.

At the request of the U.S. State Department, Dunham traveled to the African nation of Senegal

Katherine Dunham in *Bamboche* (1962)
(Library of Congress, neg. no. USZ62-123620)

there to display the costumes from her performances and the objects from many cultures she had collected during her world tours.

To show her commitment to the project, Dunham herself took a home in East St. Louis, although she continued to live part of the year in Haiti. Her love of the country and the people lead her to establish a medical center at her villa to provide basic health care to the poorest Haitians. In the early 1990s, Dunham also drew international attention to the plight of Haitian refugees refused entrance into the United States by going on a hunger strike. Although the United States did not change its policy, Dunham ended the strike on its 47th day at the request of Haitian president Jean-Bertrand Aristide.

Dunham's spectacular career was celebrated in 1983 with a Kennedy Center Lifetime Achievement Award. Fourteen of her dance works were revived four years later by the Alvin Ailey American Dance Theater in a program titled *The Magic of Katherine Dunham.* Another project intended to preserve her choreography and technique for future dancers is a pair of videotapes, *Katherine Dunham: A Portrait of the Artist* and *The Dunham Technique,* which Dunham herself is helping to produce.

in 1965 to help organize the First World Festival of Negro Arts. Back in the United States, she placed all of her energies into a new project: The establishment of the Performing Arts Training Center in East St. Louis. She came up with the idea for the center while serving as an artist in residence at Southern Illinois University in 1964. Dunham was disturbed that young people in the impoverished African-American neighborhoods nearby had no constructive way to spend their time. Working with the university, she created the center as a place where neighborhood residents could learn about African cultures and receive training in the performing arts. Dunham also created a museum

Further Reading

Beckford, Ruth. *Katherine Dunham.* New York: M. Dekker, 1979.

Dunham, Katherine. *A Touch of Innocence: Memoirs of Childhood.* 1959. Reprint, Chicago: University of Chicago Press, 1994.

Rose, Albirda. *Dunham Technique: A Way of Life.* Dubuque, Iowa: Kendall/Hunt, 1990.

Recommended Recorded and Videotaped Performances

Mambo (1954). Hen's Tooth Video, VHS, 1997.

Stormy Weather (1943). Twentieth Century-Fox, VHS, 1991.

E

❖ ESTEFAN, GLORIA (Gloria Fajardo)
(1958–) *Singer*

Drawing on her Cuban roots, Gloria Estefan has been largely responsible for introducing Latin rhythms into American pop music. Born Gloria Fajardo on September 1, 1958, she left Cuba with her family the following year when Fidel Castro came to power. Her father, José, had been a bodyguard for the wife of the former president, Fulgencio Batista. After the Fajardos were settled in Miami, Florida, José was recruited for the CIA's Bay of Pigs operation in Cuba, where he was captured and imprisoned for a year and a half. Further casting a pall on Gloria's youth, José Fajardo was diagnosed with multiple sclerosis several years after his release. While her mother worked to support the family, Gloria was in charge of caring for her father and younger sister. Burdened by her responsibilities, she found her only escape in listening and singing to records.

In 1975 she met Emilio Estefan, a keyboardist who headed a local band called Miami Latin Boys. Soon after, she joined the band as the lead singer, performing on the weekends while attending the University of Miami. Somewhat plump and very shy, Gloria slowly gained confidence onstage, in

large part because of Emilio's encouragement. After she graduated from college, Gloria and Emilio married on September 1, 1978. Two years later, their son Nayib was born.

In 1980 Emilio left his day job to become a full-time manager of the band, by then renamed the Miami Sound Machine. He secured a contract with the Hispanic division of CBS Records, and the group recorded four successful Spanish-language albums. Although they had hits in Spanish-speaking countries around the world, the Miami Sound Machine made little headway in the United States. Wanting to promote the group in the lucrative American market, CBS encouraged the band to write and sing songs in English. One of their first, "Conga," became a crossover hit, making an appearance on the pop, dance, black, and Latin charts.

The band followed up with the all-English albums *Primitive Love* (1985) and *Let It Loose* (1987). Specializing in dance songs with a Latin beat, they had hits with "Bad Boys," "Words Get in the Way," "Rhythm Is Gonna Get You," and "1-2-3." Internal disagreements led several band members to leave the group, which allowed Estefan to play an increasingly important role as the frontwoman. Recognizing the public's affection for Estefan, the group's billing changed first to Gloria

Estefan and the Miami Sound Machine, then simply to Gloria Estefan. By the late 1980s, Estefan had also started singing more of the ballads she loved and fewer of the dance tunes that had made her a star.

Estefan promoted her records with constant touring, until March 20, 1990, when a tractor trailer collided with her tour bus. Estefan's back was broken in the accident. After a four-hour operation, in which steel rods were embedded along her spine, it was unclear whether or not she would be confined to a wheelchair. During her long recuperation, Estefan received an enormous outpouring of support from her fans. To the surprise of her doctors, after a year of physical therapy she made a complete recovery. In March 1991 she was once again able to set out on tour to market her album *Into the Light.*

Estefan remained remarkably prolific during the 1990s. She returned to recording in Spanish with the acclaimed *Mi Tierra* (1993); produced an album of covers titled *Hold Me, Thrill Me, Kiss Me* (1994); and reexplored heavily produced dance tracks with *Gloria!* (1998). Amidst her heavy recording schedule, she took off time to have a second child, Emily Marie, in 1994.

Driven by a need to experiment with new genres, Estefan released *Alma Caribeña,* an exploration of Afro-Caribbean music, in 2000. In addition, she began an acting career, making her movie debut as a grade-school teacher in *Music of the Heart* (1999) opposite MERYL STREEP. Estefan also appeared in the HBO film *For Love or Country: The Arturo Sandoval Story* (2000), which told the true story of a jazz musician's efforts to leave Cuba to achieve creative freedom.

Throughout her career, Estefan has helped to push Latin music into the American mainstream. In 1994, she became the first artist to sing a song in Spanish at the Grammy Awards. Six years later, she cohosted the first Latin Grammy Awards ceremony in Los Angeles.

Unafraid of entering the political realm, Estefan has drawn criticism for her support of Cuban-based artists and for visiting the Miami family of Elián Gonzáles, who sought to keep the boy in the United States against the wishes of his Cuban father. Her outspokenness has made her the United States's highest-profile representative of the Cuban-American community. Many Cuban Americans hold her in high regard as the embodiment of their American dream. Still a resident of Miami, Estefan is affectionately known in her hometown as "nuestra Glorita"—our Gloria.

Further Reading

Benson, Michael. *Gloria Estefan.* Minneapolis: Lerner, 2000.

Philips, Jane. *Gloria Estefan.* Broomall, Pa.: Chelsea House, 2001.

Recommended Recorded and Videotaped Performances

Gloria Estefan and the Miami Sound Machine: The Evolution Tour. Sony/Columbia, VHS, 1996.

Gloria Estefan: Greatest Hits. Sony/Columbia, CD, 1992.

Music of the Heart (1999). Buena Vista Home Entertainment, DVD/VHS, 2000.

F

❖ FARRELL, SUZANNE (Roberta Sue Ficker)
(1945–)   *Dancer*

The final muse of master choreographer George Balanchine, Suzanne Farrell was born Roberta Sue Ficker on August 16, 1945, in a suburb of Cincinnati, Ohio. The youngest of three sisters, she began her ballet training at eight at the Cincinnati Conservatory of Music. When she was 14, she was spotted by a talent scout from the prestigious School of American Ballet and invited to New York to audition for Balanchine. In 1960, Ficker was one of 12 students to earn a Ford Foundation scholarship to the school.

In less than a year, Ficker joined the corps of the New York City Ballet, directed by Balanchine. She soon began calling herself Suzanne Farrell, a name she found in the phone book. Within months, Farrell was dancing leading roles and emerging as one of Balanchine's favorites. In *Mediation* (1963), he created the first of many roles especially for Farrell. Two years later, she was named a principal dancer of the company, an event Balanchine celebrated by creating the evening-long ballet *Don Quixote,* in which he danced opposite Farrell.

The work was seen by many as a commentary on Balanchine and Farrell's increasingly intimate relationship. Entranced by Farrell's drive and talent, Balanchine worked closely with the dancer, developing an almost telepathic communication with her. He often made only the vaguest suggestion to Farrell, which she then translated into the movement he was looking for. Balanchine also admired Farrell's body type, calling her his Stradivarius because she was the perfect instrument for his choreography. Tall, beautiful, and long-limbed, Farrell was extremely strong yet could convey an impression of delicacy ideal for communicating Balanchine's romantic sensibility.

Balanchine had a history of marrying his favorite ballerinas—four in all—but with Farrell he had only a working relationship. Still, members of his company referred to her as the "fifth Mrs. B," with a strong whiff of jealousy. Farrell earned the resentment of more veteran dancers as she won coveted roles in ballets such as *Brahms-Schoenberg Quartet* (1966), *Jewels* (1967), and *Metastasis & Pithoprakta* (1968).

In February 1969, Farrell married fellow company member Paul Mejia. When Mejia began losing good roles, the couple became convinced that he was being punished by the possessive Balanchine. In May, they issued an ultimatum: If Mejia was not cast in a leading role in the ballet's Spring

Gala Benefit, they would both leave the New York City Ballet. Mejia lost the role, and they resigned, beginning the period Farrell would come to refer to as her "banishment."

After appearing as a guest dancer with the National Ballet of Canada, Farrell joined the Ballet of the Twentieth Century in 1970. As part of this innovative Brussels-based company led by Maurice Béjart, she toured Europe and the Middle East. Although she was the ballet's star, she missed her collaboration with Balanchine. In 1974, she wrote him, asking to return to the New York City Ballet. They were reunited the next year, and quickly Farrell reestablished herself as the company's prima ballerina. During the next eight years, Farrell originated lead roles in many of Balanchine's late masterworks, including *Tsigane* (1975), *Chaconne* (1976), and *Mozartiana* (1981). In 1982, she danced in *Variations for Orchestra,* the last work Balanchine choreographed before his death in 1983.

Farrell continued to dance for the New York City Ballet, now under the direction of her frequent dance partner Peter Martins. In 1983, they made their last appearance together in the 1,000th performance of Balanchine's *The Nutcracker.* Many declared Farrell's career was over four years later, when she had hip replacement surgery. To her fans' delight, months of grueling therapy allowed her to return to the stage in 1988. She continued to perform until her health forced her to retire the following year.

Farrell has since become a respected teacher with the New York City Ballet and the School of the American Ballet. In 2000, she began working with the John F. Kennedy Center for the Performing Arts on a touring show titled, "Suzanne Farrell Stages the Masters of Twentieth Century Ballet," featuring works by Balanchine, Béjart, and Jerome Robbins. The same year, she became the director of the Suzanne Farrell Ballet, an 18-member ensemble that made its debut at the Kennedy Center's "Balanchine Celebration." In an interview with *Dance Magazine,* she revealed how much she continues to rely on the lessons learned from her mentor: "I still ask Balanchine for guidance. . . .

Balanchine was always there for me—in a way, he choreographed my life."

Further Reading

Daniel, David. "Farrell, Suzanne." *International Encyclopedia of Dance,* edited by Selma Jeanne Cohen, vol. 2, pp. 376–378. New York: Oxford University Press, 1998.

Farrell, Suzanne, with Toni Bentley. *Holding on to the Air.* New York: Summit Books, 1990.

Recommended Recorded and Videotaped Performances

The Balanchine Library: Davidsbundlertanze (1981). Elektra/Asylum, VHS, 1995.

The Balanchine Library; The Prodigal Son/Chaconne (1978). Elektra/Asylum, VHS, 1995.

The Balanchine Library: Selections from Jewels and Stravinsky Violin Concerto (1977). Elektra/Asylum, VHS, 1996.

❖ FINLEY, KAREN
(1956–)   *Performance Artist*

In the 1990s, performance artist Karen Finley found herself and her work at the center of a national debate on censorship. Born in 1956, she grew up in Evanston, Illinois, encouraged by her parents to express herself through the arts. She was especially inspired by her father, who sold insurance but considered jazz drumming his true vocation.

Intending to become a painter, Finley left home to attend the San Francisco Art Institute. While she was visiting her parents during a break, her life was shattered when her father killed himself in the garage. Finley later maintained that the event was "where everything comes from" in her work. She explained that her father's suicide left her so full of anger that she had trouble concentrating on her painting. She instead turned to performance art as a way of turning her rage into art.

Finley arrived in New York in 1984 and soon became a fixture in the city's art scene. Her shows developed into mixtures of provocative monologues, dramas built around props, and projections of prerecorded videotapes. Nudity and obscenities, too, became familiar elements in her work. Although praised by many critics of avant-garde theater, her performances also drew sharp criticism, most notably an eloquent attack by journalist Pete Hamill that appeared in the *Village Voice* in 1986.

An even more influential diatribe against Finley's work appeared in *The Washington Post*. Syndicated columnists Rowland Evans and Robert Novak expressed outrage over the content of the work produced by artists with grants from the National Endowment for the Arts (NEA). They singled out Finley, ridiculing her as a "nude, chocolate-smeared young woman." Their criticism focused on one section of her 90-minute performance piece, *We Keep Our Victims Ready*. In this part of the performance, Finley stripped to her underwear and rubbed chocolate over her body, shrieking obscenities in the voice of several characters, including victims of rape, suicide, and poverty.

Commenting that the chocolate was a "symbol of women being treated like dirt," Finley was offended that the diatribe mentioned only a part of a much longer work, taking it entirely out of context. Evans and Novak themselves admitted that they had never seen the performance they were commenting on. Still, their criticisms were embraced by conservative politicians such as Jesse Helms and Pat Buchanan. They chose Finley's grant from the NEA as a battleground for the fight to further their political agenda.

Under pressure from conservative groups, the National Council of the Arts, which advised the NEA, rejected grants for Finley and three other artists—Holly Hughes, John Fleck and Tim Miller—on June 29, 1990. Finley, who had been an NEA grant recipient since 1984, was aghast. "I am shocked," she told the press, adding, "A year ago I was in a country of freedom of expression; now I am not."

Now known as the NEA Four, Finley, Hughes, Fleck, and Miller responded by suing the NEA. The artists won their case; each was awarded their grant money and $6,000 in compensatory damages. In the meantime, the NEA approved a new requirement for evaluating grant recipients: The agency was now to consider "general standards of decency and respect for the diverse beliefs and values of the American public." The new requirement and its subsequent appeal in the NEA case was largely seen as a concession to its conservative critics.

Despite her notoriety, Finley continued to produce provocative performance pieces, including *American Chestnut* (1997) and *Shut Up and Love Me* (1999). She also wrote three books. *Shock Treatment* (1990), published amidst the NEA debates, includes the text of two performance pieces and other writings. Her other books are works of satire. *Enough Is Enough: Weekly Meditations for Living Dysfunctionally* (1993) lampoons self-help literature, while *Living It Up: Adventures in Hyperdomesticity* (1996) offers Finley's own take on the Martha Stewart phenomenon.

In 1998, Finley was performing *Return of the Chocolate Smeared Woman,* a piece that commented on the image of her presented by the press in the thick of the 1990 NEA grant debacle. During its run, the appeal of the NEA Four case was decided by the Supreme Court. In an 8 to 1 decision, the court decided for the NEA, claiming that its decency standards constituted "advisory language" that did not violate the First Amendment, as Finley and her fellow artists alleged. Finley called the ruling "a big loss for our country." Even with the defeat, Finley has remained a symbolic leader for freedom of expression. As Laurie Stone wrote in a 1998 profile of the artist in *Ms.* magazine, "We need Finley: she doesn't duck bullets, . . . and she continues to push against her own boundaries as an artist." Seeking a fresh start, Finley left New York for Los Angeles in 1999. The same year, she posed nude for *Playboy* magazine—an ironic response to critics who saw nothing in her work but sexuality. In 2001, she debuted a new performance piece, *Shut Up and Love Me,* which explored how heterosexual women must "[try] to find a sensible way of living within a code of being desired."

Further Reading

Finley, Karen. *A Different Kind of Intimacy: The Collected Writings of Karen Finley.* New York: Thunder's Mouth Press, 2000.

Sante, Luc. "Blood and Chocolate: What Karen Finley Really Does." *The New Republic.* October 15, 1990, pp. 34+.

❖ FITZGERALD, ELLA
(1917 or 1918–1996)   *Singer*

Considered one of the best jazz singers of the 20th century, Ella Fitzgerald helped create an encyclopedia of American popular song with her influential "Songbook" recordings of the 1950s and 1960s. The joy in her voice, even when interpreting somber songs, stands in stark contrast to her impoverished youth. Born in Newport News, Virginia, on April 25 in either 1917 or 1918, Ella was raised by her mother in Yonkers, New York. Her father abandoned the family when she was an infant.

While Ella was in her teens, her mother died. An aunt in Harlem took her in after her stepfather began abusing her. Ella spent much of her time on the street, running numbers and working as a police lookout for prostitutes. Her illegal activities landed her in reform school, where she was regularly beaten by the male guards.

Despite her desperate circumstances, Fitzgerald developed a love for popular songs and aspired to become a dancer. Having prepared a dance routine, she entered an amateur contest at Harlem's famous Apollo Theater in 1934. Once on stage, she panicked. Unable to move, she started singing "The Object of My Affection," a hit by her favorite singer, Connie Boswell. Fitzgerald won first prize. In addition to $10, she was to have received a weeklong engagement at the Apollo. She was so unkempt in her hand-me-down clothes, however, that the management felt she was too unpresentable to appear at the theater.

Now hoping for a singing career, Fitzgerald snagged an introduction to bandleader Chick Webb. After hearing her voice, Webb arranged for her parole from reform school, became her legal guardian, and set about training her to perform. Fitzgerald quickly became a star attraction, playing the Cotton Club and other popular New York nightclubs. In 1935, she also began recording with Decca Records. Three years later, she had her first hit, "A-Tisket, A-Tasket," which she cowrote, basing the lyrics on a children's rhyme. In 1939, Webb died and Fitzgerald took over his band until it was forced to disband as the musicians were drafted to serve in World War II.

Fitzgerald quickly established herself as a solo artist, moving easily from swing music to the bebop rhythms pioneered by musicians Charlie Parker and Dizzy Gillespie. Renowned for her ability to mimic the sound of instruments, she also became the master of scat singing, in which she created a melody out of a rapid-fire series of nonsense syllables.

Beginning in 1946, Fitzgerald became a fixture at the annual Jazz at the Philharmonic concerts organized by promoter Norman Granz. Granz felt that the light ditties and novelty songs Fitzgerald was recording for Decca were not up to her caliber. He arranged her release from the label and founded Verve Records, with Fitzgerald as its leading artist. Between 1956 and 1964, she began recording a series of "songbooks" under Granz's direction. These album sets featured the works of the greatest American songwriters, including Cole Porter, George and Ira Gershwin, Irving Berlin, Jerome Kern, and Rodgers and Hart. Fitzgerald's recordings established a canon of the American popular song and, in many cases, became the definitive interpretation of these songwriters' works. Expressing the universal admiration for Fitzgerald's songbooks, Ira Gershwin once said, "I never knew how good our songs were until I heard Ella Fitzgerald sing them."

Continuing to record with Verve, Fitzgerald made about 150 albums and sold about 25 million records during her 60-year career. She also toured constantly and made more than 200 appearances on television. Fitzgerald sang in two films, *Pete*

Kelly's Blues (1955) and St. Louis Blues (1958). Her work won her 12 Grammy Awards, a Kennedy Center Honor, and the National Medal of Freedom. In an unprecedented run, she was voted the best female jazz singer by readers of *Down Beat* magazine for 18 consecutive years.

In addition to her huge popular following, Fitzgerald was a favorite among her peers. Vocalist Mel Tormé was quoted as saying, "Ella was the absolute epitome of everything that I've ever believed in or loved as far as popular singing was concerned," whereas Peggy Lee said simply, "She's the best singer I ever heard." Some critics, however, faulted Fitzgerald for not displaying the emotionalism of another great jazz vocalist, BILLIE HOLIDAY. For others, though, her lack of emotion was seen as a strength, allowing listeners to create their own interpretations of the lyrics she sang.

Also unlike Holiday, Fitzgerald had a relatively uneventful personal life. She was married twice— to shipworker Benny Kornegay in 1941 and to bassist Ray Brown in 1948. Her first marriage ended with an annulment; the second, with a divorce. With Brown, she adopted a son—Ray Jr.—whom she raised by herself after 1952.

In her later years, Fitzgerald was plagued by ill health. Although suffering from heart trouble and diabetes, she continued to perform as often as possible. Even as her body grew frail, her voice remained remarkably strong and confident. Fitzgerald finally retired in 1992. The next year, her diabetes forced the amputation of her legs below the knee. She spent the rest of her life in her home in Beverly Hills, California, where she died on June 15, 1996. The next month, 23 jazz greats gathered at New York's Carnegie Hall to pay tribute to the performer remembered with affection and awe as "the first lady of song."

Further Reading

Grouse, Leslie, ed. *The Ella Fitzgerald Companion.* New York: Schirmer Books, 1998.

Nicholson, Stuart. *Ella Fitzgerald: A Biography.* New York: Scribner's, 1994.

Recommended Recorded and Videotaped Performances

The Complete Ella Fitzgerald Song Books. Polygram Records, CD set, 1993.

Ella Fitzgerald: Something to Live For. Winstar Home Entertainment, VHS, 1999.

The First Lady of Song. Polygram Records, CD set, 1993.

❖ **FONDA, JANE (Jane Seymour Fonda)**
(1937–) *Actress*

Renowned for her wide range as a film actress, Jane Fonda has played similarly divergent roles off-screen. During her turbulent life, she has been an ingenue, a sex kitten, a serious performing artist, a political radical, a savvy Hollywood insider, a fitness guru, a corporate wife, and a social reformer.

Jane Seymour Fonda was born on December 21, 1937, in New York, New York. The daughter of film star Henry Fonda, she spent most of her seemingly idyllic youth in Los Angeles. Away from the public eye, however, she suffered from intense insecurities fueled by her emotionally remote father and depressed mother. When Jane was 12, her mother committed suicide. The next year, her younger brother Peter shot himself in the stomach, an incident he later described as an accident.

Emerging out of her difficult childhood, Fonda attended Vassar College, before dropping out to become a fashion model. After studying at New York City's Actors Studio, she began a career in film at 22. Most of her early movies were light comedies, most notably *Cat Ballou* (1965) and *Barefoot in the Park* (1967). Her most notorious role, however, was as the heroine of *Barbarella,* a science fiction satire directed by Roger Vadim, whom Fonda married in 1965. The film remains a cult favorite, largely because of Fonda's striptease over the opening credits.

Disturbed by her new sex symbol image, Fonda left Vadim and sought more serious acting roles. She found the ideal part in *They Shoot Horses, Don't They?* (1969), an unrelentingly grim story of competitors in a 1930s dance marathon. Fonda

Jane Fonda with director Alan Pakula
on the set of *Klute* (1971)
(© Bettmann/CORBIS)

was nominated for an Academy Award for *Horses*. Three years later, she won her first Oscar for *Klute* (1971), a thriller in which she played an emotionally troubled call girl with characteristic intensity.

By this time, Fonda had become as well known for her politics as for her acting. Expressing her support for such radical groups as the American Indian Movement and the Black Panthers, she was particularly outspoken in her opposition to the Vietnam War. In 1972, Fonda traveled to North Vietnam at the urging of Tom Hayden, leader of the Students for a Democratic Society, whom she married the next year. During her trip, she spoke out against the war on Vietnamese radio, calling American soldiers murderers. She was also pho-

tographed wearing a helmet and a smile, riding on an antiaircraft gun that she appeared to be aiming at American warplanes. Many Americans were offended by her actions and gave her the derisive nickname "Hanoi Jane." In 1988, Fonda apologized for her inflammatory rhetoric on a nationally broadcast special hosted by Barbara Walters. Nevertheless, some Americans, particularly Vietnam War veterans, have never forgiven Fonda for her stance during the war.

Initially, the film industry was also repelled by Fonda's radical politics. For several years, she had difficulty finding film roles. Finally, in 1977, *Fun with Dick and Jane* was enough of a hit to bring her back into the Hollywood fold. She followed this frothy comedy with several distinguished films, including *Julia* (1977), *The China Syndrome* (1979), and *Coming Home* (1978), for which she won her second best-actress Oscar. In these popular movies, she played a somewhat sheltered woman who during the course of the film is awakened to feminist and political issues.

Fonda publicly explored her own personal life in *On Golden Pond* (1981). The movie cast her as the estranged daughter of a cranky, dying professor, played by her father. Onscreen, Jane and Henry Fonda appeared to come to terms with their own tense relationship. Jane was nominated for a supporting-actress Oscar, while Henry was posthumously given the award for best actor.

In the 1980s, Fonda began a new career as a pioneer of the fitness videotape. She published *Jane Fonda's Workout Book* in 1981, in which she promoted exercise as her own method of keeping fit and trim. Entrepreneur Stuart Katz, encouraged by his wife, approached Fonda about turning her fitness book into a video. The resulting videotape was a sensation: It held the number-one spot on Billboard's list of best-selling videos for 53 weeks and stayed on the chart for more than five years. Its success was the start of Fonda's fitness empire, which eventually included some 20 more videotapes, a clothing line, and several exercise clubs. From her profits, Fonda contributed $17 million to political and social causes.

Fonda continued her movie career, although most of her films, such as *The Morning After* (1987), *Old Gringo* (1989), and *Stanley and Iris* (1990), failed to find an audience. Her relationship with husband Tom Hayden also began to falter. After 17 years of marriage, she and Hayden divorced in 1989. Their son Troy, as well as her daughter Vanessa from her first marriage, continued to live with Fonda.

In 1992, Fonda announced her retirement from acting after her marriage to television mogul Ted Turner. She surprised her admirers by publicly taking a back-seat to the flamboyant Turner. Fonda particularly drew criticism by performing the "tomahawk chop" as a show of support for the Atlanta Braves, a baseball team her husband owned. Offended by this perceived belittling of Indian cultures, Native American activists were stunned by the behavior of Fonda, who in the 1970s had been among the most prominent advocates for Indian rights.

After eight years of marriage, Fonda announced her separation from Turner in 2000. She continued, however, her work with the Georgia Campaign for Adolescent Pregnancy Prevention (G-CAPP)—an organization originally funded by the Turner Foundation. The G-CAPP is devoted to eliminating teenage pregnancy worldwide through education. In 2001, Fonda also donated $12.5 million to the Harvard Graduate School of Education to establish a gender studies center. In addition to her social activism and philanthropic work, she has hinted that she may return to acting, possibly in the theater.

After six decades of reinvention, Fonda expressed enthusiasm for what she called the "third act of her life" in a 2000 magazine interview with talk show host OPRAH WINFREY, "As an actress, I know how important the third act is," she explained. "You can have first acts that are interesting, but you don't know what they mean. Then a good third act pulls it all together."

Further Reading

Anderson, Christopher. *Citizen Jane: The Turbulent Life of Jane Fonda.* New York: Holt, 1990.

Collier, Peter. *The Fondas: A Hollywood Dynasty.* New York: Putnam, 1991.

Recommended Recorded and Videotaped Performances

Barbarella (1968). Paramount, VHS, 1991.
Coming Home (1978). MGM/UA, VHS, 1997.
Klute (1971). Warner Home Video, VHS, 1998.
On Golden Pond (1982). Artisan Entertainment, VHS, 1982.

❖ **FOSTER, JODIE (Alicia Christian Foster)** (1962–)   *Actress, Director*

Known for her subtle acting and fierce intelligence, Jodie Foster is perhaps the most widely respected actress in Hollywood. On November 19, 1962, she was born Alicia Christian Foster in Los Angeles, California. Only months before, her father had left her mother, Brandy. Raising Jodie and her three siblings alone, Brandy supported the family by working as a publicist, until Jodie's brother Buddy began finding jobs as a child actor. With Brandy as his manager, he appeared in many commercials and as a regular on the *Mayberry R.F.D.* television series (1968–71).

Jodie began her own career at age three. Taken along on one of Buddy's auditions, she was spotted and hired to appear in an ad for Coppertone suntan lotion. Over the next five years, she made 45 commercials. When she was eight, her mother considered her ready for acting. After her debut on *Mayberry R.F.D.*, she guested on more than 50 shows and starred in two short-lived situation comedies—*Bob, Carol, Ted, and Alice* (1973) and *Paper Moon* (1974–75). As Buddy's career stalled, Jodie's began to flourish. She was soon her family's primary breadwinner.

At 10, Jodie started acting in feature films. She became a staple of live action Disney films, appearing in *Napoleon and Samantha* (1972), *Freaky Friday* (1977), and *Candleshoe* (1977). She found more challenging work playing a spirited troublemaker in Martin Scorsese's *Alice Doesn't Live Here Anymore* (1974). Two years later, Scorsese invited her to play a far grittier role—that of a teenage prostitute in his nihilistic *Taxi Driver* (1976). Jodie initially wanted to turn down the part. "I was the Disney kid," she later explained. "I thought, 'What would my friends say?'" Brandy Foster, however, refused to let her give up the chance to work with Scorsese and the film's star, Robert De Niro. After undergoing a series of psychological tests to prove that she could cope with the movie's violence, Jodie at 14 delivered one of the most lauded performances of her career. In addition to an Oscar nomination, she won the New York Film Critics Circle and Los Angeles Film Critics awards for best supporting actress.

Under Brandy's supervision, Foster continued to choose offbeat roles. She played a vamp in the all-child musical *Bugsy Malone* (1976) and a murderer in the thriller *The Little Girl Who Lives Down the Lane* (1976). In 1980, Foster portrayed unusually complex teenagers in two well-received films, *Foxes* and *Carny*.

After 17 years in front of the camera, Foster stunned the film industry in 1980 by deciding to attend Yale University full time. Always an avid reader and brilliant student, she saw her college years as way of, at least temporarily, escaping the limelight. In a horrific twist of fate, Foster instead was thrust into the headlines when John Hinckley attempted to assassinate President Ronald Reagan on March 30, 1981. Obsessed with Foster's character in *Taxi Driver*, Hinckley stated that he was in love with Foster and had shot the president as a way of winning her affection. Subsequently receiving death threats from several other deranged admirers, Foster had to be escorted around campus by armed bodyguards.

While still at Yale, Foster acted occasionally, including taking a starring role in the film *The Hotel New Hampshire* (1984). Yet, after graduating with honors, she had difficulty finding acting jobs. Only after vigorous lobbying was she able to win the part of Sarah Tobias, a foul-mouthed gang-rape victim, in *The Accused* (1988). Endowing her character with a powerful sense of dignity, Foster was rewarded with an Oscar for best actress.

After having minor critical successes acting in *Five Corners* (1988) and *Stealing Home* (1988),

Foster took a turn at directing with *Little Man Tate* (1991). The story of a child prodigy raised by a single mother echoed many aspects of her own youth. In 1992, she formed her own production company, Egg Pictures. Her deal with Polygram Filmed Entertainment allowed her to act, direct, or produce the films made by Egg, giving her flexibility and power enjoyed by few movie actresses.

In 1991, Foster received her second Oscar for best actress, playing an FBI agent battling a serial killer in *The Silence of the Lambs*. She had less success with *Sommersby* (1993), a Civil War romance, and *Maverick* (1994), a comedy set in the Old West. In her first Egg production, *Nell* (1994), Foster was nominated for another best actress Oscar, but the film failed to find an audience. Her second directorial effort, *Home for the Holidays* (1995), met a similar fate. Even though many films in the 1990s were box-office disappointments, Foster remained one of Hollywood's leading actresses. For her performance in *Anna and the King* (1999), Foster received $15 million, a pay rate higher than that of any other film actress at the time, with the exception of JULIA ROBERTS.

Self-assured in both her private and professional life, the unmarried Foster gave birth to a boy, Charlie, in 1998. She had a second child in 2001, refusing to answer any questions regarding either's paternity. With equal confidence, Foster in 2000 bowed out of *Hannibal*, the big-budget sequel to *The Silence of the Lambs*, to direct *Flora Plum* (2002), signaling her increasing interest in working behind the camera.

Further Reading

Kennedy, Phillipa. *Jodie Foster: A Life on Screen.* New York: Birch Lane Press, 1996.
Smolen, Diane. *The Films of Jodie Foster.* Secaucus, N.J.: Carol Publishing, 1996.

Recommended Recorded and Videotaped Performances

The Accused (1988). Paramount, VHS, 1996.
Little Man Tate (1991). MGM/UA, VHS, 2000.

The Silence of the Lambs (1991). Image Entertainment, DVD, 1998.

Taxi Driver (1976). Columbia/Tristar, DVD/VHS, 1999.

❖ FRANKLIN, ARETHA
(1942–) *Singer*

Fittingly known as the Queen of Soul, Aretha Franklin has been the premier female singer of rhythm and blues for more than four decades. Franklin was born on March 25, 1942, in Memphis, Tennessee, but at age two moved with her family to Detroit, Michigan, where she still lives. The fourth of five children, she grew up surrounded by gospel music. Her father, C. L., was the minister of the 4,500-member New Bethel Baptist Church, where her mother, Barbara, often sang. When Aretha was 10, Barbara Franklin died, leaving C. L. as her primary adult influence.

Aretha sang her first solo at her father's church when she was 12. She stunned the congregation with her mature and expressive voice. By 14, she had begun recording hymns for Chess Records and traveling with her father's revival tours. Aretha's education ended when, at 15, she gave birth to her first child. She would have two more children during her teens.

Taken with the singing of DINAH WASHINGTON, Franklin decided to switch from gospel to the blues. With her father's blessing, she left for New York in 1960 to seek out a career in secular music. Her demo tape reached Columbia Records executive John Hammond, who called Franklin "the best natural since BILLIE HOLIDAY." Hammond had signed Holiday to her first record contract and did the same for Franklin. Her albums with Columbia, however, did not provide the best showcase for her talent. To make her more commercial, Hammond reined in her raw and powerful voice in a light jazz nightclub sound. Although she won the *Down Beat* magazine critic's poll for the best new vocalist of 1962, Franklin's Columbia recordings were only moderate successes.

When her contract with Columbia elapsed, Franklin signed with Atlantic. She was encouraged to find her own singing style by Ted White, who began acting as her manager after their marriage in 1961. Atlantic allowed Franklin to take an active role in choosing her material and developing its arrangement. The label also sent her to work with world-class musicians at a recording studio in Muscle Shoals, Alabama. The result was a powerful merging of gospel expression with the soul music tradition.

The first song Franklin recorded, "I Never Loved a Man (The Way I Love You)," went to number one in the spring of 1967. It was only the first in a string of hits. In 1967 and 1968, Franklin released three top 10 albums and six top 10 singles, including "Chain of Fools," "(You Make Me Feel Like a) Natural Woman," and "I Say a Little Prayer." Her signature song became "Respect," which Franklin claims she never grows tired of singing. In her voice, the Otis Redding song becomes a woman's demand for her lover to acknowledge her worth and dignity. It was adopted as an anthem by both the civil rights movement and the women's movement.

Franklin continued to record to popular and critical acclaim. Through 1975, she won at least one Grammy every year. Her success, however, strained her marriage. She and White divorced in 1969 and she had a six-year relationship with her road manager Ken Cunningham, by whom she had a son. She married actor Glynn Turman in 1978; they were divorced in 1984. Franklin suffered another blow in 1979 when her beloved father was shot by a burglar. He remained in a coma for five years before his death in 1984.

Emerging from a creative dry spell, Franklin gave her career a boost with her movie-stealing appearance in the hit film *The Blues Brothers* (1980), which helped introduce her music to a new, younger audience. The same year, she signed with a new company, Arista. After a few modestly successful records, Franklin had one of her biggest hits with "Freeway of Love," a song from the album *Who's Zooming Who* (1985). She also hit the charts in the 1980s with two duets—"Sisters Are Doing It For Themselves" (1985) with Annie

Lennox and "I Knew You Were Waiting for Me" with George Michael.

In 1987 Franklin was inducted into the Rock and Roll Hall of Fame, the first woman to be so honored. For lifetime achievement, she was also given a special Grammy in 1994, one of 17 she has earned throughout her career.

During the 1990s, Franklin began exploring new interests. She established Crown Productions, a television and film production company that optioned Jesse Jackson's autobiography as its first project.

In 1998, Franklin appeared in *The Blues Brothers 2000* and recorded the popular *A Rose Is Still A Rose,* her first album in seven years. The same year, she sang on the VH1 television special *Divas Live.* Although she shared a stage with Mariah Carey, Celine Dion, GLORIA ESTEFAN, Carole King, and Shania Twain, it was Franklin's performance that stopped the show, proving that even among popular music's royalty she still reigns as the queen. The famously shy Franklin published her own autobiography, *Aretha: From These Roots,* in 1999. In 2001, she was honored with her own VH1 special, "VH1 Divas Live: The One and Only Aretha Franklin."

Further Reading

Bego, Mark. *Aretha Franklin: Queen of Soul.* New York: St. Martin's Press, 1989.

Franklin, Aretha, and David Ritz. *Aretha: From These Roots.* New York: Villard Books, 1999.

Recommended Recorded and Videotaped Performances

Aretha Franklin: The Queen of Soul. WEA/Atlantic, VHS, 1991.

The Very Best of Aretha Franklin, Vol. 1. WEA/Atlantic/Rhino, CD, 1994.

The Very Best of Aretha Franklin, Vol. 2. WEA/Atlantic/Rhino, CD, 1994.

G

GARBO, GRETA (Greta Lovisa Gustafsson)
(1905–1990)   *Actress*

Hollywood's most enigmatic star, Greta Garbo was born Greta Lovisa Gustafsson on September 18, 1905, in Stockholm, Sweden. Raised in poverty, she began working to support her family at 14. Blessed with striking looks, she parlayed a job as shopgirl for the PUB department store into a modeling and acting career. Gustafsson appeared in several films used to advertise PUB's goods before landing a small role in an unsuccessful comedy, *Peter the Tramp* (1922).

Eager to become a serious actress, Gustafsson won a scholarship to the prestigious Royal Dramatic Theater. After a year of study, she caught the eye of Mauritz Stiller, the best-known film director in Sweden. Stiller cast her as the lead in *The Saga of Gösta Berling* (1924) and began to manage every aspect of her professional and personal life. Teaching her what to say, how to act, and how to think, he transformed the unsophisticated Greta Gustafsson into the worldly Great Garbo, the stage name she began using in 1923 at Stiller's insistence.

Due the success of *Gösta Berling* in Germany, German director G. W. Pabst asked Garbo to star in *The Joyless Street* (1925). In the grim film, she played a professor's daughter pressured to become a prostitute in post–World War I Vienna. (The film also featured as an extra MARLENE DIETRICH, who would later become Garbo's rival in Hollywood.) Although *Street* was a box-office failure, Garbo emerged from the film a favorite star of European moviegoers.

In 1925, Louis B. Mayer, the head of Metro-Goldwyn-Mayer (MGM) Studios, persuaded Stiller to come to Hollywood. Stiller agreed only on the condition that MGM would also place Garbo under contract. Convinced Garbo was too plump, Mayer had little enthusiasm for his new contract player. She was cast as a femme fatale in her first two American films, *The Torrent* (1926) and *The Temptress* (1926). Stiller was set to direct the latter but was fired for insubordination. Discouraged by Hollywood, he returned to Sweden, where he died in 1928.

Garbo had her breakthrough in her third film, *Flesh and the Devil* (1927). Like many of her later movies, the film cast her a seductress whose dangerous sexuality spells her own doom. *Flesh* was a great popular success, in large measure due to her passionate scenes with John Gilbert, then the reigning male lead in American movies. Press reports about their scorching offscreen affair delighted MGM and buoyed ticket sales.

Garbo, however, was far less enthusiastic about the publicity. Naturally shy, she refused to give interviews or be photographed, maintaining that "my private affairs are strictly private." Calling her the "Swedish Sphinx," MGM publicists used her aloofness as a marketing tool to highlight a mysterious quality about Garbo that had already attracted audiences.

With the success of *Flesh,* Garbo demanded a raise. Mayer balked, so she returned to Sweden for seven months. Desperate for another Garbo film, MGM finally relented. Garbo saw her salary increased form $600 to $5,000 a week. The story only added to her popular appeal: That she was willing to walk away from stardom became part of her mystique.

To Garbo, as important as her salary increase was the greater control she now had over her career. From that point on, MGM gave her the best directors and the most popular male leads. Cinematographer William Daniels was hired for nearly all her American films. His delicate use of light and shadow photographed Garbo's beauty to its best advantage.

Garbo's silent films continued to draw crowds. MGM, however, worried that, because of her heavy Swedish accent, sound pictures would end her career. The studio kept her in silents for two years after talkies were first introduced. Finally, MGM cast her in a sound adaptation of Eugene O'Neill's *Anna Christie* (1930), chosen because she could play the role of a young Swedish immigrant. The MGM publicity machine came up with the slogan "Garbo Talks" to advertise the film. Adding to the anticipation, Garbo did not appear until well into the picture. The camera lingered on her for nearly a minute before she uttered her first line, "Give me a whiskey. Ginger ale on the side. . . . And don't be stingy, baby." Rather than being turned off by her accent, the public responded to her husky voice as a welcome complement to her exotic, sophisticated good looks.

Anna Christie won Garbo the first of four best actress Oscar nominations and brought her to the

Greta Garbo in *Queen Christina* (1933)
(Museum of Modern Art Film Stills Archive)

height of her stardom. Over the next seven years, she made 11 pictures, including the classics *Queen Christina* (1933), *Anna Karenina* (1935), and *Camille* (1937). Her onscreen charisma made her the best-paid actress in Hollywood and allowed her to steal the all-star *Grand Hotel* (1932) from such heavyweights as John Barrymore and Wallace Beery. In the film, she spoke the line that became her trademark: "I want to be alone."

In 1939, Garbo insisted that MGM cast her as a Russian spy in *Ninotchka* (1939), a comedy directed by Ernst Lubitsch. Her previous American films had all been dramas, most featuring her as the passionate heroine in a tragic romance. Drawing on their past advertising campaign, MGM announced Garbo foray into comedy with the slogan "Garbo Laughs." The film, which effectively lampooned Garbo's ice-queen image, was a great popular success. Her next attempt at comedy, however, was a disaster. *Two-Faced Woman* (1941) had Garbo sorely miscast as an American and came under attack by the Legion of Decency, a committee of Catholic bishops, for seeming to condone adultery. It marked the end of Garbo's film career.

Having invested her earnings well, Garbo turned her back on Hollywood and moved to New York City. For the rest of her life, she denied all requests for interviews. She enjoyed a circle of friends and lovers—both male and female—but quickly banished anyone who talked about her to the press. Although often called a recluse, Garbo went on daily walks sporting dark glasses and a large hat. For decades before her death on April 15, 1990, spotting the great Garbo on the street was a sport enjoyed by her fans and neighbors.

Further Reading

Daum, Raymond W., and Vance Muse. *Walking with Garbo: Conversations and Recollections.* New York: HarperCollins, 1991.
Sands, Frederick, and Sven Broman. *The Divine Garbo.* New York: Grosset & Dunlap, 1979.

Recommended Recorded and Videotaped Performances

Camille (1937). Warner Home Video, VHS, 2000.
Grand Hotel (1932). Warner Home Video, VHS, 2000.
The Joyless Street (1925). Kino Video, VHS, 1990.
Ninotchka (1939). Warner Home Video, VHS, 2000.
Queen Christina (1933). Warner Home Video, VHS, 1998.

❖　GARDNER, AVA (Ava Lavinia Gardener)
(1922–1990)　*Actress*

One of Hollywood's greatest beauties, Ava Gardner was born Ava Lavinia Gardener on December 24, 1922. The daughter of a sharecropper, she spent her early years in Grabtown, a small, rural community outside Smithfield, North Carolina. After graduating from high school, she briefly attended Atlanta Christian College, with the intention of becoming a stenographer.

In 1941, Gardner traveled to New York to visit her older sister Bernice and her husband, Larry Tarr,

a photographer. Impressed by Gardner's beauty, Tarr took several photographs of her and placed one in the window of his studio. A clerk from the Metro-Goldwyn-Mayer (MGM) legal department spied the picture and convinced Tarr to send it to a studio talent scout. Gardner was given a silent screen test to mask her heavy Southern drawl. On seeing the test, one MGM official remarked, "She can't act; she didn't talk; she's sensational."

Contract in hand, Gardner took off for Hollywood. MGM gave their new discovery a barrage of acting and diction lessons, though in her early films she was expected to do little more than decorate her scenes. Resenting MGM's disinterest in developing her talent, Gardner claimed the studio treated her like its "prize hog." Despite her anger at MGM, Gardner took her work seriously and earned a reputation as a consummate professional.

The public, however, was more interested in her personal life. At 19, she married Mickey Rooney, then MGM's top star. His womanizing and her jealousy led to divorce 16 months later. In 1945 Gardner had second highly publicized marriage, this time to bandleader Artie Shaw. They divorced about a year later, as Gardner grew weary of Shaw's unwelcome efforts to educate her. Through the rest of her life, Gardner remained friendly with Rooney and Shaw, as she did with most of her many lovers.

After playing small roles in about 20 films, Gardner had her breakthrough part as a treacherous nightclub singer in *The Killers* (1946). Because of its success, she was typecast as a femme fatale for several years. In 1951, however, she won the plum role of Julie in an all-star production of the musical *Show Boat.* Gardner was disappointed, though, when the studio hired Annette Warren to dub her singing voice.

Also in 1951, Gardner married singer Frank Sinatra. The press was fascinated by their explosive relationship, especially their frequent public arguments. Although they divorced in 1957, Sinatra continued to regard Gardner as the love of his life. She is often credited as Sinatra's muse for his classic recordings of the 1950s.

During this decade, Gardner was given more varied and challenging roles. She displayed a talent for wisecracking in *Mogambo* (1953), for which she was nominated for an Academy Award for best actress. The next year, she starred in *The Barefoot Contessa* (1954), the story of a Spanish flamenco dancer molded into a movie star. The film's director, Joseph Mankiewicz, later remembered her telling him, "Hell, Joe, I'm not an actress, but I think I understand this girl. She's a lot like me."

Gardner was dismissive about her acting skills, often far more so than her critics. Although her highly photogenic face brought her to Hollywood, she projected an onscreen presence that, unlike those of most screen beauties, appealed to both men and women. No matter how glamorously she was made up, she remained charmingly down-to-earth. In her own words, she was just "a country girl."

Press accounts of Gardner always focused on her love of drinking, smoking, and staying up all night. She, however, considered herself shy and was deeply offended by her image, which she described as "a loudmouthed, temperamental, oversexed, sultry siren." In part to escape the press, Gardner moved to Europe in the late 1950s. While living in Spain, she became an enthusiastic fan of bullfighting and bullfighters. Gardner had many romances with matadors, including the famed Luis Miguel Dominguin.

Gardner's contract with MGM expired in 1958. In her subsequent film work, she often appeared in smaller but meatier roles. Playing a lusty widow operating a run-down Mexican hotel, Gardner had one of her best parts in *Night of the Iguana* (1964). She also had memorable turns in *The Bible* (1969) and *The Life and Times of Judge Roy Bean* (1972) before retiring from film in 1977. As her health began to fail, she became increasingly reclusive. In her London apartment, she died of pneumonia on January 25, 1990.

Further Reading

Fowler, Karin J. *Ava Gardner: A Bio-Bibliography.* New York: Greenwood Press, 1990.

Gardner, Ava. *Ava: My Story.* New York: Bantam Books, 1990.

Recommended Recorded and Videotaped Performances

The Killers (1946). Universal, VHS, 1998.

The Night of the Iguana (1964). Warner Home Video, VHS, 1992.

Show Boat (1951). Warner Home Video, DVD/VHS, 2000.

❖ **GARLAND, JUDY (Frances Ethel Gumm)**
(1922–1969) *Singer, Actress*

On film, Judy Garland largely defined the Hollywood musical during its heyday in the 1930s and 1940s. Onstage, she emerged as one of the most dynamic performers of the 20th century, earning a legion of fans whose ardor for Garland has scarcely diminished since her death in 1969.

The youngest of three sisters, she was born Frances Ethel Gumm in Grand Rapids, Michigan, on June 10, 1922. Her father managed a movie theater, where he sang between films, accompanied on the piano by Frances's mother. When still a toddler, Frances and her older siblings also began performing for moviegoers as the Gumm Sisters.

The act continued to play local theaters after the family moved to southern California in 1927. Placed in a theatrical school by her ambitious mother, Frances soon became the group's star, singled out as the "little girl with the great big voice." In 1934 while performing in Chicago, the singing Gumms adopted the name Garland, perhaps at the suggestion of vaudeville comedian George Jessel. A year later, Frances herself decided to change her first name to "Judy" after the title of a popular song.

As her reputation grew, Judy was invited to audition for movie studio head Louis Mayer in 1936. Without a screen test, he signed her to a contract with Metro-Goldwyn-Mayer (MGM), which immediately set about grooming her for stardom. Her first screen appearance was in a short titled *Every Sunday* (1936), in which she appeared with fellow teenage singing sensation Deanna Durbin. Unsure how best to use Garland, MGM then loaned her out to Twentieth Century-Fox for the campus comedy *Pigskin Parade* (1936). In her next movie, *Broadway Melody of 1938* (1937), she caught the attention of all Hollywood. Stealing the movie from stars ELEANOR POWELL and Robert Taylor, Garland memorably performed a love song to a photograph of movie heartthrob Clark Gable to the tune of "You Made Me Love You." The music was arranged by Roger Edens, a vocal coach and composer who would have a long, fruitful working relationship with Garland.

Her next great screen role was the one for which she is still best known—Dorothy in the classic musical film *The Wizard of Oz* (1939). Although the movie now seems inconceivable without Garland, she won the coveted part only because MGM could not get its first and second choices, child star SHIRLEY TEMPLE and Garland's former costar Deanna Durbin. In another irony, her performance of "Somewhere Over the Rainbow"—which later became her signature song—was nearly cut from the film at the last minute because the studio feared the song was too melancholy for a children's film. Despite their worries, both Garland and the song were embraced by the public. For her work in *Oz*, she received her only Academy Award—a special Oscar for the best juvenile performance of the year.

Garland spent much of her late teens starring in two popular series of films with former schoolmate Mickey Rooney. She appeared in three "Andy Hardy" movies as Andy's spirited but somewhat insecure pal Betsy Blake. Garland also shared star billing with Rooney in four films of the "Babes" series of lighthearted, frivolous musicals. In *Babes in Arms* (1939), *Strike Up the Band* (1940), *Babes on Broadway* (1941), and *Girl Crazy* (1943), they played would-be performers inspiring their friends to "put on a show."

Offscreen, Garland was far from the happy girl next door she so often played on film. Her boss, Louis Mayer, and her mother (who Garland later called "the real Wicked Witch of the West") dominated the young star, pushing her to meet a relentless schedule of filmmaking, recording, radio performances, and personal appearances. As a result of the stress, Garland developed insomnia. To help her sleep, she was given barbiturates. To

help her wake up and maintain her weight, she was given amphetamines. By the end of her teens, Garland was addicted to pills.

Despite her difficult personal life, Garland did much of her best film work during the 1940s. She appeared in a string of popular musicals including *For Me and My Gal* (costarring with Gene Kelly in his screen debut, 1942), *The Harvey Girls* (1946), and the classic *Meet Me in St. Louis* (1944), on the set of which she first met director Vincente Minnelli. In 1945 she wed Minnelli after dissolving her marriage of four years to composer David Rose. The couple had one child, LIZA MINNELLI, who would grow up to become an accomplished performer in her own right.

Minnelli went on to direct Garland in *The Clock* (1945), a romantic drama, and *The Pirate* (1947), a Cole Porter musical that reteamed her with Kelly. By this time, however, her working habits had grown erratic. Her drug addiction, combined with an ever-present insecurity about her talents, made her chronically late and often too frightened to leave her trailer. After filming *The Pirate*, Garland was briefly confined to a mental institution before returning to the screen in still another successful musical, *Easter Parade* (1948), opposite Fred Astaire. She was set to star again with Astaire in *The Barkleys of Broadway* (1949), but because of her mental instability, she was replaced by Astaire's old dance partner GINGER ROGERS. Her fragile condition also lost her leads in the films *Annie Get Your Gun* (1950) and *Show Boat* (1951), musical properties bought by MGM with Garland in mind.

In 1950 Garland had hit with *Summer Stock* (1950), in which she performed "Get Happy," a song that became a popular part of her repertoire. However, on the set of her next movie, *Royal Wedding* (1951), her difficult behavior compelled MGM to fire their star. Soon afterward, she made a highly publicized suicide attempt, the first of several.

With no offers from other studios, Garland, with the help of agent Sid Luft, began to perform in concert. Luft booked her for an astoundingly successful run at the Palladium in London, followed by an even greater triumph at New York's Palace Theater. She broke box-office records during her 19-week engagement, which won her a Tony Award. Her concerts also earned Garland one of the most devoted followings a singer has ever enjoyed. Singing many of the songs she made famous in her films, Garland created a sense of intimacy with her audiences with her emotionally intense performances.

Divorced from Minnelli in 1951, Garland married Luft the next year. (The couple would have two children, Lorna and Joey.) Soon after their marriage, the couple established their own production company at Warner Brothers in order to make *A Star Is Born* (1954). A musical remake of the 1937 film of the same name, the movie told the show-business story of a rising young star who eclipses her husband, a once-famous actor caught in the grip of alcoholism. The melodrama inspired perhaps Garland's most stirring dramatic performance. She was nominated for an Academy Award for best actress, but lost, possibly because Hollywood had trouble forgiving her for her past temperamental behavior. In her next film, *Judgment at Nuremberg* (1961), her brief role earned her another Oscar nomination, this time for best supporting actress.

After *A Star Is Born,* Garland returned to the concert stage, although ill health often interfered with her work. During one of several comebacks, however, she turned in possibly her greatest performance on April 23, 1961, at New York's Carnegie Hall. The live recording of the concert sold more than 2 million copies and brought her two Grammy Awards.

In September 1963, Garland made her debut in her own variety show on television. The programs varied in quality, though some episodes (such as one in which Garland sang with the then largely unknown BARBRA STREISAND) contain excellent performances. Nevertheless, the show failed to find an audience and was canceled before finishing a season.

In need of money, Garland went back to singing in concert, with mixed results. After a bitter custody battle, she divorced Luft in 1965 and married actor Mark Herron the same year. They separated after six months and divorced in 1967. Two years later, Garland wed for the fifth and last time, marrying discotheque owner Mickey Deans. While on tour in London, Deans found Garland collapsed in her hotel room on June 22, 1969. She died at 47 from an apparently accidental overdose of sleeping pills. The enormous impact she had had on American culture was evident at the outpouring of grief from her devoted fans. More than 20,000 came to her funeral to pay their last respects.

Further Reading

Clarke, Gerald. *Get Happy: The Life of Judy Garland.* New York: Random House, 2000.

Edwards, Anne. *Judy Garland.* New York: Simon & Schuster, 1975.

Frank, Gerold. *Judy.* New York: Da Capo Press, 1999.

Shipman, David. *Judy Garland: The Secret Life of an American Legend.* New York: Hyperion, 1993.

Recommended Recorded and Videotaped Performances

Broadway Melody of 1938 (1937). MGM/UA, VHS, 1992.

The Judy Garland Show Collection (1963). Pioneer Video, DVD set, 1999.

Meet Me in St. Louis (1945). Warner Home Video, VHS, 2000.

A Star Is Born (1954). Warner Home Video, DVD/VHS, 2000.

The Wizard of Oz (1939). Warner Home Video, DVD/VHS, 1999.

❖ **GISH, DOROTHY**
(1898–1968) *Actress*

In her seven-decade career, Dorothy Gish was a leading lady of the theater and a pioneer in film and television. She was born on March 11, 1898, in Dayton, Ohio, but soon moved to New York City. Burdened by business failures, her father abandoned his family, leaving her mother, Mary, alone to care for Dorothy and her older sister, LILLIAN GISH. To help make ends meet, Mary found parts for the girls in theater productions. Dorothy made her stage debut at four, playing a boy in *East Lynne.* After years of touring, she had her greatest early success playing a waif in *Dion O'Dare* (1907).

In 1912, the Gish sisters were introduced to film director D. W. Griffith by their old friend Gladys Smith, who had adopted the stage name MARY PICKFORD. Griffith immediately cast them in *An Unseen Enemy* (1912). Dorothy went on to appear in more than 60 of Griffith's movies, though he was more drawn to Lillian and generally gave her better roles. Only under pressure from Lillian did Griffith agree to cast Dorothy in his World War I epic *Hearts of the World* (1917). She stole the movie with her comic portrayal of the Little Disturber, her favorite role of her career. Her performance made her one of the most sought-after comedians in silent film.

Under the supervision of Griffith, Dorothy Gish made a string of comedies released by Paramount under the banner "the Dorothy Gish Artcraft-Paramount Series." With titles such as *Peppy Polly* (1919) and *Flying Pat* (1920), these movies took advantage of Gish's natural exuberance and gift for pantomime, which earned her the nickname "the female Chaplin." One of her most successful Paramount comedies was *Remodeling Her Husband* (1920), a romantic comedy directed by her sister and written by Dorothy Parker. Gish married her costar, James Rennie, in 1920. She and Rennie were divorced 15 years later but remained friends.

Although comedy was her forte, Gish occasionally appeared in drama. Perhaps her greatest film was *Orphans of the Storm* (1922). The Griffith classic had her starring opposite Lillian as a blind woman caught up in the turmoil of the French Revolution.

Hitting a career slump in the mid-1920s, Gish made several British films with director Herbert Wilcox, including the highly successful *Nell Gwyn* (1926). Her final English film, *Wolves* (1930), was Gish's first talking picture. Considering it a failure, Gish retreated from film work. She made only four more movies; her final film, *The Cardinal,* was released in 1964.

Dorothy Gish in 1923
(Library of Congress, neg. no. USZ62-90166)

Gish continued her acting career onstage. In 1928, she had a successful run in *Young Love,* which also starred Rennie. Among her many other Broadway triumphs were *Brittle Heaven* (1934), *Missouri Legend* (1938), and *The Magnificent Yankee* (1946). In her last theater role, she shared the stage with Lillian in *The Chalk Garden* (1952). In the 1950s, Gish began a new career, performing in live television dramas. Her television credits included "Harvest" (1953), which also starred James Dean, and "Morning's at Seven" (1956).

In the 1960s, Gish's health began to fail. She was living in a sanitarium in Rapallo, Italy, when she died of pneumonia on June 4, 1968, with her devoted sister at her bedside.

Further Reading

Basinger, Jeanine. *Silent Stars*. New York: Knopf, 1999.
Gish, Lillian. *Dorothy and Lillian Gish*. New York: Scribners, 1973.

Recommended Recorded and Videotaped Performances

The Cardinal (1963). Warner Home Video, VHS, 1994.
Harvest (1953). Timeless Video, VHS, 1996.
Orphans of the Storm (1921). Image Entertainment, DVD, 1998.

❖ GISH, LILLIAN
(1893–1993) *Actress, Director*

Born the same year the movie camera was invented, Lillian Gish was one of the most influential pioneers of the film industry. She was born in Springfield, Ohio, on October 14, 1893 (although, to make her seem younger, her birth year was later given as 1896). The Gishes soon moved to New York City, where her father abandoned the family. Left to care for Lillian and her little sister, Dorothy, on her own, Gish's mother, Mary, managed a boardinghouse for performers. There, all three were drawn into the world of the theater. "Baby Lillian," as she was billed, made her stage debut in *In Convict Stripes* in 1902. For the rest of her youth, she spent most of her time appearing in touring companies, often traveling alone from show to show.

In New York, the Gish sisters became friends with another young actress, Gladys Smith, who would soon find superstardom as MARY PICKFORD. Then working for the Biograph film studio, Smith introduced them to director D. W. Griffith, who was immediately struck by their delicate beauty. Legend has it that, without warning, he shot a prop gun over their heads. The Gish girls' horrified shrieks convinced him that they could emote onscreen. Griffith promptly hired them to work in his next film *An Unseen Enemy* (1912). They soon followed Griffith to the Mutual Film Corporation, where he and Lillian collaborated on several of the greatest films of the silent era.

Griffith always encouraged ideas and suggestions from his players, a practice that was particularly fruitful in his relationship with Lillian Gish. They both shared a commitment to film, which they viewed as legitimate art form at a time when few considered it more than a curiosity. On Griffith's advice, Gish researched her roles thoroughly, reading voraciously to prepare herself for every part, even though she had had nearly no formal education. She also took lessons in voice and dance, eventually becoming a skilled athlete able and willing to do dangerous stunt work. Her devotion to her work is clear from an anecdote recounted by an eyewitness who watched Griffith film Gish outside during a snowstorm: "D. W. would ask her if she could stand it, and she would nod. The icicles hung from her lashes, and her face was blue. When the last shot was made they had to carry her to the studio."

With Griffith's encouragement, Gish developed a particularly effective acting style that almost immediately distinguished her from her peers. Most theater actors were trained to use broad gestures that looked too mannered and stiff on the screen. Gish sensed that film required much more subtle gestures and more subdued demonstrations of feeling. Especially in close-ups, she was able to use small changes in her facial expressions to communicate deep, often even contradictory emotions. Ever since, film acting has been based on these early innovations of Gish.

In Gish's first films, she often played a young woman in danger, who is dramatically saved at the last minute. Lovely, yet frail-looking, she, under Griffith's influence, became the embodiment of innocent, female virtue. Gish's own forcefulness, however, lent an underlying strength to her idealized screen persona.

Gish emerged as a bona fide film star with the release of *The Birth of a Nation* (1915), which became the most successful silent film ever made. Controversial for its racist presentation of African Americans, *Nation* was the first narrative film epic and introduced many of the shots and techniques that now serve as the basic syntax of moviemaking. In it, Gish starred as Elsie Stoneman, a young

Lillian Gish in *Broken Blossoms* (1919)
(Museum of Modern Art Film Stills Archive)

woman suffering various travails during the chaos of the Civil War and Reconstruction. Gish also appeared in Griffith's masterpiece *Intolerance* (1916), the director's response to efforts to ban his earlier film. Its four sections, set in different time periods, were linked by the repeated image of Gish rocking a cradle.

Gish delivered perhaps her most powerful performance in *Broken Blossoms* (1919), although she begged Griffith to cast someone else in the lead. Then in her late 20s, she felt far too old to be convincing as a young girl terrorized by her violent father. Despite her hesitance, she proved convincing, especially in her climactic death scene. The intensity of her fear as her father beats her to death left audiences in a stunned silence at the picture's end. Gish also won great acclaim for Griffith's *Way Down East* (1920) and *Orphans of the Storm* (1922), the latter of which also starred her sister, Dorothy.

Gish's tenure as Griffith's muse came to end when he realized her name could sell more tickets than his. Calling her into his office, he told her he could no longer pay her what she was worth, insisting that for her own interest she needed to work elsewhere to fully capitalize on her success. Gish hesitantly went off on her own. She invested money in Inspiration Films, where she made *The White Sister* (1923) and *Romola* (1924). Gish then signed a lucrative five-movie deal with Metro-Goldwyn-Mayer (MGM) that gave her control over the stories and directors chosen for her. Her MGM films included *La Bohème* (1926), *The Scarlet Letter* (1926), and *The Wind* (1928).

In the 1930s, Gish made the transition into talking pictures with *One Romantic Night* (1930) and *His Double Life* (1933). Yet she found her popularity fading due to changes in public tastes. Audiences now wanted to see flappers like CLARA BOW and exotic beauties like GRETA GARBO—not the Victorian angels with whom Gish had become so closely associated. Gish responded by returning to the stage, where she quickly revived her career. She was well-received in a number of classic dramas, including *Uncle Vanya* and *Hamlet,* in which she played Ophelia opposite John Gielgud. She also became a fixture in New York intellectual circles owing to her friendship with critic George Jean Nathan, who repeatedly proposed marriage to her. She always refused, later explaining, "What kind of marriage would it have been to a wife who worked twelve hours a day, seven days a week."

By the mid-1940s, Gish was also working periodically in films, often in supporting roles. As a supporting actress, she was nominated for an Academy Award for her work in *Duel in the Sun* (1947). Soon she was appearing regularly on television as well, in made-for-television movies and as a guest star on series.

An advocate for film preservation, Gish wrote two books about her life in movies—*The Movies, Mr. Griffith, and Me* (1969) and *Dorothy and Lillian Gish* (1973). In 1969, she began discussing her career in a lecture series, *Lillian Gish and the Movies,* which eventually toured the United States, Canada, western Europe, and Russia. Her work was also celebrated with a special Oscar in 1971, a Kennedy Center Honor in 1982, and an American Film Institute Lifetime Achievement Award in 1984.

Gish's final film was *The Whales of August* (1987), which paired her with another screen legend, BETTE DAVIS. During the filming, the cast and crew were awed by Gish's emotive powers in a particular scene. The acerbic Davis, exasperated with the to-do, offered her own more pointed and perhaps more fitting praise for Gish's performance. "Of course, it's a great close-up. She invented the goddam shot."

On February 27, 1993, Lillian Gish died in her sleep, just months away from her 100th birthday. In her will, she established the "Dorothy and Lillian Gish Award," which each year pays the annual proceeds from her multimillion-dollar estate to a person distinguished in the arts.

Further Reading

Affron, Charles. *Lillian Gish: Her Legend, Her Life.* New York: Scribner, 2001.

Gish, Lillian. *Dorothy and Lillian Gish.* New York: Scribners, 1973.

Gish, Lillian, with Ann Pinchot. *The Movies, Mr. Griffith, and Me.* 1969. Reprint, San Francisco: Mercury House, 1988.

Recommended Recorded and Videotaped Performances

The Birth of a Nation (1915). Image Entertainment, DVD, 1998.

Broken Blossoms (1919). Image Entertainment, DVD, 1999.

Duel in the Sun (1946). Anchor Bay Entertainment, DVD/VHS, 2000/1998.

Orphans of the Storm (1921). Image Entertainment, DVD, 1998.

❖ **GOLDBERG, WHOOPI (Caryn Johnson)**
(ca. 1955–) *Actress, Comic, Talk Show Host*

With her offbeat humor and looks, Whoopi Goldberg is perhaps the film industry's most unlikely star. A native New Yorker, she was born Caryn Johnson on November 13, probably in 1955. Though raised in poverty in a housing project, she was ambitious and self-confident, sure that one day she would achieve her dream of becoming an actress. Her early ambitions were fueled by watching movies on television, often three or four a day. At eight, Caryn began her performing career with the Helena Rubinstein Children's Theater.

Caryn found school far less satisfying. Undiagnosed dyslexia made her such a poor student that she was labeled retarded. Discouraged, she dropped out and drifted into drugs, eventually becoming a heroin addict. By her late teens, she had kicked heroin with the help of drug counselor, whom she married. During their brief union, she had one child, Alexandrea.

Still determined to act professionally, Johnson moved to San Diego, California, in 1974. She joined Spontaneous Combustion, an improvisation troupe, and was a founding member of the San Diego Repertory Theater. To make a living, she worked various jobs, including hairdressing and making up corpses in a funeral parlor. Raising her daughter alone, she was forced to go on welfare for several years, an experience she remembers as humiliating. Yet, her confidence in her talents never waned. She later recalled, "Even when I wasn't making any money, I always knew I was good."

Johnson adopted the stage name Whoopi Cushion (pronounced kush-ON), but when her mother complained that it was undignified, she began using the surname Goldberg, a name from her family tree. She first used this billing in a two-character show she performed with the comedian Don Victor. Goldberg took the show to San Francisco, where she soon began working with Blake Street Hawkeyes theater troupe. There, she developed *The Spook Show,* a one-woman production in which she played a variety of characters, including a junkie and a nine-year-old African-American girl who dreams of becoming white.

While performing *The Spook Show* at a workshop in New York City, Goldberg drew the attention of director Mike Nichols. Nichols offered to produce her show and bring it to Broadway. Retitled *Whoopi Goldberg,* the show opened to admiring reviews on October 24, 1984. A videotaped performance was aired on HBO the following year.

One of Goldberg's new fans was Steven Spielberg, who hired her to star in his film *The Color Purple* (1985). Goldberg's quiet, subtle performance won her a Golden Globe Award and an Oscar nomination. The movie, and by extension Goldberg, were criticized by many African Americans, who took exception with the movie's unflattering depiction of its black male characters.

In 1986, Goldberg used her newfound fame to relieve the plight of the homeless. With Billy Crystal and Robin Williams, she began hosting an annual comedy benefit concert, Comic Relief. Goldberg has campaigned for many other social causes, including abortion rights and services for people with AIDS.

Although pronounced a new star after *The Color Purple,* Goldberg had trouble finding good parts. She made a string of movies—including *Jumpin' Jack Flash* (1986), *Burglar* (1987), and *Fatal Beauty* (1987)—in which her performance far outshone the mediocre material she was given. After appearing in several commercial failures, she was written off by many Hollywood insiders.

Goldberg proved them wrong with *Ghost* (1990), in which she played a supporting comic role as a phony psychic. The film became a surprise hit and won Goldberg a best supporting actress Oscar. She became the first African-American actress since HATTIE MCDANIEL to receive an Academy Award.

Her stardom confirmed, Goldberg threw herself into a wide variety of projects. On television, she appeared in *Bagdad Cafe* (1990), a short-lived situation comedy, and became a regular cast member of *Star Trek: The Next Generation.* In 1992, she became the host of *The Whoopi Goldberg Show,* a half-hour late-night talk show that featured one-on-one conversations between Goldberg and her guest. The show was soon canceled due to poor ratings.

In film, Goldberg scored a critical success with *The Long Walk Home* (1990), a drama set during the Montgomery, Alabama, bus boycott of the 1950s. Two years later, she again proved her ability to attract a wide audience with *Sister Act* (1992), in which she played a nightclub singer masquerading as a nun. Goldberg earned $8 million for its poorly received sequel, *Sister Act II* (1993).

While filming *Made in America* (1993), Goldberg began a widely publicized romance with her white costar, Ted Danson. To satirize the hate mail the couple was receiving, Goldberg wrote a vulgar comedy routine that Danson delivered in blackface at a Friars Club "roast," a comic tribute to one of this entertainment organization's members. Few found the performance amusing. Goldberg and Danson were slammed by offended critics.

The incident did little to dull Goldberg's popularity, however. In the late 1990s, she was chosen to host the Academy Awards several times, becoming the first African American to do so. She continued to be a sought-after film actress, appearing in *Corrina, Corrina* (1994), *Boys on the Side* (1995), and *Ghosts of Mississippi* (1995). On the set of *Corrina, Corrina,* she met union organizer Lyle Trachtenberg, to whom she was briefly married. In 1998, Goldberg returned to theater, taking over the role of Pseudolus in the Broadway revival of *A Funny Thing Happened on the Way to the Forum.* She also became a regular on the television game show *The Hollywood Squares.*

Once dismissed as too unconventional for stardom, Goldberg has become one of the hardest-working women in the American entertainment industry. As she told an interviewer in 2000, "You know, I was supposed to be a flash in the pan. I'm the longest flash Hollywood's ever seen."

Further Reading

Goldberg, Whoopi. *Book.* New York: Rob Weisbach Books, 1997.

Parrish, James Robert. *Whoopi Goldberg: Her Journey from Poverty to Megastardom.* New York: Birch Lane Books, 1997.

Recommended Recorded and Videotaped Performances

The Color Purple (1985). Warner Home Video, DVD/VHS, 1997/1999.
Ghost (1990). Paramount, VHS, 2001.
Sister Act (1992). Touchstone Video, VHS, 1996.

❖ **GRABLE, BETTY (Ruth Elizabeth Grable)**
(1916–1973) *Actress, Dancer, Singer*

"As American as apple pie and Betty Grable," a popular slogan of the 1940s, illustrates Grable's enormous popularity with a public troubled by the trials and uncertainties of the war years. Born Ruth Elizabeth Grable on December 18, 1916, she was raised in St. Louis, Missouri, one of two daughters of a successful stockbroker and his theatrically ambitious wife. Frustrated by her own failures to launch a singing career, Grable's mother, Lillian, forced on Betty a grueling schedule of acting, dancing, singing, and music instruction. "I hated every lesson," Grable later recalled.

To advance Betty's career, Lillian moved her daughter to Los Angeles. Due to her mother's persistence, by 1930 Betty had a contract with Twentieth Century-Fox, but the studio dismissed her when it discovered she was only 13. She made several shorts directed by comedian Fatty Arbuckle before delivering a breakdown performance in a comic dance number in the Fred Astaire–GINGER ROGERS vehicle *The Gay Divorcee* (1934).

Grable's career was also given a boost by her marriage to former child star Jackie Coogan in 1937. Together they appeared in two successful college comedies. Their personal relationship, however, faltered as Coogan suffered several financial setbacks. The couple divorced in 1939.

Still a star on the rise, Grable signed a new contract with Twentieth Century-Fox, beginning a 10-year association with the studio. Grable almost immediately became the studio's reigning star when she was called on to replace an ailing Alice Faye in *Down Argentine Way* (1940). The movie was a substantial hit, and soon Grable was appearing a series of lighthearted musicals filmed using the new technology of Technicolor. Although never a favorite with critics, Grable attracted legions of fans. Her wholesomely sexy image attracted men, whereas her warmth and personal charm made her equally appealing to women.

Twentieth Century-Fox, however, was most interested in promoting not Grable's personality, but her most outstanding physical asset—her shapely legs. In addition to showcasing them in her dance numbers, the studio insured Grable's legs for $1 million dollars as a publicity stunt. Her male fans, especially those sent overseas with the outbreak of World War II, responded with demands for pinups of Grable. The result was perhaps the most famous publicity still in the history of American film. Photographed from the back wearing a white swimsuit and high heels, Grable was shown with her head turned, looking coyly back at the viewer. Perfectly capturing Grable's innocence flavored with just a hint of naughtiness, the pinup became a phenomenon. More than 3 million were sent to soldiers, some of whom made their own tributes to Grable by painting the image on their PT boats and B-22 bombers.

With the war years, Grable became not only an American icon but also the highest-paid woman in the United States. Yet, despite the success she brought Twentieth Century-Fox, she was constantly at war with studio head Darryl F. Zanuck. He wanted to put her in dramas, but Grable rightly sensed that the public most wanted to see her in the lighter fare that had made her a star. In 1953 she severed ties with Zanuck after filming *How to Marry a Millionaire,* which also featured the studio's new star MARILYN MONROE.

In the years that followed, Grable found herself in growing financial difficulties. In 1943 she had married bandleader Harry James, who gambled away their earnings and amassed sizable debts. To earn a living for them and their two children, Grable often had to take substandard work in Las Vegas shows and television specials and commercials. She divorced James in 1965, after which Grable found renewed popularity performing in touring companies of Broadway musicals, such as *Hello Dolly!* On July 2, 1973, this new career was stopped short by her death at 56 from lung cancer.

Further Reading

Billman, Larry. *Betty Grable: A Bio-Bibliography.* Westport, Conn.: Greenwood Press, 1993.

Pastos, Spero. *Pin-Up: The Tragedy of Betty Grable.* New York: Putnam, 1986.

Warren, Doug. *Betty Grable: The Reluctant Movie Queen.* New York: St. Martin's Press, 1981.

Recommended Recorded and Videotaped Performances

Down Argentine Way (1940). Twentieth Century-Fox, VHS, 1989.

The Gay Divorcee (1934). Turner Home Video, VHS, 1999.

How to Marry a Millionaire (1953). Twentieth Century-Fox, VHS, 1992.

❖ GRAHAM, MARTHA
(1894–1991) *Dancer, Choreographer*

One of the most influential artists of the 20th century, Martha Graham revolutionized modern dance during her 75-year career. Through her 200 dance works, her much-studied technique, and unique and powerful passion as a dancer, she had an enduring effect not only on dance but on all the American fine arts.

The oldest of three sisters, Graham was born on May 11, 1894, in Allegheny, Pennsylvania. Even as a small child, she found stifling the puritanical society of her hometown. Martha's youth was brightened, however, by her physician father, whom she loved and revered. She credited him with the observation that would guide her life—"Movement never lies." Although the context in which he said this is unclear, his words inspired her always to place emotional honesty at the core of her art.

In 1909, Graham's life changed dramatically following her family's move to Santa Barbara, California. She bloomed in this setting, finding herself far more free to explore her creativity than she had been in New England. Although showing a decidedly artistic bent Graham received no formal dance training. Still, she was determined to pursue a dance career after her father took her to a concert of the Denishawn dancers when she was 17. Headed by RUTH ST. DENIS and Ted Shawn, Denishawn was the premier modern dance troupe of the day.

Over her family's objections, Graham went to Los Angeles to study at the Denishawn school in the summer of 1916. To her disappointment, St. Denis discounted her new pupil, because she considered the 21-year-old Graham far too old to become a serious student. St. Denis did, however, readily recruit Graham to fashion costumes for the company, which ignited her lifelong fascination with costume design.

As a dancer, Graham received much more encouragement from Shawn. He took her under his wing, helping to shape her into one of Denishawn's leading dancers. In 1920 he gave her the lead female role in his ballet *Xochitl.* Although she recognized a debt to Shawn, it was not enough to save him from becoming the target of her already notorious anger. One story holds that while dancing with Graham, Shawn once accidentally hit her head on the floor. Her immediate response was to bite him on the arm as hard as possible.

Graham toured with Denishawn for four years, then spent two more as a soloist in a New York dance troupe, the Greenwich Village Follies. In 1926, though, she decided she had to strike out on her own. To get the challenges and exposure she craved as a dancer, she realized, she would have to become her own choreographer. The move showed daring, since she had no financial resources to fall back on. In addition to teaching dance, Graham had to model furs and perform in Radio City Music Hall extravaganzas to earn enough money to survive while she pursued her new goal. In April 1926, she borrowed $1,000 to fund her debut concert, which featured herself and three students as the performers.

Graham's early works were experimental and bold. Although they seemed obscure and inaccessible to many, she soon attracted a crowd of devoted fans. Somber and stark, her dances dealt with emotions, but only in their most abstracted form. In *Lamentation* (1930), for example, she performed a solo while encased in a tube of stretch jersey. She pushed her limbs against the confining fabric to express the agony of grief.

Perhaps her greatest work of this period was *Primitive Mysteries,* which was staged in New York by the Dance Repertory Theater in 1931. Inspired by a trip to the Southwest, the dance drew from the Indian and Spanish religious rituals of the region. It was also deeply influenced by the composer, Louis Horst, who was also Graham's lover. Horst encouraged Graham to commission music with strong, simple instrumentation that would serve to focus attention on the dance itself.

In her own choreography, Graham consciously worked to eliminate the fussiness she saw in both ballet and the Denishawn tradition. Her movements were not pretty or delicate. They were powerful and intense, drawing from the animal-like ferocity Graham lent to her own performances. The technique she developed was also well suited to her body type. Though only a petite 5'2", Graham had an extraordinarily strong torso and back. These attributes were crucial to her theory of "contraction and release," which called for a dancer's body first to cave in at the center, then to open outward. Graham also favored angular positions for the arms and legs. She became so associated with angularity that one critic quipped that if she ever became pregnant, she would give birth to a cube.

In 1936, Graham's artistic direction changed suddenly when she met a young dancer named Erick Hawkins. She brought Hawkins into her company, which previously had been made up exclusively of women. His addition gave her new avenues for choreography as she began creating dances with herself and Hawkins as the principals. More important, her intense love for Hawkins, whom she would marry in 1948, moved her away from an abstraction of feelings to a more direct expression of human emotions.

Hawkins first appeared with Graham in *American Document* (1938), which was her first major success. The inventive work incorporated elements of the minstrel show to comment on racial injustice. It also signaled her growing interest in American themes, which culminated in *Appalachian Spring* (1944). Graham's most famous work, this classic is arguably the best-loved dance piece of the twentieth century. Set to a score by Aaron Copland, it depicts the marriage of a frontier bride and groom, roles originated by Graham and Hawkins. The stark set design was also one of the many fruitful collaborations between Graham and sculptor Isamu Noguchi. Noguchi's minimalist sets for Graham would have an extraordinary impact internationally on both dance and theater.

In the late 1940s, Graham headed into a new and extraordinary phase of her career. Drawing on her fascination with Jungian psychology and Greek myths, she began to look to Greek tragedies for inspiration. Monumental and highly emotional, many of her works during this period presented these stories from a woman's point of view. Graham's *Night Journey* (1947), for instance, told the tale of Oedipus from the perspective of his mother and wife, the queen Jocasta. By some devotees, Graham's "Greek period" appeared to reflect on the stage her own inner turmoil over her volatile relationship with her husband. In one example, the depiction of Medea's jealously in *Cave of the Heart* (1946) was seen to mirror Graham's fear of losing Hawkins to a younger woman.

Graham and Hawkins finally divorced in 1954. The loss was devastating to Graham both personally and professionally, since much of her most respected work had been inspired by her feelings for Hawkins. Graham's despair was only worsened by her own physical deterioration. Increasingly, her aging body was not up to the task of dancing her own works. Still, Graham refused to stop performing and stubbornly made no attempt to train younger dancers to take over her lead roles. She continued to dance long past her prime, retiring finally in 1969 when it became obvious, even to her, that she could no longer go on. Graham later recalled that after her decision to give up performing, she was so distraught she "wished to die."

After several dark years, Graham began to apply her indomitable will to a new project—preserving her legacy as a choreographer. In the mid-1970s, she began revisiting her earlier works, adapting and reinterpreting them for other dancers. She also consciously started to project to the public a persona as a living legend. Often photographed in glamour shots, Graham took to making provocatively cryptic pronouncements to the press. This era in her career was dubbed by some as her "Halston period," after one of her many celebrity friends, the fashion designer Halston, who once created gold lamé costumes for her company.

While cementing her place in dance history, Graham also was developing new dance works. For some of the most noteworthy, she abandoned her practice of commissioning scores and instead built choreography around existing musical works. For instance, *The Rite of Spring* (1984) offered Graham's own interpretation of Igor Stravinsky's classic, while her last work, *Maple Leaf Rag* (1990), drew on her love of Scott Joplin's ragtime compositions.

On April 1, 1991, Graham's long career came to an end with her death at age 96. Internationally hailed as a genius, she left virtually no aspect of dance untouched by her influence. As a choreographer, she gave the world hundreds of dance works, many of which are still staged by dance companies around the globe. As a teacher, she defined a technique that has become part of nearly every professional dancer's education. And as a performer, she set a standard of discipline, commitment, and passion that continues to inspire artists in all fields.

Further Reading

Graham, Martha. *Blood Memory.* New York: Doubleday, 1991.

De Mille, Agnes. *Martha: The Life and Works of Martha Graham.* New York: Random House, 1991.

Stodelle, Ernestine. *Deep Song: The Dance Story of Martha Graham.* New York: Schirmer Books, 1984.

Tracy, Robert. *Goddess: Martha Graham's Dancers Remember.* New York: Limelight Editions, 1997.

Recommended Recorded and Videotaped Performances

Martha Graham: The Dancer Revealed. Kultur Video, VHS, 1994.

3 by Martha Graham. Pyramid Home Video, VHS, 1991.

H

❖ HARLOW, JEAN (Harlean Harlow Carpenter)
(1911–1937)   *Actress*

Forever the embodiment of the blond bombshell, Jean Harlow became one of the greatest stars of the 1930s, although her career lasted less than a decade. On March 3, 1911, she was born Harlean Harlow Carpenter in Kansas City. After her parents divorced in 1922, her domineering mother, Jean, moved with Harlean to Los Angeles, where Jean pursued an acting career with little success. She and her daughter soon returned to Kansas City, later moving to Chicago after Jean remarried.

At a school dance, Harlean met Charles McGrew II, a wealthy student with whom she eloped at age 16. The couple set up home in Beverly Hills. Harleen quickly tired of life as a housewife. Divorcing McGrew in 1929, she began finding jobs as an extra in films such as Charlie Chaplin's *City Lights* (1931). Working her way into bit parts, she appeared in *Double Whoopee* (1929), a comedy short with Laurel and Hardy, and *Saturday Night Kid* (1929), a silent feature starring sex symbol CLARA BOW.

Now billed as Jean Harlow, she had her big break in 1930, when she was cast in Howard

Hughes's *Hell's Angels.* An enormously expensive film about World War I, it boasted fabulous aerial footage but featured woefully weak characters and plot. Critics were particularly critical of Harlow's mannered performance. Yet, despite her amateurish acting, the public was intrigued by the light-haired, green-eyed beauty. Encouraged by the touting of Hollywood's new "platinum blond" by Hughes's publicity machine, women began trying to capture the Harlow look.

Almost overnight, Harlow became a star in great demand. Hughes loaned out his find to a series of studios, which inevitably cast her as a tough, worldly woman with no hesitation to use her sexual appeal to get what she wants. After playing variations on this type in films such as *Public Enemy* (1931) and *Iron Man* (1931), she welcomed the chance to play a wealthy heiress in a Frank Capra comedy. But the film did little to change her image after it was retitled *Platinum Blonde* (1931) to capitalize on Harlow's newfound fame.

Feeling frustrated with being pigeonholed, Harlow went head-to-head with Hughes, who in retaliation sold her contract to Metro-Goldwyn-Mayer (MGM). The move to the new studio proved a great career boost. MGM recognized her comic gifts and placed her in several vehicles that showed

Jean Harlow with Louise Closser Hale and Donald Dillaway in *Platinum Blonde* (1931)
(Museum of Modern Art Film Stills Archive)

them to their best advantage. In 1932 she cemented her stardom with *Red-Headed Woman,* a comedy written by Anita Loos in which she played a gold-digging secretary out to seduce her boss. Almost unique in films of the day, in the end Harlow's bad girl got her man without having to suffer for her conniving. Harlow followed its success with *Red Dust* (1932) and *Hold Your Man* (1933), both of which paired her effectively with Clark Gable. But she found perhaps her best role in *Bombshell* (1933), a savage Hollywood satire in

which Harlow perfectly lampooned her own sex-pot image.

While she was enjoying spectacular professional success, Harlow experienced a series of personal disasters. The most public was her brief marriage in 1932 to MGM executive Paul Bern, who was twice her age. Known for acting as a kindly adviser to stars, Bern committed suicide only two months after their wedding. His suicide note, which was widely reproduced in the press, included an apology to Harlow and hinted that impotence had led him to take his own life. Hollywood gossips sensationalized Bern's death, but the resulting publicity helped rather than hurt Harlow by eliciting public sympathy for the young bride. When she insisted on returning to work on *Red Dust* after the suicide, Gable was reported to have said, "That little lady has more guts than any man in Hollywood!"

Harlow went the altar a third time the following year, wedding *Bombshell*'s cinematographer Harold Rosson, again a man many years her senior. The marriage lasted only 14 months. Harlow had a final, impassioned romance with actor William Powell, with whom she costarred in *Reckless* (1935), but the couple never married.

While filming *Saratoga* (1937) opposite Gable, Harlow became ill with blood poisoning. Only 10 days later, on June 7, 1937, she was dead at the age of 26. The news of her sudden, expected death stunned Hollywood and shocked her devoted fans. Though Harlow left behind only a handful of films, she has remained a powerful influence in cinema history for her creation of screen sirens whose allure lay as much in their wit as their sex appeal.

Further Reading

Golden, Eve. *Platinum Girl: The Life and Legends of Jean Harlow.* New York: Abbeville Press, 1991.
Stenn, David. *Bombshell: The Life and Death of Jean Harlow.* New York: Doubleday 1993.

Recommended Recorded and Videotaped Performances

Bombshell (1933). Warner Home Video, VHS, 1992.
Intimate Portrait: Jean Harlow (1999). Unapix, VHS, 2000.
Red-Headed Woman (1932). Warner Home Video, VHS, 1992.

❖ HAYES, HELEN (Helen Hayes Brown)
(1900–1993) *Actress*

Hailed as the "First Lady of the American Theater," Helen Hayes's distinguished acting career stretched over an amazing 84 years. Born Helen Hayes Brown in Washington, D.C., on October 10, 1900, her early interest in playacting and theatergoing delighted her mother, Essie. Herself a minor stage comedian, Essie soon placed her own theatrical ambitions on her daughter, who first appeared onstage at age five. At nine, Helen made her professional debut playing a prince in *The Royal Family* (1909). The part brought her to the attention of producer Lew Fields, who cast her in several New York shows. Although film was then viewed with scorn by theater people, Helen also appeared in a few movie shorts, including *Jean and the Calico Dog* (1910).

Essie and Helen returned to Washington in 1911, but Helen continued to perform in plays both there and in New York City. Now billed as Helen Hayes, she always earned enthusiastic praise from reviewers. She later claimed her reputation as an excellent child actress was due to her being a quick study. But in fact she worked hard to develop her own acting technique by studying her adult costars and receiving her mother's relentless coaching.

After graduating from high school, Hayes had her first major success with the touring production of *Pollyanna* (1918). The saccharine melodrama featured her as the ever cheery, ever optimistic title character. Standing only five feet tall and weighing only 100 pounds, Hayes was soon known for playing young, innocent waifs. In addition to helping to typecast her in these limited roles, *Pollyanna* also marked the beginning of her association with producer George C. Tyler. Under contract to Tyler, Hayes appeared in one or two Broadway shows a year, usually light fare such as Booth Tarkington's *Penrod* (1918) and James Barrie's *Dear Brutus* (1918).

Hayes was given her first star billing with *Bab* (1920). Otherwise, the show was a withering disappointment for the young actress. Critics found her performance mannered and began to speculate that Hayes had little real acting talent.

Shaken by the reviews, Hayes began to study acting and voice, as well as taking lessons in dance, fencing, and boxing. She hoped to learn to free her voice and movements so she would seem more natural on stage. In 1924 she also took the risky step of severing ties with Tyler by defying his demands that she not join the Actors' Equity union.

Liberated from Tyler's tight control over her professional and personal life, Hayes was able to pursue more substantial roles. She found parts in productions of *She Stoops to Conquer* (1924) and *Caesar and Cleopatra* (1925) before scoring hits with *What Every Woman Knows* (1926) and *Coquette* (1927). Playing a flapper in *Coquette,* Hayes emerged from its three-year run as one of America's leading young actresses. While reprising some of her best-known roles on radio, a sponsor even touted her as the "First Lady of the American Theater." The tag stuck, even though Hayes at the time felt it was mischaracterization that ignored the excellent work done by other star Broadway actresses.

In 1928, while performing in *Coquette,* Hayes married playwright Charles MacArthur, best known for cowriting the play *The Front Page* (1928). To their friends, the match appeared an odd one with little chance for lasting success. MacArthur was a witty, urbane womanizer, while Hayes was far less worldly and far more disciplined. Although MacArthur's excessive drinking would cause problems in their marriage, they both found in each other the support they needed to do their best creative work. They and their two children, Mary and James, eventually settled in a large Victorian house in Nyack, New York, where they entertained Alfred Lunt, Lynn Fontanne, Dorothy Parker, Robert Benchley, and other great wits and theatrical luminaries.

After their marriage, MacArthur and Hayes were courted by Hollywood. As he became one of the movie industry's highest-paid screenwriters, she began to star in feature films. In 1931, she won an Academy Award for best actress for her performance in *The Sin of Madelon Claudet,* the script of which was heavily doctored by her husband. She also received acclaim in *Arrowsmith* (1931) and *A Farewell to Arms* (1932). Still, the down-to-earth Hayes never quite fit the mold of the glamorous star. MacArthur, too, grew disillusioned with Hollywood, and the couple agreed to move back to New York and focus on stage work.

In 1933, Hayes made a splash in *Mary of Scotland.* Playing another British monarch, this time Queen Victoria, she reached the pinnacle of her career in *Victoria Regina* (1935). The demanding play required her to portray the queen from her teens to her old age. Owing largely to Hayes's spectacular performance, the drama ran on Broadway for two years and toured for still another two. All told, she played Victoria about 1,000 times before a total audience of approximately 2 million.

In the 1940s, Hayes appeared in a variety of serious dramas such as *Harriet* (1943), a biographical play about Harriet Beecher Stowe, and *The Glass Menagerie* (1948), Tennessee Williams's classic work about a matriarch desperately clinging to her illusions. In 1947, however, she won the first Tony Award for best actress for *Happy Birthday,* a light comedy written by her friend Anita Loos.

By this time, Hayes's teenage daughter, Mary, was a beautiful aspiring actress, who frequently appeared in her mother's plays. While preparing for a new part in 1949, Mary contracted polio and died. The loss devastated Hayes and MacArthur. Urged on by her husband, Hayes tried to conquer her sorrow by doing charity work for polio research and returning to the stage, most notably in *The Wisteria Trees* (1950), a version of Anton Chekhov's *The Cherry Orchard* set in the American South. MacArthur had more difficulty recovering after Mary's death. Always prone to depression, he was unable to work, and his drinking problem grew worse. In 1956, MacArthur died of alcohol-related illnesses. Although Hayes lived for almost 40 more years, she was never romantically linked with another man after MacArthur's death.

Though she acted occasionally on television and radio, Hayes continued to concentrate on theater work. In 1955, she appeared in *A Touch of the Poet* in a New York house renamed the Helen Hayes Theater in her honor, and in 1958, she earned her second Tony Award for *Time Remembered.* With the support of the State Department, in the early 1960s she went on a world tour, performing in *The Glass Menagerie* and *By the Skin of Our Teeth,* among other American classics.

To the surprise of many, Hayes gave up high-profile productions to join the APA-Phoenix Repertory Company in 1966. Playing both small roles and large, she performed with the troupe until financial difficulties forced it to disband two years later.

Approaching her 70s, Hayes announced in 1969 that she was leaving the theater. Yet, she was quickly lured back by revivals of *The Front Page* (1969) and *Harvey* (1970). By 1971, however, she had developed an allergic reaction to theater dust that made stage work impossible. She made her last stage appearance that year in *Long Day's Journey Into Night* in her hometown of Washington.

Hayes refocused on work in film and television. In 1970, she won a second Oscar for best supporting actress for playing a feisty stowaway in the disaster movie *Airport.* On television, she made numerous guest appearances, most notably a spot on *Hawaii 5-0,* a crime drama costarring her son, James MacArthur. She also starred briefly with Mildred Natwick in her own series, *The Snoop Sisters* (1973–74).

In 1985 Hayes retired from show business. She often traveled to receive awards and attend functions in her honor, but otherwise spent her last days at her Nyack estate. On May 17, 1993, she died there of a heart attack at the age of 92.

Ever modest, Helen Hayes once ascribed her success to "the quality of being average," a self-deprecating way of describing her gift for bonding with audiences. Whether portraying sweet ingenues, imperious queens, or impish little old ladies, she played her characters with a dignity and warmth that endeared her to the public over nine decades.

Further Reading

Barrow, Kenneth. *Helen Hayes: First Lady of the American Theater.* Garden City, N.Y.: Doubleday, 1985.

Hayes, Helen, with Katherine Hatch. *My Life in Three Acts.* San Diego: Harcourt, Brace & Jovanovich, 1990.

Murphy, Donn B., and Stephen Moore. *Helen Hayes: A Bio-Bibliography.* Westport, Conn.: Greenwood Press, 1993.

Recommended Recorded and Videotaped Performances

Arrowsmith (1931). MGM/UA, VHS, 2000.

A Farewell to Arms (1957). Image Entertainment, DVD, 1999.

The Sin of Madelon Claudet (1931). MGM/UA, VHS, 1991.

❖ HAYWORTH, RITA (Margarita Carmen Cansino, Rita Cansino) (1918–1987) *Actress, Dancer*

Dubbed the "American Sex Goddess" by *Time* magazine, Rita Hayworth was one of the 1940s' most popular film stars. Born Margarita Carmen Cansino on October 17, 1918, she was the daughter of a Spanish dancer in vaudeville and a Ziegfeld chorus girl. Hoping to break into movies, her father, Eduardo, moved the family from Brooklyn to Los Angeles when Margarita was nine. He found work teaching dance and staging film dance sequences until his adolescent daughter emerged as a great beauty. At 12, she left school to become Eduardo's professional dance partner. Billed as the "Dancing Cansinos," they performed as many as 20 shows a week.

Margarita soon drew the attention of Hollywood talent scouts. In 1934, a screen test won her a six-month contract with the Fox studio, which shortened her first name to Rita. She appeared as a dancer in one scene in *Dante's Inferno* (1935). Her other work for Fox was left on the cutting room floor.

Released from her contract, Rita Cansino put her career in the hands of Edward Judson, a shady businessman to whom she was married from 1937 to 1942. Judson found her freelance acting jobs in B movies until Columbia signed the starlet to a seven-year contract. The studio re-created Cansino, positioning her as a glamour girl instead of as an "ethnic" actress as Fox had. To complete this transformation, they raised her hairline through electrolysis and christened her Rita Hayworth. (Her new surname was a variant spelling of her mother's maiden name.) Hayworth, a shy woman who

Rita Hayworth in *Gilda* (1946)
(Museum of Modern Art Film Stills Archive)

considered herself a dancer with a flair for comedy, was not wholly at ease with her new, sexier image.

At Columbia, Hayworth continued to be cast in forgettable low-budget films before appearing as the second female lead in Howard Hawks's *Only Angels Have Wings* (1939). The role led to substantial parts in *Blood and Sand* and *The Strawberry Blonde* (both 1941). But she finally achieved stardom when cast as Fred Astaire's dance partner in the musical *You'll Never Get Rich* (1941). With its success, Hayworth performed in series of wartime musicals, playing a young, all-American beauty. The most notable included *You Were Never Lovelier* (1942), again costarring Fred Astaire, and *Cover Girl* (1944) with Gene Kelly.

During World War II, Hayworth was also famous for a photograph that appeared in the August 11, 1941, issue of *Life* magazine. Showing her facing the camera while kneeling in lingerie, the image became one of the most popular pin-ups of soldiers overseas. In a dubious tribute to Hayworth, the photograph was taped to a test atomic bomb dropped on the Bikini Atoll in 1946.

After the war, Hayworth found several of her best roles in films noir. In *Gilda* (1946), she was both smoldering and vulnerable in the title role. In perhaps her most indelible screen moment, she performed in the film a memorable striptease, pulling off long black gloves while singing "Put the Blame on Mame." (As in most of her films, her singing voice was dubbed.) The sexy image of Gilda haunted Hayworth's personal life. She was famously quoted as saying, "Every man I've known has fallen in love with Gilda and wakened with me."

Hayworth cut her trademark red hair and dyed it blond to play another femme fatale in *The Lady from Shanghai* (1948). The film's director was the acclaimed Orson Welles, who became Hayworth's second husband in 1943 and the father of her daughter Barbara. Called "the beauty and the brain" by the press, they were one of Hollywood's most sensational couples until she divorced Welles soon after their one film together was completed. Of the marriage's failure, she once said, "I just can't take his genius anymore."

The year before her divorce, Hayworth took a vacation to Europe, where she met Prince Aly Khan. Although both were married at the time, they began a public romance. The tabloid coverage on the couple made Hayworth an international celebrity. Their marriage in May 1949 and the birth of their daughter, Yasmin, seven months later were also widely reported. Like all of Hayworth's marriages, this union did not last long, probably because of Aly's philandering. They were divorced in 1953.

In 1951, Hayworth returned to Hollywood after a three-year absence. She had successes with films such as *Affair in Trinidad* (1952), *Pal Joey* (1957), and *Separate Tables* (1958), but she was unable to revive the popularity she had achieved during the 1940s. Even worse for Hayworth, she weathered two disastrous, violent marriages—the first to singer Dick Haymes (1953–55), the second to *Separate Tables* producer James Hill (1958–1961).

In 1962, Hayworth tried to boost her failing career by appearing in *Step on a Crack* on Broadway. However, the show was canceled because of the star's inability to memorize her lines and her increasingly violent mood swings and emotional outbursts. Rumors spread that Hayworth had become an out-of-control alcoholic. Still, she continued to find some film work, although primarily in Europe. Hayworth made her last film, a western titled *The Wrath of God,* in 1972.

With her mental condition deteriorating steadily, the underlying cause of Hayworth's instability was finally discovered when she was diagnosed with Alzheimer's disease in the early 1980s. In her final years, she was cared for by her daughter Yasmin, who became a leading advocate for Alzheimer's research. Hayworth died at her home in New York City on May 14, 1987.

Further Reading

Leaming, Barbara. *If This Was Happiness: A Biography of Rita Hayworth.* New York: Viking, 1989.

Ringgold, Gene. *The Films of Rita Hayworth.* Seacaucus, NJ: Citadel Press, 1991.

Recommended Recorded and Videotaped Performances

Gilda (1946). Columbia/Tristar, DVD, 2000.

The Lady From Shanghai (1948). Columbia/Tristar, DVD/VHS, 2000/1992.

Separate Tables (1958). MGM/UA, VHS, 1999.

You Were Never Lovelier (1942). Columbia/Tristar, VHS, 1992.

❖   HENIE, SONJA
(1912–1969)   *Actress*

A three-time Olympic gold medal winner, Sonja Henie used the same discipline and determination that made her an ice-skating champion to emerge as one of Hollywood's top stars of the late 1930s. She was born on April 8, 1912, in Oslo, Norway, where her father, Hans, was a successful fur salesman. Himself a former world bicycle champion, Hans encouraged Sonja and her older brother Leif to excel in athletics. Instructed by Leif, Sonja began skating at eight and won her first competition the next year. Thereafter, the Henie family devoted its time and sizable financial resources to making Sonja a skating star.

Owing to the Henies' help and Sonja's fierce competitive spirit, she was victorious at the 1928, 1932, and 1936 Olympics as well as winning 10 consecutive world championships. In the process, Henie transformed her sport. Inspired by Russian ballerina Anna Pavlova, she incorporated dance moves into skating routines for the first time. She also introduced rigorous training schedules and close attention to costuming into international skating competitions.

Again with the support of her family, Henie abandoned her amateur status in 1936 to perform in films. "I want to go into pictures, and I want to skate in them," she announced, adding, "I want to do with skates what Fred Astaire is doing with dancing." To gain the attention of studio executives, the Henies rented the Polar Palace in Los Angeles and funded two heavily advertised performances to showcase Sonja's talents. The ploy worked, and soon Henie was offered a five-year contract with Twentieth Century-Fox.

Between 1936 and 1939, Henie appeared in six highly popular light romances with plots contrived to include show-stopping skating sequences. Although her skating was the most notable feature of these films, Henie took her new role as an actress seriously. On the set, she was an avid student of filmmaking and worked hard to learn to act credibly. Audiences responded by making her the third top box-office draw of 1939, falling behind only Clark Gable and SHIRLEY TEMPLE.

Taking advantage of her film success, Henie staged the sold-out "Hollywood Ice Revue" in 1937. She also coproduced an ice show that ran in New York City for 10 years. An astute businessperson, Henie handled many of the details of managing the show herself, from making bookings to hiring and firing the staff.

In the early 1940s, the novelty of Henie's skating films faded, leading to her retirement in 1948. The war years and their aftermath were also fraught with controversy for Henie, as many Norwegians accused her of providing little financial support for her countrypeople as they suffered under Nazi occupation. Their anger was fueled by rumors of Henie's sympathy for the Nazi regime dating from her participation in the 1932 Olympics in Germany.

Henie married Daniel Topping, the owner of the Brooklyn Dodgers, and Winthrop Gardner Jr. a wealthy New Yorker, but both unions ended in divorce. In 1956, she wed a third time to Norwegian businessman and art collector Niels Onstad. With his encouragement, she invested much of her multimillion-dollar fortune in impressionist art. In 1968, they placed their collection in the Sonja Henie-Niels Onstad Art Center in Oslo as a gift to the Norwegian people. Eighteen months later, Henie succumbed to leukemia on October 12, 1969.

Further Reading

Henie, Sonja. *Wings on My Feet.* New York: Prentice-Hall, 1940.

Strait, Raymond, and Leif Henie. *Queen of Ice, Queen of Shadows: The Unsuspected Life of Sonja Henie.* New York: Stein and Day, 1985.

Wakefield, Wanda Ellen. "Henie, Sonja." In *American National Biography,* edited by John Arthur Garraty and Mark C. Carnes, vol. 10, pp. 590–591. New York: Oxford University Press, 1999.

Recommended Recorded and Videotaped Performances

Biography: Sonja Henie (1998). A&E Entertainment, VHS, 1998.

One in a Million (1937). Twentieth Century-Fox, VHS, 1994.

Sun Valley Serenade (1941). Twentieth Century-Fox, VHS, 1991.

❖ **HEPBURN, AUDREY (Edda Kathleen van Hemmstra Hepburn-Ruston)**
(1929–1993) *Actress*

During her lifetime, film star Audrey Hepburn was celebrated both for her elegant beauty on screen and for her tireless charity work. On May 4, 1929, she was born Edda Kathleen van Hemmstra Hepburn-Ruston in Brussels, Belgium. The wealth of her mother, who was a Dutch baroness, provided her with a happy, though sheltered, upbringing, even after her English father abandoned the family in 1935. As part of the divorce settlement, Edda was sent to school in England in order to be closer to him. At nine, she began taking ballet lessons with an eye toward pursuing a professional dance career.

At the beginning of World War II, Edda and her mother moved to Holland, hoping to escape Nazi control. The Nazis, however, soon invaded the country and seized her mother's fortunes. They were forced to flee into the countryside, where young Edda nearly died from malnutrition. Her life was saved only by food and supplies provided by relief workers. The experience was so traumatic that Hepburn later turned down a chance to play Holocaust victim Anne Frank, feeling that Frank's wartime experiences in Holland had too many uncomfortable parallels to her own.

After the war, Hepburn returned to London and resumed her ballet studies. Convinced she could not succeed as a ballerina, she began modeling and dancing in musical theater. She also took bit parts in English movies, including *The Lavender Hill Mob* (1951) and *Monte Carlo Baby* (1952). The filming of the latter took her the Riviera, where she had a chance meeting with the French author Colette. Colette became Hepburn's champion, insisting that the young actress be cast in the Broadway show *Gigi,* based on one of the writer's novels. Hepburn initially refused the part, convinced that with her limited acting experience she could not carry a show on her own. She was eventually persuaded to take on the role, though she was fired and rehired twice during rehearsals. Her performance steadily improved, and when the show premiered, she was hailed as a major new talent.

Hepburn's success as Gigi earned her the lead in the American movie *Roman Holiday* (1953). In it, her natural grace and charm were used to their best advantage as she played a runaway princess looking for a brief escape from her official duties during a tour of Italy. For her first major film performance, the 24-year-old Hepburn won an Academy Award for best actress. Three days later, she took home a Tony Award as well for the Broadway show *Ondine* (1954). Hepburn soon afterward married her *Ondine* costar, Mel Ferrer; the couple had a son in 1960.

Almost overnight, Hepburn emerged as one of Hollywood's greatest stars. She used the situation to negotiate an advantageous, long-term contract with Paramount. In addition to guaranteeing her the opportunity to fit theater roles into her schedule, it allowed her script approval of her movie projects. As a result, Hepburn escaped being cast just as the romantic partner for male stars. Instead, most of her movies focused on her, often telling stories of young women who grow and mature through new experiences and hardships.

In her second major role, Hepburn played the titular character in *Sabrina* (1953), a comedy that had her character bloom from an innocent into a sophisticate during a sojourn in Paris. The film improbably paired her romantically with Humphrey Bogart, who was then more than twice her age and looked it. Such "May-December" relationships became a common feature in Hepburn's movies. In nearly half of her films, her romantic partners were more than 20 years her senior. *Sabrina* brought Hepburn a second Oscar nomination. She would be so honored three more times for the films *The Nun's Story* (1959), *Breakfast at Tiffany's* (1961), and *Wait Until Dark* (1967).

During the filming of *Sabrina*, Hepburn became acquainted with the fashion designer Hubert de Givenchy, who remained her close friend throughout her life. As Givenchy's muse, Hepburn set fashion trends on- and offscreen by wearing his classic, simple designs. His sophisticated clothes on her slender frame helped create an alternative to the then-prevailing standard of Hollywood beauty as personified by curvy bombshells such as MARILYN MONROE. To this day, Hepburn's impeccable sense of style has continued to have a significant impact on popular fashion.

In the 1960s, Hepburn appeared in two of her signature roles: Holly Golightly in the romantic comedy *Breakfast at Tiffany's* (1961) and Eliza Doolittle in the musical *My Fair Lady* (1967). In both parts, she played a poor girl who re-creates herself as a fashionable urbanite, though Hepburn's innately regal manner made her fairly unconvincing as the characters before their glorious transformations. Critics were particularly hard on her for her performance in *My Fair Lady*, largely because many felt the then-lesser-known Julie Andrews, who had originated the role on Broadway, had deserved the part. Hepburn herself was disappointed when the filmmakers decided to dub over her own sweet but weak singing voice in the musical numbers.

The decade saw Hepburn in several more memorable films, including *Two for the Road* (1967) and *Wait Until Dark* (1967), which was produced by her husband Mel Ferrer. The next year, the couple divorced, and in 1969 Hepburn married Italian psychiatrist Andrea Dotti. They had a son in 1970 and were divorced in 1982.

After retiring in 1967 to spend more time with her family, Hepburn returned to the screen in the mature love story *Robin and Marian* (1976). The film costarred Sean Connery, who proved to be one of her strongest leading men. Hepburn continued to appear occasionally in small roles in feature films and made-for-TV movies. Her final screen part was an angel in Steven Spielberg's disappointing *Always* (1989).

Hepburn devoted her final years to what she regarded as her most important role: serving as the international "goodwill ambassador" for the United Nations International Children's Emergency Fund (UNICEF). Fueled by her own gratitude to the relief workers who saved her as a child, Hepburn took her position extremely seriously. She not only raised millions of dollars in relief funds, she also traveled constantly, making personal appearances in the most war-torn and disease-ridden areas of the globe to bring world attention to the miserable living conditions of the people there. Hepburn's efforts were particularly instrumental in escalating the United States's relief for famine victims in Somalia. Her devotion to

UNICEF ended only with her death from colon cancer on January 20, 1993. Later that year, the Academy of Motion Picture Arts and Sciences posthumously gave Hepburn the Jean Hersholt Humanitarian Award for her charitable works.

Further Reading:

Keogh, Pamela Clarke. *Audrey Style.* New York: Harper-Collins, 1999.

Paris, Barry. *Audrey Hepburn.* New York: Putnam, 1996.

Vermilye, Jerry. *The Complete Films of Audrey Hepburn.* Secaucus, N.J.: Carol Publishing, 1995.

Recommended Recorded and Videotaped Performances

Breakfast at Tiffany's (1961). Paramount, DVD/VHS, 1999/1996.

My Fair Lady (1964). Warner Home Video, DVD, 1998.

Sabrina (1954). Paramount, VHS, 1998.

❖ HEPBURN, KATHARINE
(1907 or 1909–) *Actress*

During her 62-year film career, Katharine Hepburn embodied the independent American woman both onscreen and off. Born in Hartford, Connecticut, on May 12 in 1907 or 1909, she was one of six children in a well-to-do New England family. From an early age, her parents encouraged her to think for herself and stand up for what she believed. Her mother was a well-regarded suffragist, while her father, a physician, was an early advocate for educating the public about venereal disease.

Katharine received an excellent private school education before enrolling at Bryn Mawr College, the alma mater of both her mother and her grandmother. By the time she graduated in 1928, she had decided to become an actress. In a 1992 interview, she explained that she chose her profession for no other reason than "I wanted to be famous."

In 1928, Hepburn married the socially prominent Ludlow Ogden Smith. She wrote in her 1991 autobiography that she was "an absolute pig" in her dealings with Smith. The couple separated after only three weeks, although they were not divorced until 1934. Hepburn never married again.

With the help of acting coaches, she gradually moved from summer stock to Broadway. In 1932, she played the role of a scantily-clad Amazon queen in the satire *The Warrior's Husband.* David O. Selznick offered her a contract with RKO. Citing this as the first overture made to her by Hollywood, Hepburn later quipped, "They didn't like me until I got into a leg show." Ambivalent about film, she asked for an outrageous salary of $1,500 a week. When RKO unexpectedly agreed to her terms, she set off for Los Angeles.

Hepburn made her film debut in *A Bill of Divorcement* (1932), opposite John Barrymore. The movie paired her with director George Cukor, with whom she would work on many of her best films. Though her acting was unpolished, she emerged from the movie a promising new talent. After suffering a popular disappointment with *Christopher Strong* (1933), she became a star with her third film, *Morning Glory* (1933), the story of an aspiring actress. The movie won Hepburn the first of three best actress Oscars.

Naturally thin and athletic, Hepburn had an aristocratic beauty unusual in 1930s Hollywood. She had her greatest successes in the decade playing assertive heroines (*Little Women,* 1933; *Stage Door,* 1937) and eccentric socialites (*Bringing Up Baby,* 1938; *Holiday,* 1938). However, her studio, RKO, seemed to have little confidence in her future. Irritated by their lack of interest in building her career, Hepburn attempted a return to theater in a disastrous production of *The Lake* (1934). The play was a commercial flop, and Hepburn's performance was critically scathed. Famously, theater critic Dorothy Parker wrote that in the play Hepburn ran "the gamut of emotion, from A to B."

In 1938, RKO wanted Hepburn to star in *Mother Carey's Chickens,* a melodrama about the struggles of a poor farm family. Feeling her studio was placing her in projects unsuitable to her talents, she bought out her contract for more than $200,000. Hepburn then returned to the stage, this time in a comedy especially tailored for her by

Katharine Hepburn in *The Philadelphia Story* (1940)
(Museum of Modern Art Film Stills Archive)

Philip Barry, who had written the play on which her film *Holiday* was based. Titled *The Philadelphia Story*, Barry's new play focused on Tracy Lord, a spoiled socialite who needed to learn to respect human weakness before she could find love. The production, in which Hepburn had invested, was an enormous hit. Controlling the movie rights herself, she sold them to Metro-Goldwyn-Mayer (MGM) at a profit with the stipulation that the film version had to star her under Cukor's direction. The resulting movie was a great commercial and critical success that brought Hepburn back to Hollywood's A-list.

Her next film at MGM was *Woman of the Year* (1942), her first of nine movies costarring Spencer Tracy. The comedy dealt with the relationship between two reporters, casting Hepburn as an accomplished professional as her movies with Tracy often did. In both comedy and drama, they usually played a couple who

constantly sparred with one another, all the while exploring the things that drive men and woman together and apart. Among their most effective pairings were *Adam's Rib* (1949), in which Hepburn was cast as a prominent lawyer, and *Pat and Mike* (1952), in which she had the chance to display her athletic talent while playing a professional athlete.

Offscreen, Hepburn and Tracy had a love affair, which they succeeded in keeping from the public eye for many years. Tracy had separated from his wife before meeting Hepburn but stayed married throughout their 25-year relationship.

By the 1950s, as Hepburn moved into her 40s, she was no longer cast as the spirited socialite or professional woman. Instead, her independence took on a more negative light. Hepburn delivered excellent performances in *The African Queen* (1951) and *Summertime* (1955), though in both romances she played a somewhat priggish spinster. She also increasingly portrayed eccentrics in films such as *Suddenly, Last Summer* (1959). The 1960s, however, brought Hepburn several memorable roles. She had perhaps her greatest critical triumph in *Long Day's Journey Into Night* (1962), in which she starred as the drug-addicted matriarch of Eugene O'Neill's autobiographical play. Hepburn also had popular successes with *Guess Who's Coming to Dinner* (1967) and *The Lion in Winter* (1968), for which she won her second and third Oscars.

Hepburn continued to act in the 1970s, though appropriate vehicles proved harder to find. She again collaborated with George Cukor in *Love Among the Ruins* (1975), a made-for-television romance that coupled Hepburn with Laurence Olivier and won her an Emmy Award. Other television roles included an adaptation of Tennessee Williams's *The Glass Menagerie* (1972) and a remake of *The Corn Is Green* (1979), her final work directed by Cukor.

Hepburn had less success on the big screen. Her most prominent film of the 1970s, *Rooster Cogburn*, had little to recommend it except the novelty of seeing her costar with the legendary John Wayne, in one of his final film appearances. However, a 1981 pairing with another acting great, Henry Fonda, brought Hepburn her last substantial role. In the film *On Golden Pond*, Hepburn played the stalwart wife of Fonda's aging professor. For her performance, Hepburn won her fourth best actress Oscar, a record that has yet to be surpassed.

After appearing in a small role in *Love Affair* (1994), Hepburn retired from film, leaving behind a legacy of 47 movies. Much of her work, particularly her performances from the 1930s and 1940s, remains fresh, largely because Hepburn and the characters she portrayed were far ahead of their time. Decades before the idea of the liberated woman was widely accepted, Hepburn had consistently played the part—both in film and in life. In a fitting tribute to her influence on American culture, a 1999 American Film Institute poll of leading critics named Katharine Hepburn the greatest female star of the movies.

Further Reading

Hepburn, Katharine. *Me: Stories of My Life*. New York: Knopf, 1991.

Leaming, Barbara. *Katharine Hepburn*. New York: Crown Publishers, 1995.

Ryan, Joal. *Katharine Hepburn: A Stylish Life*. New York: St. Martin's Press, 1999.

Recommended Recorded and Videotaped Performances

Adam's Rib (1949). Warner Home Video, DVD/VHS, 2000.

Bringing Up Baby (1938). Turner Home Video, VHS, 1997.

On Golden Pond (1982). Artisan Entertainment, DVD/VHS, 1998.

The Philadelphia Story (1940). Warner Home Video, DVD/VHS, 2000.

❖ **HOLIDAY, BILLIE (Eleanora Fagan, Lady Day)**
(1915–1959) *Singer*

Billie Holiday was arguably the most influential jazz singer of her time, although her genius has often been overshadowed by her difficult and tragic personal life. Little is known for certain about her early years. Given the name Eleanora, she was born probably in Philadelphia to Sadie Fagan, who was then 13 and unmarried. Her 15-year-old father, Clarence Holiday, soon left to pursue a career as a jazz guitarist.

When Eleanor was still an infant, Sadie moved to Baltimore, where her family lived. To find work, she soon set off for New York City, leaving Eleanor in the care of relatives. Holiday later alleged that her family beat her and that at 10 she was the victim of rape. At about the same time, she was sent to live in a reformatory because of her chronic truancy from school.

When she left the institution, Eleanora drifted into Baltimore's underworld, becoming a prostitute at 12. At the brothel where she worked, she was introduced to the music of BESSIE SMITH and Louis Armstrong, both of whom would have a great influence over her development as an artist. By about 1927, she traveled to New York, where she was reunited with Sadie. Working as a prostitute, maid, and waitress, she struggled to make a living for herself and her mother.

By the early 1930s, she was regularly finding jobs singing in small clubs and speakeasies. For her performances, she adopted the name Billie Holiday, taking the first name of her favorite screen star, Billie Dove, and the last name of her father. While singing at Monette's, a nightclub in Harlem, she was discovered by producer John Hammond. Although her voice was not strong and her range was narrow, he was immediately taken by the young singer's style. He later remembered that in her he "heard something that was completely new and fresh."

After writing an influential rave about her work in *Melody Maker* magazine, Hammond signed her to Columbia Records and arranged for her to make her first recordings with Benny Goodman in 1933. Two years later, the producer had more success by pairing Holiday with pianist Teddy Wilson. Her records with Wilson of such songs as "They Can't Take That Away from Me" and "Easy Living" were both creative and commercial triumphs.

Holiday's reputation on the club circuit was also on the rise. She became known for her flawless phrasing and expressive, unique interpretation of many standard songs. She often lent weight to light, sentimental tunes about love by investing them with irony or despair. Holiday also developed an uncanny ability to use her voice like an instrument, playing it skillfully to meet the needs of the song. She once explained, "I don't think I'm singing. I feel like I'm playing a horn. I try to improvise . . . like Louis Armstrong or someone else I admire."

Her talents brought her to the attention of Count Basie and Artie Shaw, who hired her to sing with their orchestras. While working with Shaw's band, she was one of the few African-American singers backed by white musicians. The situation led to a series of humiliations for Holiday, as she was met on the road with racial slurs and discriminatory policies.

By 1938 Holiday had decided she preferred performing as a solo act. She soon emerged as a star while singing regularly at Cafe Society, a renowned club in New York's Greenwich Village that catered to a sophisticated, interracial audience. There she established herself as a dramatic singer through her rendition of "Strange Fruit," a controversial, and powerful song about southern lynchings. She also became known for "God Bless the Child," her own classic song about taking care of oneself during hard times.

Holiday developed an important working relationship with tenor saxophonist Lester Young, whom she had first met when they both worked with Count Basie. Devoted friends, their musical partnership resulted in several memorable recordings, including "Mean to Me." In admiration of Holiday, Young called her "Lady Day," a nickname also adopted by her fans. In return, she referred to Young as "Prez."

By the early 1940s, Holiday's professional life career was soaring, but her personal life was in turmoil. In 1941 she wed nightclub manager Jimmy Monroe, but their marriage was short-lived. Still, it lasted long enough for Holiday to become addicted to heroin, which Monroe had introduced her to. Soon she was spending much of the $1,000 she earned weekly on the drug.

Her fortunes were further depleted when in 1945 she married trumpeter Joe Guy and, together, they formed their own band. Their unsuccessful tours proved an enormous financial drain. She had better luck with a series of recordings she made with Decca Records beginning in 1946. Backed by strings in slick arrangements, Holiday displayed a stronger voice than that heard in her earlier records. Also to further her profile, she appeared in *New Orleans* (1947), a movie about the city's music scene, in which she performed "Do You Know What It Means to Miss New Orleans." Holiday, however, was so dispirited by being cast as a maid that she never made another film.

In 1947 Holiday entered a clinic, hoping to free herself from her growing drug habit. Alerted to her heroin use by her hospital stay, federal agents arrested her on a narcotics charge soon after she left the clinic. In an interview with *Down Beat* magazine, Holiday observed the irony of the timing of her arrest: "Just when things were going to be so big and I was trying so hard to straighten myself out. Funny, isn't it?" At the height of her career, she was sentenced to nine months in a West Virginia reformatory.

Ten days after her release, Holiday was cheered by a sold-out crowd at a concert at Carnegie Hall. The triumph lessened the blow of losing her cabaret card, which allowed her to sing in New York clubs, because of her felony conviction. She had to confine her appearances to theaters and concert halls until John Levy, manager of the Ebony Club, illegally hired her, while the police looked the other way. Involved romantically with the volatile Levy, Holiday narrowly evaded another jail sentence in 1948 when both were arrested for opium possession. The following year, the two were married, though she soon left Levy for Louis McKay, whom she wed in 1956.

In 1952, Holiday began recording for Verve Records. These late recordings reveal that years of drug and alcohol abuse had taken a toll on her singing talents. Yet, when she was singing well, her voice was richer than before. In the Verve recordings, Holiday also showed an undiminished interest in trying new arrangements and new interpretations of old standards. She claimed that she was unable to sing the same song the same way twice, once explaining, "I just can't do it. I can't even copy me."

Late in her career, Holiday also achieved a life-long goal of performing in Europe. A 1954 tour took her to Spain, Germany, the Netherlands, France, Switzerland, and England, where she played to an audience of 6,000 at London's Royal Albert Hall.

Such successes did nothing, however, to stop her physical deterioration. Arrested again in 1956, Holiday was permitted to enter a rehabilitation facility, where she conquered her heroin addiction. However, she continued to drink heavily. At her last performance, on May 25, 1959, she had to be led off the stage after two songs.

Devastated by the death of Lester Young months earlier, Holiday collapsed on Memorial Day and was rushed to a New York hospital. She emerged from a coma, but her body, ravaged from years of abuse, had difficulty recovering. Adding to her pain, the police raided her hospital room and arrested her once again for narcotics possession. Holiday was still under house arrest when she died in the hospital on July 17, 1959. She was 44 years old.

While desperate for money, Holiday had written her autobiography, *Lady Sings the Blues* (1956), with *New York Post* reporter William Dufty. The book, and the 1972 film starring DIANA ROSS based on it, focused on her impoverished childhood, the racial discrimination she encountered, and her troubles with men and drugs. They sadly helped to foster an image of Holiday that clouded the one aspect of her life that made her exceptional: the unadulterated and contagious joy she had for singing.

Further Reading

Gourse, Leslie, ed. *Billie Holiday Companion: Seven Decades of Commentary.* New York: Schirmer Books, 1997.

Holiday, Billie, with William Dufty. *Lady Sings the Blues.* 1956. Reprint, with a new discography by Vincent Pelote, New York: Penguin, 1995.

Margolick, David. *Strange Fruit: Billie Holiday, Cafe Society, and an Early Cry for Civil Rights.* Philadelphia: Running Press, 2000.

O'Meally, Robert G. *Lady Day: The Many Faces of Billie Holiday.* New York: Arcade Publishing, 1991.

Recommended Recorded and Videotaped Performances

The Complete Billie Holiday on Verve. Polygram, CD set, 1992.

The Complete Decca Recordings. GRP, CD set, 1991.

Lady Day: The Many Faces of Billie Holiday (1991). Kultur Video, VHS, 1991.

Lady Sings the Blues (1972). Paramount, VHS, 1996.

Love Songs. Sony/Columbia, CD, 1996.

❖ HORNE, LENA (Lena Mary Calhoun Horne)
(1917–) *Singer, Actress*

Since the 1930s, Lena Horne has been charming audiences with her silky voice. She was born Lena Mary Calhoun Horne in the Bedford-Stuyvesant area of Brooklyn, New York, on June 17, 1917. After her parents separated when she was three, her mother, an aspiring actress, left Lena in the care of Lena's maternal grandparents, both of whom were active in civil rights. When Lena was two, her grandmother enrolled her in the National Association for the Advancement of Colored People (NAACP).

In about 1924, Lena joined her mother, who was a touring performer in African-American tent shows. Traveling through the South, she felt first-hand the indignities suffered by African Americans in a segregated society. The experience also piqued her interest in show business.

By the onset of the Great Depression, Horne was living with her mother and new stepfather in the Bronx. Needing to help support her family, she left school at 16 to work as a chorus girl at the Cotton Club, a famed nightclub in Harlem that presented shows starring African-American talent for a wealthy white clientele. In addition to Horne's beautiful face and shapely figure, she was hired because her light skin and Caucasian-looking features were appealing to whites.

Horne spent some of her paycheck on music lessons, a decision that paid off when she won a small role in the Broadway musical *Dance With Your Gods* (1935). The same year, she was hired as a singer for Noble Sissle's Society Orchestra. In 1937, she left the entertainment business to marry Louis Jones, a family friend. Horne and Jones settled in Pittsburgh and had two children, Gail and Teddy, before they separated in 1940.

Returning to New York, Horne started singing with the Charlie Barnet Orchestra, with whom she made her first recordings. By 1941, she was a regular performer at Cafe Society Downtown, a nightspot in Greenwich Village that drew a mixed-race audience. There, she met many of the prominent African-American New Yorkers of her day. For a time, Horne dated boxer Joe Louis. She also developed friendships with actor Paul Robeson and singer BILLIE HOLIDAY. Perhaps even more important to her career was meeting Walter White, the head of the NAACP. He encouraged her to try to break down racial barriers in films. At the time, few African-American actresses were ever cast as anything but maids.

In 1942, Horne went to Los Angeles for a nightclub job. While there, she landed a seven-year contract with Metro-Goldwyn-Mayer (MGM), becoming the first African American to sign with a major movie studio since 1915. She demanded a clause in her contract stipulating that she would not be required to play any stereotyped roles.

Horne had her most substantial film part in *Cabin in the Sky* (1943), playing the temptress Georgia Brown in this all-African-American musical. Otherwise, MGM was not quite sure what to do with Horne. Racial taboos kept her from becoming a romantic lead; since Horne was African American, the studio refused to pair her

Lena Horne with Eddie Anderson
in *Stormy Weather* (1943)
(Museum of Modern Art Film Stills Archive)

with a white man. Instead, in most of Horne's films, she was seen only in musical numbers, inevitably dressed in a tasteful evening gown. In *Stormy Weather* (1943), for instance, she sang the title song, which became her signature tune. Keeping Horne's film appearances restricted to short scenes also allowed MGM to cut her out of prints shown in the South, where moviegoers were more apt to object to seeing an African American on screen.

During World War II, Horne became the favorite pinup girl of African-American soldiers. She was also a popular entertainer in USO tours, though she would not perform if African Americans were denied admittance to her show. At the beginning of one performance, she walked off-stage when she realized that African-American troops had been seated behind German prisoners of war. The USO pulled her from its tours, so Horne began entertaining troops on tours she financed herself.

After the war, Horne married white conductor-arranger Lennie Hayton in Paris in 1947. They kept their relationships secret until the press exposed it in 1950. As a result, Horne received numerous death threats. She also became a target of Senator Joseph McCarthy's communist witch-hunts during the 1950s.

Nevertheless, Horne remained a star, particularly as a nightclub performer and recording artist. Her album *Lena Horne at the Waldorf-Astoria* became the top-selling recording by a female artist ever produced by RCA Records. Horne also performed frequently on television, on such programs as *The Ed Sullivan Show* and *The Tonight Show*. In the 1960s, she also made regular appearances in marches and rallies for civil rights, including the March on Washington in 1963.

Horne separated from Hayton, though they remained close friends. She found the love of her life, however, in Billy Strayhorn, a famed arranger-composer who died in 1967. The years ahead would bring more sorrow to Horne. During an 18-month period in 1970–71, she saw the deaths of her father, her son Teddy, and Hayton. Through the early 1970s, Horne stayed out of the public eye as she recovered from her grief.

In 1974, Horne was lured back to Broadway, where she costarred with Tony Bennett in the show *Tony and Lena.* She also appeared as Glinda the Good Witch in *The Wiz,* the film version of an all-black Broadway musical based on *The Wizard of Oz.* The unsuccessful movie was directed by her son-in-law, Sidney Lumet.

Horne went on what she considered her farewell concert tour in 1980, but ironically one of her greatest professional triumphs was yet to come. In 1981, she starred in *Lena Horne: The Lady and Her Music.* Her still powerful voice, combined with her personal warmth and sense of humor, made it the longest running one-woman show in Broadway history. Calling the show "the best thing that ever happened to me," Horne won a special

Tony for her performance and a Grammy for the album recorded from it.

After more than 10 years, Horne returned to the recording studio in the 1990s. In addition to *An Evening with Lena Horne: Live at the Supper Club* (1995), she made two well-received studio albums, *We'll Be Together Again* (1994) and *Being Myself* (1998). In a culmination of seven decades in the entertainment industry, she gave an acclaimed performance at the 1997 JVC Jazz Festival to celebrate her 80th birthday.

Further Reading

Buckley, Gail Lumet. *The Hornes: An American Family.* New York: Knopf, 1986.

Haskins, James, with Kathleen Benson. *Lena: A Biography of Lena Horne.* Chelsea, Mich.: Scarborough House, 1991.

Horne, Lena, with Richard Schickel. *Lena.* New York: Doubleday, 1965.

Recommended Recorded and Videotaped Performances

Cabin in the Sky (1999). Warner Home Video, VHS, 1943.

Stormy Weather (1991). Twentieth Century-Fox, VHS, 1943.

The Wiz (1978). Universal, DVD/VHS, 1999/1998.

❖ HOUSTON, WHITNEY
(1963–) *Singer, Actress*

Recording artist Whitney Houston began her record-setting career with the best-selling debut album ever released by a female singer. Born in East Orange, New Jersey on August 9, 1963, she was groomed for stardom at an early age. Her mother was the famed gospel artist Cissy Houston, and her cousin was pop singer DIONNE WARWICK. Family friends included ARETHA FRANKLIN, Roberta Flack, and Gladys Knight.

In her teens, Houston began her professional career singing backup for the singers Chaka Khan and Lou Rawls. Her beauty and lean figure also won her modeling work, including appearances on the covers of *Seventeen* and *Glamour* magazine. Houston dabbled in acting as well. She made numerous television commercials and played small roles on the situation comedies *Silver Spoons* and *Gimme a Break.*

At 19, Houston was signed to Arista Records by president Clive Davis, who was known for his careful nurturing of talent. For two years, she and Davis worked closely together to mold her pop sound and elegant look. The result was *Whitney Houston* (1985). The album sold more than 13 million copies and spawned three number-one singles—"How Will I Know," "The Greatest Love of All," and "Saving All My Love for You," for which she won a Grammy Award for best pop vocal performance. Not all critics, however, were enthusiastic about Houston's triumphant appearance on the music scene. Her detractors complained that her voice, through technically flawless, showed little true emotion.

For the next two years, Houston toured and developed material for her second album, titled simply *Whitney* (1987). It became the first album by a female artist to enter the charts at number one. Houston also scored four more number-one singles, including "I Wanna Dance with Somebody" and "So Emotional." Her next album, *I'm Your Baby Tonight* (1990) went triple platinum, yet it was considered a disappointment because its sales were not as phenomenal as its predecessors.

In July 1992, Houston married recording artist Bobby Brown, with whom she had one daughter, Bobbi Kristina. The same year, she made her acting debut playing a singing star in the romantic thriller *The Bodyguard.* The film was an international success, earning more than $400 million worldwide. Just as sensational was the response to the movie's soundtrack album, which featured six songs by Houston. The best-selling soundtrack ever, the album included the DOLLY PARTON–penned love song "I Will Always Love You," which became the biggest hit of Houston's career.

Houston continued acting in the films the hit *Waiting To Exhale* (1995) and *The Preacher's Wife* (1996), which proved one of the few failures in her career. In 1997, she also starred in *Cinderella,* a highly rated television musical in which she played the Fairy Godmother.

Houston unveiled a new sound in 1998's *My Love Is Your Love,* her first album in eight years. Moving away from the pure pop that made her a star, the recording showed Houston experimenting with hip-hop and with rhythm and blues. It also featured Houston singing with several younger artists, including Missy Elliot, Faith Evans, and Lauryn Hill.

Although beloved by legions of fans, Houston has been the subject of tabloid gossip, often focusing on the drug use of her husband. In 2000, Houston herself was charged with marijuana possession in Hawaii (the charges were dismissed the next year). She also drew harsh criticism when she was pulled from performing at the 2000 Academy Awards ceremony because of her erratic behavior during rehearsals for the telecast. Houston, did see one triumph that year, however—the release of *Whitney: The Greatest Hits.* The briskly selling career retrospective showed that her private problems had done little to diminish the public's enthusiasm for her work.

Further Reading

Bowman, Jeffery. *Diva.* New York: Harper, 1995.

Cox, Ted. *Whitney Houston,* Philadelphia: Chelsea House, 1997.

Recommended Recorded and Videotaped Performances

The Bodyguard (1992). Warner Home Video, DVD/VHS, 1997/1999.

Whitney: The Greatest Hits. BMG/Arista, DVD/VHS, 2000/2000.

Whitney: The Greatest Hits. BMG/Arista, CD set, 2000.

❖ HUMPHREY, DORIS
(1895–1958)   *Dancer, Choreographer*

Passionate and uncompromising, Doris Humphrey was one of the greatest innovators of American modern dance. Born on October 17, 1895, she was raised in Oak Park, Illinois, in a financially struggling family. Nevertheless, her parents found funds to provide her with an excellent progressive education. At the Francis W. Parker School in Chicago, Doris was first exposed to folk and interpretive dance. At home, she received musical training from her mother, who gave piano lessons to supplement the Humphreys' income.

Soon after Doris graduated from high school, her father lost his job at a run-down theatrical hotel. She was then called upon to become the family's primary breadwinner. With her mother, Humphrey established a school with classes in ballroom dancing. The work was profoundly unsatisfying to Humphrey. After four years, the school had become profitable enough for her to leave for Los Angeles to pursue a professional dancing career.

In 1917 she enrolled at the Denishawn school, which was operated by dance legend RUTH ST. DENIS and her husband, Ted Shawn. Immediately impressed by Humphrey's talents, St. Denis delighted her new student by declaring she was born to be a dancer, not a teacher. Soon Humphrey was a lead dancer with the Denishawn company. She also worked as a teaching assistant and, with St. Denis's enthusiastic encouragement, made her first forays into choreography.

After seven years with Denishawn, Humphrey grew disenchanted with its emphasis on theatricality as she imagined a new style of dance expressive of more modest human emotions and experiences. In 1928 she left the company to establish a school in New York City with friends and fellow former Denishawn dancers Charles Weidman and Pauline Lawrence. The three partners lived together and, after Humphrey's marriage in 1932, were joined by her husband, Charles Francis Woodford, and their son.

As other disgruntled Denishawn alumni joined their ranks, the three partners established the Humphrey-Weidman dance company. Working with this company, Humphrey began developing her own theory of dance in early works such as *Water Study* (1928) and *Life of the Bee* (1929). She sought to create dance "from the inside outside," allowing the emotions she wanted to communicate to dictate the movements she chose. Often she choreographed a dance in silence and commissioned music later, so as not to let music, rather than emotion, guide her.

Humphrey's primary theory of movement came to be known as "fall and recovery." She held that all human movement fell within the "arc between two deaths"—the "deaths" being the body in a prone position and the body standing erect. Her work often required dancers to make motions that put themselves off-balance and then to use the resulting momentum to restore control over their bodies. In this pattern, Humphrey saw a broader meaning. Influence by German philosopher Friedrich Nietzsche, she saw life as a constant tension between the desire for security and the lure of adventure, an idea represented in her dance through the "fall and recovery" movements. Another prominent theme of Humphrey's work was the quest for social harmony. Resisting a trend toward abstraction in modern dance, throughout her career she held fast to the notion that dance could inspire tolerance and peace between peoples.

In the early 1930s, Humphrey joined other noted modern dancers—including MARTHA GRAHAM, AGNES DE MILLE, and HELEN TAMIRIS—in popular showcases organized by the Dance Repertory Theater. She also taught at Bennington College's pioneering dance program. At Bennington, she premiered two pieces from her highly ambitious *New Dance Trilogy* (1935–36). Each dance in the trilogy lasted for more than 40 minutes, far longer than most dance pieces of the time. Because the extraordinary demands the trilogy placed on dancers, all three parts were never staged in the same performance.

After some 15 years in operation, the Humphrey-Weidman company disbanded following its final performance of Humphrey's *Inquest* (1944) at Swarthmore College in Pennsylvania. With her company's demise, Humphrey began working with her former student José Limón. As the artistic director of Limón's company, she choreographed a number of dances, including *Day on Earth* (1947), which explored an everyman figure's relationship with his first love, wife, and daughter. With Limón, she also spent summers as an artist in residence at Connecticut College.

In 1951, Humphrey became a teacher and choreographer at the Juilliard Dance Theater, a newly founded arm of the prestigious Juilliard School of Music in New York City. She could no longer dance due to severe arthritis in her hip, yet through her work at Juilliard she continued to have a profound influence over the next generation of modern dancers and choreographers. Humphrey also documented her theories of dance in *The Art of Making Dances* (1959), a volume that was 30 years in the making. She was only able to find the time to finish it after cancer left her bedridden and unable to teach. The illness took her life on December 29, 1958. An obituary in the *New York Times* summed up her life's work by declaring, "Doris Humphrey is an enduring part of the dance in America, as the granite under the soil is enduring."

Further Reading

Humphrey, Doris. *The Art of Making Dances.* Edited by Barbara Pollack. New York: Rinehart, 1959.
———. *Doris Humphrey, an Artist First: An Autobiography.* Edited and completed by Selma Jeanne Cohen. 1977. Reprint, Pennington, N.J.: Princeton Book Company, 1995.
Siegel, Marcia B. *Days on Earth: The Dance of Doris Humphrey.* New Haven: Yale University Press, 1987.

Recommended Recorded and Videotaped Performances

The Doris Humphrey Legacy. Dance Horizons Video, VHS set, 1997.
Doris Humphrey Technique: The Creative Potential. Dance Horizons Video, VHS, 1992.

❖ JACKSON, MAHALIA
(1911–1972) *Singer*

The United States's most famous gospel singer, Mahalia Jackson was born in New Orleans on October 26, 1911. After her mother died when she was five, Mahalia went to live with an aunt. The strict upbringing she received included frequent attendance at a Baptist church, where Mahalia learned the standard repertoire of hymns while singing in the choir. She was even more influenced, however, by the music she heard coming out of the church next door to her house. Its members were of the Holiness sect, which attempted to revitalize slave religious traditions. In her 1966 autobiography, *Movin' On Up,* Jackson later recalled, "Everybody in there sang and they clapped and stomped their feet and sang with their whole bodies. . . . Their music was so strong and expressive it used to bring the tears to my eyes."

Eager to escape the racial segregation of the South, Jackson moved to live with relatives in Chicago in 1928. While working as a laundress and a maid, she became a soloist in the choir at the Greater Salem Baptist Church. With other members, she formed the Johnson Gospel Singers and began touring small churches and revival meetings.

Although most large African-American churches were moving toward increasingly sedate services, she found a ready audience for her exuberant and uninhibited performing style in smaller venues. While shouting out in her strong, bold voice, Jackson swayed from side to side, using her whole body to express her religious fervor. Often she rushed down from the stage, creating a sense of connection with the members of the congregation by singing among them.

In 1938 Jackson married Isaac Hockenhull, a chemist who created cosmetics that his wife then sold. With money from the business and from her singing engagements, she soon opened Mahalia's Beauty Shop and an adjoining flower shop. Hockenhull, however, pressed her to take one of her many offers to give up gospel music for more lucrative blues singing. Although her music borrowed heavily from the rhythms of the blues, ragtime, and jazz of New Orleans, Jackson steadfastly refused, maintaining she cared little about money. This sore point between her and her husband contributed to their divorce in 1943. (Jackson's second marriage, in the mid-1960s to musician Sigmund Galloway, also ended in divorce.)

Meanwhile, Jackson's singing career continued to blossom. From 1937 to 1946, she worked closely

Mahalia Jackson in about 1965
(Library of Congress, neg. no. USZ62-114990)

with Thomas A. Dorsey, then the premier composer of gospel songs. In addition to acting as her accompanist, he helped Jackson shape her talent, particularly by advising her on how to build her performances to a climax.

Jackson first began recording in 1937, but her records did not reach a mass audience until Chicago radio personality Studs Terkel began playing her rendition of "I'm Goin' to Tell God All About It One of These Days." This exposure led to a contract with Apollo Records in 1946. The next year, her "Move On Up a Little Higher" sold more than 2 million copies.

By the 1950s, Jackson had become a national celebrity. She gave concerts at New York's Carnegie Hall, made regular television guest appearances, and began recording with a full orchestra on Columbia Records, though she continued to resist continual efforts to make her sing more secular fare. In Chicago, she had her own television show on CBS but could not convince the network to televise it nationally for fear of offending southern white audiences.

Jackson's reputation grew when she became involved in the civil rights movement. In 1956 she traveled to Montgomery, Alabama, to show her support for the African-American bus boycott led by Martin Luther King Jr. She remained a close associate of King's, notably performing during the 1963 March on Washington just before King delivered his famous "I Have a Dream" speech. Sadly, she also sang at his and Robert F. Kennedy's funerals in 1968.

In the 1960s, Jackson also launched several successful tours of Europe, where she had a substantial following. Her health, however, became increasingly fragile due to a heart condition. It finally took her life on January 27, 1972, At her funeral, ARETHA FRANKLIN—one of the many young artists she had championed—sang "Take My Hand, Precious Lord," one of Jackson's best-loved songs.

Further Reading

Jackson, Mahalia, with Evan McLeod Wylie. *Movin' On Up.* New York: Hawthorne Books, 1996.

Schwerin, Jules. *Got to Tell It: Mahalia Jackson, Queen of Gospel.* New York: Oxford University Press, 1992.

Recommended Recorded and Videotaped Performances

The Best of Mahalia Jackson. Sony/Columbia, CD, 1995.

Gospels, Spirituals, and Hymns. Sony/Columbia, CD, 1998.

Jazz on a Summer's Day (1958). New Yorker Films, DVD/VHS, 2000.

❖ JAMES, ETTA (Jamesetta Hawkins) (1938–) *Singer*

Rich and rough, Etta James's booming voice has put its stamp on nearly every popular music genre—from blues to jazz to rock. On January 25, 1938, James was born Jamesetta Hawkins in Los Angeles, California. Her 14-year-old mother, Dorothy, was more interested in the club scene than in raising her infant. For much of her youth, Jamesetta lived with her grandparents, devout churchgoers who placed her in their church choir. At six, Jamesetta was singing solos and appearing on gospel radio shows.

In her teens, Jamesetta went to live with Dorothy Hawkins in San Francisco. Like her mother, Jamesetta had a taste for street life and a knack for getting into trouble with the law. She also shared with Dorothy a passion for the jazz singing of BILLIE HOLIDAY.

When she was 15, Jamesetta started her own singing group, the Creolettes, with two friends.

She bullied her way into an audition with bandleader Johnny Otis, who was wowed by her powerful voice. Still a minor, Jamesetta forged her mother's name on a release form, and the Creolettes started touring with Otis billed as the Peaches. Rearranging the syllables of her name, Otis also rechristened Jamesetta as Etta James.

Soon, the Peaches had their first hit. An answer to Hank Ballard and the Midnighters' song "Work with Me Annie," "Roll with Me, Henry" hit number two on the rhythm and blues charts. Because the original title was considered by some to be too raunchy for airplay, the song was also titled "The Wallflower."

With her newfound success, James went solo. She toured with Little Richard and sang backup for Marvin Gaye and Chuck Berry. Once she had the honor of sharing a stage with her idol Billie Holiday, who was then dying from health ailments resulting from her drug addiction. With her hands and feet hideously swollen, Holiday whispered some words of advice to the young singer: "Just don't ever let this happen to you."

In 1960, James moved to Chicago and began recording for Chess Records. She had 10 charting hits between 1960 and 1963, making her one of the top artists in rhythm and blues. In records such as "At Last" (1961) and "Something's Got a Hold on Me" (1962), James displayed her wide range, moving easily from ballads to jazz songs to pop tunes. Despite her success during this period, James was unable to crossover to sizable white audiences like her contemporary DIANA ROSS, whose singing style was much inspired by James. James's records also had an enormous influence on JANIS JOPLIN, Rod Stewart, the Rolling Stones, and other white artist who rose to fame later in the decade.

Through the late 1960s and early 1970s, James's recording schedule became erratic as a longtime heroin habit began to take over her life. In 1974, she finally kicked her addiction after entering a rehabilitation clinic in Tarzana, California. Slowly, James set about rebuilding her career, playing small clubs and occasionally appearing at jazz and blues festivals. By the mid-1980s, she was touring with the Rolling Stones. She returned to recording after a seven-year hiatus, releasing *The Seven Year Itch* in 1988.

Now considered a legend, James was inducted into the Rock and Roll Hall of Fame in 1993. In the 1990s, James began spending more time in the studio, creating recordings in a variety of genres. The most successful was *Mystery Lady* (1994), which featured James's take on songs made famous by Billie Holiday. The album, which James said she had wanted to make for 30 years, earned her a Grammy for best jazz vocal. Also well-received were *Love, Life and Blues* (1998) and *Matriarch of the Blues* (2001), on which she was backed by her two grown sons, Donto and Sametto.

Now settled in Los Angeles with her husband Artie Mills, James documented the many ups and downs of her life in her autobiography, *Rage to Survive* (1995). In it, she said she had learned to live with the rage that inspired much of her work. "In some ways, it's my rage that keeps me going," she wrote. "Without it, I would have been whipped long ago. With it, I got a lot more songs to sing."

Further Reading

"Etta James." In *Contemporary Black Biography.* Vol. 13. Detroit: Gale Research, 1996.

James, Etta, and David Ritz. *Rage to Survive: The Etta James Story.* New York: Villard, 1995.

Recommended Recorded and Videotaped Performances

Etta James, The Best: The Chess 50th Anniversary Collection. MCA, CD, 1997.

Jammin' With the Blues Greats (1982). Image Entertainment, DVD/VHS, 1998/1995.

20th Century Masters: The Best of Etta James. MCA, CD, 1999.

❖ JAMISON, JUDITH
(1944–)   *Dancer, Choreographer*

Long the lead dancer of the Alvin Ailey American Dance Theater (AAADT), Judith Jamison was born in Philadelphia on May 10, 1944. With a keen interest in the arts, her parents enrolled her in the Judimar School of Dance when she was six. Almost immediately, she emerged as a prodigy. During her 11 years at the school, she received a firm grounding in ballet as well as instruction in tap, jazz, and acrobatics.

After graduating from high school, Jamison received a scholarship to Fisk University in Nashville, where she studied psychology. She completed her freshman year before deciding to renew her commitment to dance. Jamison returned home and began attending the Philadelphia Dance Academy (now the University of the Arts). While taking a master class in 1964, she was discovered by noted choreographer AGNES DE MILLE, who invited the young dancer to perform her ballet *The Four Mays* with the American Ballet Theater at New York's Lincoln Center.

Once the ballet closed, Jamison decided to stay in New York City. She took a job operating the log flume ride at the 1964 World's Fair, while she tried out for professional dance companies. On one audition, Jamison danced for choreographer Donald McKayle for a spot on a television special. In the audience was McKayle's friend, dancer and company director Alvin Ailey. Three days after seeing Jamison, Ailey called her with an invitation to join his multiracial company.

From 1965 to 1980, Jamison was Ailey's principal dancer as well as his close friend. Her controlled technique and dynamic stage presence—showcased in early Ailey works such as *Blues Suite* (1958) and *Revelations* (1960)—earned an excellent reputation in the dance world. Graceful and elegant, Jamison was described by one critic as "a marvelous all-around performer—extravagantly tall with a purring kind of strength and a leap that looks as if she had been poured upward."

In 1972, Jamison became an international star with the premiere of Ailey's *Cry*, a 15-minute solo piece he choreographed with Jamison in mind. Dedicated to "black women everywhere, especially our mothers," the work explored the sorrows and joys experienced by African-American women throughout history. Other Ailey dances that furthered Jamison's fame included *Pas de Duke,* which she performed with Mikhail Baryshnikov to music by Duke Ellington, and *Spell,* which paired her with ballet great Alexander Godunov.

After 15 years with the Ailey company, Jamison left to star in the Broadway show *Sophisticated Ladies* with tap dancer Gregory Hines. She also turned her attention to teaching and, with Ailey's encouragement, to choreography. Her first work, *Divining,* debuted with his company in 1984.

Jamison briefly considered retiring but instead decided to work toward realizing her longtime dream of starting a dance company of her own. In 1988, she formed the 12-member Jamison Project. Just as the new company was beginning to establish itself, Ailey fell ill. He asked Jamison to take over his company after his death, and she agreed. In December 1989, she became AAADT's artistic director, merging her own fledging group into the more established company. At the time she explained, "Somebody said to me these are big shoes to fill. But that's not what this is about. This about trying to wear my own shoes."

As AAADT's director, Jamison has dedicated herself to raising funds to take the company out of debt and to showcase both new works by young choreographers and the classic dances created by Ailey. To preserve Ailey's legacy, in 1993, she herself choreographed *A Hymn for Alvin Ailey.* For this dance work, she collaborated with performance artist Anna Deavere Smith, who added remembrances of Ailey company members to the piece. In 1999, Jamison won an Emmy Award for choreography after *Hymn* was filmed for the PBS series *Dance in America.* The same year, her career as a dancer and company director was celebrated when she became the recipient of a Kennedy Center Honor for lifetime achievement in the arts.

Further Reading

Jamison, Judith, with Howard Kaplan. *Dancing Spirit: An Autobiography.* New York: Doubleday, 1993.

Maynard, Olga. *Judith Jamison: Aspects of a Dancer.* Garden City, N.Y.: Doubleday, 1982.

Recommended Recorded and Videotaped Performances

An Evening with the Alvin Ailey Dance Theater (1986). Image Entertainment, DVD, 2001.

A Tribute to Alvin Ailey (1990). Kultur Video, DVD/VHS, 2000/1997.

❖ **JOPLIN, JANIS** (Janis Lyn Joplin)
(1943–1970) *Singer*

The first woman to become a rock superstar, Janis Lyn Joplin was born into a middle-class family in Port Arthur, Texas, on January 19, 1943. A loner as a child, she developed an enthusiasm for art and music. By her teens, Joplin eschewed the pop music favored by her peers, drawn instead to the classic blues recordings of BESSIE SMITH and Leadbelly. Coarse and sexually assertive, she also began rebelling against the conventional views of femininity defined by her Texas upbringing.

After graduating from high school, Joplin left home with a vague ambition to seek out a singing career. She drifted from Houston to Los Angeles to New York City, playing occasional gigs and periodically signing up for college classes. She finally gravitated to San Francisco and immersed herself in the growing counterculture there.

Discouraged by her lack of success as a singer, Joplin returned to Port Arthur in 1965. Now dependent on drugs and alcohol, she tried to kick her habits and build a new life in her hometown. Although she was briefly engaged, her efforts to become a Port Arthur matron failed. As she told *Rolling Stone* magazine in 1970, "Texas is OK if you want to settle down and do your thing quietly, but it's not for outrageous people, and I was always outrageous."

In 1966, Joplin was called back to San Francisco by the manager of Big Brother and the Holding Company, a hard rock band looking for a lead singer. Though unconventional, the pairing of Joplin's raw, raspy blues singing with a rock sound immediately clicked. Her amplified backup band also helped define a new performance style for Joplin. She

117

became wildly animated on stage, conveying a passion that her audiences found contagious.

Already a name performer in San Francisco, Joplin burst onto the national scene with Big Brother's performance at the 1967 Monterey Pop Festival. She was hailed, not only for her unique sound, but also her stage persona. Called by the *Village Voice* "a sex symbol in an unlikely package," she presented a new brand of female emotionalism and assertiveness. This image was heightened by the press, which with her encouragement reported on her penchant for one-night stands and indulgence in alcohol. Onstage and off, a bottle of Southern Comfort in her hand became one of her trademarks.

Following Monterey, Joplin signed up with manager Albert Grossman, who became an important adviser throughout the rest of her career. Her new fame also helped make *Cheap Thrills* (1968), her second album with Big Brother, a million-seller. Although it featured some of her best-known songs—including "Piece of My Heart" and her rendition of George and Ira Gershwin's "Summertime"—the studio records failed to capture the dynamism of Joplin's stage performances. She herself grew unhappy with Big Brother's lack of discipline and left the band. Trying to find a backup group to better showcase her singing, she subsequently formed two bands of her own, the Kozmic Blues Band in 1969 and the Full-Tilt Boogie Band in 1970.

Though increasingly plagued by alcohol and drug abuse, Joplin developed a deeper, more controlled style as she began work with Full-Tilt Boogie on a new album, titled *Pearl* after her nickname among her friends. Her personal life also seemed to be entering a new phase with her engagement to Seth Morgan, a Berkeley student from a wealthy New York family. While finishing recording *Pearl* (1971) in Los Angeles, however, Joplin at 27 suffered a fatal accidental overdose of heroin on October 4, 1970. The album, released posthumously, gave Joplin her only number-one single, "Me and Bobby McGee," a song of lost love and regret penned by her ex-lover Kris Kristofferson.

Despite Joplin's early death, her legend as one of rock's greatest performers has endured. She continues to be regarded as the leading white female interpreter of blues-influenced rock, while her personal image was a harbinger of the 1960s and 1970s feminist call for abandoning restrictive definitions of "ladylike" behavior. Another part of her legacy that would no doubt have pleased Joplin herself was finding a young, wide audience for WILLIE MAE THORNTON, BESSIE SMITH, and the other blues greats who helped inspire Joplin's own unique style.

Further Reading

Dalton, David. *Piece of My Heart: The Life, Times, and Legend of Janis Joplin.* New York: St. Martin's Press, 1985.

Echols, Alice. *Scars of Sweet Paradise: The Life and Times of Janis Joplin.* New York: Metropolitan Books, 1999.

Friedman, Myra. *Buried Alive: The Biography of Janis Joplin.* 1973. Reprint, New York: Harmony Books, 1992.

Recommended Recorded and Videotaped Performances

Cheap Thrills (1968). Sony/Columbia, CD, 1999.

Janis (1974). MCA, VHS, 1990.

Monterey Pop (1967). Rhino, VHS, 1997.

Pearl (1970). Sony/Columbia, CD, 1999.

Woodstock: Three Days of Peace and Music (1970). Warner Home Video, DVD/VHS, 1997.

K

KELLY, GRACE (Princess Grace, Grace Patricia Kelly)
(1929–1982)   *Actress*

Although Grace Kelly's film career lasted only five years, she remains one of the most luminous stars in Hollywood history. On November 12, 1929, she was born Grace Patricia Kelly into a wealthy Philadelphia family. Her mother was a former model, and her banker father had been a champion oarsman in the 1920 Olympics. Although shy as a girl, she made her stage debut at the age of 10.

A blue-eyed blond with aristocratic features, Kelly embarked on a successful modeling career while studying at New York's American Academy of Dramatic Arts in the late 1940s. She longed to act on the stage, a goal aided by her uncle George, a Pulitzer prize–winning playwright. Kelly first appeared on Broadway in 1949 in August Strindberg's *The Father* but, to her disappointment, had trouble landing other stage roles, perhaps because of her weak voice. She had much more success in television. In 1949 and 1950, she appeared in some 60 television programs.

In 1950 Kelly set her sights on feature films. Moving to Los Angeles, she appeared in *Fourteen Hours* (1951) before being cast in her breakthrough role as Gary Cooper's Quaker wife in the classic western *High Noon* (1952). Signed to a contract with Metro-Goldwyn-Mayer (MGM), Kelly was nominated for an Academy Award for best supporting actress for *Mogambo* (1953), in which she acted opposite Clark Gable. The following year, she won the best actress Oscar for *The Country Girl* (1954), beating out the favorite, JUDY GARLAND. In the film, she played down her stunning beauty to portray the bitter wife of an alcoholic.

More characteristic of her film roles were the three movies she subsequently made with director Alfred Hitchcock: *Dial M for Murder* (1954), *Rear Window* (1954), and *To Catch a Thief* (1955). In these films, Hitchcock made the most of her "ice queen" facade that always suggested a red-hot passion smoldering just beneath the surface. The director once characterized Kelly's unique appeal as "sexual elegance."

By 1955, Kelly was the most popular female star in American film. That spring, while attending the Cannes Film Festival in France, she met Prince Rainier III during a photo shoot for the French magazine *Paris Match*. Hailing from one of Europe's oldest royal families, Rainier ruled over Monaco, a tiny country smaller than the MGM lot in Los Angeles. The two met again months later at the house of a friend of the Kelly family. Within a week, they announced their engagement.

On April 19, 1956, Kelly married Rainier in a televised ceremony and thereafter became known to the world as Princess Grace. Her professional career effectively came to an end. Her final two films, *High Society* and *The Swan,* were both released in 1956.

As Princess Grace, Kelly devoted the rest of her life to raising her three children—Caroline, Stephanie, and Albert—and to performing charity work. She earned the affection of the people of Monaco and, through her glamour, helped revive the country's tourist industry, particularly by making its casinos a favored destination of the rich. Although she was said to be living a fairy tale, she seemed to have missed acting. It is rumored that Hitchcock offered her the lead role in *Marnie* in 1964, but she hesitantly turned it down because her husband objected. (The role then went to Tippi Hedren, who bore a superficial resemblance to Kelly.) In her final years, Kelly took an apartment in Paris and began spending less and less time at her husband's palace.

On September 12, 1982, while driving home to Monaco with her daughter Stephanie, Kelly lost control of her car, which plunged off the twisting mountain road. Stephanie was largely unhurt, but Kelly sustained substantial injuries. Two days later, she died without regaining consciousness. Doctors later determined that she had probably suffered a mild stroke just before the crash. The sudden death of Grace Kelly stunned her fans around the world, who could scarcely believe that such a seemingly charmed life could end so tragically.

Further Reading

Bradford, Sarah. *Princess Grace.* New York: Stein and Day, 1984.

Lacey, Robert. *Grace.* New York: G. P. Putnam's Sons, 1994.

Spada, James. *Grace: The Secret Life of a Princess.* Garden City, N.Y.: Doubleday, 1987.

Recommended Recorded and Videotaped Performances

The Country Girl (1955). Paramount, VHS, 1998.

High Noon (1952). Republic, DVD, 1999.

Rear Window: Collector's Edition (1954). Universal, DVD/VHS, 2001/2000.

❖ KEMBLE, FANNY (Frances Anne Kemble, Frances Anne Butler)
(1809–1893) *Actress*

While bringing a new respectability to female entertainers, the life and career of Fanny Kemble had an even more far-reaching influence over American society. At the dawn of the first women's rights movement, she showed 19th-century Americans that a woman could live a public life and earn her own keep, all the while retaining her dignity and virtue.

On November 27, 1809, Frances Anne Kemble was born into England's most famous theatrical family. Her father, Charles Kemble, was a well-known actor and the manager of London's Covent Garden Theater. Her aunt, Sarah Siddons, was the best-loved British actress of her day. Despite her distinguished lineage, young Fanny had little interest in a stage career and instead set her sights on becoming a writer.

Her wishes, however, were unimportant to Charles Kemble, when in 1829, mounting debts threatened to close his theater. To save the Covent Garden, he hatched a plan to stage a production of *Romeo and Juliet* starring members of the Kemble family. He enlisted 19-year-old Fanny to play the female lead, even though she had never acted professionally. Reluctantly, Fanny spent three weeks frantically studying the play and learning about stage acting.

On October 5, the night the production premiered, she still felt woefully unprepared. Backstage, she began to cry out of fear and nearly had to be pushed onto the stage when it was time for Juliet's first appearance. But despite Kemble's terror, she made one of the most spectacular debuts in theater history. Her natural stage presence more than made up for her lack of experience. Literally overnight, she became the most acclaimed actress in England.

Fanny Kemble as Juliet in about 1830
(Library of Congress, neg. no. USZ62-112016)

Three years later, she duplicated her triumph across the Atlantic with a spectacular tour of the United States. A new vogue in America for the works of Shakespeare helped contribute to her success. Yet more important was Fanny herself. Her audience was struck not only by her talent but also by her charm, honesty, and self-confidence. President Andrew Jackson, Daniel Boone, and Daniel Webster were all admirers. Poet Walt Whitman cited her as an early inspiration for his masterpiece *Leaves of Grass.* Perhaps most ardent were her many young female fans. Even those who never saw her perform rushed to buy small figurines of Kemble and lithographs, plates, and handkerchiefs stamped with her image. Many also fashioned their hair after hers and took up horseback riding, which the athletic Kemble recommended as exercise.

Despite her unparalleled popularity, Kemble retired from the stage after appearing in the United States for only two seasons. In 1834, she abandoned acting to marry Pierce Butler, a young man from a wealthy Philadelphia family. Kemble never warmed to the stage. She possibly saw allying herself to Butler as her best chance to give up the theater life while still securing enough funds to keep her father's theater in operation.

Whatever her motives, it was clear almost immediately that her marriage was to be a disaster. Butler was everything Kemble was not: small-minded, conventional, and mean-spirited. Soon he set about sabotaging her pet project—the publication of her journal kept during her initial trip to America. Butler first tried to censor the manuscript, and when that did not work, he offered to pay her publisher $2,500 to reject the work. Despite his efforts, *Journal of Frances Anne Butler* (1835) was published and caused a sensation. Some enjoyed her breezy narrative style, while others were insulted by some of her less-than-charitable offhand remarks about American habits and customs.

More damning than Butler's schemes to destroy her writing career was the revelation that his family's money came from a Georgia plantation operated using slave labor. In 1838, she accompanied Butler to the plantation and was appalled by what she saw. In response, she wrote a scathing account of how the Butlers' slaves were treated titled *Residence of a Georgian Plantation in 1838–1839.* This time, however, Butler succeeded, at least initially, in suppressing the book's publication. (The book finally appeared in 1863. It had a substantial influence on the British government's decision not to back the Confederacy in the Civil War.)

As their marriage deteriorated, increasingly the couple's two daughters were used as pawns in Butler's attempt to control his wife. He drove Kemble from their home and allowed her to see her children for only an hour a day. Adding to her troubles, she was destitute, as her husband, not she, was the legal owner of all income from her writings. Desperate, Kemble returned to England in 1845 to stay with relatives. In 1847, she decided to revive her stage career, but her return to the theater was not well-received. During her 13-year hiatus, she had grown too plump to play ingenues convincingly, and most likely her lack of genuine interest in the venture dampened her audience's enthusiasm as well.

In the same year, Butler sued for divorce, citing Kemble's trip to Europe as proof of desertion. In the widely reported trial, he was given custody of their daughters for 10 months of the year. Although the court awarded her an allowance from her husband, she refused to accept it. Instead, to make her livelihood, she launched an American tour during which she gave two-hour readings from Shakespeare's plays. With no theater managers to placate and no jealous actors to appease, she found these readings exciting and creatively satisfying. The public also responded favorably. Fans flocked to her recitals, which earned her a substantial income in an era when few women did paying work. Even more startling was that fact that perhaps her greatest professional success came on the heels of her well-publicized divorce at a time when the sanctity of marriage was valued above all else.

Earning her living as a writer and a reader, Kemble shuttled between the United States and England until 1879, when she settled permanently in the land of her birth. There, she made her home a salon, entertaining many of the luminaries of her time, including George Sand and Henry James. There, too, on January 15, 1893, she died peacefully at the age of 83, having lived a long life full of the freedom and passion that, from seeing her example, many American women had come to crave for themselves.

Further Reading

Blainey, Ann. *Fanny and Adelaide: The Lives of the Remarkable Kemble Sisters.* Chicago: Ivan R. Dee, 2001.

Clinton, Catherine. *Fanny Kemble's Civil Wars.* New York: Simon & Schuster, 2000.

Furnas, J. C. *Fanny Kemble: Leading Lady of the Nineteenth-Century Stage.* New York: Dial Press, 1982.

L

❖ **LEE, GYPSY ROSE (Rose Louise Hovick, Louise Hovick)**

(1914–1970)   *Stripper*

Born Rose Louise Hovick on January 9, 1914, Gypsy Rose Lee succeeded in using the striptease as a vehicle to international stardom. When Louise was four, her parents divorced, leaving her mother Rose to support Louise and her younger sister, June. Rose decided to manage her daughters in stage careers, a goal she set to with uncompromising determination. Through her relentless drive, Rose succeeded in booking their act, called "Dainty June and Her Newsboy Songsters," in vaudeville theaters throughout the country. Both daughters, however, resented Rose's domineering personality. In 1929, at 13, June finally escaped her mother's control by eloping with one of the "newsboys" hired by Rose.

Rose and Louise continued the act without June, but found few bookings as vaudeville's popularity faded. They were forced to start working far more unseemly theaters featuring burlesque shows. One night in Toledo, the headlining striptease artist landed in jail, and the 17-year-old Louise was pushed to take her spot. Perhaps out of nervousness, she removed her clothes slowly and wrapped herself in the stage curtain at the end of her act. More suggestive than most strip acts, her performance was a hit with the audience. Renaming herself Gypsy Rose Lee, she embarked on a new career as America's most famous stripper.

Appearing in the Ziegfeld Follies and other popular shows, Lee removed fewer pieces of clothing than other striptease stars. Her act, hailed by intellectuals and high society, entertained instead by gently making fun of sexual mores and inhibitions. While slowly slithering out of her dress, the statuesque Lee would talk to the crowd, making witty and sophisticated observations. As she herself said of her stage performance, "You don't have to be naked to look naked. You just have to think naked."

Under the name Louise Hovick, Lee appeared in several movies, but she had far greater success as a writer. Entirely self-educated, she wrote *The G-String Murders* in 1941, which became one of the year's best-selling novels. The following year, when Mayor Fiorello La Guardia closed New York's burlesque houses, Lee increasingly turned to writing. She wrote a second mystery novel (*Mother Finds a Body*, 1942), a comic play (*The Naked Genius*, 1943), and many articles for *Collier's, The New Yorker,* and other popular magazines.

Her greatest literary success, however, was *Gypsy: A Memoir* (1957). Rather than being a strict autobiography, the book focused on her youth in vaudeville and burlesque with the character of her mother Rose at center stage. Two years after it was published, *Gypsy* became the basis of a critically and popularly acclaimed Broadway musical starring ETHEL MERMAN as Rose. (The part was later played by ROSALIND RUSSELL in a 1961 film and by BETTE MIDLER in a 1993 television production.) Its success helped fund Lee's passion for art and antiques, which filled her lavish 26-room Manhattan townhouse.

To capitalize on *Gypsy*'s success, Lee put together *A Curious Evening with Gypsy Rose Lee,* her own one-woman show that premiered in New York City and then traveled to Los Angeles in 1961. She decided to settle permanently in Beverly Hills, where she hosted a slightly risqué television talk show. Still celebrated for her witticisms long after her stripping days were over, Lee died of lung cancer at 56 on April 26, 1970. Married and divorced three times, Lee had one child, a son named Erik; he was adopted by his father, film director Otto Preminger, after her death.

Further Reading

Archer, Stephen M. "Lee, Gypsy Rose" In *American National Biography,* edited by John Arthur Garraty and Mark C. Carnes, vol. 13, pp. 371–372. New York: Oxford University Press, 1999.

Lee, Gypsy Rose. *Gypsy: A Memoir.* 1957. Reprint, Berkeley, Calif.: Frog, Ltd., 1990.

Recommended Recorded and Videotaped Performances

Gypsy (1962). Warner Home Video, DVD/VHS, 2000.
Gypsy (1993). Pioneer Video, DVD/VHS, 2000/1999.

❖ LEGINSKA, ETHEL (Ethel Liggins)
(1886–1970)   *Musician, Composer*

Concert pianist Ethel Leginska helped open doors for women seeking careers as orchestra musicians. She was born Ethel Liggins in Yorkshire, England, on April 13, 1886. Ethel soon emerged as a musical prodigy and performed her first concert when she was only seven. Winning the support of a wealthy patron, she began studying piano in Frankfurt, Vienna, and Berlin in 1900.

By 1906 Liggins was performing recitals throughout Europe as Ethel Leginska. She perhaps took the new surname because she believed its Polish sound would give her more legitimacy as a musician. The next year she married Roy Emerson Whittern, an American music student. The couple had one son, Cedric, before divorcing in 1918.

Leginska made her American debut in New York in 1913. She was immediately a popular and critic success. Impressing her audiences by her demanding repertoire, Leginska was dubbed the "Paderewski of women pianists," a nickname that compared her to one of Poland's most famed musicians.

Leginska also became known for her opposition to the handicaps female musicians and other professional women faced. Angry over her own unsuccessful custody fight for her son, she spoke out against the lack of child care options as well as the inadequate educational opportunities for women. In concert, she eschewed ball gowns for practical, comfortable clothing, making it clear to her audiences that she regarded herself not as an ornament, but as an artist.

Although Leginska was more than willing to challenge society's prejudice against female concert performers, she was unable to conquer her own personal obstacles. After suffering three nervous breakdowns, she abandoned the concert stage in 1926. Leginska instead began to concentrate on her work as a composer and conductor. Since the early 1920s, she had tried to carve out her conducting career, a field previously closed to women. Drawing on her contacts in the music world, she secured engagements as a guest conductor of many of Europe's finest orchestras by promising to play a concerto as part of the program.

In 1925, she returned to the United States to conduct the New York Symphony Orchestra, following with successful engagements in Boston and Los Angeles. The novelty of a female conductor first drew in audiences, though soon Leginska's obvious talents were earning her universal acclaim.

The ambitious Leginska also devoted herself to establishing the Boston Philharmonic Orchestra (1926–27) and the Boston English Opera Company (1927–1929). In addition to directing the Chicago Women's Symphony Orchestra, she also founded the National Women's Symphony Orchestra in New York in 1931.

By the late 1930s, Leginska increasingly turned to teaching. In 1940, she settled in Los Angeles where she established a studio and gave lessons for more than a decade. She frequently staged concerts featuring her students as soloists and herself as conductor. In 1957 Leginska also conducted a Los Angeles orchestra in performing *The Rose and the Ring,* an opera she had composed in 1932. Having become the first woman to have a distinguished career as a pianist, conductor, and composer, Ethel Leginska died on February 26, 1970, at the age of 83.

Further Reading

Conlon, Paula. "Ethel Leginska." In *American National Biography,* edited by John Arthur Garraty and Mark C. Carnes, vol. 13, pp. 432–433. New York: Oxford University Press, 1999.

Neuls-Bates, Carol. "Leginska, Ethel," In *The New Grove Dictionary of American Music.* Edited by H. Wiley Hitchcock and Stanley Sadie. New York: Grove's Dictionaries of Music, 1986.

Recommended Recorded and Videotaped Performances

Columbia Masters. Ivory Classics, CD, 2001.

The Pupils of Leschetizky: A Gallery of Great Pianists. Pearl Opal, CD, 1992.

❖ LEIGH, VIVIEN (Vivian Mary Hartley)
(1913–1967) *Actress*

Although renowned for her interpretation of classic stage roles, Vivien Leigh will always be best remembered for two of her film roles—the Civil War–era belle Scarlett O'Hara and the fading southern beauty Blanche DuBois.

On November 5, 1913, Leigh was born Vivian Mary Hartley in Darjeeling, India, where her affluent father worked in a brokerage firm. When Vivian was seven, her family returned to England, and she was enrolled in convent school. The next year, her role as a fairy in a production of *A Midsummer Night's Dream* convinced her that she wanted to become an actress. As a teenager, Vivian continued her education in finishing schools throughout Europe. Sophisticated and cultured, she emerged also as a great beauty before enrolling in London's distinguished Royal Academy of Dramatic Art in 1931.

Her career was put on hold in December 1932 after she married Herbert Leigh Holman, a prominent lawyer. The following October, Leigh had her only child, Suzanne. In 1934, she returned to acting, taking the stage name Vivien Leigh. She made her film debut with a one-line role in *Things Are Looking Up* (1934). The next year, Leigh began appearing in small parts onstage. She had her first starring role in *The Mask of Virtue.* The play was a failure, but it made her a star overnight. Film producer Alexander Korda signed the ingenue for a five-year contract.

Korda cast her in *Fire over England* (1937). During the filming, she met costar Laurence Olivier, beginning one of film history's most sensational romances. Their affair was well publicized, as both began seeking a divorce. In 1938, Leigh followed her lover to Los Angeles, where he was to star in a film adaptation of *Wuthering Heights* (1939).

While in Hollywood, Olivier arranged for Leigh to visit the set of *Gone With the Wind* (1939). Based on Margaret Mitchell's best-selling novel, the historical spectacle had begun filming, even though the lead role—the conniving and beguiling Scarlett O'Hara—had yet to be cast. Producer David O. Selznick had launched a two-year, $100,000 search to find the perfect actress. He considered more than 2,000 candidates, including nearly every prominent actress in the United States.

On the set, Selznick was introduced to Leigh by his brother Myron, who, Hollywood legend has it, pushed her forward, announcing, "I want you to meet Scarlett O'Hara." After a screen test, Selznick agreed that Leigh was the best choice for the role. Both steely and vulnerable, Leigh's Scarlett was hailed by moviegoers and critics. Few were surprised when her first American film role won her an Oscar for best Actress.

Their divorces granted, Leigh and Olivier married in 1940. Considered the most glamorous couple on both sides of the Atlantic, they appropriately appeared on Broadway playing Romeo and Juliet. With the escalation of World War II, they returned to England, where Olivier joined the Royal Army. During the war years, they made one movie together—*That Hamilton Woman* (1941), about the ill-fated romance between Lord Admiral Nelson and Lady Emma Hamilton. British prime minister Winston Churchill claimed it was his favorite film.

Following the war, Leigh returned to the stage, appearing in many classic roles with the prestigious Old Vic repertory company. She also resumed her movie career, though films such as *Caesar and Cleopatra* (1946) and *Anna Karenina* (1948) drew a far smaller audience than *Gone With the Wind* had. She had greater success with *A Streetcar Named Desire* (1951), in which she starred opposite Broadway sensation Marlon Brando. Her sensitive portrayal of the fragile Blanche DuBois won her a second Academy Award.

Through the early 1950s, Leigh devoted herself to stage work, often appearing with her husband. In 1957, the English government awarded her the knight's cross of the Legion of Honour for her work. While her professional career remained strong, her personal life began to crumble. Her health began to fail due to tuberculosis, which she had contracted in 1945. Even more devastating, Leigh was suffering from mental illness, often nearing a complete nervous collapse. Her instability was a contributing factor to her divorce from Olivier in 1960.

Even without Olivier, Leigh continued to be a star of the stage. In 1963, she had an unexpected success in the musical comedy *Tovarich,* for which she won a Tony Award. She also appeared in two high-profile films—*The Roman Spring of Mrs. Stone* (1961) and *Ship of Fools* (1965)—in which she played desperate older women. While in rehearsal for a London stage production of Edward Albee's *A Delicate Balance,* Vivien Leigh died suddenly from tuberculosis on July 8, 1967. That night, the theaters of London's West End district turned off their lights for an hour to honor her distinguished career.

Further Reading

Edwards, Anne. *Vivien Leigh: A Biography.* New York, Simon & Schuster, 1977.

Molt, Cynthia Marylee. *Vivien Leigh: A Bio-Bibliography.* Westport, Conn.: Greenwood Press, 1992.

Walker, Alexander. *Vivien: The Life of Vivien Leigh.* New York: Weidenfeld & Nicolson, 1987.

Recommended Recorded and Videotaped Performances

Gone With the Wind (1939). Warner Home Video, DVD/VHS, 2000/2001.

The Roman Spring of Mrs. Stone (1961). Warner Home Video, VHS, 1995.

A Streetcar Named Desire (1951). Warner Home Video, DVD/VHS, 1997/1996.

❖ **LEITZEL, LILLIAN (Lillian Alize Elianore)**
(ca. 1891–1931)   *Circus Performer*

The most renowned female performer of the American circus, Lillian Leitzel was born Lillian Alize Elianore in Breslau, Germany, in about 1891. Her mother, a well-known circus aerialist who was often on tour, left Lillian to be raised by her grandparents. They saw that she received a solid education that included instruction in five languages and rigorous training in music and dance. Although Lillian was being groomed for a career as a concert musician, she became more interested in learning her mother's acrobatic tricks.

When she was about nine, Lillian joined her mother and two aunts in a circus act called

Lillian Leitzel in 1931
(Library of Congress, neg. no. USZ62-122867)

"Leamy's Ladies" after their manager. The act made its way to the United States in about 1910. Lillian's relatives soon returned to Europe, but she decided to stay and seek her fortune as a solo performer in vaudeville. Under the stage name Lillian Leitzel, she toured with various shows before being discovered by an agent of Ringling Brothers, one of the best American circuses. She became famous soon after her debut in 1915. By 1919, when Ringling Brothers merged with its rival, Barnum and Bailey, Leitzel was the undisputed queen of the circus.

Her act generally had two parts. In the first, she performed acrobatic moves on gymnasts' rings suspended 50 feet in the air. In the second, she twirled her body around rope hanging from the center of the circus big top. She usually made as many as 100 revolutions, which the audience helped the announcer count out loud.

By circus standards, the routine was not particularly difficult or dangerous. What made it a crowd-pleaser was Leitzel's sense of the dramatic. She demanded that she always appear in the center ring and was often escorted on stage by a large man to emphasize her own tiny 4'9" frame. And as Leitzel descended the rope at her act's end, she frequently fell into a feigned swoon, often into the arms of a male circus performer.

Her offstage antics were flamboyant as well. Ever the prima donna, she insisted on being the only performer with a private tent for a dressing room and with a private car on the circus train. They were often filled with flowers and expensive gifts from the many suitors who vied for her attention. Leitzel had three marriages, the last in 1928 to a fellow star, trapeze artist Alfredo Codona.

While Leitzel was performing in Copenhagen, the rope holding one of her gymnast rings snapped, plunging her 29 feet to the ground. Two days later, on February 15, 1931, she died of her injuries. Remembered both as a graceful athlete and a larger-than-life personality, she was among the greatest performers to appear in the "Greatest Show on Earth."

Further Reading

Albrecht, Ernest. "Leitzel, Lillian." In *American National Biography,* edited by John Arthur Garraty and Mark C. Carnes, vol. 13, pp. 459–460. New York: Oxford University Press, 1999.

Taylor, Robert Louis. *Center Ring: The People of the Circus.* Garden City, N.Y.: Doubleday, 1956.

❖ **LOMBARD, CAROLE (Jane Alice Peters)**
(1908–1942)   *Actress*

A master of the screwball comedy, Carole Lombard was born Jane Alice Peters on October 6, 1908. Her prosperous family lived in Fort Wayne, Indiana, until 1914, when her parents separated. Jane's mother then moved with her and her two older brothers to Los Angeles.

Always a tomboy, Jane at 12 was spotted playing baseball on the street by director Allan Dwan. He subsequently cast the girl in her first film, *A Perfect Crime* (1921). Though Jane was eager to become a professional actress, her career did not take off until another chance meeting occurred four years later. Now a slender beauty, Jane caught the attention of a Fox studio executive while dancing at a Hollywood nightclub. When the studio signed her to a contract, she opted to change her name to Carole Lombard, taking the surname of a family friend.

After several screen appearances, Lombard was in a car accident that plunged a shard of glass in her cheek. She underwent several plastic surgeries, but was still left with a small, yet noticeable scar. Determined, nevertheless, to continue her career, she gave herself a thorough education on movie lighting and camera angles to ensure that she would be photographed flawlessly.

After making several comedies for producer-director Mack Sennett, Lombard signed a contract with Paramount in 1930. There, she made two films with William Powell, whom she married in 1931. Although the couple divorced two years later, they remained friends.

In 1934, Lombard appeared in *Twentieth Century,* the film that made her a star. Playing a former shopgirl turned movie star, she keenly displayed her precise comic timing and unparalleled talent for combining glamour and pratfalls. She owed her next great film role to her ex-husband, who recommended her for the female lead in *My Man Godfrey* (1936). The pinnacle of both Lombard's and Powell's careers, the film is perhaps the greatest example of a screwball comedy, a genre in which Lombard excelled. Popular throughout the 1930s, screwball comedies combined physical humor with fast-paced, sophisticated dialogue and often lampooned the manners of the rich. Among Lombard's other noteworthy contributions to the genre were William Wellman's *Nothing Sacred* (1937) and Alfred Hitchcock's *Mr. and Mrs. Smith* (1941).

At the height of her success, Lombard in 1939 married actor Clark Gable during a break in the filming of *Gone With the Wind.* The couple had one of the most publicized romances in movie history. Though they had acted together in *No Man of Her Own* in 1932, Lombard and Gable did not fall in love until 1936, when they met again at a party. Widely considered a "man's man," Gable was attracted to Lombard's rare combination of earthiness and elegance, characteristics that also endeared her to both the actors and crew members she worked with. After her marriage, Lombard cut back on her work schedule in order to spend more time with her husband. They moved to a ranch in Encino, California, where Lombard eagerly took up Gable's favorite pastimes, including hunting and fishing.

Soon after the United States entered World War II, Lombard finished work on *To Be or Not to Be* (1942), Ernst Lubitsch's black comedy that pitted a Polish acting troupe against the Nazis. Lombard demonstrated her own commitment to an Allied victory by embarking on a tour to sell war bonds. After an appearance in Indianapolis, she boarded a plane headed home. On January 16, 1942, as the plane approached Las Vegas, it crashed into a mountain, killing everyone on board instantly. Her sudden death stunned Hollywood and devastated her grieving husband. Although Gable remarried twice, he was buried next to Lombard following his own death in 1960.

Further Reading

Maltin, Leonard. *Carole Lombard.* New York: Pyramid, 1976.

Matzen, Robert D. *Carole Lombard: A Bio-Bibliography.* New York: Greenwood Press, 1988.

Swindell, Larry. *Screwball: The Life of Carole Lombard.* New York: William Morrow, 1975.

Recommended Recorded and Videotaped Performances

My Man Godfrey (1936). Madacy Entertainment, DVD, 1998.

To Be or Not To Be (1942). Warner Home Video, VHS, 1996.

Twentieth Century (1934). Columbia/Tristar, VHS, 1991.

❖ LUPINO, IDA
(1918–1995) *Actress, Director*

A leading actress in American film noir, Ida Lupino today is best remembered as one of the few female movie directors of the 1940s and 1950s. She was born on February 4, 1918, in London, England, into a family whose show-business roots could be traced to the Renaissance. According to Hollywood legend, Lupino secured her first film role when she accompanied her mother, musical comedy actress Connie Emerald, to an audition. Ida was cast in the movie, while her mother walked away empty-handed.

While still in her teens, Lupino signed a contract with Paramount. Following a string of ingenue roles, she found her greatest screen roles in the early 1940s, playing determined, often desperate women in popular melodramas, most notably *They Drive By Night* (1940) and *High Sierra* (1941). As her star was rising, she married actor Louis Hayward in 1938. The couple divorced seven years later.

Though Lupino was enjoying a successful acting career, by the mid-1940s she was looking to work behind the camera. In a 1945 interview, she stated, "I see myself developing new talent. . . . I am genuinely more interested in the talent of others than I am in my own." With this in mind, she founded Emerald Productions (later named Film-

makers) with her second husband, Collier Young, whom she married in 1948. On the production company's first effort, *Not Wanted* (1949), Lupino was credited as producer and coscreenwriter. She had also, however, taken over the director's chair, after the credited director, Elmer Clifton, had a heart attack.

Filmmakers Productions made seven more features, which Lupino and Young cowrote and coproduced. Six were also directed by Lupino. Lupino's films, made on tight budgets with no stars, were distinguished by the tough social issues they addressed, including single motherhood, female sexuality, and bigamy. Unlike most Hollywood fare, they not only presented modern problems but also offered no easy answers to how they might be solved. Although none of Lupino's features were highly profitable, she did produce two films now considered classics of film noir— *The Bigamist* (1953) and *The Hitch-Hiker* (1953).

After a misguided attempt to become a film distribution company, Filmmakers was dissolved in 1954. Lupino subsequently directed only one other film, *The Trouble with Angels* (1966). During the 1960s, however, she found a new career in directing episodes of television series. With a reputation for working quickly, Lupino directed more than 100 programs, including episodes of *The Donna Reed Show, Gilligan's Island,* and *Alfred Hitchcock Presents.* Somewhat to her dismay, Lupino was eventually typed as an action director and was most often sought after to work on westerns, such as *Have Gun, Will Travel* and *Gunsmoke.*

Lupino also appeared on television as an actress. Her most notable role was as the costar of the short-lived series *Mr. Adams and Eve* (1957–58), which was also starred Howard Duff, whom she married after divorcing Young in 1950. (Lupino and Duff had one daughter but were also divorced in 1984.) From time to time, Lupino guest-starred on series as well, including her final acting performance on an episode of *Charlie's Angels* in the mid-1970s.

Ida Lupino with Humphrey Bogart in *High Sierra* (1944)
(Museum of Modern Art Film Stills Archive)

In her final years, she lived to see her directorial career reexamined by film scholars in the 1970s and 1980s. Although she resisted being seen as a feminist director, she enjoyed that, fitting with her own preferences, her directing came to overshadow her more publicized success as an actress. Lupino died on August 3, 1995, in Burbank, California.

Further Reading

Donati, William. *Ida Lupino: A Biography.* Lexington: University Press of Kentucky, 1996.

Kuhn, Annette, ed. *Queen of the 'B's: Ida Lupino: Behind the Camera.* Westport, Conn.: Greenwood Press, 1995.

Recommended Recorded and Videotaped Performances

They Drive by Night (1940). Warner Home Video, VHS, 2000. (V).

The Hitch-hiker (1952). Kino Video, DVD/VHS, 2000/1997.

Biography: Ida Lupino. A&E Entertainment, VHS, 1998.

❖ **LYNN, LORETTA (Loretta Webb)**
(1935–) *Singer, Songwriter*

Loretta Lynn's warmth and honesty helped make her a top country music star of the 1960s and 1970s. She was born Loretta Webb on April 15,

1935, in Butcher Hollow, Kentucky. Loretta was raised in poverty, the second of eight children living in a small cabin without running water or electricity. A bright spot of her youth was listening to the Grand Ole Opry, the Saturday night radio show featuring the best acts in country and western music.

In 1949, 14-year-old Loretta met Oliver Vanetta Lynn, who was also known by the nicknames "Doolittle" and "Mooney" (the latter a reference to his affection for moonshine whiskey). After a month-long courtship, the two were married. Mooney took Loretta to live in Custer, Washington, where he worked in the timber industry. By the time she was 18, she had four children to care for.

Encouraging Loretta's love of singing, Mooney bought her a 20-dollar guitar, which she taught herself to play by listening to records by country legend Kitty Wells. Mooney soon was pressuring her to play and sing in public. Though initially Loretta was too shy to enjoy performing, slowly she began to warm to playing in clubs and on a local television show hosted by singer Buck Owens.

In 1959, Loretta Lynn inspired a wealthy fan to establish Zero Records, solely to market her music. To sell her first record, "Now I'm a Honky Tonk Girl," she and Mooney took to the road. In their 1955 Ford, they covered some 80,000 miles, traveling from radio station to radio station to promote "Honky Tonk Girl" to disc jockeys. Amazingly, their grassroots efforts moved the single up the country charts, where it peaked at number 10.

The Lynns moved to Nashville, and Loretta secured a record deal with Decca in 1962. The next year, she was made a member of the Grand Ole Opry. Singing regularly in clubs and at fairs, she often opened for PATSY CLINE, who took the young singer under her wing. After Cline's death in a plane crash in 1963, Lynn effectively took over her spot as the leading female country singer.

Like other female stars of the genre, Lynn primarily sang about the troubles of rural women in traditional marriages. Unlike them, however, her songs were often rally cries for assertiveness, many of which she wrote herself, drawing on her own experiences. Among her hits that had special meaning for her female fans were "Don't come Home A-Drinkin' with Lovin' on Your Mind," "One's on the Way," "Fist City," and "You Ain't Woman Enough (To Take My Man)." Particularly notorious was Lynn's song "The Pill" (1975), a celebration of the personal freedom birth control gave to women. Released at the height of the women's movement, the record was deemed so controversial that many radio stations refused to play it.

After a string of hits, including a series of popular duets with Conway Twitty, Loretta Lynn emerged as crossover phenomenon by the mid-1970s. Although her sound remained faithful to traditional country, she appealed to a mainstream audience, in large part because of the homespun wit she displayed in her concerts and in television appearances. The public's fascination with Lynn as a personality peaked in 1976 with the publication of her best-selling autobiography *Coal Miner's Daughter*. Her engaging rags-to-riches story became a successful film in 1980.

Her popularity took its toll on her health, however. Exhausted by constant touring, Lynn collapsed onstage several times and suffered from migraines and ulcers. In the 1980s, she began to slow her pace; at the same time country music began to embrace a pop sound. One example of the new style of country was the music of Lynn's younger sister, Crystal Gayle, who had become one of the genre's brightest stars. As the music scene changed, Lynn began to restrict her public appearances, especially after the drowning death of her son Jack Benny in 1984.

In 1993 Lynn teamed up with two other country legends—TAMMY WYNETTE and DOLLY PARTON—to record the album *Honky Tonk Angels*. During the rest of the decade, however, little was heard from Lynn. She retreated to her mansion outside of Nashville to care for Mooney, who was ill from diabetes. Over six years, he lost his eyesight, his hearing, and both of his legs before dying from the disease in 1996.

Four years later, Lynn made her long-awaited return to studio recording with *Still Country,* her first album of new songs since 1988. She also wrote a second autobiography, *Still Woman Enough* (2001). While promoting her comeback projects, Lynn acknowledged that, during her absence from the music business, country had become more slick and pop-infused than ever before. But with characteristic confidence, she refused to recast herself to suit popular tastes. "I never left country music, everyone else did," Lynn claimed in a 2000 interview. "It's made me a good livin'. Why should I go in another direction?"

Further Reading

Lynn, Loretta, with George Vecsey. *Coal Miner's Daughter.* Reprint. New York: Da Capo Press, 1996.

Recommended Recorded and Videotaped Performances

Biography: Loretta Lynn. A&E Home Video, VHS, 1996.
Coal Miner's Daughter (1980). Universal, VHS, 2000.
Honky Tonk Girl: The Loretta Lynn Collection. MCA, CD, 1994.
Loretta Lynn: In Concert. Mercury Nashville, VHS, 1992.

M

❖ MABLEY, MOMS (Loretta Mary Aiken, Jackie Mabley)
(ca. 1894–1975)   *Comic, Actress*

Called the "funniest woman in the world," Moms Mabley was the first African-American comedian to find a wide audience. She was born Loretta Mary Aiken in Brevard, North Carolina, in either 1894 or 1897. Few details are known about her early life. Raised among 12 siblings, she apparently had two children, both the products of rapes, as a young teenager. The children were put up for adoption, and on the advice of her grandmother, Aiken left home to find her fortune.

Living first in Cleveland, she made friends with some performers, who, because of her beauty, suggested she go into show business. By 1908, Aiken was singing, dancing, and appearing in comic skits in a minstrel show in Pittsburgh. For the next decade, she found work in many African-American theatrical revues, one of which briefly made it to Broadway. During these years, she became friendly with fellow entertainer Jack Mabley. Although they never married, she took his name and began billing herself as Jackie Mabley.

By the early 1920s, Mabley was a regular on the "chitlin' circuit," the network of black-owned southern clubs and theaters. There she developed her most famous character—an elderly woman wearing baggy clothes and a toothless grin with an insatiable taste for younger men. In one of her most quotable lines, her comic persona insisted, "There ain't nothing an old man can do for me but bring me a message from a young one." Offstage, far from her shabby character, Mabley was an elegant young woman with a love of furs and fashionable clothes.

To further her career, Mabley came to New York City in the mid-1920s. Soon she was a headliner, playing the Savoy Ballroom and Cotton Club with musical stars such as BESSIE SMITH, Louis Armstrong, and Cab Calloway, with whom she was romantically involved. She also began playing small parts in films, most notably a role as a madam in *The Emperor Jones* (1933), starring Paul Robeson. Mabley made frequent appearances on Broadway as well, including a performance in *Fast and Furious* (1931), which also featured writer Zora Neale Hurston.

In 1939 Mabley made history by becoming the first comedienne to play the famed Apollo Theater in Harlem. Before large crowds, she honed her routine, perfecting her comic timing and improving her gift for ad-libbing. Mabley often complained that white male comedians came to her

Moms Mabley in 1962
(Library of Congress, neg. no. USZ62-117535)

shows, notebooks in hand, ready to steal her best material. Among her fellow performers, though, she gained a reputation for generosity and compassion, traits that earned her the nickname "Moms."

In her standup comedy, Mabley often dealt with racial divisions head on, pioneering the social commentary that would later become a staple of black comedians. She was also known for her off-color language and risqué humor. In part because of her "blue" humor, Mabley found it more difficult to find a mainstream audience than many other African-American performers.

It was not until her recording career began that Mabley gained widespread recognition outside of black nightspots. In 1960 Chess Records released *Moms Mabley: Funniest Woman in the World,* which recorded a live performance Mabley gave in Chicago. A surprise hit, the album sold more than 1 million copies. Mabley went on to perform on 25 more comedy records.

In the late 1960s, Mabley found a still greater audience on television. She made her television debut in 1967 on *A Time for Laughter,* a special produced by Harry Belafonte featuring an all-black cast. Mabley soon became a regular guest on variety and talk shows, such as *The Smothers Brothers Show* and *The Mike Douglas Show.*

An overnight television star after 50 years in show business, Mabley was offered her first starring film role in *Amazing Grace* (1974), the story of an elderly busybody who tries to reform a corrupt city government. While filming the comedy, she suffered a heart attack but recovered. Soon after the movie's release, however, she fell ill and died on May 23, 1975. Her groundbreaking career has since been the subject of several off-Broadway plays, including Alice Childress's *Moms: A Praise for a Black Comedienne* (1987).

Further Reading

Watkins, Mel. *On the Real Side.* New York: Simon & Schuster, 1994.
Williams, Elsie A. *The Humor of Jackie "Moms" Mabley: An African American Comedic Tradition.* New York: Garland Publishing, 1995.

Recommended Recorded and Videotaped Performances

On Stage: Funniest Woman in the World. MCA, CD, 1990.

❖ MacDONALD, JEANETTE (Jeannette Anna McDonald)
(1903–1965)   *Actress, Singer*

Known as the "Lingerie Queen of the Talkies" and as one half of "America's Singing Sweethearts," Jeanette MacDonald found fame onscreen both as a sophisticated comedian and a wholesome romantic lead. Born Jeanette Anna McDonald on June 18, 1903, in West Philadelphia, she was the youngest of three girls. All were starstruck at an early age. Under the tutelage of one of her sisters, Jeannette began singing at local churches and lodges at age four.

In 1919, she left high school to perform in the stage show *Demi Tasse Revue* in New York City. Now spelling her name Jeanette MacDonald, she began appearing regularly in Broadway choruses, slowly moving up the ranks to featured roles in musicals. Her stage work drew the attention of Paramount Studios, which asked her to do a screen test.

While casting his first talkie, German-born director Ernst Lubitsch saw MacDonald's test and recognized a kindred soul. He offered her the lead opposite French actor Maurice Chevalier in *The Love Parade* (1929), a comic operetta. The film led to a series of romantic farces reteaming MacDonald with Lubitsch. Remarkably in sync with her director's style of subtle, sly wit, she consistently displayed a fresh combination of innocence and erotic readiness. MacDonald turned in one of her best performances in Lubitsch's ambitious *Merry Widow* (1934), but the film was a box-office failure and spelled the end of this phase of her career.

MacDonald found far greater success in a pair of concert tours she made through Europe in the early 1930s. Although popular in the United States, she was a sensation across the Atlantic. The French were especially enthusiastic fans, in part because through Berlitz courses she had learned to sing and speak in fluent French. When she first arrived in France, she was greeted by crowds whose size were said to rival those that met aviator Charles Lindbergh in 1927.

On returning to the United States, MacDonald was signed to a contract by Metro-Goldwyn-Mayer (MGM). Studio head Louis B. Mayer set about cleaning up her somewhat risqué image by teaming her with Nelson Eddy in *Naughty Marietta* (1935). With the film's enormous success, MacDonald and Eddy became the most popular screen duo of the depression era. Their films together were lavish productions intended as family fare, with the actors expressing their romantic feelings toward each other through song. Their most famous duet, "Indian Love Song" in *Rose Marie* (1936), was well-loved in their day but has since been frequently parodied for its saccharine sweetness.

Jeanette MacDonald in *Naughty Marietta* (1935)
(Museum of Modern Art Film Stills Archive)

By 1939, MacDonald was the highest-paid actress in Hollywood. The MacDonald-Eddy musicals, however, had nearly run their course. Happily married to actor Gene Raymond (whom she had wed in 1937), MacDonald responded by setting off on a series of concerts. Always longing to be accepted as an opera singer, MacDonald experienced one of her greatest personal triumphs in 1944 when she made her debut with the Chicago Opera Company. Even in the face of the public's rapidly changing musical tastes, she continued to tour well into the 1950s. With her devoted husband by her side, Jeanette MacDonald died on January 14, 1965, at the age of 61.

Further Reading

Knowles, Eleanor. *The Films of Jeanette MacDonald and Nelson Eddy.* South Brunswick, N.J.: A. S. Barnes, 1975.

Parish, James Robert. *The Jeanette MacDonald Story.* New York: Mason/Charter, 1976.

Turk, Edward Baron. *Hollywood Diva: A Biography of Jeanette MacDonald.* Berkeley: University of California Press, 1998.

Recommended Recorded and Videotaped Performances

Merry Widow (1934). Warner Home Video, VHS, 1989.

Naughty Marietta (1935). Warner Home Video, VHS, 1992.

Rose Marie (1936). Warner Home Video, VHS, 1992.

❖ MADONNA (Madonna Louise Ciccone)
(1958–) *Singer, Actress, Dancer, Songwriter*

A pop icon on the level of Elvis Presley and MARILYN MONROE, Madonna was arguably the most influential female performer of the late 20th century. Born Madonna Louise Ciccone on August 16, 1958, she was the third of six children in a Roman Catholic family living in Pontiac, Michigan. When Madonna was six, her mother also named Madonna, died of cancer. As the eldest daughter in the Ciccone household, she was largely responsible for taking care of the home and her younger siblings, even after her father remarried. Hemmed in by her religion and her father's discipline, she later recalled that she "grew up feeling repressed. I was really a good girl." An honor student and cheerleader, Madonna also studied ballet with instructor Christopher Flynn. He provided Madonna with welcome relief from her oppressive home life by taking her to dance clubs in downtown Detroit.

Madonna won a dance scholarship to the University of Michigan. She soon dropped out, however, to seek her fortune in New York. Madonna arrived in the city the summer of 1978 with $37 in her pocket. To earn her rent, she worked as an artists' and photographers' model, while performing in the third company of the Alvin Ailey American Dance Theater.

In the thick of New York's underground culture, Madonna soon gravitated toward the music scene. With the encouragement of her live-in boyfriend, musician Dan Gilroy, she began learning to play the drums and the guitar and experimenting with writing songs. She also sang with various bands, having a brief stint in Paris as a singer in a French disco group. Back in New York, her singing caught the attention of Mark Kamis, a disc jockey at Danceteria, then one of the city's leading clubs. With Kamis's help, Madonna cut a demo recording of the song "Everybody," which landed her a contract with Warner Brothers.

Her first album, *Madonna* (1983), initially sold badly. Sales took off only after three of its tracks—"Holiday," "Lucky Star," and "Borderline"—became dance club favorites. Adding to the appeal of her disco-influenced pop sound was her fashion sense. In music videos played on the then-fledgling cable station MTV, Madonna presented herself as streetwise urchin. Badly dyed, teased hair, lace gloves, underwear worn as outerwear, and crucifixes were all hallmarks of her early style.

With the success of her first album, Madonna was able to insist on having the best producers and musicians work on her next, *Like a Virgin* (1984). The album and two singles from it—the title track and "Material Girl"—charted at number one. Again Madonna successfully used MTV to market her music. As in the video for "Like a Virgin," she wore a white wedding dress to perform the song on the MTV Video Music Awards. Writhing on stage as if in sexual ecstasy, Madonna's performance was considered shocking at the time. In her music video for "Material Girl," Madonna was made up as MARILYN MONROE in a clever send-up of the film *Gentlemen Prefer Blondes* (1953). Giving up her usual dance club look for a glamorous red ball gown, Madonna went through the first of the many physical transformations that define her career.

In 1985 Madonna made her first foray into film with a small part in *Vision Quest.* She became a full-fledged movie star with *Desperately Seeking Susan* (1985), playing a fashionable free spirit, a character who closely resembled herself. The same year, she made her stage debut in David Rabe's *Goose and Tom-Tom,* opposite Sean

Penn. Madonna and Penn were married for four tumultuous years before divorcing in 1989.

Madonna continued her recording career with two more hit albums, *True Blue* (1986) and *Like a Prayer* (1989). Turning to slightly more serious material, she provoked national controversies with several songs. "Papa Don't Preach," from *True Blue*, confounded Madonna's conservative critics by telling the story of a pregnant teen who opts for motherhood instead of abortion. The title track on *Like a Prayer* angered the Catholic Church because of the video's provocative images, which included Madonna kissing an African-American Christ and dancing in a field ablaze with burning crosses. Because of the uproar over the video, Pepsico pulled its sponsorship of Madonna's upcoming tour, though the singer was able to keep her $5 million fee.

In the late 1980s, Madonna repeatedly struck out at the box office. Her films *Shanghai Surprise* (1969), *Who's That Girl* (1987), and *Bloodhounds of Broadway* (1989) were all commercial flops. She had better luck playing the small part of Breathless Mahoney in *Dick Tracy* (1990), starring Warren Beatty, with whom she had a well-publicized romance. Tying into the film, she released the album *Breathless,* featuring the single "Vogue." Revered in the gay community, Madonna introduced mainstream America to "voguing," a dance involving posing like a fashion model that was popular in gay clubs in the mid-1980s.

Also in 1990, Madonna released *The Immaculate Collection,* a greatest hits album. It featured several new songs, including "Justify My Love." Because of its suggestions of voyeurism, bisexuality, and group sex, its video was banned from play on MTV before 11 o'clock at night. The resulting publicity helped sell some 250,000 copies of the "Justify My Love" videotape and propelled *The Immaculate Collection* to number one. Madonna also delighted her fans with *Truth or Dare* (1991), a documentary film she commissioned about her "Blond Ambition" world tour. Presenting Madonna as every inch a star, the film contained Beatty's memorable assessment of the melding of her life and art: "She doesn't want to live off camera."

In 1992, Madonna signed a seven-year, $60 million contract with Time Warner that gave her nearly total creative control over her recordings and films. It also gave her her own record label, Maverick. Unlike most vanity labels fronted by stars, it would become highly profitable, signing such artists as Alanis Morissette, Candlebox, and Me'Shell Ndegéocello.

In the wake of her Time Warner deal, Madonna's *Sex* (1992) was released. The $50 coffee table book contained photographs of a mostly nude Madonna acting out her sexual fantasies. Though condemned as an attention-getting stunt by her critics, the book's first run sold out quickly. Her album *Erotica* (1992), however, was a disappointment, suggesting to some in the music industry that Madonna's popularity was fading. Her movie career provided further evidence. Though she appeared in a small role in the successful *A League of Their Own* (1992), her star vehicle *Body of Evidence* (1993) was a disaster.

Perhaps sensing that she had gone too far, Madonna displayed a softer, more soulful sound on the album *Bedtime Stories* (1994). A year later, she released *Something to Remember,* a collection of her hit ballads. Hoping to finally establish herself as a movie draw, she also lobbied hard for the role of Eva Perón in the musical *Evita*. Although the movie received a lukewarm response from critics and audiences, it helped to establish Madonna as a credible actress.

During the filming, Madonna became pregnant by her boyfriend and personal trainer, Carlos Leon. On October 14, 1996, she gave birth to Lourdes Maria Ciccone Leon and later described the experience to *People* magazine as "the greatest miracle of my life." In addition to motherhood, Madonna publicly embraced the Jewish kabbalah and Far Eastern religions and culture. She showcased her new spiritual side on *Ray of Light* (1998), which many critics consider her best album.

Madonna had another success with her next album, *Music* (2000), which marked a return to the playful dance songs that had made her a star. A month before its release, she had her second child,

Rocco. Madonna married Rocco's father, British film director Guy Ritchie, in December 2000. The following year, her Drowned World tour—the first tour since 1993—sold out across Europe and the United States.

In an MTV interview, Madonna once said, "The whole reason I got into show business wasn't because I thought I had a spectacular voice. It was because I thought I had something to say." Since her early days as a performer, the public has been listening. A worldwide sensation for more than two decades, Madonna now has generations of fans who consider her the last word on what's next in popular culture.

Further Reading

Benson, Carol, and Allan Metz, eds. *The Madonna Companion: Two Decades of Commentary.* New York: Schirmer Books, 1999.

Bego, Mark. *Madonna: Blonde Ambition.* Updated edition. New York: Cooper Square Press, 2000.

Recommended Recorded and Videotaped Performances

Evita (1996). Hollywood Pictures Home Video, DVD/VHS, 1998.

The Immaculate Collection (1991). Warner/Electra, DVD/VHS, 1991/1999.

The Immaculate Collection. Warner Brothers, CD, 1990.

Madonna: Truth or Dare (1991). Artisan Entertainment, DVD/VHS, 2000/2001.

Ray of Light. Warner Brother, CD, 1998.

❖ MARTIN, MARY
(1913–1990) *Actress, Singer*

Best known for her stage portrayal of Peter Pan, Mary Virginia Martin was born on December 1, 1913, in Weatherford, Texas. Under her mother's tutelage, she learned to play the violin and studied voice. Throughout her youth, she gave frequent singing performances at local churches and social clubs.

At 14, Martin began dating Benjamin Hagman. Though her parents sent her to finishing school in Nashville to end the romance, she married Hagman in 1930 on her 17th birthday and gave birth the next year. Her son, Larry Hagman, would grow up to become a popular television actor best known for his roles in *I Dream of Jeannie* and *Dallas.* Martin and Benjamin Hagman divorced in 1936.

Martin settled in Weatherford, where she established a dance school. To receive more dance training herself, she traveled to Los Angeles in 1932. The trip kindled her desire for a movie career. She spent several years going to auditions and making screen tests but had more luck finding work in nightclubs. While performing at the Trocadero, she was discovered by Broadway producer Lawrence Schwab. Martin headed for New York City and was soon cast in Cole Porter's musical *Leave It to Me.* Coached by stage singer SOPHIE TUCKER, Martin won over audiences with a suggestive rendition of "My Heart Belongs to Daddy."

Her Broadway triumph at last won her a Hollywood contract. At Paramount Studio, she made eight films, but none were memorable. Her foray into film, however, did allow her to meet movie executive Richard Halliday. They married in 1940 and had one daughter, Heller. During their long, happy marriage, Halliday gave up his career to manage Martin's.

Following his advice, Martin decided to focus on stage work. She had an early success in *One Touch of Venus* (1945), in which she played a statue of Venus that came to life. In 1946, Martin also had hits with *Lute Song* and *Pacific 1860,* both of which were written with her in mind. She lost the starring role in the Broadway musical, *Annie Get Your Gun* to ETHEL MERMAN, but became a bona fide stage star when she played the part during its 1947–48 tour.

In 1949 Martin starred in *South Pacific* playing Nellie Forbush, a spirited young woman forced to confront her own prejudices. Her legendary performance featured two show-stopping songs, "I'm in Love with a Wonderful Guy" and "I'm Gonna Wash That Man Right Out of My Hair." After *South Pacific,* she was offered, but turned down, roles in many of Broadway's best-regarded musicals, including *Oklahoma!, My Fair Lady,* and *Kiss Me Kate.* She broadened her audience, however, by appearing on television in several early variety shows.

In 1954 Martin scored on the stage once again as the star of *Peter Pan,* which later she named as her favorite role. She appeared in the part in various productions over the next six years. The musical was also filmed for television in 1955 and 1956.

In 1959, Martin originated another classic role, that of Maria von Trapp in *The Sound of Music.* She also toured much of the globe in a State Department–sponsored production of *Hello Dolly!* Her last musical role came in 1966, when she starred with Robert Preston in *I Do! I Do!*

After that show, citing exhaustion, she went into semiretirement and moved with her husband to Brazil, where they had frequently vacationed. Following his death in 1973, she returned to California, where in the 1980s she hosted *Over Easy,* a PBS television series dealing with issues relating to the elderly. She also made a final stage appearance in 1986, costarring with her longtime friend Carol Channing in the drama *Legends.* Martin died of cancer on November 3, 1990, at the age of 77.

Further Reading

Martin, Mary. *My Heart Belongs.* New York: Morrow, 1976.

Rivadue, Barry. *Mary Martin: A Bio-Bibliography.* New York: Greenwood Press, 1991.

Recommended Recorded and Videotaped Performances

Birth of the Blues (1941). Universal, VHS, 1995.
Mary Martin Sings, Richard Rodgers Plays. RCA, CD, 1990.
My Heart Belongs to Daddy. Pearl-Koch, CD, 2000.
Peter Pan (1960). Goodtimes Home Video, DVD/VHS, 1999.

❖ McDANIEL, HATTIE (Hi-Hat Hattie)
(1895–1952) *Actress, Singer*

Hattie McDaniel will always be inseparable from her best-known role—that of Mammy in *Gone With the Wind* (1939). Her performance as the worldly wise slave made her the first African American to win an Academy Award.

Born on June 10, 1895, in Wichita, Kansas, McDaniel was one of 13 children of her Baptist minister father and gospel singer mother. Both of her parents were former slaves. Hattie, who early displayed a talent for singing, quit school at 15 to become a full-time performer with a minstrel show organized by her father. During the 1920s, after the show disbanded, she joined several vaudeville troupes that toured the West. In 1925 in Denver, Colorado, she became one of the first African Americans ever to perform on the radio.

Left jobless after the 1929 stock market crash, McDaniel moved to Milwaukee, where she worked as a bathroom attendant at the Club Madrid. The nightspot only hired white singers but was finally persuaded to give McDaniel a chance to sing after patrons familiar with her work insisted. Her rendition of "St. Louis Blues" was such a hit that she became the club's star performer for two years.

In 1931, McDaniel followed the example of three of her siblings and moved to Hollywood to seek her fortune in the movies. While looking for film work, she took jobs as a domestic and as a radio singer performing under the name Hi-Hat Hattie. Hattie played several bit parts before landing her first credited film role in *Judas Priest* (1934). In the film, she sang a duet with star Will Rogers, who later insisted McDaniel stole the show. With this success, she finally got the attention of Hollywood. Throughout the 1930s, McDaniel had steady work, although the range of work offered to her was limited. In the some 40 movies she acted in during the decade, she played a maid or a cook, then generally the only parts open to African-American actresses.

After reading the best-selling *Gone with the Wind,* McDaniel campaigned to play Mammy, a house slave of the novel's O'Hara family, in the much-heralded film adaptation. Against stiff competition, she handily won the role that made her famous. In her many scenes with VIVIEN LEIGH as Scarlett O'Hara, McDaniel's wise and moral

Mammy stood in contrast to the impulsive and selfish Scarlett. When McDaniel accepted the best supporting actress Oscar for her performance, she said, "I sincerely hope that I shall always be a credit to my race, and to the motion picture industry."

Despite the strength and dignity McDaniel brought to Mammy, she was criticized by some African Americans for playing this and other roles that were considered demeaning to blacks. McDaniel defended her career, once pointing out, "It's better to get $7,000 a week for playing a servant than $7.00 a week for being one." Her stance, in addition to her performance in the much disparaged *Song of the South* (1946), led the National Association for the Advancement of Colored People (NAACP) to denounce her.

During this period, McDaniel also suffered several personal difficulties. Left a widow by a brief first marriage in the 1920s, McDaniel had been married and divorced three times by 1950. In 1944, she had been delighted to find herself pregnant by her second husband. In her eighth month, her doctors, however, discovered that they mistook diabetes and other ailments for a pregnancy. Friends say McDaniel never fully recovered from this grave disappointment.

Adding to her sadness, she saw film studios, leery of charges of racism, growing less and less willing to cast any African-American actors. As her movie career waned, McDaniel returned to radio. In 1947, she was cast as the title character in the popular program "Beulah," a role previously played by white actors. "Beulah" was a comedy about a quick-witted African-American maid working for a white family. Sensitive about previous criticism of her work, McDaniel demanded that her contract stipulate that no black dialect would be used on the show and that she would be able to strike out any dialogue she found objectionable. It also gave her a starting salary of $1,000 a week.

A television version of "Beulah" appeared in 1950 with ETHEL WATERS in the title role. When Waters left the show the next year, the public demanded that McDaniel take over the part. Soon after beginning filming, she fell ill, first

with a heart attack, then with terminal breast cancer. McDaniel died on October 26, 1952, at the age of 57.

In her will, McDaniel asked that she be laid to rest in a white casket, covered by a white shroud with a white gardenia in her hair. She also wanted to be buried in the Hollywood Memorial Park Cemetery, the resting place of many fellow stars, but the cemetery denied the request because of her race. In 1999, however, the cemetery, under new ownership, finally approved McDaniel's reinterment there and erected a massive granite monument in her honor.

Further Reading

Harmetz, Aljean. *On the Road to Tara: The Making of Gone With the Wind.* New York: Harry N. Abrams, 1996.

Jackson, Carlton. *Hattie: The Life of Hattie McDaniel.* Lanham, Md.: Madison Books, 1989.

Recommended Recorded and Videotaped Performances

Gone With the Wind (1939). Warner Home Video, DVD/VHS, 2000/2001.

Show Boat (1951). Warner Home Video, DVD/VHS, 2000.

❖ **MERMAN, ETHEL (Ethel Zimmerman)**
   (1909–1984) *Actress, Singer*

One of America's greatest musical actresses, Ethel Merman was born Ethel Zimmerman (sometimes spelled Zimmermann) in Queens, New York, on January 16, 1909. After graduating from high school, by day she was a secretary, while by night she slowly carved out a career as a nightclub singer. Shortening her last name to Merman, she was soon working with veteran showmen, including Jimmy Durante and Eddie Jackson.

While performing at a Brooklyn theater, Merman was spotted by a Broadway producer who brought composer George Gershwin to see her act. Gershwin was so struck by her powerful voice that he gave her a part in his musical *Girl Crazy* (1930) and even offered to rewrite some of his songs to better suit her. In the show, Merman caused a sensation with her dynamic performance of "I Got Rhythm," which became one of her signature songs.

Merman quickly became a Broadway star, appearing in shows put together by the day's top musical directors. Her early musicals were loosely structured vehicles short on narrative but peppered with soon-to-be-classic songs that she introduced to the American public. For instance, in her five shows featuring music by songwriter Cole Porter, Merman was the first stage interpreter of "Anything Goes," "I Get a Kick Out of You," "You're the Top," and "Down in the Depths of the 90th Floor."

Bold and booming, Merman's voice proved ideal for Broadway theaters with poor acoustics. She was also heralded for her extraordinary presence, which kept theater audiences enthralled as she belted out her numbers. Her larger-than-life stage demeanor, however, played less well on film. She made nine movies in the 1930s—including *Anything Goes* (1935) and *Alexander's Ragtime Band* (1938)—but she still was known primarily for her stage work.

In 1940, Merman married Hollywood agent William Smith. A year later, the union ended in divorce, as did her three subsequent marriages (Robert D. Levitt, 1941–52; Robert F. Six, 1953–60; and Ernest Borgnine, 1964–65). With Levitt, Merman had two children, Ethel Merman Levitt and Robert D. Levitt Jr.

Merman's career reached a zenith with her appearance in Irving Berlin's *Annie Get Your Gun* (1946). Much more than her earlier shows, this musical, based on the life of Wild West sharpshooter ANNIE OAKLEY, required Merman to hone her skills as an actress. It also gave her the show-stopping song, "There's No Business Like Show Business," an anthem to the thrill of performing with which Merman has been associated ever since. Its title was used for a 1954 filmed celebration of Berlin's music starring Merman.

Merman had another triumph in 1959 with *Gypsy,* a musical about the early life of burlesque queen GYPSY ROSE LEE. Merman had the starring role as the performer's overbearing stage mother,

Ethel Merman in *Annie Get Your Gun* (1946)
(© Bettmann/CORBIS)

Rose. The part was ideal for Merman, whose brassiness well presented Rose's bullying while her tenderness ably revealed her character's underlying vulnerability. Merman was particularly hailed for her performance of "Rose's Turn," which was considered by many fans to be her finest moment on stage.

Merman's last major stage role was in *Hello Dolly!* In 1969 Merman took over the title part, which was originated by Carol Channing on stage. Merman put her own indelible stamp on the role until the show closed after nearly 3,000 performances.

In the 1960s and 1970s, Merman appeared frequently on television. In addition to performing songs on variety shows and specials, she was a guest star on programs such as *Batman* and *That Girl* and a regular on talk shows and game shows.

Merman's stellar stage career was honored by a lifetime achievement award given to her at the

1972 Tony Awards. She died 12 years later at her Manhattan home on February 15, 1984.

Further Reading

Bryan, George B. *Ethel Merman: A Bio-Bibliography.* New York: Greenwood Press, 1992.

Merman, Ethel, and George Eells. *Merman: An Autobiography.* New York: Simon and Schuster, 1978.

Thomas, Bob. *I Got Rhythm! The Ethel Merman Story.* New York: Putnam, 1985.

Recommended Recorded and Videotaped Performances

Alexander's Ragtime Band (1938). Twentieth Century-Fox, VHS, 1994.

There's No Business Like Show Business: The Ethel Merman Collection. Razor and Tie Entertainment, CD, 1997.

❖ **MIDLER, BETTE**
(1945–) *Singer, Actress*

A remarkably likeable and versatile entertainer, Bette Midler has been described by *Time* magazine critic Richard Corliss as "the most dynamic and poignant singer-actress of her time." Named after actress BETTE DAVIS, she was born in Honolulu, Hawaii, on December 1, 1945, to a working-class family. Fascinated with Hollywood musicals, she dreamed of becoming a performer, an ambition her mother encouraged with dance and music lessons.

While attending the University of Hawaii, Midler was hired as an extra on the set of the film *Hawaii* (1966). The experience was exciting enough to persuade her to move to Los Angeles. There, she worked as an extra until she saved enough money to head to New York City to pursue a career as a serious stage actress.

After playing several small roles, Midler won a part in the chorus of the Broadway musical *Fiddler on the Roof* in 1966. She stayed with the show for three years, gradually working her way through the ranks until she was hired for the prominent role of Tzeitel. While performing in *Fiddler,* Midler also began working on a club act, in which she sang a wide variety of pop, rock, and jazz tunes. Onstage, she spiced up her act with bawdy jokes between songs.

Midler worked at a few Greenwich Village clubs before she was hired in 1970 to perform at the Continental Baths, a public bathhouse with a largely gay male clientele. With help from her pianist, Barry Manilow, Midler developed a brassy onstage persona. Combining sexy, often vulgar comedy monologues with her eclectic musical tastes, she created a tight bond with her audience. She later recalled, "The more outrageous I was, the more [they] liked it. It loosened me up."

As word spread about her act, she began to play larger venues. She also was invited to perform on several national TV talk shows, including *The Tonight Show* hosted by Johnny Carson. Midler's fame was cemented by the release of her debut album, *The Divine Miss M,* in late 1972. The record yielded an unlikely top 10 hit—a cover of the Andrews Sisters song "Boogie Woogie Bugle Boy." Midler went on to star in the Broadway revue *Clams on the Half Shell* (1973–74) and record several less successful albums. Among them were *Bette Midler* (1973) and *Broken Blossoms* (1977).

In 1979 Midler moved into film with *The Rose,* the story of a fictitious self-destructive rock star loosely based on JANIS JOPLIN. Midler's performance was a great critical success and earned her an Oscar nomination. She also won a Grammy Award for the movie's title song.

From this high point, Midler's career took a sharp turn downward in the early 1980s. *Divine Madness* (1980), a filmed version of her club act, was a box-office disappointment. Even more badly received was her next movie, *Jinxed* (1982). The film was a flop, and offscreen battles between Midler and her costar Ken Wahl earned her a reputation for being temperamental. The experience was so bitter that Midler began to doubt her choice of career. "I thought maybe they are right, maybe I don't have what it takes," she said, recalling the critical response to the movie.

Midler began to regain her equilibrium with her 1984 marriage to investor and performance artist Martin von Haselberg. Soon afterward, she signed a contract with Disney. The film studio reined in her risqué persona and molded her into a comedy star with appeal for a mass audience. Her new image was showcased in a series of hit comedies, including *Ruthless People* (1986) and *Outrageous Fortune* (1987). With these films, Midler became the top female box-office draw of the late 1980s.

Midler also had a solid success with *Beaches* (1988), an old-fashioned tearjerker that paired her with Barbara Hershey as lifelong friends. She followed it up with two other "women pictures"—*Stella* (1990) and *For the Boys* (1991). Although a popular failure, *For the Boys,* produced by Midler's company, All Girls Productions, earned her her second Oscar nomination. Midler also won acclaim for her performances in *Gypsy* (1993), a television adaptation of the classic musical about the life of GYPSY ROSE LEE, and *First Wives Club* (1996), a satire costarring Goldie Hawn and Diane Keaton. In 1992, she made show-business history as Johnny Carson's last guest before his retirement from *The Tonight Show.* Her appearance won her an Emmy Award.

While concentrating on film and television, Midler has continued her recording career, delivering pop hits well into middle age. Her most successful singles were "Wind Beneath My Wings" (1988) and "From a Distance" (1990). In 1998, Midler received enthusiastic reviews for *Bathhouse Betty* (1998), an album that revisited the bouncy, campy songs that made her a club phenomenon decades earlier.

Frustrated by the movie roles she was offered, Midler turned to series television in 2000. In the situation comedy *Bette,* she played a hyperactive, insecure version of herself. Though heavily hyped, the series was cancelled in March 2001. Many critics blamed the writing, citing that even with mediocre material, Midler's charm as a performer still found a way of shining through.

Further Reading

Bego, Mark. *Bette Midler, Outrageously Divine: An Unauthorized Biography.* New York: New American Library, 1987.

Mair, George. *Bette: An Intimate Biography of Bette Midler.* Secaucus, N.J.: Carol Publishing Group, 1995.

Recommended Recorded and Videotaped Performances

Divine Madness (1980). Warner Home Video, DVD/VHS, 1999.

The Divine Miss M (1972). Atlantic, CD, 1995.

Experience the Divine: Bette Midler Greatest Hits. Atlantic, CD, 1993.

For the Boys (1991). Twentieth Century-Fox, VHS, 1995.

The Rose (1979). Twentieth Century-Fox, VHS, 1996.

❖ **MILLS, FLORENCE (Florence Winfree)** (1896–1927) *Singer*

One of most popular singers of the Jazz Age, Florence Mills was born Florence Winfree in Washington, D.C., on January 25, 1896. Entered in dance contests while still a toddler, she made her professional debut at seven, billed as Baby Florence Mills in the touring revue *Sons of Ham.* She was taken under the wing of the star Aida Overton Walker, who taught her to sing her own song, "Miss Hannah from Savannah." Mills quickly became a staple of the African-American vaudeville circuit.

As a teenager, Mills began touring with her sisters Olivia and Maude as the Mills Sisters. After the group broke up, she moved to Chicago and started singing at nightclubs. Mills formed a trio with Ada Smith and Cora Green to play the Panama Club, where disregarding the mores of the day, African Americans and whites danced together. Mills briefly returned to vaudeville as a singer and dancer with the Tennessee Ten. In 1923, she married another member of the group, Ulysses S. "Slow Kid" Thompson.

In 1921, Mills was asked to star in *Shuffle Along,* a musical comedy by Noble Sissle and Eubie Blake. The show was the first African-American revue to attract a large white audience. It is credited with introducing to jazz rhythms and dance into the mainstream of American culture. With the musical's success, Mills became a star among African Americans and whites. With a petite frame and a high, birdlike voice, she consistently stole the show with her rendition of "I'm Craving for That Kind of Love."

In 1922, white showman Lew Leslie hired Mills to perform at his Plantation Club. He also made her the star of the *Plantation Revue,* which opened on Broadway. The next year, Mills took her act to London and appeared in the stage show *From Dover Street to Dixie.* Renamed *From Dixie to Broadway,* the revue was relocated to New York, where it became the first African-American musical comedy performed in a Broadway theater. The show gave Mills her signature song, "I'm a Little Blackbird Looking for a Blue Bird."

Leslie built his next musical, *Blackbirds of 1926,* around his star. After playing six weeks in Harlem, the revue traveled to Paris and London. The show was sensation among the British elite. The Prince of Wales claimed to have seen it more than 20 times. The fashionable widely imitated Mills's personal style, particularly her slick bobbed haircut.

Mills withdrew from the show due to ill health and returned to New York in September 1927. The next month, she had two emergency operations for appendicitis. Mills died of paralytic ileus resulting from her illness on November 1, 1927. The fans of her short career were stunned by her sudden death. More than 5,000 people attended her funeral, while some 150,000 mourners crowded the streets of Harlem to pay their respects.

Further Reading

Moore, James Ross. "Mills, Florence." In *American National Biography,* edited by John Arthur Garraty and Mark C. Carnes, vol. 15, pp. 547–548. New York: Oxford University Press, 1999.

Sampson, Henry T. *Blacks in Blackface: A Source Book on Early Black Musical Shows.* Metuchen, N.J.: Scarecrow Press, 1980.

Woll, Allen L. *Black Musical Theater.* Baton Rouge: Louisiana State University Press, 1989.

❖ MINNELLI, LIZA

(1946–   )   *Actress, Singer, Dancer*

Embodying show business glamour and excess, Liza Minnelli seemed born to be a star. Born on March 12, 1946, in Los Angeles, California, she was the daughter of singer JUDY GARLAND and director Vincente Minnelli. Before her third birthday, she had already made her film debut in *In the Good Old Summertime* (1949), which starred her mother. Growing up in Hollywood, she spent much of her youth on movie sets. She especially enjoyed watching dancers, particularly Gene Kelly and Fred Astaire. Liza herself took dance lessons from Metro-Goldwyn-Mayer's choreographer, Nico Charisse.

Liza's parents divorced in 1951, though she remained close to both. In her relationship with the emotionally unstable Garland, however, she increasingly seemed more than like the mother than the child. With Garland battling addictions to alcohol and pills and weathering a string of failed marriages, Liza began running the household, while trying to guard her mother from mental collapse.

In 1962, Minnelli dropped out of school to pursue her own show business career in New York. At 16, she made her off-Broadway debut in *Best Foot Forward* and then toured with other musicals for several years. Although Minnelli wanted to build a career without her parents' help, she agreed to appear in concert with Garland at the London Palladium in November 1964. Minnelli was terrified at being compared with her superstar mother. But in the middle of the concert, she began to relax as she realized that Garland was acting "like a lioness that owned the stage and suddenly found somebody invading her territory." Minnelli saw her mother's competitive instinct as the ultimate compliment. As she later said, "It was like Mama suddenly realized I was good."

In 1965, Minnelli returned to the New York stage in *Flora, the Red Menace.* The show flopped, but it won the 19-year-old Minnelli a Tony Award for best actress, the youngest performer ever to receive the honor. Through *Flora,* she also began a working relationship with songwriters Fred Ebb and John Kanter. With their help, she developed a nightclub act that showcased her strong voice and boundless energy.

After a small role in the film *Charlie Bubbles* (1968), Minnelli starred in *The Sterile Cuckoo* (1969). Playing an emotionally needy college student, she proved herself an able dramatic actress and earned her first Oscar nomination. Minnelli also had success taking her club act to television in the special *Liza with a Z* (1972), for which she won an Emmy Award.

Minnelli was cast in perhaps her greatest role in *Cabaret* (1975), the film version of Ebb and Kanter's musical set in Weimar Germany. Playing an American cabaret singer, Minnelli was able to both sing and show off her acting skills. Her dynamic performance earned her an Oscar for best actress.

From this high point, Minnelli's film career took a downward turn as she repeatedly failed to find the right vehicle for her talent. *Lucky Lady* (1975), a high-budget action comedy that paired her with Burt Reynolds and Gene Hackman, failed at the box office. *A Matter of Time* (1976), a fantasy directed by Vincente Minnelli, fared even worse. Playing an innocent chambermaid, Liza Minnelli received some of the worst reviews of her career. She seemed finally to have found an ideal role when she was cast opposite Robert De Niro in *New York, New York* (1977), director Martin Scorsese's attempt to recreate a 1940s-style movie musical. The film, however, was met with indifference by both critics and the public.

While floundering in film, Minnelli remained a star onstage. In addition to her concert tours, she appeared in several musicals. She won Tony Awards for her work in *The Act* (1977) and *The Rink* (1983). When Hollywood had all but given up on her star power, Minnelli had a surprise hit with *Arthur* (1981), a film comedy in which she played the love interest of Dudley Moore.

In the 1970s and 1980s, Minnelli was frequently the subject of gossip columns. Her tumultuous private life included marriages to singer Peter Allen, film executive Jack Haley, and artist Mark Gero. Each ended in divorce. A frequent visitor to high-profile nightclubs, Minnelli also developed an addiction to alcohol and prescription drugs. In 1984, she entered Washington, D.C.'s Betty Ford Clinic for treatment.

Minnelli continued to appear in film—most notably in *Arthur 2: On the Rocks* (1988) and

Stepping Out (1991)—but increasingly she devoted herself to live performances. She became one of the highest-paid concert performers, having particular success on her 1988 tour with Frank Sinatra and Sammy Davis Jr. By the late 1990s, however, health problems repeatedly threatened her ability to sing and dance. In addition to continuing problems with alcohol and drugs, she had several hip and knee operations, after which she had to relearn how to walk. In 1997, Minnelli was again hospitalized to have polyps removed from her vocal chords.

Despite an early prognosis that she would never be able to sing again, Minnelli returned to Broadway in 1999 in *Minnelli on Minnelli*. The popular show included reminiscences about her parents and songs made famous in their films. A 17-city tour was scheduled for the next spring, but Minnelli had to cancel it after suffering from both hip problems and double pneumonia. In November 2000, she had an even more severe health scare when she was rushed to the hospital with viral encephalitis. Long a survivor of personal and professional setbacks alike, Minnelli recuperated quickly from the near-fatal illness. Not surprisingly, her friend, gossip columnist Liz Smith, told the press after visiting the recovering star, "All she talks about now is working again."

Further Reading

Mair, George. *Under the Rainbow: The Real Liza Minnelli.* Secaucus, N.J.: Carol Publishing Group, 1996.

Spada, James, with Karen Swenson. *Judy and Liza.* Garden City, N.Y.: Doubleday, 1983.

Recommended Recorded and Videotaped Performances

Cabaret (1972). Warner Home Video, DVD/VHS, 1998/2000.

Judy Garland: Live at the London Palladium (1964). Laserlight Video, VHS, 1997.

Liza with a "Z": A Concert for Television (1972). Sony/Columbia, CD, 1988.

Minnelli on Minnelli. Angel, CD, 2000.

New York, New York (1977). MGM/UA, VHS, 2000.

❖ MIRANDA, CARMEN (Maria do Carmo Miranda da Cunha)
(1909–1955) *Singer, Actress*

Billed as the "Brazilian Bombshell," Carmen Miranda's zesty singing and outrageous costumes helped make her a film star in the 1940s. On February 9, 1909, she was born in Portugal as Maria do Carmo Miranda da Cunha (though she was immediately nicknamed Carmen). When she was three, her family moved to Rio de Janeiro, Brazil. She left school at 14 to work in a hat shop and soon was singing in parades. Developing an act in which she imitated popular Brazilian singers, Miranda became a favorite nightclub performer and recording artist.

As tourists caught her act, word of Miranda reached the entertainment industry in the United States. At the recommendation of film star SONJA HENIE, Broadway producer Lee Shubert hired her for his revue *The Streets of Paris*. Miranda appeared for only six minutes, performing the song "South American Way," but she became a sensation. When she returned home, however, she discovered that many of her old fans objected to her act, believing it made a mockery of Brazilian culture for American audiences.

Miranda came back to the United States, this time beckoned by Hollywood. Signing a contract with Twentieth Century-Fox, she made a huge impact in her first picture, *Down Argentine Way*

Carmen Miranda in *Down Argentine Way* (1940)
(Museum of Modern Art Film Stills Archive)

(1940), reprising her song "South American Way." In her follow-up film, *That Night in Rio* (1941), her two songs—"I Yi Yi Yi Yi (I Like You Very Much)" and "Chic Chica Boom Chic"—both became major hits with American record buyers.

Miranda was featured in 12 more films, usually as a supporting comic character. In her musical numbers, she became known for extravagant outfits, many of which were exaggerated versions of the costumes she had worn onstage in Brazil. She was particularly known for her seven-inch-high wedge-heel shoes and high headdresses adorned with bananas and other tropical fruit.

Perhaps her best-remembered film appearance was in *The Gang's All Here,* directed by Busby Berkeley, who was famous for his musical extravaganzas. In her "The Lady in the Tutti-Frutti Hat," number, she entered in a cart pulled by gold oxen surrounded by 60 chorus girls playing Brazilians on a banana plantation. The act ended with Miranda standing against a backdrop covered with hundreds of bananas, making her fruit hat grow to impossible heights. The comic flamboyance of Miranda's film appearances made her then and now a popular figure of parody, especially among cabaret performers.

Although the novelty of Miranda's film persona started growing thin by the mid-1940s, she remained a top-draw act in theaters and nightclubs. In 1947 she married her agent, David Sebastian, who was able to book her for successful runs at London's Palladium Theater and at Las Vegas casinos. Her health, however, began to suffer in the early 1950s, when she was diagnosed with heart problems. On August 5, 1955, the day after she taped a strenuous song-and-dance routine for television's *Jimmy Durante Show,* she died suddenly of a heart attack at the age of 46. Her body was returned for burial in Brazil, where a national day of mourning was declared.

Further Reading

Gil-Montero, Martha. *Brazilian Bombshell: The Biography of Carmen Miranda.* New York: Donald Fine, 1989.

Thomas, Tony, and Jim Terry, with Busby Berkeley. *The Busby Berkeley Book.* Greenwich, Conn.: New York Graphic Society, 1973.

Recommended Recorded and Videotaped Performances

Carmen Miranda: Bananas Is My Business (1995). Fox Lorber, DVD/VHS, 2000/1997.
Copacabana (1947). Republic Entertainment, VHS, 1989.
Down Argentine Way (1940). Twentieth Century-Fox, VHS, 1989.

❖ MITCHELL, JONI (Roberta Joan Anderson)
(1943–   )   *Singer, Musician, Songwriter*

Revered as one of the greatest popular singer-songwriters, Joni Mitchell created a seamless melding of folk, rock, and jazz in her classic albums *Blue* (1971) and *Court and Spark* (1974). Born Roberta Joan Anderson on November 7, 1943, she grew up in poverty in rural Alberta, Canada. Living in a shack without indoor plumbing, she endured a series of ailments as a child. She suffered from a burst appendix and a near-fatal case of measles before contracting polio at age nine. Paralyzed by the illness, she endured a year of painful rehabilitation to recover her ability to walk. Mitchell later maintained the experience made her an artist, explaining, "Staring into the eyes of death as a young person deepens you a lot."

Moving with her family to Saskatoon, Saskatchewan, Joan Anderson developed a passion for music and painting in her teens. At 13, she started calling herself Joni, largely because she liked the look of it when she signed her artwork. Working as a model, she earned enough money to enroll in the Alberta College of Art in Calgary. Her studies were halted, however, when at 20 she became pregnant by a fellow student. Together, they moved to Toronto but soon separated. An unwed mother with no income, Anderson hastily married folk singer Chuck Mitchell. Moving to Detroit, the couple stayed together for only two years. After they separated, Joni Mitchell gave up her daughter for adoption.

Hoping to become a folk singer, Mitchell headed for Manhattan and tried to break into the music scene. Although the folk movement of the early 1960s was by then dying out, other singers encouraged her. Soon artists such as BUFFY SAINTE-MARIE and Judy Collins were regularly performing covers of her songs. Through the help of a friend, singer David Crosby, Mitchell secured a contract with Reprise Records. Her first album, *Joni Mitchell: Song to a Seagull* (1968), did moderately well. It was followed with *Clouds* (1969), which like many of her albums to come featured a painting by Mitchell on the cover. The album was a critical and popular success, buoyed by Judy Collins's hit cover of Mitchell's song "Both Sides Now." Collins's recording became the eighth best-selling single of 1968. Mitchell's reputation grew with *Ladies of the Canyon* (1970). It included the songs "Big Yellow Taxi," which later became a hit for Mitchell, and "Woodstock," a hippie anthem successfully covered by Crosby, Stills, Nash, and Young.

Mitchell won her greatest acclaim yet for her album *Blue* (1971). The lyrics recounted her failed love affairs, including romances with rock artists Jackson Browne, James Taylor, and Graham Nash. The intimacy of her confessional songs jolted her audience. As Mitchell once said, "At the time of *Blue,* our pop stars never admitted these things."

After *Blue,* Mitchell took a hiatus from performing, though she continued to record on the Asylum label. In 1972, Mitchell's weariness with the music business revealed itself in *For the Roses,* which she thought might be her farewell album. Instead, she returned to the studio to produce *Court and Spark* (1974). Backed by Tom Scott and the L.A. Express, the album had a jazz sound then rarely heard in popular rock. With this band, she also recorded a successful live album, *Miles of Aisles* (1974).

Throughout the rest of 1970s, she continued adding jazz elements into her work in such albums as *Hejira* (1976) and *Don Juan's Reckless Daughter* (1977). Not all of Mitchell's fans appreciated her new sound. Her experiments also confounded critics who had previously championed her work. *Rolling Stone* magazine went as far as naming her album *The Hissing of Summer Lawns* the worst record of 1975. Her musical courage, however, won the admiration of one of her idols, jazz great Charles Mingus. Mingus and Mitchell began collaborating on an album, but he died before it was completed. Mitchell released *Mingus* (1979) as a tribute to her friend. Too jazz-influenced for rock fans and too rock-influenced for jazz enthusiasts, the album was a critical and commercial disappointment.

Mitchell once contended that *Mingus* "pretty much cost me my airplay, my radio presence." Certainly, her albums of the 1980s—such as *Wild Things Run Fast* (1982) and *Chalk Mark in a Rain Storm* (1988)—were largely ignored by critics and record buyers alike. For Mitchell, the decline in her popularity proved liberating. "Once I realized that I had fallen out of favor, I decided to stretch out," she later explained. Encouraging her musical experiments was Larry Klein, a record producer she had married in 1982.

By the 1990s, record buyers who had grown up with her music from the 1970s were coming into power in the music industry. Largely because of their support, *Night Ride Home* (1991) was her most well-received recording in a decade. Her next album, *Turbulent Indigo* (1994), won even broader acclaim. Once shunned by music insiders, Mitchell was awarded the Grammy for the best album of the year.

Mitchell's career upswing coincided with a period of personal turmoil. In 1992, Mitchell and Klein divorced. By the middle of the decade, she was beginning to suffer from post-polio syndrome, leaving her with muscle and joint aches that made performing increasingly difficult. After beginning a search for the daughter she had put up for adoption, Mitchell had a well-publicized reunion with her child, now named Kilauren Gibb.

Mitchell has since returned to the studio, releasing *Taming the Tiger* (1998) and *Both Sides Now* (2000), the latter an album mostly of standards from the 1940s and 1950s. Through her music, both old and new, Mitchell continues to inspire new artists with her emotional honesty and fearless experimentation.

Further Reading

Fleischer, Leonore. *Joni Mitchell*. New York: Flash Books, 1976.

Luftig, Stacey, ed. *The Joni Mitchell Companion*. New York: Schirmer Books, 2000.

Recommended Recorded and Videotaped Performances

Blue (1971). Warner Brothers, CD, 1987.

Court and Spark (1974). Elektra Entertainment, CD, 1987.

Joni Mitchell: Painting with Words and Music (1998). Image Entertainment, DVD/VHS, 1999.

Mingus (1979). Elektra Entertainment, CD, 1987.

Turbulent Indigo. Warner Brothers, CD, 1994.

❖ MONK, MEREDITH

(1942–) *Performance Artist, Composer, Choreographer*

"I combine forms weaving together music, movement, film, object, light and ambiance," wrote Meredith Monk in 1996 of the performances that have made her a leading force in the American avant-garde. On November 20, 1942, Monk was born in Lima, Peru, where her mother, a professional singer, was on tour. She has claimed that she learned to sing before she could talk. At three she began taking dancing lessons, and at 16 she began composing music.

Monk formally studied performing arts at Sarah Lawrence College, where she embraced the school's interdisciplinary approach. In addition to studying composition, opera, and chamber music, she concentrated on dance, learning both classical ballet and the modern dance techniques pioneered by DORIS HUMPHREY and Merce Cunningham.

After graduating in 1964, Monk moved to New York City, where she joined the innovative Judson Dance Theater and became involved in happenings and off-Broadway theater. Monk also began creating her own works, which combined music, dance, theater, and film. Early solo pieces included *Break* (1964), during which she moved across the stage accompanied by an audio tape of car crashes, and *16 Millimeter Earrings* (1966), in which a film was projected onto her body.

In 1968, Monk founded her own company, The House. Ten years later, it was expanded to include the Meredith Monk Vocal Ensemble to perform her vocal compositions. In many of her early experiments with The House, she created site-specific performances designed for nontraditional spaces. *Juice* (1969), for example, was performed over three nights—the first at the Guggenheim Museum, the second at a Barnard College theater, and the third at Monk's loft. Another piece, the Opie-award winning *Vessel* (1971), about Joan of Arc, began in Monk's home and ended in a parking lot.

Monk's work drew the attention of a larger audience with the success of *Quarry* (1976), which earned her a second Opie. It dealt with a sickly girl's perceptions of World War II and the Holocaust. Monk again explored the effects of war in *Specimen Days* (1981), in which performers playing two Civil War–era families—one from the North, the other from the South—occupied separate sections of the stage.

More recently, Monk has been acclaimed for *Atlas* (1991), a full-length opera that premiered at the Houston Grand Opera. It examined the spiritual journey of a woman played by Monk and inspired by explorer Alexandra David-Neel. Also well-received were *American Archaeology No. 1: Roosevelt Island* (1996) and *Politics of Quiet* (1996). In 1995 Monk was given a MacArthur Foundation "genius" grant, just one of the many honors she has received for her pioneering work.

Further Reading

Jowitt, Deborah, ed. *Meredith Monk*. Baltimore Md.: Johns Hopkins University Press, 1997.

Kreemer, Connie, ed. *Further Steps: Fifteen Choreographers on Modern Dance*. New York: Harper & Row, 1987.

Recommended Recorded and Videotaped Performances

Four American Composers: Meredith Monk (1983). Unapix, VHS, 1991.

Our Lady of Late. Wergo, CD, 2000.

❖ **MONROE, MARILYN** (Norma Jean Mortenson, Norma Jean Baker)
(1926–1962)   *Actress*

With the possible exception of Elvis Presley, no performer has become a greater American icon than film star Marilyn Monroe. Born as Norma Jean Mortenson in Los Angeles on June 1, 1926, Monroe was raised as Norma Jean Baker in a series of foster homes and orphanages. Her unmarried mother, Gladys, was mentally ill and unable to care for her. Gladys was ultimately committed to a mental institution and diagnosed as a schizophrenic.

Largely to escape living with still another foster family, Baker at 16 married James Dougherty in 1942. He soon left to join the merchant marine, while Baker found a wartime job with the Radio Plane Company in Van Nuys, California. There, she was spotted by army photographers, who chose her as their model for photos to accompany an article about female factory workers in *Yank* magazine. Her freshness, beauty, and ease in front of the camera attracted other photographers, and she began to model regularly for advertisements and promotions.

Eager for a Hollywood career, Baker divorced her husband in 1946 and convinced Twentieth Century-Fox to give her a silent screen test, designed to showcase her looks while de-emphasizing her lack of acting experience. The studio signed her up, assigning her Marilyn as her new first name. She herself chose Monroe, her mother's maiden name.

Fox placed Monroe in bit parts in two films before letting her go. She was briefly picked up by Columbia Pictures, where she made *Ladies of the Chorus* (1949). Without a studio, she made an appearance in the Marx Brothers' *Love Happy* (1949), but had to resort to posing for nude photographs when no more film work came her way. After she achieved stardom, these photographs resurfaced in 1955 in the first issue of *Playboy* magazine.

Monroe had better luck after she became romantically involved with Johnny Hyde, a powerful Hollywood agent. Hyde taught her how to handle herself in the film industry, but more important, he found parts for her in two distinguished films, *The Asphalt Jungle* (1950) and *All About Eve* (1950). The roles were small, but in them Monroe showed herself to be an accomplished scene-stealer. Her enthusiastic fan mail convinced Twentieth Century-Fox to re-sign the actress, this time to a seven-year contract.

Now confident in Monroe, Fox made her the center of a publicity campaign that sold her to the public as a classic "dumb blonde." Her first starring role, however, was in a thriller, *Don't Bother to Knock* (1952), in which she played a psychotic babysitter. The next year, she stayed closer to her image, playing a beautiful gold digger in both *Gentlemen Prefer Blondes* and *How to Marry a Millionaire.* Also in 1953, Monroe solidified her growing star status in *Niagara,* in which she played a scheming adulteress.

Monroe's fame was furthered by her marriage to baseball star Joe DiMaggio in January 14, 1954. Her studio-created reputation as a sexpot, however, soon came between them, as DiMaggio grew increasingly uncomfortable with the unrelenting attention she received from the public and press. He was particularly repelled by the publicity surrounding *The Seven Year Itch* (1955), a comedy that cast her as a young actress who inspired romantic fantasies in her married neighbor. A famous shot, exploited by the studio, had Monroe standing atop a street grating, allowing the wind to blow her skirt up. Although the film showcased Monroe's budding skill as a comedian, it infuriated and offended DiMaggio, thereby contributing to the end of their nine-month marriage.

Monroe herself grew weary of playing a blonde bombshell. Always embarrassed about her lack of formal education, she became determined to be taken seriously as an actress not by Hollywood but by the intellectual elites of the theater world. Breaking her contract with Fox, she left for New York City to study acting with Lee and Paula Strasberg, the directors of the Actors Studio and leading proponents of the "Method" acting technique. At the Strasbergs' suggestion, Monroe began to undergo psychoanalysis to help relieve her personal and professional insecurities. While in New York, she also met playwright Arthur Miller, whom she married in 1956.

Eager to keep one of their most popular stars, Fox renegotiated Monroe's contract. She agreed to make four more pictures for the studio, but only if she could also appear in movies made by her own company, Marilyn Monroe Productions. The advantageous contract ushered in the most creatively successful era of Monroe's film career. Though she continued to play beautiful but dim women, her roles better allowed her to comment on this image. In 1956, she appeared in *Bus Stop* as Cherie, a saloon singer frustrated by men's inability to see the woman behind her sexual facade. In 1959, in perhaps her best performance, Monroe hilariously parodied herself in *Some Like It Hot*. And in 1961, she had her most complex role in *The Misfits* as the sensitive and disillusioned Roslyn, a part written especially for her by Miller.

Despite these successes, Monroe grew increasingly disturbed. Her natural emotionalism combined with overuse of alcohol and pills helped brand her as one of the film industry's most "difficult" actresses. She was unpredictable on the set and chronically late, if she showed up for work at all. While filming *Some Like It Hot*, director Billy Wilder had to write her lines on furniture to aid her failing memory and focus. It took scores of takes for her deliver the simple line, "It's me, Sugar." Contributing to her personal difficulties were a series of miscarriages and her troubled marriage to Miller, which ended in divorce in 1961.

After a brief stay in a mental institution the same year, she went back to work on the film *Something's Got to Give*. Her working habits, though, were so erratic that Fox fired her in June 1962. On August 5, Monroe's housekeeper discovered her body at her home in Brentwood, California. At 36, she had died of a drug overdose. The tragedy invited various interpretations. Many people assumed she committed suicide, while others speculated that she was murdered, perhaps because of an affair she had with President John F. Kennedy. Most Monroe biogra-

phers, however, have since concluded that the overdose was accidental.

The life and death of Marilyn Monroe have inspired countless books, films, plays, paintings, and songs. Many have attempted to "explain" Monroe, though frequently their interpretations say less about their subject than the authors' own agendas. She is most often seen as a waif victimized and ultimately destroyed by the film industry and her adoring public. Her movie legacy, however, shows something more extraordinary: a performer with presence so luminous it has rarely been equaled on film.

Further Reading

McCann, Graham. *Marilyn Monroe.* New Brunswick, N.J.: Rutgers University Press, 1987.

Monroe, Marilyn. *My Story.* New York: Stein and Day, 1974.

Spoto, Donald. *Marilyn Monroe: The Biography.* New York: HarperCollins, 1993.

Recommended Recorded and Videotaped Performances

Gentlemen Prefer Blondes (1953). Twentieth Century-Fox, VHS, 1998.

The Misfits (1961). MGM/UA, VHS, 1996.

The Seven Year Itch (1955). Twentieth Century-Fox, VHS, 1998.

Some Like It Hot (1959). MGM/UA, DVD/VHS, 2001/1999.

❖ MONTEZ, LOLA (Eliza Rosanna Gilbert)
(1818–1861)   *Dancer, Actress*

One of the most famous and flamboyant celebrities of the 19th century, Lola Montez was born Eliza Rosanna Gilbert in Limerick, Ireland, in 1818. When she was four, her parents moved to Calcutta, India, where her father soon died of cholera. Her mother quickly remarried, and her new stepfather sent Eliza to Scotland to live with his relatives. Studying in Paris, France, and Bath, England, she received an excellent education, although she had trouble following her schools' strict dictates.

When she was 19, her mother paid her a visit, accompanied by Thomas James, a young officer in the Indian army. Learning that her mother wanted to marry her off to a wealthy, elderly man in India, Gilbert rebelled by convincing James to elope with her. She accompanied James back to India, but their marriage fell apart within months. After obtaining a legal separation (but not a divorce), Gilbert set off for England. On the trip, she had a shipboard liaison that she did little to keep secret. Her adultery became one of the many public scandals she would inspire throughout her life.

Cut off financially by her mother after her elopement, Gilbert chose the most impractical way possible of making a living: She decided to become a dancer. After a few months in Spain, she returned to England transformed. She had cast off Eliza Gilbert to become Lola Montez, an exotic Spanish dancer with a fantastic fictional biography. In June 1843, her new persona made her London stage debut. Although her talents as a dancer were limited, she excited the crowd by her suggestive and eccentric performance. She ran into trouble, however, when a newspaper reported that several audience members recognized Montez as none other than the scandalous Eliza Gilbert.

Her London engagement canceled, Montez began a tour of the continent, playing venues in Dresden, Berlin, Warsaw, and St. Petersburg. She enjoyed enormous success both as a performer and a personality. Glamorous and beautiful, she insinuated herself into the highest levels of European society and took a series of famous lovers, including Franz Liszt and Alexandre Dumas *père*.

Her greatest conquest, however, was Ludwig I, king of Bavaria. Already known for his weakness for women of the stage, the king fell hard for Montez, who was soon bullying him into making liberal government reforms. Her arrogance and imperiousness, though, infuriated his subjects, especially after she persuaded Ludwig to make her a countess even though she was not a Bavarian citizen. During the political unrest of 1848, she was forced to flee, first to Switzerland, then to England.

Lola Montez in 1852
(Seaver Center for Western History Research, Los Angeles County Museum of Natural History)

Still living off funds from the love-besotted king, Montez married the wealthy George Trafford Heald in 1849. His relatives spearheaded her arrest for bigamy, but quickly the marriage broke up of its own accord. By the end of the whole affair, Montez had lost Ludwig's support. With no other income, she went back to work, writing a biography full of outlandish fabrications and touring France and Belgium. American showman P. T. Barnum tried to arrange a tour of the United States, but when their negotiations soured, Montez decided to head across the Atlantic on her own.

When Montez arrived in New York in 1851, newspaper accounts of her European antics had already made her famous and infamous to Americans. After her Broadway debut, she began traveling through the East, making a sensation wherever she went. Her tours earned her a healthy $1,000 a week.

In the United States, Montez modified her act to include dramatic performances of plays such as Oliver Goldsmith's *School for Scandal.* After 1852, her signature piece became *Lola Montez in Bavaria,* a play she commissioned based on her supposed adventures. Savaged by critics for being a self-serving fiction, the public loved it, and it became a regular part of her repertoire.

Another crowd-pleaser was Montez's notorious Spider Dance, which concluded many of her performances. A loose variant on an Italian folk dance, it involved Montez, dressed in an elaborate costume, pretending that spiders were crawling over her body and into her clothes. Her frenzied dance, in which she often pulled up her skirt to expose her shapely legs, was considered highly erotic in her day.

In 1853, Montez took her act west. En route to San Francisco, she met newspaper editor Patrick Purdy Hall, whom she married soon after her arrival. Predictably, the marriage lasted only a few months.

Onstage, she duplicated her success in the East. The Spider Dance was particularly a hit in the mining camps she toured. For a time, Montez, entranced by the California countryside, lived in a small cottage in Grass Valley, where she raised a menagerie that included a pet grizzly bear cub. But growing restless, she gave up her bucolic experiment and set off for a final tour of Australia in 1855. Montez played a few more shows in New York after her return, but by 1857 she had largely given up her stage act. Even she recognized that she was growing too old for the Spider Dance. Her health, too, was suffering after many years of immoderate living.

Although she had been well paid for her stage work, her extravagances had exhausted her fortunes. Still pressed to earn a living, she began a new career as a lecturer in the United States and England. With titles such as "Beautiful Women," "Chivalry," and "Wits and Women of Paris," her talks drew large audiences, though many were more eager to see the legendary Lola Montez than to hear what she had to say. As her health faded, she had to give up the lecture circuit, even though she had already spent most of her profits. Relying on the benevolence of her many friends, Lola Montez spent her last days in New York City, where she died on January 17, 1861, at the age of 42.

Further Reading

Foley, Doris. *The Divine Eccentric: Lola Montez and the Newspapers.* Los Angeles: Westernlore Press, 1969.

Varley, James F. *Lola Montez: The California Adventures of Europe's Notorious Courtesan.* Spokane, Wash.: The Arthur H. Clark Company, 1996.

❖ MOORE, MARY TYLER
(1936–) *Actress*

In the television characters Laura Petrie and Mary Richards, Mary Tyler Moore helped define the modern American woman of the 1960s and 1970s. Born in Brooklyn, New York, on December 29, 1936, she had a difficult childhood hampered by an alcoholic mother and emotionally distant father. Moving to Los Angeles when she was eight, Mary dreamed of becoming a professional dancer.

At 18, Moore married Dick Meeker, a salesman. At about the same time, she landed her first job, a series of appliance commercials in which she portrayed a dancing fairy named "Happy Hotpoint." She soon had to be replaced when she grew too obviously pregnant to wear her tight costume. In 1955, she gave birth to a son, Richard.

In 1959, Moore was cast in her first television series, *Richard Diamond, Private Detective* (1957–60), as Sam, Diamond's receptionist. To give the character an air of mystery, only her legs were seen on screen. Feeling unchallenged, Moore left the series and began making television guest spots. She auditioned for a variety of series roles, including that of Laura Petrie, the wife of comedian Dick Van Dyke's character in *The Dick Van Dyke Show* (1961–66). With an engaging blend of wholesomeness and sexuality, Moore's Laura became an idealized version of a 1960s housewife. Although only 23 when the series began, Moore displayed a keen comic timing that allowed her to hold her own with her far more experienced costars. Her performance won her two Emmy Awards. During the series' five-year run, Moore divorced Meeker and married television executive Grant Tinker. Also in this period, a routine blood test revealed that Moore suffered from diabetes. She has since been an active advocate for diabetes research and a chairperson for the Juvenile Diabetes Foundation.

When *The Dick Van Dyke Show* ended, Moore struggled to find a successful vehicle in theater and film. She was cast opposite Richard Chamberlain in a stage musical of *Breakfast at Tiffany's* (1966), but the show closed soon after it opened. Moore was also ill-served by weak ingenue roles in the films *Thoroughly Modern Millie* (1967) and *A Change of Habit* (1969).

Moore returned to the small screen in 1969 to cohost the television special "Dick Van Dyke and the Other Woman, Mary Tyler Moore." Its positive reception led CBS to offer Moore a 13-episode contract for a new comedy series. She accepted on the condition that she and Tinker would produce the show through their company, MTM Enterprises.

With the help of writers Allan Burns and James L. Brooks, they created *The Mary Tyler Moore Show* (1970–77). Moore played Mary Richards, a woman in her thirties who, escaping a bad romantic relationship, finds a job as an assistant news producer at Minneapolis television station. Like *The Dick Van Dyke Show,* Moore's series depicted her home life and work life, giving an equal emphasis to each.

The series was an immediate hit. It also struck a cultural chord, as one of the first portrayals of a career woman who enjoyed her job and had no overriding desire to get married. As *TV Guide* declared in 1973, "Thirty-three, unmarried and unworried—Mary is the liberated women's ideal." Moore was also surrounded by a talented cast including Ed Asner as her crusty boss Lou Grant, Valerie Harper as her witty neighbor Rhoda Morgenstern, and Gavin MacLeod as her caustic coworker Murray Slaughter. Much of the show's success was due to the performers' and writers' ability to flesh out these characters with concerns

and anxieties that matched the tenor of the time. Several of the characters, including Lou Grant and Rhoda Morgenstern, were so embraced by the television viewers that MTM spun them off into successful series of their own.

Moore chose to end the series in 1977, when it was still highly popular. She then made two efforts revive the variety show format, *Mary* (1978) and *The Mary Tyler Moore Hour* (1979), but audiences seemed to want to see her only as Mary Richards. Though short-lived, *Mary* is remembered for introducing viewers to newcomers David Letterman, Michael Keaton, and Swoosie Kurtz.

Beginning in the late 1970s, Moore worked to establish herself as a serious actress. In the television movie *First, You Cry* (1978), she won an Emmy Award for her portrayal of a breast cancer survivor. On Broadway, she took over the role of an angry quadriplegic in *Whose Life Is It Anyway?* (1979) and received a special Tony Award for her performance. On film, she delivered another tour de force, playing an emotionally dead mother in *Ordinary People* (1980). When casting her, director Robert Redford said he wanted to show the world the "dark side of Mary Tyler Moore." For the role, she earned an Oscar nomination.

These professional successes coincided with personal troubles. In 1978, Moore's sister died of a drug overdose, and in 1980, she and Tinker were divorced. The same year, her son, Richard, died from an accidentally self-inflicted gunshot wound. Moore's life took a turn for the better in 1982 when she met and married Robert Levine, a cardiologist. He helped convince her to get treatment for alcohol abuse at Washington, D.C.'s Betty Ford Clinic in 1984. Four years later, Moore became one of the wealthiest women in show business when she sold her share of MTM Enterprises for an estimated $113 million.

Moore appeared in three more television series—*Mary* (1985), *Annie McGuire* (1988), and *New York News* (1995)—but each was quickly canceled. She was better received in television movies, including *Gore Vidal's Lincoln* (1988) and *Stolen Babies* (1993), for which she won her seventh

Emmy. Critics also hailed Moore for her portrayal of Ben Stiller's neurotic mother in the comedy *Flirting with Disaster* (1996).

A 1998 reunion with Valerie Harper on *The Rosie O'Donnell Show* convinced Moore that it was time to revive the Mary Richards character. Two years later, she and Harper starred in the television film *Mary and Rhoda*. The movie received a lukewarm response, but it did little to tarnish Mary Richards's status as one of television's most beloved characters.

Further Reading

Alley, Robert S. *Love Is All Around: The Making of the Mary Tyler Moore Show.* New York: Delta, 1989.

Moore, Mary Tyler. *After All.* New York: Putnam, 1995.

Recommended Recorded and Videotaped Performances

Dick Van Dyke Show Box Set. Diamond Entertainment, VHS, 1997.

Ordinary People (1980). Paramount, DVD/VHS, 2001/1996.

The Very Best of the Mary Tyler Moore Show. New Video Group, VHS, 1998.

❖ MORENO, RITA (Rose Dolores Alverio, Rosita Moreno)

(1931–   ) *Actress, Singer, Dancer*

Rita Moreno is one of the few performers ever to win an Oscar, a Tony, an Emmy, and a Grammy. On December 11, 1931, she was born Rosa Dolores Alverio in Humacao, Puerto Rico. After her parents' divorce, her mother moved to New York City to find work and left her in the care of relatives. At five, Rosa was reunited with her mother and placed in an American kindergarten without knowing a word of English.

The next year, Rosa began taking dance lessons. After years of performing at recitals and weddings, she made her Broadway debut at 13 in *Skydrift* (1944). She continued her performing career by singing in nightclubs and dubbing stars such as ELIZABETH TAYLOR and Margaret O'Brien for Spanish versions of Hollywood films.

Spotted by a talent scout, she signed a contract with Metro-Goldwyn-Mayer in 1950. Using her stepfather's last name, she was billed first as Rosita Moreno, then as Rita Moreno. Moreno was quickly stereotyped, playing spirited Mexican and Indian women in B movies. During her first decade in film, her few standout roles included small parts in *Singin' in the Rain* (1952) and *The King and I* (1956).

Moreno finally had her breakthrough in the role of Anita in *West Side Story* (1961). Particularly memorable was her performance of the song "America," in which her character, a young Puerto Rican woman, celebrates the social freedom she has living in the United States. Moreno won an Academy Award for best supporting actress for her performance.

Moreno followed this success with challenging nonsinging film roles in *Summer and Smoke* (1961), *The Night of the Following Day* (1969), and *Carnal Knowledge* (1971). She also appeared regularly onstage. One of her most memorable roles was that of Googie Gómez, a comically inept Puerto Rican singer in Terrence McNally's *The Ritz* (1975). The role allowed her to lampoon the stereotypical Hispanic characters she played earlier in her career. It also won her a Tony for best supporting actress.

In the 1970s, Moreno spent much of her time on television. She joined the cast of *The Electric Company* in 1971. This PBS series featured comic skits designed to help elementary students learn to read. Moreno and her other cast members won a Grammy for a children's album based on the show. Moreno also won two Emmy Awards for guest appearances on *The Muppet Show* in 1977 and *The Rockford Files* in 1978. Moreno starred in two short-lived television series—*The Rita Moreno Show* (1978) and *Nine to Five* (1982–83)—and played recurring roles on several others, including *B. L. Stryker* (1989) and *The Cosby Mysteries* (1994). Since 1997, Moreno has portrayed a streetwise nun on *Oz*, the gritty HBO series set in a maximum-security prison.

Moreno continues to make occasional appearances onstage and onscreen. She frequently costars

Rita Moreno in *West Side Story* (1961)
(Library of Congress, neg. no. USZ62-116064)

in plays with Fernanda Luisa, her daughter by husband Leonard Gordon, whom Moreno married in 1965. Moreno's recent films include *I Like It Like That* (1994) and *Blue Moon* (2000).

In 1997, Moreno entered another phase in her career by making her debut as a cabaret singer. She has since appeared at the top clubs throughout the United States, performing a 70-minute act featuring her favorite ballads, pop songs, and show tunes. In a 2000 interview, the versatile Moreno spoke of her confidence in taking this new path: "There's nothing I don't do, short of juggling. And I'm working on that."

Further Reading

"Rita Moreno." In *Dictionary of Hispanic Biography*. Detroit: Gale Group, 1996.

Suntree, Susan. *Rita Moreno*. New York: Chelsea House Publishers, 1993.

Recommended Recorded and Videotaped Performances

Carnal Knowledge (1971). MGM/UA, DVD/VHS, 1999.

The King and I (1956). Twentieth Century-Fox, DVD/VHS, 1999.

The Ritz (1976). Warner Studios, VHS, 1992.

West Side Story (1961). MGM/UA Studios, DVD/VHS, 1999.

N

❖ NORMAN, JESSYE
(1945–) *Singer*

One of America's greatest opera singers, Jessye Norman was born on September 15, 1945, in Augusta, Georgia. With her parents encouraging her interest in music, she started singing in church choirs at four. Soon after, she began taking piano lessons. As a child, she was first exposed to opera by listening to a radio broadcast from New York's Metropolitan Opera. Norman later recalled, "I was nine and didn't know what was going on, but I just loved it."

Her singing voice won her a full scholarship to Howard University, from which she graduated with honors. She continued her musical studies at the Peabody Conservatory in Baltimore and the University of Michigan in Ann Arbor. In 1968, she won the International Music Competition in Munich, Germany. Based on the tremendous reception she received there, she moved to Europe to build her career. The following year, Norman made her debut with the Deutsche Opera in Berlin in Richard Wagner's *Tannhäuser.* She was soon playing the best European opera houses. In 1972, she made her first appearances at La Scala in Milan and at the Royal Opera House in London.

The same year, Norman performed Verdi's *Aïda* at the Hollywood Bowl in Los Angeles. She followed this triumph with her first major appearance in New York City in 1973. Part of the "Great Performers" series at Lincoln Center, her performance was hailed by the *New York Times* for its "extraordinary intelligence, taste and emotional depth."

After touring around the world, Norman retreated from opera singing in 1975. Concentrating on recitals, she explained she wanted to take some time to develop her voice. In Hamburg, Germany, in 1980, Norman took the stage in *Ariadne auf Naxos,* her first opera performance in five years. Three years later, Norman delighted her American fans by making her debut with the Metropolitan Opera in its 100th season in September 1983. Another career triumph came in 1987, when she received a 10-minute ovation after performing a program of songs by Richard Strauss with the Boston Symphony Orchestra.

Norman is almost as well known for her regal bearing as for her technically perfect voice. With a dramatic personality and a large physique, she offers a commanding, sometimes even intimidating presence both on and off the stage. The word *diva* has often been used to describe Norman. In fact, she was rumored to be the inspiration for the opera singer in the popular French film *Diva* (1982), a romantic thriller.

Norman also has a reputation for searching out unusual projects and interesting collaborations. Among her more than 50 recordings are *With a Song in My Heart* (1984), an album of show tunes, and *I Was Born in Love with You* (2000), a collection of songs by French composer Michel Legrand. Onstage, Norman sang a concert of spirituals with Katherine Battle in 1990 and performed an experimental dance and song piece with choreographer Bill T. Jones in 1998. March 2000 saw the Carnegie Hall premiere of woman.life.song. Combining song and spoken word, this innovative work was commissioned by Norman and included music by composer Judith Weir and text by writers Toni Morrison, Maya Angelou, and Clarissa Pinkola Estes.

Throughout her career, Norman has received numerous honors, including more than 30 honorary degrees and several Grammy Awards. In 1997, at 52 she became the youngest recipient of a Kennedy Center Honor, the highest honor the United States bestows on artists.

Further Reading

"Jessye Norman." In *Contemporary Black Biography,* Vol. 5. Detroit: Gale Group, 1993.

Michener, Charles. "Diva Fever." *Vanity Fair.* February 1989. 52: 2, 150+.

Recommended Recorded and Videotaped Performances

Jessye Norman at Notre Dame (1991). Philips, VHS, 1992.
Jessye Norman: Sacred Songs. Philips, CD, 1997.
Jessye Norman Sings Carmen. Philips, VHS, 1990.
Strauss: Four Last Songs. Philips, CD, 1987.

❖ NORMAND, MABEL
(1892–1930) *Actress*

The greatest screen comedienne of the silent era, Mabel Ethelreid Normand was born in Staten Island, New York, on February 9, 1982. Given almost no formal education, she started working in her early teens for the Butterick dress pattern company, but soon her beauty attracted the attention of several commercial artists including Charles Dana Gibson. Her image was used to sell young women soft drinks, cold cream, and a host of other products.

At the suggestion of a friend, she decided to try film acting, largely because it paid more than modeling. Hired by the Biograph studio, Normand appeared in her first short in 1910. She soon developed a romantic relationship with Biograph director Mack Sennett and started working for his new studio, the Keystone Film Company, two years later.

At Keystone, Normand became a staple in Sennett's slapstick comedies. It is fabled that she invented a favorite Sennett bit when, during filming, she once impulsively slammed a pie into costar Ben Turpin's face. Petite, pretty, and spirited, Normand became one of the studio's best-known stars.

Using her influence over Sennett, she insisted that she have a say in directing her own films. She essentially codirected a series of successful pictures with fellow star Charles Chaplin. Among them were *Mabel at the Wheel* (1914), *Mabel's Busy Day* (1914), and *Mabel's Strange Predicament* (1913), in which Chaplin debuted his famous "Little Tramp" character. When Chaplin insisted on complete control over his movies, Normand found a more fruitful collaboration with Roscoe "Fatty" Arbuckle. Together, they directed seven popular "Mabel and Fatty" comedies.

Wanting more exposure in full-length films, Normand persuaded Sennett to found the Mabel Normand Feature Film Company in 1916. The company's first effort, *Mickey* (1918), showcased Normand in a different type of role. She played a young orphan mistreated by others in her town, a part that resembled those that had made her screen rival MARY PICKFORD a star. *Mickey* proved incredibly popular and made millions, little of which Normand saw. Furious at Sennett, she left to work for the Samuel Goldwyn Company.

Without Sennett at her side, Normand's tendency for high living grew more destructive. She spent her money extravagantly, loved all-night parties, and freely enjoyed drugs and alcohol. Her recreational habits had already begun to interfere with her work, when on February 2, 1922, they seemed to threaten her very career. On that night, director William Desmond Taylor, with whom she was romantically involved, was murdered. Normand was the last to see Taylor alive, and though she was cleared of any direct connection with his death, rumors spread that he had been protecting Normand from a drug dealer who was blackmailing her. Coming on the heels of the 1921 Fatty Arbuckle scandal, during which her former co-star was accused of murdering a starlet, the incident fueled a popular backlash against Normand. Three years later, she was involved in a second scandal, when her chauffeur shot an oil millionaire in a dispute over her. This time, the bad press destroyed her career.

Amidst several failed comeback attempts, Normand eloped with actor Lew Cody in 1926. His alcoholism appeared to increase her own alcohol problem. Her health failing throughout the rest of the 1920s, Normand died of tuberculosis on February 23, 1930, at the age of 37.

Further Reading

Fussell, Betty Harper. *Mabel*. New Haven, Conn.: Ticknor & Fields, 1982.

Sherman, William Thomas. *Mabel Normand: A Source Book to Her Life and Films*. Seattle, Wa.: Cinema Books, 1994.

Recommended Recorded and Videotaped Performances

Tillie's Punctured Romance (1914). Image Entertainment, DVD, 1999.

OAKLEY, ANNIE (Phoebe Ann Moses)
(1860–1926) *Wild West Show Performer*

Known to the public as "Little Sure Shot," Annie Oakley became an international celebrity through her astounding displays of sharpshooting in Buffalo Bill's famous Wild West show. Although she was considered by many to be the epitome of a western woman, she was born on August 13, 1860, near the village of Woodland, Ohio, about 70 miles north of Cincinnati. Her given name was Phoebe Ann Moses, but she was always known as Annie by her family.

The fifth of seven children, Annie suffered a difficult childhood. Her parents were barely able to scrape by as farmers. When she was six, her father died suddenly of pneumonia, and her mother, unable to feed her large family, had to find new homes for her children. Annie was sent to live and work first at an orphanage, then on a family farm. Unwilling to endure the family's physical abuse of her, she ran away, hitched a ride on a train, and returned to her mother's home.

As a child, she helped her family by engineering crude traps to catch small animals for food. She soon taught herself to use her father's gun, learning to shoot game animals in the head so as not to damage the meat. Annie became such a skilled hunter that she began selling her catch to restaurants in Cincinnati. Years later, she spoke with pride of being able to pay off her mother's mortgage with the money she made.

While visiting a sister in the city, Annie was chosen to show off her shooting in a contest with a professional marksman, Frank Butler. (Although the year of the contest is often cited as 1875, it may have occurred as late as 1881.) To Butler's dismay, his tiny challenger bested him. Once he got over his embarrassment, he invited her to a show in which he was performing. The next year, he and Annie were married.

Soon Annie joined Frank's act, taking the stage surname Oakley after a Cincinnati suburb. After playing vaudeville theaters and circuses for several years, Butler approached William "Buffalo Bill" Cody, the owner of a show featuring trick riding, roping, and sharpshooting. In 1885, he convinced Cody to hire Oakley, who became the first white woman to perform in his Wild West show.

Ten years her senior, Butler largely left the limelight to manage Oakley and teach her everything he knew about showmanship. Under his loving tutelage, she developed a thrilling act during which she used her gun to shatter glass balls thrown in the air, snuff out the flames of candles attached to a revolving wheel, tear in two a playing card held in the hand of a trusting assistant, and even pluck an apple off the head of her beloved dog.

Annie Oakley in about 1885
(Buffalo Bill Historical Center,
Cody, Wyo./Vincent Mercaldo Collection)

In addition to constantly thinking up new tricks, she and Butler also created a crowd-pleasing stage persona. Oakley dressed in a western costume, usually topped with a large hat, its brim upturned to show a silver star. She insisted on always wearing skirts to let her audience know that she was a lady. Oakley's gentle demeanor helped make her favorite with the crowd: It allowed them to enjoy her expertise at a traditionally male enterprise whereas they may have been put off by the same display of strength and skill performed by a less overtly feminine woman. Because of her ladylike appearance, Cody usually placed her early in the program, reasoning that seeing her would comfort women and children made uneasy by all the loud shooting in the show.

Working for Cody's show for 16 seasons, Oakley toured throughout the United States and Europe. She particularly caused a sensation in England, where she was presented to Queen Victoria. In addition to the thousands who saw her act, many were able to enjoy Oakley's tricks recorded on an early nickelodeon film she made for Thomas Edison in 1894.

After suffering a serious injury in a 1901 train accident, Oakley left Buffalo Bill's Wild West show. The next year, she had a great stage success, playing the lead in *The Western Girl.* Her character triumphed over evil by shooting a liquor bottle out of the hand of a drunk and lassoing a villainess to keep her from committing murder. Oakley also spent time participating in shooting matches. By setting many new records, she helped open the sport to women. She also appeared regularly in shows for charities, especially for orphans' homes.

After a brief comeback with *Vernon Seaver's Young Buffalo Show,* she retired from show business for good in 1913. She continued to participate in shooting matches, however, even after she was left partially paralyzed by an automobile accident in 1922. With Butler, an ailing Oakley returned home to Ohio in 1926. There she died in her sleep on November 3, 1926. Butler followed her to the grave less than three weeks later and was buried next to his wife of some 50 years. Since her death, Oakley's life has become a legend, told in myriad books and most famously in the stage musical *Annie Get Your Gun* (1946). This musical also had a successful run starting in 1999 with Bernadette Peters in the starring role. Country singer Reba McEntire performed the role in 2001.

Further Reading

Kaspar, Shirl. *Annie Oakley.* Norman: University of Oklahoma Press, 1992.
Riley, Glenda. *The Life and Legacy of Annie Oakley.* Norman: University of Oklahoma Press, 1994.

Recommended Recorded and Videotaped Performances

Annie Get Your Gun (1950). Warner Home Video, DVD/VHS, 2000.
Annie Oakley: Crack Shot in Petticoats. A&E Home Video, VHS, 2000.

P

PARTON, DOLLY
(1946–   )   *Singer, Songwriter, Actress*

Moving from country music to pop songs to movie stardom, Dolly Parton charmed America with her flamboyant, yet folksy persona. She was born on January 19, 1946, in a rural community in Sevier County, Tennessee. The fourth of 12 children, she grew up in a close but poor sharecropping family, an experience that inspired many of her early songs.

Dolly first sang publicly in a church where her grandfather preached. At six, she began playing guitar and writing songs. At 10, she made her first radio appearance and three years later sang on the Grand Ole Opry, a country music radio revue that was broadcast throughout the South. Although ferociously ambitious, she put her music career on hold until she finished high school, becoming the first in her family to receive a diploma. The morning after graduation, she headed off to Nashville to make her fortune.

While struggling to become a singer, she met and married Carl Dean, a contractor, in 1966. The next year, she first entered the charts with the song "Dumb Blonde." Appearing on *American Bandstand,* Parton became a local hero because of her

modest success. In Sevier County, October 7, 1967, was declared Dolly Parton Day, during which the aspiring singer was honored with a parade.

Parton also received her big break in 1967, when she was chosen as the new girl singer on the television program *The Porter Wagoner Show.* Wagoner, an established country star, soon began recording a string of successful duets with Parton, including "The Last Thing on My Mind" (1967) and "If Teardrops Were Pennies" (1973). On the strength of both her work with Wagoner and her solo career, Parton became a member of the Grand Ole Opry in 1969.

During her seven-year stint on *The Porter Wagoner Show,* Parton's relationship with Wagoner slowly deteriorated, as she began to long for greater things, while he wanted her to remain his protégée. In 1974, she finally quit the show. Supposedly, she wrote her most famous song—"I Will Always Love You"—about ending her professional relationship with Wagoner.

On her own, Parton found immediate success. In 1975 and 1976, the Country Music Association named her Entertainer of the Year. Parton, however, set her sights on pop stardom. She fired her band in 1977 and hired a management firm in Los Angeles to take charge of her career. The move provoked criticism from some country fans, who thought she was forgetting her roots and selling out for fame and fortune. Particularly irksome was her carefully packaged appearance, which featured tight-fitting, flashy gowns and bouffant blonde wigs. The costume seemed a parody of country music style, ripe for mocking by the genre's detractors. Parton herself attributed her look to her own sense of good fun. As she told *Vogue* magazine, "It's a good thing I was born a woman or I'd a been a drag queen."

Parton had a mainstream pop hit with "Here You Come Again," which won her a Grammy Award in 1978. She followed it with the chart-topper "9 to 5" (1980), the theme song to her first movie, which costarred JANE FONDA and LILY TOMLIN. She had less success in her next film outing, *The Best Little Whorehouse in Texas* (1982), for which she rerecorded her earlier hit "I Will Always Love You." When the new version rose to the top of the charts, Parton became the first artist to hit number one twice with the same song. The tune would return to the charts in 1992 in a cover by WHITNEY HOUSTON that ultimately earned Parton more than $1 million in royalties.

After *Whorehouse* proved a box-office disaster, Parton retreated from the public eye, suffering from physical ailments and weight gain. She reemerged with the hit duet "Islands in the Stream" (1984) with Kenny Rogers. Parton also tried her hand at hosting a television variety show, *Dolly* (1987), but it was quickly canceled "because it sucked," Parton's own clear-eyed assessment. Her film career also continued to flounder with the flops *Rhinestone* (1984) and *Straight Talk* (1992). She had hit with *Steel Magnolias* (1989), but she was only one member of a strong ensemble cast. Parton herself came to doubt her ability to carry a movie "'cause I'm not that fine of an actress."

Despite her career setbacks, Parton developed an unerring business sense, which has made her one of the wealthiest women in show business. Against the wishes of her financial advisers, in 1986 she invested $6 million in Dollywood, an amusement park in Pigeon Forge, Tennessee, near her childhood home.

The park has been an extraordinary success, bringing in approximately $30 million in profits a year. In 2001, Parton expanded the facility to include a full water park. Parton's other successful business concerns include two production companies and five music publishing businesses that handle the estimated 3,000 songs she has written throughout her career. Arguably her most important legacy to popular music, her song catalog earns her substantial annual royalties.

Although Parton's recent recordings have been uneven, she has had several successes collaborating with other stars, a strategy that emerged from her frustration with getting little airplay for her solo material. "I'm commercial minded," she once explained in an interview, adding, "If I can't get my own hit, I'm not too proud to hang onto somebody else's coattails." On *Trio* (1987) and *Trio II* (1999), she sang with Emmylou Harris and Linda Ronstadt, while on *Honky Tonk Angels* (1994), she collaborated with TAMMY WYNETTE and LORETTA LYNN. As a solo artist, Parton scored an unexpected success with *Treasures* (1996), an album of covers that yielded several dance club hits, including a remixed version of Cat Stevens's "Peace Train" featuring Ladysmith Black Mambazo. Parton also scored a critical victory with *The Grass Is Blue* (1999) and *Little Sparrow* (2001). These forays into the notoriously noncommercial genre of bluegrass reminded her diehard fans that regardless of how often Parton journeys into the mainstream, at heart she is never far from her country roots.

Further Reading

Mahony, Judith Pasternak. *Dolly.* MetroBooks, 1998.
Parton, Dolly. *Dolly: My Life and Other Unfinished Business.* New York: HarperCollins, 1994.

Recommended Recorded and Videotaped Performances

The Essential Dolly Parton. RCA, CD, 1995. (CD)
The Essential Dolly Parton, Vol 2. RCA, CD, 1997. (CD)
9 to 5 (1980). Twentieth Century-Fox, VHS, 1995. (V)
Steel Magnolias (1989). Columbia/Tristar, DVD/VHS, 2000.
Trio. Warner Brothers, CD, 1987.

❖ **PEARL, MINNIE (Sarah Ophelia Colley, Mrs. Henry Cannon)**
(1912–1996) *Comic*

For more than 50 years, Sarah Ophelia Colley charmed listeners of the Grand Ole Opry radio show with her comic character Minnie Pearl. Born on October 12, 1912, Colley grew up in a cultured, wealthy family in Centerville, Tennessee. As a child, she enjoyed vaudeville, but while attending Ward-Belmont College in Nashville, Tennessee, she became enamored with serious theater. Her ambition was to have a theatrical career like her idol, KATHARINE HEPBURN.

After several years of teaching dramatics in Centerville, Colley was hired in 1934 as a director by Wayne P. Sewell Productions. The company staged productions in rural areas to benefit local charities. During one of these shows, Colley boarded with an elderly mother of 16 children in Baileyton, Alabama. The woman amused Colley with old folk stories about the families living on Baileyton Mountain. "After 10 days with her," Colley later remembered, "I began to quote her and people would laugh." Incorporating her own experiences in the South, Colley crafted her friend's tales into a comic persona from Grinder's Switch, a small, fictional town named after a railroad switching station near Centerville. She named her alter ego "Minnie Pearl" because "there was always an Aunt Minnie or a Cousin Pearl back where I came from."

Returning to Nashville, Colley auditioned as Minnie Pearl for WSM, the high-watt radio station that broadcast the Grand Ole Opry throughout the South. Though somewhat put off by an educated woman playing a broad country character, the station managers agreed to put her on late in the show. The fan response was so positive that she soon became a fixture on the show. Greeting the audience with "Howdyyy! I'm just so proud to be here," Minnie Pearl was a cheery, country spinster, full of stories about Uncle Nabob and Aunt Ambrosia and ever on the hunt for a "feller." The character's trademark was her flower-covered, dime store hat, with a price tag dangling from its brim. Although Minnie Pearl's cornball jokes provoked groans as often as laughs, she struck a chord with fans nostalgic for old country ways quickly disappearing in the rural South.

In addition to appearing on the Opry, Pearl toured frequently, often as an opening act for her friend and mentor, musician Roy Acuff. In 1947, she married Henry Cannon, a former army pilot who supported her career by flying Pearl to out-of-town engagements. Pearl also recorded comedy records but had only one hit, "Giddyup Go—Answer" (1966). More successful were her television appearances. In the 1970s, she reached an audience that had never heard of the Opry on the nationally syndicated country music variety show *Hee Haw*. She was a regular on the series for 22 years.

In Nashville, Pearl was revered by country music professionals, especially by the newcomers she often took under her wing. Singers Garth Brooks and Amy Grant both named their daughters after her. She also became one of city's most prominent civic leaders, a position symbolized by her well-appointed home next to the Tennessee governor's mansion. After successfully battling breast cancer in the 1980s, Pearl also became an advocate for the American Cancer Society.

Inducted into the Country Music Hall of Fame in 1975, Pearl retired from performing in 1991 following a stroke. She died five years later, on March 4, in Nashville, at the age of 83.

Further Reading

Kenworthy, Kevin, comp. *The Best Jokes Minnie Pearl Ever Told*. Nashville, Tenn.: Rutledge Hill Press, 1999.
Pearl, Minnie, with Joan Dew. *Minnie Pearl*. New York: Simon & Schuster, 1980.

Recommended Recorded and Videotaped Performances

The Best of Minnie Pearl. Questar, VHS, 1994.
Minnie Pearl: The Starday Years. Starday, CD set, 1998.
Queen of the Grand Ole Opry. Legacy-DNA, CD, 1993.

❖ **PICKFORD, MARY (Gladys Louise Smith, Little Mary)**
(1892–1979) *Actress*

The modern film industry is difficult to imagine without the influence of Mary Pickford. As the first international movie star, she helped invent screen acting, pioneered now-widely-used special effects, and was instrumental in creating a movie studio whose role was crucial in moving film from the silent to the sound era.

Pickford was born Gladys Louise Smith in Toronto, Ontario, on April 8, 1892. When she was four, her father, a ship's steward, died in an accident, leaving her family's economic fortunes in doubt. In order to survive, her mother, Charlotte, pushed Gladys and her siblings, Jack and Lottie, to act in touring theatricals. From the beginning, Gladys—billed as "Baby Gladys Smith"—was the most successful. Even as a child, she felt the heavy burden of supporting her family, instilling in her early a determination always to be paid as much as her talents were worth.

Driven to earn more, at 16 Gladys Smith approached Broadway producer David Belasco and persuaded him to hire her for his show *The Warrens of Virginia*. The show had a lengthy run, providing Smith—now acting under the stage name Mary Pickford—with a steady paycheck for two years. The show's closing, however, sent her mother into a panic. She insisted that Pickford look for work in the new film industry, even though Pickford feared that taking a job in film, then considered an unsavory branch of show business, would destroy her chances to become a stage star. At Charlotte's insistence, though, Pickford interviewed with director D. W. Griffith at the Biograph studio. He immediately saw her potential and offered her $5 a day. She said she wanted $10 and got it.

When Pickford began working in films, studio executives did not give players billing, because they were afraid that if the audience started recognizing the actors' names, the actors would start demanding more money. But even without knowing who they were, filmgoers had already begun to embrace certain performers. Pickford was one of the first to earn the public's affection. Some fans referred to her as "Little Mary," as the title cards called her character in her first film, *The Little Teacher* (1909). Others simply called her the "girl with the curls" because of the head of ringlets she wore.

In 1910 Pickford married fellow actor Owen Moore. The same year, she left Biograph to work for the newly founded Independent Motion Picture Company (IMP). IMP vigorously promoted the actress, using the slogan "Mary Pickford is an imp now!" Her name established, she returned to Biograph the next year, now commanding a salary of $150 a week. After a brief stint at the studio, Pickford returned to the stage in *A Good Little Devil* (1912). The show was a hit, largely because the fans of her films flocked to see "Little Mary" in person. After the show, she signed on with the Famous Players film company at $500 a week to star in the movie version of the play. Pickford had learned a lesson: Her future lay in film, not theater.

As her star rose, Pickford continually demanded salary increases from Famous Players head Adolph Zukor. Negotiating without an agent or a manager, she became legendary for her business acumen. (Sam Goldwyn of Metro-Goldwyn-Mayer once quipped, "It took longer to make one of Mary's contracts than it did to make one of Mary's pictures.") By 1916, she famously announced that she could not afford to work for less than $10,000 a week. Zukor agreed not only to her salary demands but also to her insistence that she have creative control over her movies. For instance, her contracts gave her approval over the actors and directors she worked with.

Pickford's gain of control over her star vehicles ushered in the height of her career. Dubbed "America's Sweetheart," she solidified her most successful screen persona in *Poor Little Rich Girl* (1917) and *Rebecca of Sunnybrook Farm* (1917). Her characters were young, plucky girls whose high spirits and innate goodness helped them triumph over adversity. Freed from directors' mandates, Pickford rejected the exaggerated gestures used by most film actors, using instead restrained expressions and subtle movements to communicate emotion. She also inspired creativity in the more technical aspects of filmmaking. In *Poor Little Rich Girl,* for example, to make the 25-year-old Pickford more credible as her 11-year-old character, the props and set designs were oversized to make her appear smaller. In *Stella Maris* (1918), a split screen was used for one of the first times to allow Pickford to play dual roles.

Seeking even more control over her films, Pickford left Famous Players and briefly signed with First National, which created a new division called the Mary Pickford Company. In 1919, she took an even greater step toward autonomy by banding with Griffith and actors Douglas Fairbanks and Charlie Chaplin to form United Artists (UA). With her new film company, Pickford had the power to choose her own projects, oversee their promotion and distribution, and share directly in their profits. Although she may not have initiated the idea of forming UA, by most accounts she was the shrewdest of its four original partners, thus instrumental to its success.

Though in public Pickford seemed in total control of her career, in private she was terrified that her personal life would destroy her success. Her marriage to Owen Morris, an abusive alcoholic, was in shambles, but she worried that her fans would reject her if she got a divorce. Even worse, she had fallen in love with the married Fairbanks. At his insistence, Pickford and he divorced their spouses and married in a secret ceremony in 1920.

Anxiously awaiting filmgoers' reactions, the couple set off on a European honeymoon. To their shock, as news spread of their wedding, the public responded not with outrage over the dissolution of their former marriages, but with delight over the romance between two of their favorite stars. Pickford and Fairbanks were mobbed by well-wishers as they disembarked their ship. Their appearance in London even incited a riot by rowdy fans eager to get a glimpse of the fairy-tale couple.

The experience revealed to Pickford the extent of her celebrity. As her stepson, Douglas Fairbanks

Jr., later assessed, she and her husband "enjoyed a status in the world's imagination that is . . . inconceivable and incomparable by today's standards." One of the most famous women in the world, Pickford herself came to understand that to her audience she was no longer Gladys Smith or even the character "Little Mary," but a concept called Mary Pickford. Remembering her reception in Europe, she wrote, "Ovations, I have come to believe, are seldom or never accorded to persons, but to ideas."

Pickford's celebrity grew even greater when she and Fairbanks settled on a grand Los Angeles estate they called Pickfair. It soon became famous as a palace befitting the closest thing America had to a royal couple. There, Pickford and her husband entertained often, playing host to such luminaries as Alfred Einstein, H. G. Wells, Amelia Earhart, and F. Scott Fitzgerald.

Pickford's first films for UA did little to tarnish her star. *Pollyanna* (1920) and *Little Lord Fauntleroy* (1921), for example, were solid hits. Nearing age 30, however, Pickford was growing uncomfortable playing children and adolescents. She attempted to play adult roles in *Rosita* (1923) and *Dorothy Vernon of Haddon Hall* (1924), but both were box-office disappointments. For several years, Pickford returned to playing the juvenile characters her fans loved. But in 1928, she finally and dramatically abandoned her little girl persona by cutting off her curls and shipping them off to a museum.

At the same time, Pickford faced another daunting challenge as an actress: the advent of sound pictures. Her first talkie was *Coquette* (1929), which was based on a stage play that actress HELEN HAYES had made famous. Wearing her new bobbed hairstyle, Pickford played a flapper and won an Academy Award for best actress for her performance. Nevertheless, the film was a critical failure and Pickford herself disliked it.

Hoping for a guaranteed crowd-pleaser, Pickford chose as her next film an adaptation of Shakespeare's *Taming of the Shrew* costarring Fairbanks. The lavish 1929 extravaganza was a costly disaster. Pickford was justifiably unhappy with her shrill

Mary Pickford with Douglas Fairbanks in *The Taming of the Shrew* (1929)
(Museum of Modern Art Film Stills Archive)

performance. The production also marked the beginning of the end of her marriage. As tensions increased between Pickford and Fairbanks, he spent most of his time traveling, leaving his wife alone at Pickfair. The couple was divorced in 1935.

Unable to find her footing in sound pictures, Pickford made her last film, *Secrets,* in 1933. Although she remained active in the management of UA until 1953, she devoted most of her time to her third husband, actor Buddy Rogers (whom she married in 1937) and their two adopted children. Increasingly, Pickford became a recluse, making only rare public appearances. She was last seen before the public in 1975, when she was awarded an honorary Academy Award. Pickford, however, refused to come to the ceremony, preferring instead to accept the Oscar at Pickfair in a filmed segment. During the ceremony, the year's best

actor winner, Jack Nicholson, paid his own tribute to the screen legend by thanking Pickford in his acceptance speech for being "the first actor to get a percentage of [the profits made by] her pictures."

By the time of her death on May 29, 1979, Mary Pickford's films were largely unseen. She controlled the rights to the movies and refused to allow them to be screened, perhaps sensing that they and her pure and innocent screen image belonged to a different era. But, even if her characters belonged to an old world, Pickford had ironically ushered in a new one—a world in which a woman could control her professional destiny, make her own fortune, and enjoy the fruits and suffer the sorrows of the modern celebrity culture.

Further Reading

Brownlow, Kevin. *Mary Pickford Rediscovered: Rare Pictures of a Hollywood Legend.* New York: Abrams, 1999.
Eyman, Scott. *Mary Pickford: America's Sweetheart.* New York: Donald Fine, 1990.
Whitfield, Eileen. *Pickford: The Woman Who Made Hollywood.* Lexington: University Press of Kentucky, 1997.

Recommended Recorded and Videotaped Performances

Coquette (1929). Warner Home Video, VHS, 1993.
Daddy Long-Legs (1919). Image Entertainment, DVD, 1999.
Mary Pickford: A Life on Film (1999). Tapeworm, VHS, 2000.
Stella Maris (1918). Image Entertainment, DVD, 2000.
The Taming of the Shrew (1929). Madacy Entertainment, VHS, 1995.

❖ POWELL, ELEANOR
(1912–1982) *Dancer, Actress, Singer*

Hailed "the world's greatest female tap dancer" by *Time* magazine, Eleanor Powell was born on November 21, 1912, in Springfield, Massachusetts. After her parents' divorce, Eleanor developed a painful shyness, which she tried to overcome by taking lessons in ballet and acrobatics. In 1925, she and her mother moved to Atlantic City, where she was hired to dance at local nightspots.

While still a teenager, Powell set out to conquer Broadway. In New York, however, she discovered that she needed to become a tap dancer to find work. As formal training, she took 10 lessons at the dance studio of Jack Donahue, who tied two sandbags around her waist to force her to resist her natural impulse toward high-stepping. On her own, Powell learned to tap off the beat by dancing to boogie-woogie records.

Powell's efforts paid off when she was hired for *Fine and Dandy* (1930), a musical comedy that made her a star. While working on this and other Broadway shows, she became known for her marathon rehearsals, which often lasted for more than six hours. Her show-stealing routines soon caught the attention of Louis B. Mayer at the Metro-Goldwyn-Mayer (MGM) movie studio. Signed for a small role in *Broadway Melody of 1936,* Powell immediately became one of the MGM's most popular stars.

With a seven-year contract with MGM, Powell began starring in a series of light musicals, including *Born to Dance* (1936), *Rosalie* (1937), and *Honolulu* (1939). Her acting was stilted and her singing was often dubbed, but Powell's dancing provided these pictures' highlights. Particularly popular were the spectacularly staged finales, during which Powell danced solo against extravagant sets populated by hundreds of extras. Powell did much of her own choreography and had each dance filmed four times. In post-production, she worked with the film editors to ensure that her film performances were as close as possible of perfection.

Unlike most female dancers of her day, Powell's enthusiastic performances were characterized by an aggressive, powerful physicality. Her style made it difficult for MGM to find a male partner who would not be overpowered by her. In fact, most of her leading men were nondancers, such as James Stewart and Nelson Eddy. She was most successfully paired, however, with Fred Astaire, who appeared with her in *Broadway Melody of 1938* (1937). Their dance to "Begin the Beguine" was not only the highlight of Powell's career but also considered by many as the greatest dance sequence ever captured on film. In his book *Steps in Time,* Astaire remembered Powell fondly, writing that "she 'put 'em down' like a man, no ricky-ticky-sissy stuff with Ellie. She really knocked out a tap dance in a class by herself."

Although Powell continued to be popular through the war years, after filming *Thousands Cheer* (1943), her last MGM musical, her contract was not renewed. She had her last starring role in *Sensations of 1945* (1944), in which she performed incredible routines with a horse and a pinball machine as her partners. Powell then largely retired from film to spend time with her husband, actor Glenn Ford (whom she married in 1943), and their son. After she and Ford divorced in 1959, Powell spent several years touring with a nightclub act and became a regular guest on television specials and programs. She made her final appearance on the American Film Institute's televised tribute to Fred Astaire in 1981. Remembered for her relentless energy and consummate professionalism, Powell died the next year in Beverly Hills on February 11.

Further Reading

Levin, Alice B. *Eleanor Powell: First Lady of Dance.* Potomac, Md.: A. B. Levin, 1997.

Schultz, Margie. *Eleanor Powell: A Bio-Bibliography.* Westport, Conn.: Greenwood Press, 1994.

Recommended Recorded and Videotaped Performances

Born to Dance (1936). Warner Home Video, VHS, 1990.
Broadway Melody of 1938 (1937). MGM/UA, VHS, 1992.
Thousands Cheer (1944). Warner Home Video, VHS, 1992.

❖ POWELL, MAUD
(1868–1920) *Musician*

Maud Powell, the United States's first great concert violinist, was born on August 22, 1868, in Peru, Illinois, and raised in the nearby town of Aurora. With her mother as her teacher, she learned to play simple pieces on the piano at four. At eight, she mastered Mozart's violin concertos and soon began performing in public. The next year, she began taking weekly trips to Chicago to study with members of the city's chamber music society.

Seeing her promise, the people of Aurora in 1881 helped Powell's family fund a year of study in Leipzig, Germany. Powell then continued her musical education at the Paris Conservatory. She later maintained that in Germany she learned to be a musician, while in France she learned to be an artist.

In 1883, at 15, Powell embarked on an extended concert tour in England, where she played for the royal family. After another year of instruction in Germany, she performed with the Berlin Philharmonic in 1885. Later the same year, she made her American debut with the New York Philharmonic Society.

Courted by an artist's manager, Powell contracted to tour throughout the American West in 1887. Playing in venues large and small, she introduced her audiences to many violin masterworks then virtually unknown in the United States. In an era when few women were professional musicians, Powell also promoted other female concert performers and female composers. She set forth her views in a paper titled "Women and Music," which she delivered at the 1893 Chicago World's Fair.

In 1894 Powell made history by being the first woman to lead male musicians in a chamber ensemble. Known as the Maud Powell Quartet, her string ensemble embarked on a series of tours after making their debut at New York City's Carnegie Hall. The same year, Powell made another historic first by becoming the earliest musician to record with the Victor Talking Machine Company's Red Seal label. By 1919, she had had more than 70 recordings made of her performances.

After the Maud Powell Quartet disbanded in 1898, Powell performed throughout the world, returning each year for a tour of the United States. In 1904 she married H. Godfrey Turner, a concert manager who took control of her professional affairs. Throughout the rest of her life, Powell maintained a relentless concert schedule that often took her to schools, colleges, and other unconventional venues for concert performances. The rigorous schedule exhausted her, and Powell's health

Maud Powell in about 1919
(Library of Congress, neg. no. USZ62-110623)

began to suffer. On January 8, 1920, she died of a heart attack at the age of 51. During her lifetime, she had successfully dispelled conventional wisdom by proving that both an American and a woman could possess the talent to become a world-class classical musician.

Further Reading

Karpf, Juanita. "Powell, Maud." In *American National Biography,* edited by John Arthur Garraty and Mark C. Carnes, vol. 17, pp. 781–782. New York: Oxford University Press, 1999.

Shaffer, Karen A. *Maud Powell: Pioneer American Violinist.* Ames: Iowa State University Press, 1988.

Recommended Recorded and Videotaped Performances

The Recorded Violin, Vol. 1: The History of the Violin on Record. Pearl, CD set, 1993.
Great Violinists, Vol. 1. Pearl-Koch, CD, 1992.

❖ **PRICE, FLORENCE (Florence Beatrice Smith)**
(1888–1953) *Musician, Composer*

The first African-American woman to compose a symphony, Florence Price was born Florence Beatrice Smith in Little Rock, Arkansas, on April 9, 1888. She was raised in a middle-class family and received her early instruction in music from her mother, a former schoolteacher. Florence gave her first public performance on the piano at four and had her first composition published at 11.

After graduating from high school, Florence Smith attended the New England Conservatory of Music in Boston, studying piano, organ, and music composition and theory. She returned to the South once she earned her degree and began teaching music on the college level. In 1912 Smith left her job as head of the music department at Atlanta's Clark University to marry Little Rock attorney Thomas J. Price. While raising two daughters, she gave private music lessons and began to compose in earnest.

Responding to rising racial tensions in Little Rock, the Price family moved to Chicago in 1927. The culturally rich environment of the city had an enormous influence on Florence Price's musical developments. She became acquainted with many fellow musicians and composers and further studied composition at several area schools, including the American Conservatory of Music and the University of Chicago. Price also gave frequent piano and organ performances and taught lessons. She was a particularly important mentor to student Margaret Bonds, who later became a noted composer in her own right.

Living in Chicago, Price also developed contacts with music publishers. They published many of her works, having noteworthy success with her short piano pieces for beginning students. Also in demand were her songs, which often drew on African-American folk material, especially the rhythms of black spirituals. Price's popular songs included *My Soul's Been Anchored in the Lord* and *Songs to a Dark Virgin;* the latter was set to a poem by her acquaintance Langston Hughes. African-American singers such as MARIAN ANDERSON and LEONTYNE PRICE often sang Price's works in concert.

Price also gained a reputation for her longer, symphonic works, many of which won major music awards. In 1932, four of her works, including Symphony in E Minor, won prizes at the Wanamaker Competition. The next year, her award-winning symphony was performed by the Chicago Symphony Orchestra at the Chicago World's Fair. Some of Price's other works were subsequently performed by orchestras in New York, Detroit, and Pittsburgh.

Price continued to perform, compose, and teach until her death from a stroke on June 3, 1953. Although in her lifetime she was largely unknown outside of the Chicago area, today she is considered one of the outstanding African-American musicians and composers of the 20th century.

Further Reading

Friedberg, Ruth C. "Price, Florence B." In *American National Biography,* edited by John Arthur Garraty and Mark C. Carnes, vol. 17, pp. 858–859. New York: Oxford University Press, 1999.
Green, Mildred Denby. *Black Women Composers: A Genesis.* Boston: G. K. Hall, 1983.
Jackson, Barbara Garvey. "Florence Price: Composer." *The Black Perspective in Music* 5 (spring 1977), 30–43.

Recommended Recorded and Videotaped Performances

Black Diamonds: Althea Waites Plays Piano Music by African-American Composers. Cambria Records, CD, 1993.
The Negro Speaks of Rivers: Art Songs by African-American Composers. Musicians Showcase, CD, 2000.

❖ **PRICE, LEONTYNE (Mary Violet Leontyne Price)**
(1927–) *Singer*

The first African American to become an international opera star, Mary Violet Leontyne Price was born on February 10, 1927, in Laurel, Mississippi. At nine, Leontyne attended a concert of singer MARIAN ANDERSON in nearby Jackson, an event she later cited as inspiring her to want a career in music. After years of singing in church and school groups, Leontyne left Mississippi to attend Central State College in Wilberforce, Ohio. Initially, she hoped to be a music teacher but soon decided to become a professional singer instead.

After graduating in 1948, Price headed for New York City to attend the prestigious Juilliard School of Music on a full scholarship. She also took private lessons from vocal coach Florence Page Kimball, who would remain a mentor throughout Price's career. While at Juilliard, Price performed in several school productions, including one of *Falstaff* in which she played Mistress Ford. Impressed by Price's performance, composer Virgil Thomson asked her to appear on Broadway in the revival of his musical *Four Saints in Three Acts.* Price was then hired for the role of Bess in a popular revival of *Porgy and Bess* that toured the United States and Europe from 1952 to 1954. During its run, she married her costar William Warfield; they were divorced in 1973, although the couple separated much earlier.

In New York, Price was acclaimed for her concerts, especially her 1954 appearance at Town Hall. Although she showed herself adept at interpreting modern works, she was determined to build a career in grand opera. In 1955 she appeared as Floria in an NBC production of *Tosca.* The performance marked the first time an African American had ever played a major operatic role on American television. Price subsequently performed in several other operas on NBC, including *Magic Flute* (1956) and *Don Giovanni* (1960).

Performing with the San Francisco Opera, Price made her opera debut on stage in 1957 as Madame

Leontyne Price in about 1965
(Library of Congress, USZ62-103119)

Lidoine in *Dialogues of the Carmelites.* The same year, she was selected to perform the lead in the company's production of *Aïda* when the original star had an emergency appendectomy. From then on, *Aïda* became a standard part of her repertoire. She performed the opera at La Scala in Milan, where she achieve another milestone by becoming the first African American to perform on its stage. Price soon emerged as an international opera star. Eventually, she would perform at nearly every major opera house in the world.

On January 27, 1961, Price had one of her greatest successes with her debut with New York's Metropolitan Opera. Performing the role of Leonora in *Il Trovatore,* she received an astounding 42-minute ovation, the longest in the opera company's history. *Il Trovatore* was only the first of 118 Met productions in which Price would appear before the end of the decade. One of her favorites was Samuel Barber's *Antony and Cleopatra* (1966), the production chosen to inaugurate the Met's new opera house at Lincoln Center. The role of Cleopatra was written with Price in mind.

During the 1970s, Price became increasingly choosy about which parts she would play. Some in the opera world labeled her as difficult, but her selectiveness helped her preserve her voice, which has remained remarkably strong. Price continued to perform opera until age 57. She gave her final performance in *Aïda* at Lincoln Center in 1985.

Since her retirement from opera, Price has continued to give recitals, a format she has always enjoyed since it allows her play different characters and experiment with different musical styles in a single performance. She has also become a respected teacher of master classes. Price maintains that helping nurture new talent is what "keeps me young." She has received an array of awards including a Kennedy Center Honor and the Spin-

garn Medal from the National Association for the Advancement of Colored People. Price has also been honored with *The Essential Leontyne Price* (1996), a set of 11 CDs of recordings made throughout her distinguished career.

Further Reading

Blier, Steven. "Time After Time: Throughout Her Long Career, Leontyne Price Has Inspired Fans and a New Generation of Singers." *Opera News.* October 1996, pp. 10+.

Lyon, Hugh Lee. *Leontyne Price: Highlights of a Prima Donna.* New York: Vintage Press, 1973.

Recommended Recorded and Videotaped Performances

The Essential Leontyne Price: Highlights. RCA, CD, 1997.

The Essential Leontyne Price: Spirituals, Hymns, and Sacred Songs. RCA, CD, 1997.

Leontyne Price: The Complete Bell Television Hour Performances. Video Artists International, VHS, 2000.

R

❖ RADNER, GILDA
(1946–1989)   *Comic, Actress*

A gifted comedian with a talent for creating lovable characters, Gilda Radner was born into an affluent family in Detroit, Michigan, on June 28, 1946. Her father earned his fortune smuggling alcohol into the United States from Canada during Prohibition. Among his subsequent investments was a hotel popular with performers such as Frank Sinatra and George Burns when they visited Detroit. Gilda had a tense relationship with her mother, especially as she began to gain weight as a young child. At 10, she was given Dexedrine, the first of many diet aids Radner would use during her life.

In 1960, her father died of brain cancer, leaving Gilda a substantial fortune. After high school, she attended the University of Michigan, where she studied drama for six years without graduating. She then moved to Toronto and drifted into a show business career. Radner worked as a children's clown for several years, before appearing in a production of *Godspell*. Also in the cast were Paul Shaffer, Martin Short, Eugene Levy, and Andrea Martin—all of whom, like Radner, would later achieve fame in television sketch comedy.

Radner soon landed a spot in Second City, a Toronto improvisational comedy troupe. Based on her Second City work, Lorne Michaels, the producer of a new, late-night variety series, *Saturday Night Live,* hired Radner as the show's first cast member in 1975. After a rocky first season, *Saturday Night Live* became a solid hit and made Radner a star. Among her most popular characters were Emily Litella, a hard-of-hearing television editorialist; Lisa Loopner, a hopelessly gawky high school nerd; and Roseanne Roseannadanna, a commentator given to making repulsive observations about everyday life.

Unlike the often aggressive comedy of male cast members such as John Belushi and Dan Akroyd, Radner's bits always contained an affection for the characters she portrayed. In addition to her gentle humor, Radner won over audiences with an almost waiflike vulnerability. *Saturday Night Live* writer Alan Zweibel once described Radner's appeal: "You felt like you knew her. She was a star, but she was your sister."

Radner won an Emmy Award in 1978 for her work on *Saturday Night Live*. She also appeared in a Broadway show—*Gilda Radner Live From New York* (1979)—featuring her favorite characters. Radner left the cast of *Saturday Night Live* in 1980, the same year she married the show's bandleader, G. E. Smith. They were divorced two years later.

Radner tried to make the move from television to movies but had limited success. She appeared in *First Family* (1980) and *It Came from Hollywood* (1982), both box-office failures. On the set of *Hanky Panky* (1982), she met actor Gene Wilder. The two married in France in 1984 and appeared in two more films together, *The Woman in Red* (1984) and *Haunted Honeymoon* (1986).

After feeling ill for nearly a year, Radner was diagnosed with ovarian cancer in 1986. Chemotherapy and radiation treatments temporarily put her illness in remission. She wrote of her struggle with cancer in her 1989 autobiography, *It's Always Something*, which she described as a "seriously funny" book. She also founded Gilda's Friends, a support group for cancer patients. In 1988, she made her last onscreen performance playing herself in an episode of *It's Garry Shandling's Show*, for which she received an Emmy nomination.

Gilda Radner died in Los Angeles on May 20, 1989. After her death, Wilder expanded her support group by establishing Gilda's Clubs, centers offering cancer patients free counseling, throughout the United States and Canada.

Further Reading

Radner, Gilda. *It's Always Something*. New York: Simon & Schuster, 1989.

Zweibel, Alan. *Bunny Bunny*. New York: Villard Books, 1994.

Recommended Recorded and Videotaped Performances

Biography: Gilda Radner (1987). A&E Entertainment, VHS, 1995.

Gilda Live (1980). Warner Home Video, VHS, 1993.

❖ RAINEY, MA (Gertrude Malissa Nix Pridgett, Gertrude Rainey, Madame Rainey)
(1886–1939) *Singer*

Hailed as the "Mother of the Blues," Ma Rainey was born Gertrude Malissa Nix Pridgett on April 26, 1886. Raised in Columbus, Georgia, she began her career at 14 when she sang in a local talent show. She already had begun working in tent shows, touring entertainments for southern black audiences, when she married fellow performer William Rainey in 1904. Together they began appearing in tent and minstrel shows, vaudeville houses, and honky-tonks, billed as "Ma and Pa Rainey, Assassinators of the Blues." In time, she began performing on her own as "Madame Rainey," though her fans still referred to her by the more intimate "Ma."

By accounts of those who saw her, Rainey was a magnetic performer. A large woman whose features were often described as homely, she complemented her love of the theatrical with flamboyant costumes. She often wore flashy beaded dresses and earrings fashioned from gold dollar coins.

Ma Rainey performed traditional folk songs, favorite vaudeville tunes, and novelty ditties, but she was best known for singing the blues. Rainey's blues told stories of love, sex, infidelity, drunkenness, depression, revenge, superstition, and murder—subjects familiar to her audiences. Later known as classic blues, Rainey's songs described the difficult day-to-day experiences of rural southern blacks living in poverty in the days of lynchings and resurgence of the Ku Klux Klan. Fitting with the lyrics she sang, Rainey's style was earthy, and her voice was often harsh. Her rough country blues would help give birth to the more polished, urban interpretation popularized by BESSIE SMITH, whom Rainey knew and greatly influenced.

Though a favorite on the southern circuit, Rainey was largely unknown in the North until 1923. She then traveled to Chicago to make a series of recordings for Paramount, which marketed them to African Americans as "race records." Over the next five years, Rainey recorded 92 songs, only a small portion of her repertoire. The most famous of these include "Bo-weevil Blues," "Those All Night Long Blues," and the risqué "Ma Rainey's Black Bottom." Because of the primitive equipment used, these records hardly captured the dynamism of her live performances. Nevertheless, they succeeded in greatly expanding her audience and encouraging record companies to record other, younger blues artists.

Soon, however, Rainey's performing career was on the wane. The Great Depression and competition from radio hit the vaudeville and minstrel circuit hard. Finding bookings fewer and farther between, Rainey returned to Columbus, Georgia, in 1935, to live in the house she had bought for her family. She spent her last years operating two theaters she owned in the nearby city of Rome. On December 22, 1939, Ma Rainey died in her hometown of a heart attack. She is now remembered as the first woman to make a living from singing the blues.

Further Reading

Davis, Angela Y. *Blues Legacies and Black Feminism: Gertrude "Ma" Rainey, Bessie Smith, and Billie Holiday.* New York: Pantheon Books, 1998.

Lieb, Sandra R. *Mother of the Blues: A Study of Ma Rainey.* Amherst: University of Massachusetts Press, 1981.

Stewart-Baxter, Derrick. *Ma Rainey and the Classic Blues Singers.* New York: Stein and Day, 1970

Recommended Recorded and Videotaped Performances

Ma Rainey: The Complete Recorded Works. Vols. 1 to 5. Document, CD, 1998.

❖ RAND, SALLY (Helen Gould Beck, Billy Beck)
(1904–1979)   *Dancer, Actress*

Famed for her titillating "fan dance," Sally Rand was born Helen Gould Beck on January 2, 1904, in Elkton, Missouri. When she was a child, her father, a retired army colonel, separated from her mother. To help support her family, Helen left home at 13 and made her way to Chicago. There, while studying ballet, she worked as a cigarette girl and nude art model. Still in her teens, she returned to Missouri and began her show-business career as a chorus girl in Kansas City and an acrobat in Ringling Brothers Circus.

Sally Rand in 1941
(Library of Congress, neg. no. USZ62-112038)

By her 20th birthday, Beck was in Hollywood, playing bit parts in silent movies. She was billed as Billy Beck until director Cecil B. DeMille gave her the name Rand after glancing at a Rand McNally atlas on his desk. She christened herself Sally, believing the name would look good on a marquee.

After sound was introduced to film, Rand had difficulty finding acting jobs. By the early 1930s, she had started working nightclubs with a six-minute act known as the fan dance. Bathed in blue light, Rand stood on stage naked, seductively moving two seven-foot-long ostrich feathers in front of her body to the music of Debussy and Chopin.

In 1933, Rand began performing her act at the Chicago World's Fair for $125 a week. Overall, fair attendance was disappointing, but Rand and her fan dance were an immediate hit. As newspaper articles about Rand made her a celebrity nationwide, her weekly salary rose to $5,000. With Rand's fame came notoriety. Although the fan dance was more teasing than revealing, she was arrested many times for indecency charges. In September 1933, she was brought to trial and found guilty. Sentenced to a year in prison, Rand appealed, and her conviction was overturned.

Rand's act was also debated on the floor of the U.S. Congress. In 1934, Congress considered pulling its funding for the reopening of the World's Fair later that year. The fair was supposed to be educational, but its main attraction was anything but intellectually uplifting. Congress finally agreed to fund the fair, on the proviso that Rand would not perform. Without Rand, the fair had such trouble attracting visitors that its concession operators rioted. By July, Rand was invited back to introduced the bubble dance, performed with a 60-inch balloon in place of her ostrich feathers.

After the fair, Rand returned to Hollywood for one picture, *Bolero* (1934). But aside from an occasional foray into regional theater, her career continued to revolve around the fan dance. Touring as many as 40 weeks a year, she took the act to fairs and nightclubs across the nation. The twice-divorced Rand continued performing the fan dance well into her 70s. One year after retiring from show business, Sally Rand died of heart failure at her home at Glendora, California, on August 31, 1979.

Further Reading

Bailey, Beth. "Rand, Sally." In *American National Biography*, edited by John Arthur Garraty and Mark C. Carnes, vol. 18, pp. 104–105. New York: Oxford University Press, 1999.

Wilmeth, Don B. "Sally Rand." In *Dictionary of American Biography, Supplement 10: 1976–1980*. New York: Charles Scribner's Sons, 1995.

❖ **RIVERS, JOAN (Joan Alexandra Molinsky)**
   (1933–   ) *Talk Show Host, Comic*

A seminal stand-up comedian who found her greatest success as a talk show host, Joan Rivers was born Joan Alexandra Molinsky on June 8, 1933. The daughter of a successful physician, she spent her youth in Brooklyn and Larchmont, New York.

In 1954, Molinsky graduated Phi Beta Kappa from Barnard College, where she performed in many school productions. Although she craved a show business career, she instead worked in the fashion industry. While a fashion coordinator for the Bond clothing stores, she married her boss's son, James Sanger. The marriage was annulled six months later.

Against her parents' wishes, Molinsky quit her job and began performing stand-up comedy in New York clubs under the name Joan Rivers. Supporting herself with secretarial work, she spent seven years on the club circuit with little success. Her big break finally came when she landed a spot on *The Tonight Show* in 1965. Four months later, she married producer Edgar Rosenberg. They had a daughter, Melissa, in 1968.

Throughout the 1960s and 1970s, Rivers was a frequent guest on *The Tonight Show* and other variety and talk programs. She helped pioneer the daytime talk show as the host of the short-lived *That Show* (1968–69). Rivers also tried writing for the stage and screen. She coauthored the unsuccessful Broadway play *Fun City* (1972) and wrote the television movie *The Girl Most Likely To . . .* (1973). Rivers and Rosenberg mortgaged their house to help finance *Rabbit Test* (1978), a film comedy cowritten and directed by Rivers. To her disappointment, the movie received mediocre reviews. She had better luck with the humor book *The Life and Hard Times of Heidi Abromowitz* (1984), which became a best-seller. She has since written two well-received autobiographies and several self-help books drawing on incidents in her own life.

In 1983, Rivers became the permanent guest host of *The Tonight Show,* often drawing better ratings than its regular host, Johnny Carson. She was particularly hailed for her monologues. Early in her career, she relied heavily on self-deprecating humor ("I was such an ugly baby a furrier tried to club me"). As her star rose, she increasingly made the rich and famous the targets of her one-liners. Rivers was especially ruthless in her humorous attack on ELIZABETH TAYLOR's weight gain ("Mosquitos see her and scream 'Buffet'"). She once explained her brand of comedy, saying "I am telling the truth in a very angry age. . . . And I succeed by saying what everyone else is thinking."

Lured by a $3 million contract from the fledging Fox network, Rivers became the host of her own late-night talk show, *The Late Show Starring Joan Rivers,* in 1986. The show failed, and soon afterward her husband suffered a nervous breakdown. He committed suicide in 1987. Adding to her sorrow, Rivers found herself nearly broke because of bad investments and watched her relationship with her daughter Melissa deteriorate. She later chronicled this difficult time in the television movie *Tears and Laughter: The Joan and Melissa Rivers Story* (1994), in which she and Melissa Rivers played themselves.

Rivers returned to television in the syndicated *The Joan Rivers Show* (1989–94), for which she won a 1990 daytime Emmy Award as best talk show host. In 1989, she also began designing and selling her own line of jewelry on the QVC cable shopping channel, an enterprise that has greatly improved her financial situation. In the 1990s, Rivers started appearing on E!, a cable entertainment news network. Since 1994, she has hosted E!'s most successful program—a pre–Academy Awards show during which she and Melissa offer humorous remarks about movie stars' sense of style or lack thereof.

Further Reading

Rivers, Joan, with Richard Meryman. *Enter Talking.* New York: Delacorte, 1986.

———. *Still Talking.* New York: Turtle Bay Books, 1991.

Recommended Recorded and Videotaped Performances

Joan Rivers: Abroad in London (1992). Paramount, VHS, 1995.

Joan Rivers' Shopping for Fitness (1996). ABC Home Video, VHS, 1996.

❖ ROBERTS, JULIA
(1967–)   *Actress*

Since her meteorite rise to fame in 1990, Julia Roberts has been one of the few actresses considered "bankable" by the Hollywood elite. The youngest of three children, she was born on October 28, 1967, in Smyrna, Georgia. Her parents ran a theatrical workshop for actors and writers in Atlanta. As a child, Julia wanted to become a veterinarian, but Roberts admits the idea of acting was "just kind of there in my mind all the time."

Her parents divorced in 1971, and her father died of cancer five years later—two events that cast a pall over an otherwise happy childhood. In her teenage years, Roberts developed a contentious relationship with her stepfather. Eager to leave home, she moved to New York City just days after her high school graduation. There, she joined her sister Lisa, who was pursuing an acting career. Her brother Eric had already found success starring in such films as *Star 80* (1983) and *The Pope of Greenwich Village* (1984).

Roberts intended to study acting but after a few classes concluded that they were not "very conducive to what I wanted to do." For a year, she signed on with a modeling agency and auditioned for acting roles with little success. Eric helped her get her first part playing his sister in *Blood Red* (1988), a drama that was not released until Roberts became a star. After a guest spot on the television series *Crime Story,* she appeared in the films *Satisfaction* (1988) and *Baja Oklahoma* (1988). Her breakthrough role came in *Mystic Pizza* (1988), in which she stole the picture playing a sexy Portuguese-American waitress. She then won the part of Shelby, a doomed diabetic, in *Steel Magnolias* (1989). Playing opposite such veteran actresses as Sally Field, Shirley MacLaine, and Olympia Dukakis, Roberts was the only cast member to receive an Academy Award nomination.

Roberts's next film—*Pretty Woman* (1990)—made her a star. In this romantic comedy, Roberts played a prostitute who enchants a ruthless tycoon (Richard Gere). Although dismissed by critics as formulaic, the movie was an enormous success with moviegoers, becoming the year's second most successful film. Much of its popularity was due to Roberts, who was hailed for the warmth and humor that she brought to her role. Critic Roger Ebert prophetically wrote, "[Roberts] gives her character an irrepressibly bouncy sense of humor. . . . Actresses who can do that *and* look great can have whatever they want in Hollywood."

Now Hollywood's hottest actress, Roberts appeared in two thrillers—*Flatliners* (1990) and *Sleeping with the Enemy* (1991). Both were box-office hits, largely because of her star power. However, her films *Dying Young* (1991) and *Hook* (1991) failed to find an audience.

Beginning in 1991, Roberts took a two-year hiatus from film. Tabloids spread unfounded rumors that, feeling the pressure of sudden fame, she was headed for a breakdown. The press also widely reported her affairs with costars Liam Neeson and Dylan McDermott and her last-minute decision not to marry actor Kiefer Sutherland. Her brief marriage to singer Lyle Lovett also fed the rumor mills.

In 1993, Roberts returned to acting in *The Pelican Brief* (1993), a popular legal thriller that paired her with Denzel Washington. Over the next few years, her career stumbled with a series of box-office failures, including *I Love Trouble* (1993), *Something to Talk About* (1995), and *Mary Reilly* (1996). Just as some critics began to dismiss Roberts' early success as a fluke, she had a hit with the romantic comedy *My Best Friend's Wedding* (1997). Roberts stayed with the genre for her next two films, both of which were great commercial successes. In *Notting Hill* (1999), Roberts played a world-famous actress uncomfortable with her fame, a role that seemed to echo her own experiences. In *Runaway Bride* (1999), she played a marriage-shy young woman opposite her *Pretty Woman* costar Richard Gere.

Roberts's next role was the title character in *Erin Brockovich* (2000), the story of a crusading law office clerk who uncovers a pollution scandal involving a utility company. For her work, Roberts earned $20 million, at the time the highest paycheck ever given to an American actress. The film became her eighth movie to earn more than $100 million, firmly reestablishing her as one of the most popular movie stars in the world. In 2001, Roberts won the Academy Award for best actress for her role in *Brockovich*.

Further Reading

Heath, Chris. "Portrait of a Trash-Talking Lady." *Rolling Stone.* April 13, 2000, pp. 70–80+.

Recommended Recorded and Videotaped Performances

Erin Brockovich (2000). Universal/MCA, DVD/VHS, 2000.
Mystic Pizza (1988). MGM, DVD/VHS, 2001.
Pretty Woman (1990). Buena Vista Home Entertainment, DVD/VHS, 2000.
Steel Magnolias (1989). Columbia/Tristar, DVD/VHS, 2000.

❖ ROGERS, GINGER (Virginia Katherine McMath)
(1911–1995) *Actress, Dancer, Singer*

Known best for her famous dance routines with onscreen partner Fred Astaire, Ginger Rogers became a master of the film musical, comedy, and drama, making her one of the most versatile actresses of her day. She was born in Independence, Missouri, on July 16, 1911, as Virginia Katherine McMath, but was nicknamed Ginger by her parents. Soon after her birth, the McMaths divorced, initiating a bitter custody battle during which her father kidnapped her twice. With Ginger secure in the care of her mother, Lela, they moved first to Hollywood, then to New York City, where Lela looked for work as a screenwriter. They eventually relocated to Fort Worth, Texas. There, Lela married John Rogers, and Ginger took the name of her new stepfather.

Like Lela, Ginger had show business ambitions at an early age. At her mother's relentless urging, at 14 she entered and won a statewide Charleston contest, which led to a three-year tour with a vaudeville act. With an eye toward becoming a big-band singer, Ginger moved to New York City in 1929. Almost immediately, she found parts in Broadway musicals, most notably George and Ira Gershwin's *Girl Crazy* (1930). Playing an ingenue, she introduced America to two classic Gershwin songs—"Embraceable You" and "But Not for Me." In *Girl Crazy,* she also had her first professional contact with Astaire, who was hired to beef up the show's choreography.

Rogers's Broadway roles soon drew the attention of Hollywood. A screen test won her a part in her first film, *Young Man of Manhattan* (1930). Her sassy reading of the line, "Cigarette me, big boy," made it a favorite catchphrase of the era. In Hollywood, Rogers established herself as a leading interpreter of the tough, wise-cracking gal in movies such as *42nd Street* and *Gold Diggers of 1933* (both 1933).

Rogers found her breakthrough role in *Flying Down to Rio* (1930). As supporting players, she and Astaire stole the movie with their performance of a dance known as the Carioca. The public's enthusiastic response to the pairing led to a series of eight musical comedies with Rogers and Astaire as the stars. The formulaic plots of these films functioned largely to fill time between their accomplished, romantic dance sequences, each of which took as long six weeks to develop. Rogers and Astaire's films together included *The Gay Divorcee* (1934), *Top Hat* (1935), and *Shall We Dance?* (1937). Rogers always named *Swing Time* (1936) as her personal favorite, once explaining, "It gave me a bigger role than Mr. Astaire!" Although Rogers and Astaire reportedly harbored hostility toward each other, in fact they were generally cordial and developed a strong working relationship based on a shared sense of discipline and professionalism.

Despite her talents, Rogers was not as well-trained as many of Astaire's dancing partners. She was, however, a quick study, able to master whatever the perfectionism of Astaire demanded. But far more important than her technical expertise was the warmth and liveliness she brought to the

Ginger Rogers with Fred Astaire in *Top Hat* (1935)
(Museum of Modern Art Film Stills Archive)

screen duo. KATHARINE HEPBURN once made the now often-quoted observation about Astaire and Rogers that "he gave her class and she gave him sex." Rogers later challenged this assessment, observing, "Nobody can give you class. . . . You've either got it or you ain't."

While working with Astaire, Rogers also distinguished herself in nonmusical films. She was a standout as a caustic young actress in the star-filled *Stage Door* (1937) and skillfully played a woman trying to masquerade as a 12-year-old in the broad comedy *The Major and the Minor* (1942). She also displayed her range as an actress by taking on dramatic roles. Playing the lead in *Kitty Foyle* (1940), a melodrama about a working girl's struggles, Rogers won an Academy Award for best actress.

While continuing her film career, Rogers in the 1950s returned to the stage, often touring in revivals of musicals such as *Annie Get Your Gun* and *Mame.* She was particularly praised for her performance in *Hello, Dolly!,* in which she starred on Broadway for a year and a half. In the late 1970s, Rogers also found success with *The Ginger Rogers Show,* a musical celebration of her career that toured through the United States and Europe.

A devout Christian Scientist and political conservative, Rogers generally led a quiet, scandal-free personal life. She did, however, marry and divorce five times, as well as having serious romances with some of Hollywood's most eligible leading men, including Cary Grant and James Stewart. In her final years, though, she lived alone, spending most of her time on a ranch in Oregon. Three years after receiving a Kennedy Center Honor for her contribution to American popular culture, Rogers died of natural causes on April 25, 1995.

Further Reading

Croce, Arlene. *The Fred Astaire and Ginger Rogers Book.* New York: Outerbridge & Lazard, 1972.

Faris, Jocelyn. *Ginger Rogers: A Bio-Bibliography.* Westport, Conn.: Greenwood, 1994.

Rogers, Ginger. *Ginger: My Story.* New York: Harper-Collins, 1991.

Recommended Recorded and Videotaped Performances

Flying Down to Rio (1933). Turner Home Video, VHS, 2000.

The Gay Divorcee (1934). Turner Home Video, VHS, 1999.

Kitty Foyle (1940). Turner Home Video, VHS, 1998.

Swing Time (1936). Turner Home Video, VHS, 1999.

❖ ROSEANNE (Roseanne Barr, Roseanne Arnold)
(1953–) *Actress, Comic, Talk Show Host*

Through her long-running television series, Roseanne injected a dose of reality into the situation comedy genre. Born Roseanne Barr on November 3, 1953, she grew up feeling like an outsider as one of the few Jews in Salt Lake City, Utah. While still in her teens, she survived a near-fatal car accident and a mental breakdown that required months of hospitalization.

At 19, Barr moved to Colorado, where she married postal clerk Bill Pentland. While raising their three children, she worked a series of low-paying jobs, living the life of the working poor she later chronicled in her comedy. During the 1970s, she became active in the women's movement. Her commitment to feminism was at the center of a stand-up act she developed in 1981. Insisting on being called a "domestic goddess" instead of a homemaker, Barr joked about the abuses women suffered at the hands of their selfish husbands and children. The look of her onstage persona was itself radical: She stood before her audiences unabashedly frumpy and overweight, refusing to make quips at the expense of her own appearance, unlike most female stand-ups.

After performing at comedy clubs throughout the West, Barr appeared at Los Angeles's Comedy Club. The gig won her a spot on *The Tonight Show* in 1983. Barr starred in several HBO comedy specials before being lured to ABC to star in her own situation comedy.

Premiering in 1988, *Roseanne* softened Barr's stand-up character and placed her at the center of the Conner family, which included two working-class parents and their three smart-mouthed children. Although Barr exuded more warmth onscreen than onstage, the show had an edge that distinguished itself from other sitcoms of the time. Rather than painting a idealized portrait of family life, *Roseanne* looked clear-eyed at the Conners' constant economic and personal struggles. The show's comedy arose naturally as these intelligent characters used humor to help them cope. According to *Entertainment Weekly, Roseanne* quickly emerged as "the finest, truest, most nuanced, and best-acted sitcom about blue-collar people since 'The Honeymooners.'"

The show was an instant hit, even though, behind the scenes, Barr was launching an all-out war for creative control. Midway through the first season, she succeeded in elbowing out Matt Williams, who was billed as *Roseanne's* cocreator.

Throughout the show's nine-year run, Barr would repeatedly fire producers and writers. While she was criticized as a prima donna, some insiders credited her actions with keeping the scripts fresh and innovative.

Offscreen, Barr also generated controversy. In 1990, she was asked to sing "The Star-Spangled Banner" before a baseball game at San Diego's Jack Murphy Stadium. Singing off-key amidst booing from the crowd, she ended her appearance by grabbing her crotch and spitting in imitation of professional sports stars. What she thought was a comic performance sparked a national debate. Many Americans branded her as unpatriotic, including President George H. W. Bush, who called Barr's rendition of the national anthem "disgraceful."

Barr's massive success continued to inspire increasingly extreme behavior. She had repeated plastic surgeries, claimed to be possessed by 24 different personalities, and revealed that she had been the victim of sexual abuse as a child, a charge her family vehemently denied. Divorcing Pentland, Barr married comic Tom Arnold in 1990 and alienated many of her associates by her vigorous promotion of Arnold as the star of two failed sitcoms, *The Jackie Thomas Show* and *Tom*. Calling herself Roseanne Arnold, she stunned her fans by announcing that she and Arnold were "marrying" her young female assistant. By 1994, her relationship with Arnold had ended in an ugly divorce, and she changed her stage name to simply Roseanne. She subsequently married her bodyguard Ben Thomas, with whom she had a son, Buck, in 1995. Roseanne filed for a divorce from Thomas three years later.

While still appearing on her series, Roseanne tentatively started a big-screen career. She performed to lukewarm reviews in *She-Devil* (1989), *Even Cowgirls Get the Blues* (1994), and *Blue in the Face* (1995). She had more success providing the voice of a baby girl in *Look Who's Talking Too* (1990) and acting in two popular television films costarring Tom Arnold—*Backfield in Motion* (1991) and *The Woman Who Loved Elvis* (1993). Roseanne also served as the executive producer of the late-night sketch comedy series *Saturday Night Special* (1996) and as the guest editor of an issue of *The New Yorker* magazine in 1995. She made the bestseller list with two autobiographies, *Roseanne: My Life as a Woman* (1989) and *My Lives* (1994).

In 1997, after a critically savaged final season during which the Conner family won the lottery, *Roseanne* went off the air. Roseanne returned to television the next year with *The Roseanne Show,* a syndicated daytime talk show. Although she received her first Emmy nomination for her hosting, the show failed to find an audience and was canceled in 1999. Even the provocateur, she has since announced her intention to appear in a nude centerfold to show off her 75-pound weight loss.

Further Reading

Arnold, Roseanne. *My Lives.* New York: Baltimore Books, 1994.

Barr, Roseanne. *Roseanne: My Life as a Woman.* New York: Harper & Row, 1989.

Recommended Recorded and Videotaped Performances

She-Devil (1989). MGM/UA, VHS, 2000.

The Roseanne Barr Show (1987). HBO Home Video, VHS, 1990.

Roseanne Arnold: Live from Trump Castle (1992). Columbia/Tristar, VHS, 1996.

❖ ROSS, DIANA
(1944–)   *Singer, Actress*

With extraordinary talent and fierce ambition, Diana Ross has become one of the most successful recording artists in history. Born on March 26, 1944, she grew up in Detroit, Michigan, the second of six children. Her family was so poor that all the children had to share the same bed, but Ross remembers her childhood as a happy one. She later described the Brewster-Douglass housing project in which she lived as "a warm, loving family environment."

Through her church choir, Ross became acquainted with Florence Ballard and Mary Wilson, members of the local vocal group the Primettes. (The male counterpart, the Primes, was founded by Eddie Kendricks, later a member of the Temptations). After joining the Primettes, Ross and her friends began to hang out at the Motown recording studio, hoping to be discovered. Once they had graduated from high school, Ross, Wilson, and Ballard were signed to the record label by Motown head Berry Gordy and renamed the Supremes.

Initially, the Supremes sang backup during performances by headliners such as Marvin Gaye and Mary Wells. But when the group was paired with the songwriting team of Eddie Holland, Lamont Dozier, and Brian Holland, they began to develop their own unique sound. After a few moderately successful recordings, they hit number one with "Where Did Our Love Go" (1964) and quickly became Motown's hottest act. With Ross's girlish voice in lead vocals, their pop tunes easily crossed over into mainstream market. To make the Supremes more marketable to whites, Gordy dressed them in evening gowns in live performances. They quickly became icons of glamour to both black and white fans.

Between 1964 and 1967, the Supremes had 14 top 10 hits, including the classics "Baby Love" (1964), "Stop! In the Name of Love" (1965), and "You Keep Me Hangin' On" (1966). In 1967, Florence Ballard was replaced by Cindy Birdsong. In the same year, the group was officially renamed Diana Ross and the Supremes, reflecting Ross's increasing push toward the center stage. Few were surprised when Ross announced in 1970 that she was going solo. Her last hit with the Supremes— "Someday, We'll Be Together" (1969)—was the group's 12th number-one song.

With the strong support of Berry Gordy, Ross began developing her solo career, scoring an early success with the hit "Ain't No Mountain High Enough" (1970). Concentrating on ballads, she would have a dozen top 10 singles between 1970 and 1985. Among her hits were "Touch Me in the Morning" (1973), "Love Hangover" (1976), and "Endless Love" (1981), a duet with former Commodores lead singer Lionel Richie.

Ross also found success in films. In 1972, she appeared as BILLIE HOLIDAY in *Lady Sings the Blues*. Although the reaction to the film was mixed, her performance won universal acclaim and was honored with an Academy Award nomination for best actress. Ross's star power also propelled *Mahogany* (1975), a slight story of the trials of a fashion designer, into a commercial hit. Her recording of the theme from *Mahogany* received an Oscar nomination for best song. Ross had less success with the film version of the theatrical musical *The Wiz* (1978), based on the movie *The Wizard of Oz* (1939). Critics savaged her for playing Dorothy, although the 34-year-old Ross has the character changed from a girl to a teacher to better suit her age.

Despite her active career, Ross worked hard to create a family life. In 1971, she married manager Robert Silberman, with whom she had three daughters. Ross and Silberman were divorced in 1975. Ten years later, Ross wed Norwegian shipping tycoon Arne Naess Jr. They had two sons before terminating their marriage in 2000.

In the 1990s, Ross suffered several personal and professional setbacks. Her brother Arthur, a successful songwriter, was found murdered in his house in 1996. Four years later she was arrested for assault after a scuffle with a security officer at London's Heathrow Airport. Ross was also drawn into a controversy involving the 2000 concert series billed as the "Return to Love" tour. Promoted as a Supremes reunion, the tour was originally intended to bring Ross together with Wilson and Ballard's replacement, Cathy Birdsong. When Wilson and Birdsong balked at their proposed compensation, Scherrie Payne and Lynda Laurence were hired to replace them. Payne and Laurence had performed with the Supremes only after Ross had left the group. Audiences, eager to see the original Supremes, were unenthusiastic about the tour lineup. Due to low ticket sales, the concert tour was canceled midway in July 2000.

During the 1990s, Ross had also seen her share of career triumphs. In the television movie *Out of the Darkness* (1994), she solidified her reputation as a dramatic actress in her skilled performance as a schizophrenic. She also had a popular success with *Double Platinum* (1999), a television movie that cast her as the celebrity mother of an aspiring singer, played by the pop star Brandy. In celebration of 30 years as a recording artist, the box set *Forever, Diana* (1993) brought together her greatest hits. Equally well-received was her performance on "VH1 Divas 2000: A Salute to Diana Ross," a cable television special that reached an audience of more than 20 million. Singer, actress, and diva, Diana Ross remains as beloved an artist now as she was in the 1960s.

Further Reading

Ross, Diana. *Secrets of a Sparrow*. New York: Villard, 1993.

Taraborrelli, J. Randy. *Call Her Miss Ross: The Unauthorized Biography of Diana Ross*. New York: Birch Lane Press, 1989.

Recommended Recorded and Videotaped Performances

Double Platinum (1999). Columbia/Tristar, DVD/VHS, 1999.

Forever, Diana. Motown, CD set, 1993.

Lady Sings the Blues (1972). Paramount, VHS, 1996.

The Wiz (1978). Universal Studios, DVD/VHS, 1999/1998.

❖ **RUSSELL, LILLIAN (Helen Louise Leonard)**

(1861–1922) *Singer, Actress*

In the Gay Nineties, Lillian Russell reigned as the great beauty of the American stage. On December 4, 1861, she was born Helen Louise Leonard in Clinton, Iowa. Four years later, her family moved to Chicago, where she attended finishing school. The youngest of five daughters, Helen received her earliest musical training at home. She later recalled, "Our family was a musical one. . . . [A]ll my sisters had exceptionally fine voices, which were carefully trained."

Her mother, an ardent feminist, divorced her husband in 1877 and moved the girls to New York

City. There, Leonard took formal voice lessons with the intention of becoming an opera singer. To her mother's chagrin, she instead made her stage debut in the chorus of a Brooklyn Academy of Music production of Gilbert and Sullivan's *HMS Pinafore*. Two weeks into its run, she married orchestra leader Harry Braham. After the death of their infant son, the couple divorced.

Hearing Leonard sing at a party, producer Tony Pastor hired her to sing at his theater. He renamed her Lillian Russell and billed her inaccurately as "the English Ballad Singer," grandly adding that she was "a Vision of Loveliness" with "a Voice of Gold." Certainly, from her 1880 debut, she was as much a sensation for her beauty as for her soprano singing. After appearing in *The Pie Rats of Penn Yan* (a burlesque of Gilbert and Sullivan's *The Pirates of Penzance*), she found great success in comic operas such as *The Snake Charmer* (1881) and *Patience* (1881).

Early in her career, Russell showed a tendency to sign whatever contracts came her way, paying little attention to how they might conflict with one another. To escape various commitments she made, Russell traveled to England in 1883, bringing showman Edward Solomon in tow. They married in 1884 and had one child, Dorothy, before it was discovered that he was not divorced from his first wife. Russell denounced Solomon during the ensuing scandal and had their marriage annulled in 1893.

Russell returned to New York in 1885, having taken the English stage by storm. She was offered an extraordinary $20,000 a season to perform at the Casino, the city's leading venue for light opera. Russell won kudos in a series of shows, particularly for her performance in *The Grand Duchess* (1890). During its run, she participated in the first long-distance phone call, singing a song from the show over the line to President Benjamin Harrison in Washington, D.C. Russell also won acclaim in *The Princess Nicotine* (1893). Her costar, tenor John Haley Augustin Chatterton, became her third husband. They separated only four months after their marriage, after viciously attacking each other in the press.

Lillian Russell in about 1897
(Library of Congress, neg. no. USZ62-94048)

Russell also made news as the friend of "Diamond Jim" Brady, a wealthy financier with a taste for extravagant living. Together, they became icons of the conspicuous consumption rampant in 1890s New York. They held spectacular parties and maintained lavish homes. Published reports of their spending sprees only added to their celebrity.

In 1896, Russell starred in *An American Beauty,* which along with "airy Fairy Lillian," became a popular nickname for her. By this period, however, Russell was gaining weight just as fashion was beginning to favor a more waiflike physique in women. As her popularity as a musical star began to fade, she moved

into a new career in burlesque. In 1890, she joined the company of comedians Joe Weber and Lew Field, appearing in such shows as *Fiddle-dee-dee, Whoop-dee-doo,* and *Hoity Toity.* While working for Weber and Fields, Russell became forever associated with the popular song "Come Down, My Evenin' Star," which she sang in nearly every show.

In 1904, Weber and Field went their separate ways. After appearing in *Lady Teazle,* a musical version of *The School for Scandal,* Russell moved into vaudeville, where she was paid as much as $100,000 a season. She also appeared in nonsinging stage roles with varying success. Her greatest triumph was the melodrama *Wildfire* (1908). Russell's only performance preserved on film was in the 1915 movie version of this play, in which she appeared opposite Lionel Barrymore.

In 1912, Russell married Pittsburgh publisher Alexander P. Moore, who encouraged her interest in Republican politics. In addition to writing and lecturing on health and beauty, she spent her final years lending her celebrity to war bond drives and the presidential campaign of Warren P. Harding. In 1922, Harding sent her to Europe to study immigration issues. Returning to United States, she suffered a fall on an ocean liner, from which she never fully recovered. On June 2, 1922, the actress still remembered as "the American Beauty" died in Pittsburgh, Pennsylvania, at the age of 60.

Further Reading

Burke, John. *Duet in Diamond: The Flamboyant Saga of Lillian Russell and Diamond Jim Brady in America's Gilded Age.* New York: Putnam, 1972.

Fields, Armond. *Lillian Russell: A Biography of "America's Beauty."* Jefferson, N.C.: McFarland, 1999.

Schwartz, Donald Ray, and Anne Aull Bowbeer. *Lillian Russell: A Bio-Bibliography.* Westport, Conn.: Greenwood Press, 1997.

❖ RUSSELL, ROSALIND
(1912–1976) *Actress*

Known for playing wisecracking career women, Rosalind Russell was born into a wealthy family in

Waterbury, Connecticut, on June 4, 1912. After two years at Marymount College, she enrolled at the American Academy of Dramatic Arts. Russell spent years in summer stock before landing her first Broadway role in the unsuccessful *Company's Coming* (1931). Three more years would pass before she was discovered by a Hollywood talent scout. An impressive screen test led to a seven-year contract with Metro-Goldwyn-Mayer.

Russell made her film debut in *Evelyn Prentice* (1934). She languished in supporting roles, often playing the "other woman," until landing the lead in *Craig's Wife* (1936), in which she portrayed a memorably obsessive housewife. Russell soon came into her own in two classic comedies—*The Women* (1939) and *His Girl Friday* (1940). Both films showcased her skill at playing fast-taking, fearless, and impeccably dressed professionals. Russell proved to be her best in larger-than-life roles. Describing her own strengths, she once told *Life* magazine, "It's okay to have talent, but . . . you've got to have vitality. . . . Sometimes what you have to do is almost claw your work onto film."

In 1942, Russell was nominated for an Academy Award nomination for the romantic comedy *My Sister Eileen*. For much of the 1940s, however, she was cast in dramas. She also acted in several movies produced by Frederick Brisson, whom she married in 1941. They had one child.

Russell's next two Oscar nominations were received for *Sister Kenny* (1946), a biography of the acclaimed polio nurse, and *Mourning Becomes Electra* (1947), the film version of Eugene O'Neill's classic play. Yet, her robust acting style was not well-suited for subtle dramatic roles, and her film career began to falter.

In the 1950s, she returned to Broadway to make her comeback. Although she could not sing or dance, she found her niche in musical theater. Russell had an enormous hit with *Wonderful Town* (1953), the musical adaptation of her film *My Sister Eileen*. Her performance, which earned her a Tony Award, was "a triumph of personality over technique," according to *Time* magazine.

Even greater was her success in *Auntie Mame* (1956), the story of a boy's adventures with his flamboyant, eccentric aunt. Russell also played the part in the 1958 movie version, for which she received her last Academy Award nomination. Her other successful late film roles included a desperate spinster in *Picnic* (1955) and the domineering mother of GYPSY ROSE LEE in the musical *Gypsy* (1962), a part played by ETHEL MERMAN on the stage.

Over the next decade, Russell appeared in many minor films and television programs. She gave her final film performance in the television movie *The Crooked Hearts* (1972). The next year, Russell received the Jean Hersholt Humanitarian Award for her charitable work. She died in Beverly Hills, California, on November 28, 1976, at the age of 64.

Further Reading

Leitner, Samuel L. "Rosalind Russell." In *Dictionary of American Biography, Supplement 10: 1976–1980*. New York: Charles Scribner's Sons, 1995.

Russell, Rosalind, and Chris Chase. *Life Is a Banquet*. New York: Random House, 1977.

Recommended Recorded and Videotaped Performances

Auntie Mame (1958). Warner Studios, VHS, 1998.
His Girl Friday (1940). Columbia Tri-Star, DVD, 2000.
Gypsy (1962). Warner Studios, DVD/VHS, 2000.
The Women (1939). Warner Studios, VHS, 1996.

❖ ST. DENIS, RUTH (Ruth Dennis)
(1878–1968) *Dancer*

Ruth St. Denis, one of the pioneers of American modern dance, was born Ruth Dennis at an artist's colony near Perth Amboy, New Jersey, on January 20, 1878. Her unconventional parents encouraged Ruth's early interest in performing. In 1893, she ran away from boarding school to give her first formal performance in a production staged by her mother, Emma. When Ruth was 15, Emma took her to New York to audition as a dancer. There, Ruth performed in private concerts and revues for the next 10 years.

Considering herself a serious artist, Ruth struggled with the frivolity and low status of popular dance. In 1904, she was inspired to create her own style of dance after seeing an image on an advertisement for Egyptian Deities cigarettes. Fascinated by ancient religions and the Orient, she became a student of Egyptian and Indian dance. Her efforts resulted in *Radha,* the first Western dance piece to attempt to interpret Eastern dancing traditions. At its first performance in 1906, she adopted a new stage name—Ruth St. Denis.

Like many other American artists of the time, St. Denis believed she needed to work in Europe to establish her legitimacy. From 1906 to 1909, she toured the continent, then returned home an international success. She established a studio in New York City, where in 1914 she met Ted Shawn when he auditioned to become her student. Later the same year, the two married, and in 1915 they moved to Los Angeles to establish their own school of dance, which they called Denishawn.

As the first school to teach modern dance in the United States, Denishawn had an enormous influence. It legitimized the idea that forms of dance that were not based on classical ballet could nevertheless be considered serious artistic expressions. It also helped train several of the greatest modern dancers of the next generation, including MARTHA GRAHAM and DORIS HUMPHREY. In addition, tours of the Denishawn dancers introduced people throughout the country to modern dance, thus helping to develop a popular interest for this then experimental art form.

By 1930, the school's finances were in disarray, and St. Denis's marriage was floundering. She and Shawn separated (although they never divorced), and he formed his own troupe of male dancers. St. Denis founded a new school, the Society of Spiritual Arts, that taught dance as a form of worship. Although tastes shifted away

Ruth St. Denis is about 1929
(Library of Congress, neg. no. USZ62-115533)

from the theatrical dances she enjoyed staging, St. Denis continued to be respected among her peers. In 1938, she was hired as the dance director of Adelphi College, but returned to Los Angeles in 1942. There, for more than 20 years, she continued to give dance concerts, including one with Shawn in 1964 to commemorate their golden wedding anniversary. Her reputation in the dance world secure, St. Denis died from a stroke on July 21, 1968.

Further Reading

Miller, Kamae A., ed. *Wisdom Comes Dancing: Selected Writings of Ruth St. Denis on Dance, Spirituality, and the Body.* Seattle, Wa.: Peaceworks, 1997.

Shawn, Ted. *Ruth St. Denis: Pioneer and Prophet.* San Francisco: J. Howell, 1920.

Shelton, Suzanne. *Divine Dancer: A Biography of Ruth St. Denis.* Garden City, N.Y.: Doubleday, 1981.

Recommended Recorded and Videotaped Performances

Denishawn: The Birth of Modern Dance (1988). Kultur Video, VHS, 1992.

❖ SAINTE-MARIE, BUFFY (Beverly Sainte-Marie)
(ca. 1941–) *Singer, Songwriter, Musician, Actress*

Best-known for her searing protest songs of the 1960s, Buffy Sainte-Marie, a Cree Indian, was born on February 20 in either 1941 or 1942 on the Piapot Reserve in Saskatchewan, Canada. While still an infant, she was orphaned and later adopted by Albert and Winifred Sainte-Marie of Wakefield, Massachusetts. Though her given name was Beverly, she soon was known to her parents by the nickname "Buffy."

By four, Buffy had taught herself to play her family's secondhand piano and started setting her own poems to music. In her teens, she similarly mastered the guitar. Through her experimentation with the instrument, she developed her own unique playing techniques as well as discovering 32 ways of tuning a guitar, each of which created a different type of sound.

After graduating with honors from the University of Massachusetts, Sainte-Marie moved to New York City and began playing her music at folk clubs in Greenwich Village. An early performance attracted the attention of singer Bob Dylan, who helped arrange for her debut at the Gaslight Cafe on August 17, 1963. Enthusiastic reviews won her a contract with Vanguard Records, the premier recording company in the burgeoning folk music scene. Her first album, *It's My Way* (1964), was a huge popular and critical success, earning her the title "Best New Artist of the Year" from *Billboard* magazine.

In performance, Sainte-Marie was hailed for her dynamism. A reviewer in the *New York News* described her power onstage, writing, "She sings in a clear, husky-timbered voice that can be sweet, low-down, bitter, compassionate, sprightly, sexy, or

Buffy Sainte-Marie in 1992
(EMI Records Group)

wryly humorous. She can purr or belt, warm you into a smile or near chill you with a trembling intensity." She was equally admired as a songwriter. In the public mind, Sainte-Marie became most closely associated with her protest songs, especially those that exposed the United States's mistreatment of Native Americans, including "Native American Child," "Now That the Buffalo's Gone," and "My Country 'Tis of Thy People You're Dying." She also showed her commitment to Indian issues by lecturing and performing in benefit concerts on reservations throughout the country.

In addition to protest songs, Sainte-Marie also penned a number of works in a wide array of styles that were hits for other performers. One of the best known was "Universal Soldier," which, when recorded by Donovan, became an unofficial anthem of the 1960s antiwar movement. She also found great commercial success with two love ballads: "Until It's Time for You to Go" (1965), which has been covered by hundreds of performers, and "Up Where We Belong," which as the theme for the film *An Officer and A Gentleman* earned her an Academy Award in 1982.

Although the popularity of folk music in the United States was fading by the late 1960s, Sainte-Marie continued to find an audience overseas. After the birth of her son Dakota, however, she gave up her recording career in 1975 to explore working in television and film. From 1976 to 1981, Sainte-Marie was a cast member on the children's television series *Sesame Street.* She also scored two films, *Harold of Orange* (1986) and *Where the Spirit Lives* (1989), and narrated *Broken Rainbow* (1985), an Academy Award–winning documentary about land disputes between the Hopi and Navajo Indians.

In the 1980s, Sainte-Marie returned to school, earning a Ph.D. in fine arts from the University of Massachusetts. She also taught herself about the latest advances in computer technology and used her knowledge to create a recording studio at her home in Kauai, Hawaii. There, she created *Coincidence and Likely Stories* (1992), her first new album in more than a decade.

Sainte-Marie's interest in computers has also carried her in other new directions. Using the computers to manipulate 19th-century photographs of Indians, she has created a series of digital paintings that were featured in a one-woman exhibit at Santa Fe's Institute of American Indian Arts Museum in 1996. In the same year, Sainte-Marie also established the Cradleboard Foundation, one of many charitable organizations benefiting American Indians with which she has been involved. To promote tolerance, the Cradleboard Foundation allows Indian students and non-Indian students to learn about one another through communication over the Internet.

Further Reading

Sainte-Marie, Buffy. *The Buffy Sainte-Marie Songbook.* New York: Grosset and Dunlap, 1971.
Sonneborn, Liz. "Buffy Sainte-Marie." In *Performers.* American Indian Lives series. New York: Facts On File, 1995.

Recommended Recorded and Videotaped Performances

The Best of Buffy Sainte-Marie (1970). Vanguard, CD, 1987.

The Best of Buffy Sainte-Marie, Vol. 2 (1971). Vanguard, CD, 1991.

Buffy Sainte-Marie: Up Where We Belong (1996). Image Entertainment, DVD/VHS, 2000.

❖ **SARANDON, SUSAN (Susan Abigail Tomalin)**
(1946–) *Actress*

Known for depicting complex, independent, and sensual women, film star Susan Sarandon was born Susan Abigail Tomalin on October 4, 1946, in Metuchen, New Jersey. The eldest of nine children, she left home to attend Catholic University in Washington, D.C., where she majored in drama. While still in college, she married her first love, actor Chris Sarandon. During this time, she also became politically active. As a student, she was arrested several times for participating in civil rights and antiwar rallies.

Susan Sarandon won her first movie role when she accompanied her husband to a casting call for *Joe* (1970). She was given the female lead, playing an ill-fated young hippie. Soon Sarandon was being offered an array of ingenue roles. As she later admitted, she at first had trouble taking acting seriously, which led her to accept insubstantial parts that showcased her beauty more than her talent. Her best early role came in *The Rocky Horror Picture Show* (1975), the cult horror movie spoof that gave Sarandon a rare chance to sing on screen.

Sarandon found her breakout roles in two films directed by Louis Malle, with whom she was romantically linked after her 1979 divorce from Chris Sarandon. In *Pretty Baby* (1978), she played a prostitute in early 20th-century New Orleans, and in *Atlantic City* (1980), she depicted a croupier longing for a more glamorous life. Her appearance in these ambitious, offbeat films showed Sarandon's growing interest in unconventional parts. One of her most daring choices was to star in *The Hunger* (1983), a moody horror film in which she played a love scene with French star Catherine Deneuve.

In *Compromising Positions* (1985), a slight comic murder mystery, Sarandon proved that she could carry a movie on her own. Still, she had to lobby hard to earn the part of Annie Savoy, a passionate baseball fanatic, in the romantic comedy *Bull Durham* (1988). At 42, Sarandon was initially thought to be too old to play the role. She changed the mind of director Ron Sheldon by coming to a meeting in a tight red-and-white dress. "It was fabulous. It was like something Sophia Loren would have worn," Sheldon later remembered. With the success of *Bull Durham,* Sarandon challenged the Hollywood assumption that the public wanted to see only young women in sexy roles.

On the set of *Bull Durham,* Sarandon met costar Tim Robbins, who became her long-term partner. The couple has had two children, Jack Henry and Miles. Their family also includes Sarandon's daughter, Eva Maria Livia Amurri, from an earlier relationship with director Franco Amurri.

Sarandon and Robbins have worked together on several projects, including *Bob Roberts* (1992) and *The Cradle Will Rock* (1999), both written and directed by Robbins. They also share an interest in social causes, such as women's rights, homelessness, and help for people with AIDS. They angered many film industry insiders by speaking out against the United States's immigration restrictions on Haitians while presenting an award at the 1993 Academy Awards ceremony.

Sarandon's political activism, however, seemed to have no ill effect on her career. At an age when many actresses have trouble finding work, she was offered some of her most interesting roles. In 1991, she costarred with Geena Davis in *Thelma and Louise,* a story of two friends on the lam from the police that sparked a national debate on the state of American feminism. Other notable parts included a frantic mother of a dying child in *Lorenzo's Oil* (1992), a sympathetic drug dealer in *Light Sleeper* (1992), and a struggling lawyer in *The Client* (1994).

Perhaps Sarandon's most powerful performance of the 1990s was in *Dead Man Walking* (1995). Written and directed by Robbins, the film told the true story of a nun who befriended a killer on death row. After four Oscar nominations, Sarandon's deft handling of the challenging and unglamorous lead role finally won her the Academy Award for best actress.

Sarandon has since earned critical acclaim in such serious films as *Safe Passage* (1995), while also scoring popular hits with such crowd-pleasers as *Stepmom* (1998) and *Rugrats in Paris: The Movie* (2000). At the same time, she has emerged as one of Hollywood's best character actors by seeking out a wide array of parts. As Sarandon herself has explained. "[T]he whole point of acting is to experiment and learn—it's like living hundreds of lives in one lifetime."

Further Reading

Smith, Gavin. "Susan Sarandon: Uncompromising Positions." *Film Comment.* March 1993. 29: 2, pp. 44+.

Spines, Christine. "Icon: Susan Sarandon." *Premiere.* "Women in Hollywood" supplement, 1999, pp. 82–84+.

Recommended Recorded and Videotaped Performances

Atlantic City (1981). Paramount, VHS, 1992.
Bull Durham (1998). MGM/UA, VHS, 2000.
Dead Man Walking (1995). MGM/UA, DVD/VHS, 2000/1999.
The Rocky Horror Picture Show (1975). CBS/Fox Home Video, DVD/VHS, 2000.

❖ **SHORE, DINAH** (Frances Rose Shore)
(1917–1994)   *Singer, Talk Show Host, Actress*

A talented radio singer who found her greatest success on television, Dinah Shore was born as Frances Rose Shore on March 1, 1917 in Winchester, Tennessee. When still an infant, Franny's family moved to Nashville, where she contracted polio at two. Only through intense physical therapy did she regain use of her legs. The experience left Franny with two lifelong characteristics: a passion for athletics and a drive to succeed that helped fuel her career.

Wearing her older sister's party dress, 14-year-old Franny lied about her age to make her singing debut in a Nashville nightclub. Unknown to her, her parents were in the audience. At their insistence, she put her singing ambitions aside until, as a sophomore at Vanderbilt University, she gave her first radio performance on Nashville's WSM.

After graduating with a degree in sociology, Shore moved to New York City, where she found occasional work in radio. On auditions, she often sang the song "Dinah," making her so identified with the name that she adopted it as her own. Shore's early radio performances caught the attention of bandleader Xavier Cugat. In 1939, he arranged for her to make her first recordings with RCA Victor. Initially, Shore sang in a bluesy, sultry style that earned her comparisons to ETHEL WATERS. As her career progressed, however, her singing became much more fast-paced and sunny. She later attributed her longevity less to her singing talent than to her ability to adapt to changing public tastes.

In the 1940s, Shore tried to parlay her success as a singer into a new career in Hollywood. There, she met and married actor George Montgomery in 1943. After appearance in several lackluster films, she had a nose job and dyed her brown hair blond. Her Hollywood makeover did little to boost her movie reputation. In 1952, she gave up trying to achieve fame in films.

Shore decided she was not photogenic enough for movies. Her failure, however, was probably partly due to the fact that scripted films were poor showcases for her natural, unstudied charm. Her talents were much better suited to television, on which she started to make regular appearances in 1950. The next year, she was given her own 15-minute variety show. The popular program, expanded to an hour-long format in 1956, was sponsored by General Motors. Shore's rendition of "See the U.S.A. in Your Chevrolet" became one of advertising's most recognizable jingles.

Following her 1962 divorce from Montgomery, Shore left her career to concentrate on caring for her two children, Melissa and John. She married again in 1963 to tennis star Maurice Fabian Smith, but the marriage lasted less than a year. Slowly, Shore was lured back to television, first in the late 1960s for a series of specials for NBC, then in 1970 for a talk show initially titled *Dinah!*

A pioneer of the talk show genre, Shore discovered that it played to her strengths. An easygoing conversationalist with a lilting southern accent, she seemed the consummate hostess, able to strike up interesting banter with celebrities of all backgrounds. The show often highlighted her own interest in cooking, which she parlayed into three successful cookbooks. It also stirred up unexpected controversy when she began dating film heartthrob Burt Reynolds after he appeared as a guest. Tabloid accounts of the May–December relationship did little to diminish Shore's wholesome reputation. Most likely, her viewers, many of whom were older women, quietly enjoyed the ability of the ever youthful-looking Shore to attract a handsome star almost 20 years her junior.

Shore's last daytime show went off the air in 1984, but she hosted various shows on cable's Nashville Network from 1989 to 1991. She then largely retired from public life, only appearing occasionally at women's golf tournaments. On February 24, 1991, Dinah Shore died of cancer at her home in Beverly Hills with her children and ex-husband George Montgomery at her side.

Further Reading

Cassiday, Bruce. *Dinah!: A Biography.* New York: Franklin Watts, 1979.

Sochen, June. *From Mae to Madonna: Women Entertainers in Twentieth-Century America.* Lexington: University Press of Kentucky, 1999.

Recommended Recorded and Videotaped Performances

Dinah Shore: Sealed with a Kiss. A&E Home Video, VHS, 2000.

16 Most Requested Songs. Sony/Columbia, CD, 1991.

16 Most Requested Songs: Encore. Sony/Columbia, CD, 1995.

Till the Clouds Roll By (1947). Warner Home Video, VHS, 1990.

❖ **SILLS, BEVERLY (Belle Miriam Silverman)** (1929–) *Singer*

As opera's premier coloratura soprano, Beverly Sills became an international celebrity in the 1970s. Born Belle Miriam Silverman on May 25, 1929, she grew up in Brooklyn, New York. Her father hoped she would become a teacher, but her mother had different plans for Bubbles, Belle's childhood nickname. When she was three, her mother entered her in a talent contest, in which Bubbles won the title "most beautiful baby in Brooklyn" for 1932. At six, she was regularly performing on New York radio. At the suggestion of the family friend, her mother gave Bubbles the stage name Beverly Sills.

In her radio performances, Beverly often sang popular songs. Her own tastes, however, ran to opera. Listening to her parents' small collection of opera records, she began memorizing Italian arias when she was only seven. Her mother soon had Beverly studying with Estelle Liebling, one of New York's most well-regarded opera teachers. At 12, Beverly decided to retire from radio to devote herself completely to her opera studies.

By the time she graduated from New York's Professional Children's School, Beverly Sills had mastered some 60 operas. In 1945, she joined a touring company that specialized in Gilbert and Sullivan operettas but found the constant traveling grueling. Two years later, she returned to New York, hoping to carve out a career in grand opera.

In 1947, Sills sang her first operatic role, appearing as Frasquita in *Carmen* with the Philadelphia Opera Company. For several years, she played nightclubs and toured with several small opera companies before landing an audition with the New York City Opera. In 1955 she made her debut with the company in *Die Fledermaus* to unanimous acclaim. Sills also made her name in modern American operas. She received some of her best notices in Douglas Moore's *The Ballad of Baby Doe* (1958). Sills later maintained, "[M]y vintage years . . . began with Baby Doe."

Sills married newspaper editor Peter Greenough in 1956. The couple had two children, both of whom suffered from medical problems. Their daughter, Muffy, was progressively hard of hearing, and their son, Peter, was autistic. In the early 1960s, Sills left the public arena to care for her children. With Greenough's encouragement, however, she soon returned to opera, having her greatest triumph to date as Cleopatra in the New York City Opera's 1966 production of *Julius Caesar*. The role brought Sills to the top ranks of American opera stars.

Among opera aficionados, Sills was hailed for her natural acting ability. She was also blessed with an excellent memory that allowed her to develop an astounding repertoire. At her height, she had mastered more than 100 roles. Also unusual for an American opera singer, Sills was well-established before making her European debut. Starting in 1967, she began appearing at major opera houses abroad, extending her reputation around the world.

Sills, however, did not make her formal debut at New York's Metropolitan Opera until 1975. Her performance was greeted with an 18-minute ovation. By this time, she was also well-known through her frequent appearances on public television arts programs. She won an Emmy in 1975 for hosting *Profiles in Music*.

Amidst complaints that her voice was deteriorating, Sills gave her final performance on October 17, 1980, in *La Loca*. With no regrets, she gave up $8 million worth of performing contracts to retire at the top of her game. The day after she left the stage for good, she started a new career as the director of the New York City Opera. At the time, the company was more than $5 million in debt and on the verge of financial collapse. Sills immediately proved herself an able administrator and skilled public relations expert. Using her celebrity, she found corporate sponsors to rescue the company from its financial crisis. She also shook up its repertoire, adding new works and reinterpretations of classics to make the company more exciting to avid operagoers. Sills also pioneered the use of projected "supertitles" to help make foreign-language operas more accessible to opera newcomers.

In 1989 Sills retired from the New York City Opera directorship. However, she continued to work actively with the March of Dimes and the Multiple Sclerosis Society, charities with which she had long been associated. Sills also served on the corporate boards of Warner Communications, Macy's, and American Express.

Sills returned to work in 1994 as the chairman of New York's Lincoln Center for the Performing Arts. The first performing artist to serve on its board, she threw herself into fund-raising and promotion, most visibly as the host of *Live from Lincoln Center*. In a 2000 interview, the opera great explained her love of working behind the scenes: "Unlike a great many famous singers, the stage wasn't my only life. Perhaps that is why when I left it, I had just as much enthusiasm for doing other things."

Further Reading

Sills, Beverly, and Lawrence Linderman. *Beverly: An Autobiography*. New York: Bantam Books, 1987.
Winokur, L. A. "Catching Up With Beverly Sills." *Wall Street Journal*, November 6, 2000, p. 5.

Recommended Recorded and Videotaped Performances

The Ballad of Baby Doe. Deutsche Grammophon, CD set, 1999.
Beverly Sills in Gaetano Donizetti's 'The Daughter of the Regiment' (1974). Video Artist International, VHS, 1992.
Beverly Sills in Verdi's 'La Traviata' (1976). Video Artists International, VHS, 1992.
The Three Queens. Deutsche Grammophon, CD set, 2000.

❖ SLICK, GRACE (Grace Wing)
(1939–) *Singer, Songwriter*

More than any vocalist, Grace Slick defined the psychedelic rock sound of the late 1960s. She was born Grace Wing on October 30, 1939, in Evanston, Illinois, though she spent much of her youth in Palo Alto, California. Both Grace's musical talent and rebellious nature were evident in her early years. Her parents tried to nurture the former with guitar and piano lessons, while squelching the latter by sending her to New York City's Finch College, a conservative school where First Daughter Tricia Nixon was one of her classmates.

At 20, Wing married film student Jerry Slick. For a brief time she worked as a floor model at the I. Magnin department store in San Francisco, though she had little ambition to be anything other than a housewife. Frequenting San Francisco clubs, Grace Slick set out on a new path after seeing the successful local rock group Jefferson Airplane. As she later explained, "I realized they made more for two hours than I made in a week, and they had a lot more fun." She soon formed her own band, the Great Society, with her husband and her brother-in-law Darby. With Slick's riveting vocals as the main attraction, the band played in San Francisco for the next year. Among their popular songs were "Somebody to Love," written by Darby Slick, and "White Rabbit," composed by Grace Slick, drawing inspiration from Maurice Ravel's "Bolero" and Lewis Carroll's *Alice in Wonderland.*

In 1966 the members of Jefferson Airplane—then Paul Kanter, Marty Balin, Jorma Kaukonen, Jack Casady, and Spencer Dryden—asked Slick to join the band. With Jefferson Airplane poised for national success, she had no trouble abandoning the Great Society to become the group's vocalist. The next year, Jefferson Airplane released the classic album *Surrealistic Pillow* (1967). It featured "Somebody to Love" and "White Rabbit," both of which became radio hits. "White Rabbit," particularly, emerged as a generational anthem. Even though it promoted drug use for mind-expansion, its lyrics were enigmatic enough to protect it from censorship.

Rivaling JANIS JOPLIN, Slick became one of the most famous women in rock. Her voice was hard and loud, much better equipped to compete with an electric guitar than that of most female singers. To Slick, however, it was her energy rather than her sound that made her stage presence magnetic. Summing up her talents, she once said, "I always had more drive and fire than voice."

In followup albums such as *After Bathing at Baxter's* (1967) and *Volunteers* (1969), Jefferson Airplane became more political and more strident.

Tensions within the band escalated as well. Jorma Kaukonen and Jack Casady left to form Hot Tuna, while Marty Balin began to work on his own material. Romantically involved with Kanter, Slick continued to record with him under the Jefferson Airplane name. In 1971, Slick divorced her first husband and gave birth to a daughter by Kanter. They initially called the baby god but later renamed her China.

By 1974, Kanter had also renamed his band Jefferson Starship. Creating a much more mainstream pop-rock sound, the group, then also featuring Marty Balin, recorded the successful album *Red Octopus* (1975), which included the hit ballad "Miracles." Slick felt uncomfortable with the band's new, softer style and she angered her bandmates with her alcohol-fueled aggressive behavior. In 1976, she married the group's lighting director, Skip Johnson. With his encouragement, Slick broke from Jefferson Starship to record several solo albums, including *Dreams* (1980) and *Welcome to the Wrecking Ball* (1981). In the early 1980s, however, she rejoined the group, now called merely Starship. Slick sang supporting vocals on the band's mid-decade top 40 hits "We Built This City" (1985), "Sara" (1986), and "Nothing's Gonna Stop Us Now" (1987) before quitting again in 1988. After a 1989 Jefferson Airplane reunion tour, she retired from performing. Explaining her decision, she said, "Rock 'n' roll is still a young person's medium, and an older women just can't get away with [it]."

In the early 1990s, Slick experienced a series of personal setbacks. Her house burned to the ground in 1993. At about the same time, she and Johnson divorced after 18 years of marriage. Slick also found herself in the tabloids in 1994, when she was arrested for pointing a rifle at a sheriff's deputy who was trying to break up a drunken argument between Slick and her boyfriend.

In 1998, Slick recounted her life story in *Somebody to Love?,* which a reviewer for the *New York Times* described as "messy, muddled, indulgent, and occasionally amusing." She has since devoted herself to her new passions—campaigning against laboratory animal research and painting. Much of her artwork includes portraits of Janis Joplin, Jimi Hendrix, Jerry Garcia, and other 1960s pop icons. Now sober and out of the rock and roll scene, she admits that her life is much more sedate, but insists her raucous personality remains intact. As Slick said in a 1993 interview, "The bus may be different but it's the same trip."

Further Reading

Gleason, Ralph J. *The Jefferson Airplane and the San Francisco Sound.* New York: Ballantine Books, 1969.

Slick, Grace, with Andrew Cagan. *Somebody to Love?: A Rock and Roll Memoir.* New York: Warner Books, 1998.

Recommended Recorded and Videotaped Performances

Jefferson Airplane, Jefferson Starship, Starship: Hits. RCA, CD set, 1998.

Monterey Pop (1967). Rhino, VHS, 1997.

Surrealistic Pillow (1967). RCA, CD, 1988.

❖ SMITH, BESSIE
(1894–1937) *Singer*

Considered by many to be the greatest blues singer of all time, Bessie Smith was born into poverty in Chester, Pennsylvania, on April 15, 1894. One of seven children, she was orphaned by the time she was eight and thereafter taken care of by her eldest sister, Viola. At about the same time, Bessie started singing on the street for the spare change of passersby.

With the help of one of her brothers, in 1912 she was given an audition for a traveling show. Accepted into the troupe as a dancer, Smith was taken under the wing of a fellow performer, GERTRUDE "MA" RAINEY. Rainey helped guide Smith into the world of show business, while possibly introducing her to Rainey's own style of rural blues singing. Smith and Rainey remained lifelong friends.

Becoming a singer herself, Smith spent a decade traveling with African-American troupes and on the vaudeville circuit, performing mostly at tent shows and carnivals to a black audience. Her aggressive singing style soon attracted a large fol-

Bessie Smith
(© Bettman/CORBIS)

lowing. During this period, she married Earl Love in 1920; he died only two years later.

Smith made several unsuccessful attempts at recording her music before Columbia Records signed her to a contract in 1923. Her first record, "Down-hearted Blues," sold more than 800,000 copies in six months. Over the next seven years, she made approximately 160 recordings for Columbia, becoming the best-selling African-American recording artist of her day. Her records proved so successful that Smith singlehandledly saved the fledging record company from bankruptcy.

Just before her recording career took off, Smith married Jack Gee, a night watchman, in 1923. From the beginning, the relationship was volatile, full of violent arguments that often ended with

Gee beating his wife. Smith's wild behavior, particularly her heavy drinking and frequent affairs with young men and women, infuriated Gee, though he never hesitated to accept the expensive gifts Smith often gave him to smooth things over.

As her records broadened her audience, Smith was in even more demand as a live performer. Billed as the Empress of the Blues, she took to wearing extravagant costumes while she sang songs about poverty, loneliness, despair, and sex, some of which she wrote herself. In 1928, she was hired to appear in a Broadway musical, *Pansy*, but, despite critical praise for her, the show was slammed by reviewers. At the invitation of composer W. C. Handy, she was also featured in a 17-minute film in which she acted out her signature song, "St. Louis Blues." While her professional life continued to thrive, Smith's marriage was falling apart. She separated from Gee in 1930 after she discovered he had stolen money from her to finance a show for his mistress.

With the onset of the Great Depression, Smith's career also started to falter. The national economic crisis left the recording industry in shambles, while at the same time, vaudeville was being replaced by radio, and the blues was losing much of its audience to swing music. Dropped by Columbia Records, Smith had to return to touring shows, though she also appeared in revues at New York's Cotton Club and Apollo Theater. In 1933, jazz enthusiast John Hammond arranged for Smith to record some new songs, primarily intended for the European market. Although she tried to update her sound by experimenting with swing, the recordings enjoyed little success.

In the fall of 1937, Smith was touring the South in the *Broadway Rastas* revue. After performing in Memphis, Tennessee, she and her lover Richard Morgan set off in the middle of the night of September 26, driving toward her next stop in Darling, Mississippi. On the dark road, Morgan accidentally drove Smith's car into a slow-moving truck. Morgan was unharmed, but Smith's body was crushed. Within minutes, a white doctor driving along the road stopped and gave Smith emergency care while they waited for an ambulance to arrive. The ambulance took her to a nearby black hospital, where within hours Smith died of her injuries.

In the aftermath of her sudden death, a myth grew around its circumstances. Smith was said to have been taken to a white hospital, denied admission because of her race, and then transported to a black hospital, by which time her condition was so bleak that she could not be saved. Ironically, Smith's death inspired more news coverage in white papers than her career ever had. The mythic story of her death was also popularized in the play *The Death of Bessie Smith* (1960) by Pulitzer Prize–winning writer Edward Albee.

Although Bessie Smith's life met an abrupt and tragic end, her music continued to influence performers as diverse as BILLIE HOLIDAY, MAHALIA JACKSON, ELLA FITZGERALD, and JANIS JOPLIN. In 1970, Joplin paid her own tribute to Smith by helping finance a tombstone for Smith's previously unmarked grave in Sharon Hill, Pennsylvania. It reads, "The greatest blues singer in the world will never stop singing."

Further Reading

Albertson, Chris. *Bessie: Empress of the Blues.* New York: Stein and Day, 1972.

Brooks, Edward. *The Bessie Smith Companion: A Critical and Detailed Appreciation of the Recordings.* New York: Da Capo Press, 1982.

Davis, Angela Y. *Blues Legacies and Black Feminism: Gertrude "Ma" Rainey, Bessie Smith, and Billie Holiday.* New York: Pantheon Books, 1998.

Recommended Recorded and Videotaped Performances

The Ladies Sing the Blues (1988). View Video, VHS, 1989.

Bessie Smith: The Complete Recordings. Vols. 1–5. Sony/Columbia, CD set, 1991–96.

The Essential Bessie Smith. Sony/Columbia, CD set, 1997.

❖ SMITH, PATTI
(1946–) *Singer*

Considered by many the mother of alternative rock music, Patti Smith was born on December

31, 1946, in Chicago, Illinois, but spent most of her youth in Pitman, New Jersey. Growing up in a blue-collar family, she became a fan of pop music, especially the songs of Little Richard, the Ronettes, and Martha and the Vandellas. She had equal enthusiasm for the work of the French symbolist poet Arthur Rimbaud, which she discovered in high school.

Smith attended Glassboro State Teachers College but dropped out when she discovered she was pregnant. She gave up the child for adoption and moved to New York City briefly before heading to Paris to study art. She hoped to become a painter, but as she developed a cartoon-like style, she discovered she was more compelled by words than by images. Smith returned to New York, determined to devote herself to writing.

Living at the Chelsea Hotel, Smith became acquainted with the leading figures of New York's avant-garde, including Andy Warhol and William Burroughs. She became romantically involved with playwright Sam Shepard, with whom she cowrote the play *Cowboy Mouth.* In addition to three books of poetry, she also wrote poems and essays for *Rolling Stone, Creem,* and other music magazines.

In May 1971, Smith started giving poetry readings accompanied by guitar music played by her friend Lenny Kaye. Music became increasingly important in her performances, especially after she started a relationship with Allen Lanier, the keyboardist for the band Blue Öyster Cult. With Lanier's encouragement, Smith began experimenting with writing songs and developing more confidence as a performer. By 1975, Smith was backed by a five-person band, billed as the Patti Smith Group, and making regular appearances at top rock clubs, such as Max's Kansas City and CBGB. Onstage, Smith was animated and charismatic, stunning audiences used to the far more demure style of most female singers of the day. In *Mademoiselle,* writer Amy Gross described her shock at seeing "this 27-year-old skinny punk who hammered out dirty poetry and sang surreal folk songs. Who never smiled. Who was tough, sullen, bad, didn't give a damn. . . . I felt both ravaged and exhilarated."

Patti Smith on *Saturday Night Live* in 1976
(© Owen Franken/CORBIS)

The Patti Smith Group was considered one of the most exciting bands in New York's underground scene. But largely because of Smith's unconventional style and looks, no record company wanted to sign them. They finally were given a contract by Clive Davis at Arista Records. In the fall of 1975, the label released Smith's first album, *Horses,* featuring on its cover a portrait of Smith by her friend, photographer Robert Mapplethorpe. Universally hailed by critics, it was one of the most auspicious debuts in popular music history. Smith's rough and gritty vocalizations on *Horses* unexpectedly found a large mainstream audience and became a powerful influence on future generations of rock artists. Citing the album's importance in his own career, Michael Stipe of REM once wrote, "I bought *Horses* the day it came out, and that was the end of one chapter of my life and the beginning of another."

After a successful tour, Smith issued her second album, *Radio Ethiopia* (1976). The record was a disappointment commercially and critically. Many of Smith's admirers believed she was becoming too self-conscious because of her new status as a rock star. Smith herself came to agree, after she fell from a 12-foot stage onto her head during a 1977 performance. Having broken her neck, she spent her long convalescence reevaluating her art and coming to terms with her stardom. On her return to performing, she told a journalist of her new sense of confidence, saying "I feel equal to anyone in rock 'n' roll." Smith was at the top of her form with her next album, *Easter* (1978). It featured her only top 20 hit, "Because the Night," which she cowrote with fellow New Jersey native Bruce Springsteen. Suffering by its comparison to *Horses* and *Easter,* her next album, *Wave* (1979), was not as well received.

In the 1980s, Smith surprised her fans by giving up performing and recording. With her husband, Fred "Sonic" Smith, the former guitarist for the bands MC5 and Sonic's Rendezvous, she moved to Detroit to start a family. She devoted herself to raising their children, Jesse and Jackson, though she continued to write poetry for herself. Smith considers this period out of the public eye as her most creatively productive years. In 1988, Smith returned to the recording studio to produce *Dream of Life,* but the new album failed to find an audience.

In the early 1990s, Smith suffered a series of personal catastrophes. At 45, her husband, Fred, died suddenly from a heart attack in 1994. His death was soon followed by those of her brother Todd and old friend Robert Mapplethorpe. Smith poured her grief into a new album, *Gone Again* (1996), which she had begun working on with her husband before his death. Returning to New York, Smith moved away from personal material, instead dealing increasingly with political subjects in her next two albums, *Peace and Noise* (1998) and

Gung Ho (2000). In a 1997 interview in *The Progressive,* she expressed her continued faith in the power of her chosen art form: "Rock 'n' roll is great because it's the people's art. It's not an intellectual art. It's totally accessible."

Further Reading

Bockris, Victor, and Roberta Bayley. *Patti Smith: An Unauthorized Biography.* New York: Simon & Schuster, 1999.

Smith, Patti. *Patti Smith Complete: Lyrics, Reflections & Notes for the Future.* New York: Doubleday, 1998.

Recommended Recorded and Videotaped Performances

Gung Ho. Arista, CD, 2000.
Horses (1975). Arista, CD, 1996.
Masters: The Collected Works. Arista, CD set, 1996.

❖ STANWYCK, BARBARA (Ruby Katherine Stevens)
(1907–1990)   *Actress*

Perhaps the most versatile actress of Hollywood's golden age, Barbara Stanwyck was born Ruby Katherine Stevens on July 16, 1907. She was raised in Brooklyn, New York. Her mother died in a streetcar accident when she was three, and her father left her to work on the Panama Canal when she was five. She subsequently lived sometimes in foster homes and sometimes with her older sister Mildred, who worked as a chorus girl.

When Ruby was 15, she followed in Mildred's footsteps, taking her first job as a dancer. After a stint with the Ziegfeld Follies, she found small parts in musical revues and plays, soon appearing under the stage name Barbara Stanwyck. She had her first lead in *Burlesque* (1928), and the next year she married vaudeville star Frank Fay. Together, they headed out to Hollywood.

Fay persuaded director Frank Capra to watch a screen test Stanwyck had made. Moved by her performance, Capra hired her for the starring role in *Ladies of Leisure* (1930) and cast her again in several other of his early features, including *The Miracle Woman* (1931) and *The Bitter Tea of General Yen*

(1933). As Stanwyck was emerging as an important new actress, her husband had trouble finding work and became alcoholic and abusive. They divorced in 1935. Stanwyck later claimed that the 1937 version of the film romance *A Star Is Born* was based on their relationship. Stanwyck's second marriage, to actor Robert Taylor in 1939, also ended in divorce.

In 1937 Stanwyck had an enormous success with *Stella Dallas,* a melodrama in which she played a working-class mother willing to make any sacrifice for her daughter. Although she was playing a woman far older than herself, she delivered a performance that was among her best and the one she later declared her favorite. It earned her the first of her four Oscar nominations.

Having established herself as a star, Stanwyck proved her comedic skills in several classic screwball farces, including Preston Sturges's *The Lady Eve* (1941) and Howard Hawks's *Ball of Fire* (1942). She also became one of the screen's most memorable femme fatales. Her most acclaimed "bad girl" was Phyllis Dietrichson, the unhappy, manipulative, and homicidal wife in Billy Wilder's film noir masterpiece *Double Indemnity* (1944). The year of its release, her salary was the highest of any woman in the United States.

Largely due to her versatility, Stanwyck continued to find memorable roles in film as she grew older, often working with the industry's top directors. She was regarded by her coworkers as a consummate professional who was always on time and prepared. From her earliest days in movies, she made it a practice to memorize not only her own lines but those of every other actor as well. Once called "the most popular woman in Hollywood" by gossip columnist Hedda Hopper, Stanwyck was also known for her generosity toward younger performers. While appearing as a presenter alongside Stanwyck at the 1977 Academy Awards, actor William Holden told the crowd how she had fought to keep him from being fired from his first film, maintaining that he owed his career "to this lovely human being."

As Stanwyck found film roles harder to come by in the 1960s, she turned to television. She briefly hosted *The Barbara Stanwyck Show* (1960–61) and had a substantial hit playing a western matriarch in *The Big Valley* (1965–69). She earned Emmy Awards for both series and was awarded a third for her performance in the 1983 miniseries *The Thorn Birds.* Stanwyck also was a regular on the nighttime soap opera *The Colbys* (1985–86).

In 1982, Stanwyck was honored with a special Oscar celebrating her long and varied career. Eight years later, she died of a heart attack on January 20, 1990 at the age of 82.

Further Reading

Madsen, Axel. *Stanwyck.* New York: HarperCollins, 1994.

Smith, Ella. *Starring Miss Barbara Stanwyck.* New York: Crown Publishers, 1974.

Recommended Recorded and Videotaped Performances

Double Indemnity (1944). Universal, VHS, 1998.

The Lady Eve (1941). Universal, VHS, 1998.

Stella Dallas (1937). MGM/UA, VHS, 2000.

The Strange Love of Martha Ives (1946). Kino Video, VHS, 1998.

❖ STREEP, MERYL (Mary Louise Streep)
(1949–) *Actress*

Arguably Hollywood's most respected actress, Meryl Streep was born Mary Louise Streep in Summit, New Jersey, on June 22, 1949. Her first foray into the performing arts came at 12, when she began studying with renowned singing teacher Estelle Liebling. In high school, she took on what might be called her first acting role, when she decided to transform herself into "the perfect *Seventeen* magazine knockout." As she would do so many times in the future, she played her part well, becoming a popular cheerleader and the homecoming queen.

Streep became more serious about acting while attending Vassar College. Her acting teacher Clinton Atkinson, who cast her in her first lead role in *Miss Julie,* once described her talents as "hair-raising, absolutely mind-boggling." On a scholarship, Streep continued her education at Yale Drama School, yet she had doubts about pursuing an acting career. "I still didn't think it was a legitimate way to carry on your life," she later recalled.

By the time Streep graduated from Yale, she already had a reputation as one of the country's best young actresses. She fulfilled her early promise first on the stage, appearing in several Shakespeare plays directed by Joseph Papp. During a production of *Measure for Measure,* Streep began a romantic relationship with costar John Cazale. For her performance in Tennessee Williams's *27 Wagons of Cotton* (1976), she was nominated for a Tony Award.

Streep was soon lured to Hollywood, making her first appearance on film in the television movie *The Deadliest Season* (1977). She made her feature film debut the same year in a small role in *Julia.* The movie's star, JANE FONDA, immediately recognized her promise and told director Sydney Pollack, "This girl is great. This girl is a genius."

In 1978, Streep won an Emmy Award for the miniseries *Holocaust.* That year, she also had in her first major role in *The Deer Hunter.* Although her character appeared on only seven pages of the script, Streep made an indelible impression, subtly playing a quiet, working-class woman with a strong sense of dignity. Streep received the first of many Academy Award nominations for her performance. The movie also starred Cazale, who became ill with bone cancer during the filming. Streep nursed him until his death in March 1978. Six months later, she married sculptor Don Gummer, with whom she has four children.

Perhaps the most pivotal year in Streep's career was 1979. She played three high-profile supporting roles that, taken together, showcased her extraordinary range. In *Manhattan,* she was a sophisticated New Yorker; in *The Seduction of Joe Tynan,* a sexy southerner; and in *Kramer vs. Kramer,* a young mother on the verge of mental collapse. Her part in *Kramer* also displayed her willingness to play complex and often unsympathetic women. Her risk-taking in this role paid off with her first Oscar for best supporting actress.

After only three years of working in film, Streep had established herself as one of the leading actresses in Hollywood by the beginning of the 1980s. She became renowned for being able to disappear into nearly any role. She proved equally convincing as a working-class martyr in *Silkwood* (1983), a Danish aristocrat in *Out of Africa* (1985), and a skid-row alcoholic in *Ironweed* (1987). During the decade, she received an astounding six Academy Award nominations. She had her only win with *Sophie's Choice* (1982), for which she awarded the best actress Oscar.

Although almost universally hailed as a great actress, Streep had her detractors. Her flawless technique left some critics cold, while the public often had trouble warming to the serious, often depressing projects she seemed to favor. Streep's amazing felicity at mastering accents became almost a cliché in Hollywood. She herself grew somewhat defensive: "For me, it's the least interesting part of the discussion of my work," she once insisted in an interview.

Perhaps responding to criticism of her downbeat roles, Streep experimented with lighter fare in the early 1990s. She appeared in the comedies *Defending Your Life* (1991) and *Death Becomes Her* (1992) and sang a country tune at the conclusion of the comedy-drama *Postcards from the Edge* (1990). These films, however, were only moderately successful, and by the end of the decade Streep had returned to drama, most notably in *The Bridges of Madison County* (1995), *Marvin's Room* (1996), and *One True Thing* (1998).

In 2000, Streep made film history when she was nominated for a best actress Oscar for *Music From the Heart* (1999). With 12 nominations, she tied the record set by KATHARINE HEPBURN. Notably, it took 50 years for Hepburn to become the most frequently nominated actress, while Streep earned nominations in less than half that time. With Streep still in mid-career, she seems poised to become the most honored American film actress of not only her generation but perhaps of all time.

Further Reading

Harris, Mark. "Depth Becomes Her." *Entertainment Weekly.* March 24, 2000, pp. 50+.

Maychick, Diana. *Meryl Streep: The Reluctant Superstar.* New York: St. Martin's Press, 1984.

Recommended Recorded and Videotaped Performances

Kramer vs. Kramer (1979). Columbia/Tristar, VHS, 2000.

Out of Africa (1985). Universal, DVD/VHS, 2000/1999.

Silkwood (1983). Anchor Bay Entertainment, DVD/VHS, 1999/1998.

Sophie's Choice (1982). Artisan Entertainment, DVD/VHS, 1998/2000.

❖ STREISAND, BARBRA (Barbara Joan Streisand)

(1942–) *Singer, Actress, Director*

The definitive superstar, Barbra Streisand has conquered stage, screen, and the recording industry, amassing millions of devoted fans along the way. Born Barbara Joan Streisand on April 24, 1942, she was raised in the neighborhood of Williamsburg in Brooklyn, New York. She never knew her father, a high school teacher who died when she was only 15 months old. Five years later, her mother remarried. Barbara's aloof relationship with her stepfather made her eager to leave home. At 16, after graduating from high school with honors, she fled for Manhattan, where she hoped to become an actress.

Changing the spelling of her first name to the more distinctive Barbra, she found work in a series of unsuccessful off-Broadway shows. When not working she and her friend Brian Dennen developed a nightclub act, in which Streisand sang the songs of FANNY BRICE, the renowned star of the Ziegfeld Follies. Although Streisand considered herself more of an actress than a singer, the act took off. She played long-running engagements at popular clubs such as Bon Soir and the Blue Angel and toured briefly as the opening act for the pianist Liberace.

While performing at the Blue Angel, Streisand was spotted by the producer of *I Can Get It for You Wholesale.* In the 1962 musical, she was cast as Miss Marmelstein, a saucy secretary. The show, which ran for nine months, made Streisand a star. During its run, she met costar Elliot Gould, whom she married in 1963. Streisand and Gould had one child, Jason, before divorcing in 1971.

Streisand's popularity only grew with the release of her first record, *The Barbra Streisand Album.* It became the top-selling album by a female artist in 1963 and earned her Grammy Awards for best album and best female vocal. The next year, she won the role of a lifetime when she was given the lead in *Funny Girl,* a musical romance based on the life of Fanny Brice. Streisand had to audition seven times, beating out CAROL BURNETT and MARY MARTIN for what would become her signature role. After the show's enormous success on Broadway, however, she was the only choice to play the part in the movie version of *Funny Girl* (1968). For her movie debut, Streisand won the Oscar for best actress in a tie with KATHARINE HEPBURN.

For the times, Streisand made an unconventional movie star. With slightly crossed eyes and long nose, she had unusual features that distinguished her from other film starlets. Often playing an ugly duckling turned into a beautiful swan by her own charisma, Streisand helped reshape the standards of Hollywood beauty.

Having established herself in film, Streisand then turned to television. The first of many television specials, *My Name Is Barbra* (1965) provided a well-crafted showcase for her musical talents. The special drew a huge audience and won five Emmy Awards.

Streisand returned to the musical genre in her next two movies, *Hello Dolly!* (1969) and *On a Clear Day You Can See Forever* (1970). She found equal success as she moved into straight comedy with films such as *The Owl and the Pussycat* (1970) and *What's Up Doc* (1972). Her biggest hit of the early 1970s, however, was *The Way We Were* (1973), a romantic drama that paired her with Robert Redford. The film and its theme, sung by Streisand, were enormous popular hits, making her the biggest female star in Hollywood during the 1970s.

In 1976, Streisand began working behind the camera with *A Star Is Born* (1976), a third remake of *What Price Hollywood?* (1937). She served as the film's executive producer, while her boyfriend Jon Peters, a former hairdresser, was billed as its producer. In addition to starring in *Star,* Streisand wrote the music for its Oscar-winning love theme, "Evergreen." She was also credited as the film's wardrobe consultant and designer of "musical concepts." During the filming, press accounts accused her of egomania, a taunt Streisand believed smacked of sexism. She has frequently maintained that her supposed pushiness and arrogance would be seen as ambition if she were a man. Although critically savaged, *Born* was a huge box-office success.

Streisand acted in two undistinguished movies—*The Main Event* (1979) and *All Night Long* (1981)—before appearing in her dream film, *Yentl* (1983). Based on a story by Isaac Bashevis Singer, the movie cast her as a young Jewish woman who disguises herself as a boy so she can receive a religious education denied to female students. Spending five years on the project, Streisand directed, cowrote, and coproduced the movie. A modest hit that was well-received by critics, *Yentl* established Streisand as a director to watch.

Her next directorial effort, *The Prince of Tides* (1991), won even greater acclaim. The film received seven Academy Award nominations, including one for best picture. Streisand's direction, however, was not given an Oscar nod—a fact that, to many in Hollywood, revealed the film industry's bias against women in positions of authority. She also weathered criticism for photographing herself in a glamorizing haze, even though her costar Nick Nolte was shot in the same manner.

The year 1991 saw the released of *Just for the Record,* a four-CD collection of her recordings since the 1960s. She has released more than 50 albums, including 12 that have gone multiplatinum. Throughout her career, she has also recorded many successful singles, including hit duets with Neil Diamond, Donna Summer, Barry Gibb, and Celine Dion.

In 1992, Streisand returned to the concert stage for her first tour in 25 years. She had abandoned live performances in 1967, when an anti-Semitic death threat left her with a paralyzing case of stage fright. Her tour was a sensation. In addition to paying astronomical prices for tickets, her fans bought millions of dollars worth of tour memorabilia sold at Barbra Boutiques across the country.

Also in 1992, Streisand established the Streisand Foundation to promote social and political causes of interest to her. A friend of Bill and Hillary Clinton, she emerged in the 1990s as Hollywood's leading spokesperson for liberal politics. She had been a particularly vocal advocate of gay rights. In 1995, she mixed filmmaking and politics by coproducing *Serving in Silence: The Margarethe Cammermeyer Story,* a television movie that criticized the U.S. military's ban on homosexuals in its ranks.

Streisand returned to the big screen in 1996 with *The Mirror Has Two Faces,* in which she again directed herself. The light romantic comedy proved only a modest success. Her fans were much more excited by her real-life romance to actor James Brolin. The couple was married in a highly publicized ceremony in 1998.

Streisand brought in the millennium with a New Year's Eve concert at the MGM Grand in Las Vegas. She has since announced her retirement from live performing. In October 2000, she gave four farewell concerts, with ticket prices selling for as much as $2,500. Streisand continues to work in film and television as a producer, director, and performer. Choosing only projects close to her heart, Streisand has earned a reputation as a consummate professional driven equally by passion and perfectionism. The elite of Hollywood came out to celebrate her trailblazing career in February 2001, when in a gala ceremony she became the first female director honored with the American Film Institute's lifetime achievement award.

Further Reading

Cunningham, Ernest W. *The Ultimate Barbra.* New York: Renaissance Books, 1999.

Edwards, Anne. *Streisand.* Boston: Little, Brown, 1997.

Nickens, Christopher, and Karen Swenson. *The Films of Barbra Streisand.* Secaucus, N.J.: Carol Publishing, 1998.

Waldman, Allison J. *The Barbra Streisand Scrapbook.* Secaucus, N.J.: Carol Publishing, 1995.

Recommended Recorded and Videotaped Performances

Barbra: The Concert (1994). Sony/Columbia, VHS, 1994.
Funny Girl (1968). Columbia/Tristar, VHS, 1997.
Timeless: Live in Concert. Sony/Columbia, CD set, 2000.
The Way We Were (1973). Columbia/Tristar, DVD/VHS, 1999/1999.
Yentl (1983). MGM/UA, VHS, 1989.

❖ SWANSON, GLORIA (Gloria May Josephine Svensson)
(ca. 1897–1983)   *Actress*

Born Gloria May Josephine Svensson on March 27, 1897 (or 1898), actress Gloria Swanson epitomized Hollywood glamour during the silent film era. She was raised in Chicago, where, while still a teenager, she was hired by the Essanay film studio as a movie extra. She caught the eye of actor Wallace Beery, who insisted that she pursue a film career. Accompanied by her mother, Svensson moved to Hollywood in 1915. The next year, she married Beery, but the couple divorced in 1918. It was the first of her six failed marriages.

Performing under the name Gloria Swanson, she slowly learned film acting techniques while under contract to the Keystone and Triangle studios. Swanson was already a leading lady when she was signed by Paramount, but it was there, working with directors Cecil B. DeMille and Allan Dwan, that she became a star. Swanson was usually cast as sophisticated seductress, carefully posed and lit to highlight her beautiful features and perfect figure.

By the mid-1920s, Swanson was one of Hollywood's most popular actresses. She owed much of her fame to her offscreen antics, which she engineered to complement her glamorous onscreen image. Swanson always dressed lavishly and expen-

Gloria Swanson in *Sadie Thompson* (1928)
(Museum of Modern Art Film Stills Archive)

sively, making her a regular feature in the day's fashion magazines. Perhaps with her image in mind, she made a French marquis her third husband in 1924. Returning to the United States after her marriage, she organized a parade in her honor that drew tens of thousands of well-wishers.

When her contract with Paramount expired, Swanson rejected an extravagant salary and left the film company to found her own. In 1927, she established Swanson Producing Corporation with the financial backing of her lover Joseph P. Kennedy (the father of future president John F. Kennedy). Ignoring the opposition of film censor Will Hays, Swanson adapted W. Somerset Maugham's novel *Rain* as *Sadie Thompson* (1928). Playing a unrepentant prostitute, Swanson delivered one of her best performances and earned her first Academy Award nomination for best actress.

Inspired by *Sadie Thompson*'s success, Swanson began work on a lavish production of *Queen Kelly,* the story of an innocent girl sent to live with her brothel-running aunt. The movie was directed by Erich von Stroheim, a Hollywood veteran well-known for his disregard for budgets. The production became a fiasco. Although Swanson poured more than $750,000 into the film, it was never completed.

Swanson briefly bounced back with *The Tres-passer* (1929), for which she received her second Oscar nomination. But several unsuccessful movies followed, forcing her to shut down her production company. By the late 1930s, Swanson was largely retired. The following decade, she made numerous attempts at a comeback in films, onstage, and on television, but her efforts went largely unnoticed.

Not until 1950 did Swanson find the right vehicle to bring her back into the limelight. The movie was *Sunset Boulevard*, a biting black comedy about behind-the-scenes Hollywood directed by Billy Wilder. Wilder considered several older actresses, including LILLIAN GISH and MAE WEST, for the lead role of Norma Desmond, an aging film star who refuses to admit her career is over. But as the epitome of the silent movie queen, Swanson won the part and was again nominated for an Oscar for her performance. Alternately pathetic and magnificent, Swanson's Desmond became one of American film's memorable characters. With her silent films now largely forgotten, it also became the role for which Swanson is now best remembered.

After this final triumph, Swanson acted in a few unmemorable films before returning to retirement. From time to time, she appeared on television talk shows, often promoting her health food diet. Three years after the publication of her autobiography *Swanson on Swanson* (1980), she died in New York City on April 4, 1983.

Further Reading

Quirk, Lawrence J. *The Films of Gloria Swanson.* Secaucus, N.J.: Citadel Press, 1984.

Simms, L. Moody, Jr. "Swanson, Gloria." In *American National Biography,* edited by John Arthur Garraty and Mark C. Carnes, vol. 21, pp. 190–192. New York: Oxford University Press, 1999.

Swanson, Gloria. *Swanson on Swanson.* New York: Random House, 1980.

Recommended Recorded and Videotaped Performances

Queen Kelly (1929). Kino Video, VHS, 1989.

Sadie Thompson (1928). Kino Video, DVD/VHS, 2001/1997.

Sunset Boulevard (1950). Paramount, VHS, 1996.

T

❖ **TALLCHIEF, MARIA (Elizabeth Marie Tallchief)**
(1925–) *Dancer*

As the muse of choreographer George Balanchine, Maria Tallchief was the first American ballerina to achieve international fame. Born Elizabeth Marie Tallchief on January 24, 1925, she was raised on the Osage Indian Reservation in Oklahoma. Her father, Alexander, was one of many Osage Indians who grew rich after oil was discovered on the tribe's land. At the insistence of her strict mother, the family fortune financed a rigorous regime of lessons in dance and music, which Tallchief and her sister Marjorie began nearly as soon as they were able to walk.

When Tallchief was seven, her family moved to Los Angeles, attracted by the superior training the girls could receive in the entertainment capital. She had regularly appeared in dance recitals for many years before becoming a student of Bronislava Nijinska, a famed Russian ballerina and choreographer. After five years of intense study, Tallchief began her professional career with the Ballet Russe de Monte Carlo, then the world's best-known ballet company. At 18, she performed her first solo with the company in Nijinska's *Chopin Concerto.*

Two years after joining the Ballet Russe, she met George Balanchine, who was hired as the company's ballet master. A brilliant Russian-born choreographer, he would become Tallchief's greatest influence. Although she did not have the extraordinarily long limbs Balanchine usually favored in dancers, he was impressed by her strength, her speed, and most importantly, her incredible commitment to her art. Almost immediately, she became Balanchine's favorite ballerina, a position that earned her leads in many of his ballets, including *Danses Concertantes* (1944), *Le Somnambulist* (Night Shadow, 1946), and *Le Baiser de la Fée* (The Kiss of the Fairy, 1946). Their personal relationship blossomed as well: Tallchief and Balanchine were married on August 16, 1946.

The following spring, Tallchief was invited to join the Paris Opera for a season as a guest artist, becoming the first American to perform on its stage in more than a century. After returning from Paris, she left the Ballet Russe to joined the Ballet Society (later renamed the New York City Ballet), a new company founded by Balanchine. The struggling company had its first major success with *Firebird* in 1949. Dancing the title role, Tallchief emerged as an international star. In just one of the many enthusiastic reviews of her performance,

Maria Tallchief in *Firebird* (1949)
(Dance Collection, The New York Public Library of the Performing Arts, Astor, Lenox and Tilden Foundations)

Walter Terry wrote, "In off-center spins, in sudden lifts, [her movements] seem to defy gravity, and in their alert, graceful, and sharp explorations of space, they define the characteristics of a magical, air-borne creature."

Firebird was followed by a string of successful collaborations between Tallchief and Balanchine, including *Swan Lake* (1951), *Serenade* (1952), *Scotch Symphony* (1952), and *The Nutcracker* (1954). Their marriage, however, faltered. Separated in 1950, they had their marriage annulled the next year.

In 1954, Tallchief left the New York City Ballet to rejoin the Ballet Russe for a salary of $2,000 a week, making her the highest-paid ballerina in the world. Soon, however, she found that she missed Balanchine's creative energy and returned to his company after only a season. She remained with

the New York City Ballet for 10 years, but grew more and more unsatisfied with her position as Balanchine began passing plum roles on to younger dancers. In 1965, she announced that she was leaving the company to devote more time to her daughter, Elisa, and her second husband, Henry Pashchen Jr. a Chicago construction company executive whom she had married in 1956.

The Lyric Opera of Chicago lured Tallchief out of retirement in 1974. Initially asked only to train its singers to enter and exit the stage gracefully, she soon founded the Ballet School of the Lyric Opera. With Balanchine's encouragement, in 1980 Tallchief also established the Chicago City Ballet, which concentrated on performing her mentor's major works. Although she distinguished herself as a teacher, Tallchief was less successful as the artistic director of her own company. She severed ties with the Chicago City Ballet in 1987, and two years later it was disbanded due to lack of funds. Tallchief, however, remains a powerful force in the world of ballet, particularly as a strong advocate for the proper performance of Balanchine's works. The U.S. government recognized her distinguished contribution to American culture by awarding her a Kennedy Center Honor in 1996 and a National Medal of Arts in 1999.

Further Reading

Maynard, Olga. *Bird of Fire: The Story of Maria Tallchief*. New York: Dodd, Mead, & Company, 1961.
Tallchief, Maria, with Larry Kaplan. *Maria Tallchief: America's Prima Ballerina*. New York: Henry Holt, 1997.

Recommended Recorded and Videotaped Performances

Dancing for Mr. B: Six Balanchine Ballerinas (1989). Elektra/Asylum, VHS, 1995.

❖ TALMADGE, NORMA
(1897–1957) *Actress*

One of the most popular film stars of the silent era, Norma Talmadge was born on May 2, 1897, in Jersey City, New Jersey. The eldest of three sisters, she grew up in Brooklyn, New York, near the Vitagraph movie studio. After her father abandoned the family, her mother, Peg, became determined to mold her girls into film stars. She succeeded with her beautiful older daughters, Norma and Constance, and achieved the next best thing with her youngest, Natalie, who became the wife of screen legend Buster Keaton.

Norma was the first of the Talmadge sisters to break into the film business. At 14, she began working at Vitagraph. She had her first role of note in *A Tale of Two Cities* (1911) and was given her first lead two years later in *Under the Daisies.* During her five years at Vitagraph, Norma Talmadge made more than 100 films.

After leaving Vitagraph, Talmadge made several movies with the Triangle Film Corporation, which was headed by Thomas Ince, Mack Sennett, and D. W. Griffith. But she did not achieve full-fledged stardom until she met and married Joseph M. Schenck, manager of Loew's Theatrical Enterprises, in 1916. Schenck took charge of both Norma and Constance Talmadge's careers. He helped Norma set up her own film studio, the Norma Talmadge Film Corporation, which produced the hugely successful *Panthea* (1917) as its first movie.

Talmadge remained a top box-office draw throughout the 1920s, bested only in popularity by MARY PICKFORD. Though not an accomplished actress, she excelled at two types of roles. In the majority of her films, she played a long-suffering heroine, often thrust into a cruel world and forced to make her own way. These melodramas were the precursors of what became known in Hollywood as "women's pictures." Talmadge also often appeared as exotics. Playing an Arab dancing girl, an Indian princess, or a tropical beauty, she was an effective fantasy figure for her fans.

Talmadge's life also excited the imagination of her audience. She and her sisters lived in high style, and the clothing they wore in their films set a standard for young, fashionable women. Norma and Constance were a favorite subject of fan magazines. For a time, Norma became a regular writer for *Photoplay,* in which she offered readers fashion advice.

Despite her glamorous lifestyle, Norma Talmadge was notoriously hardworking, appearing in more than 250 movies during her career. Characteristically, she took the advent of sound film seriously. Talmadge made no movies in 1929 so that she could concentrate on her studies with a vocal coach. The effort, however, was a waste. Talmadge made two sound pictures—*New York Nights* (1929) and *Dubarry, Woman of Passion* (1930)— both of which were commercial disasters. Rich from solid real estate investments, Talmadge decided to leave the film business. An old Hollywood legend holds that the retired Talmadge was once pestered for an autograph by a fan while leaving a restaurant. Content with no longer having to play the star, she responded, "Get away, dear. I don't need you anymore."

In 1934, Talmadge divorced Schenck and, a month later, married vaudeville star George Jessel. They were divorced in 1939, and Talmadge married Carvel M. James, a physician, in 1946. She died on December 24, 1957, leaving behind an estate worth more than $3 million.

Further Reading

Basinger, Jeanine. *Silent Stars.* New York: Alfred A. Knopf, 1999.

Loos, Anita. *The Talmadge Girls: A Memoir.* New York: Viking, 1978.

Recommended Recorded and Videotaped Performances

Secrets (1924). Home Vision, VHS, 2000.

❖ **TAMIRIS, HELEN** (Helen Becker)
(ca. 1902–1966)   *Dancer, Choreographer*

One of modern dance's greatest champions, Helen Tamiris was born Helen Becker on April 23 of 1902 or 1903. Raised on New York City's Lower East Side, she tried to escape the trials of tenement life by studying interpretive dance at the Henry Street Settlement House. By 15, she was a professional dancer with the Metropolitan Opera Ballet. She soon quit the Metropolitan to join the Bracale Opera Company on a tour through South America. There, a lover rechristened her "Tamiris" after an ancient Persian queen. She subsequently adopted first Tamiris, then Helen Tamiris as her stage name.

Feeling hemmed in by the highly regimented ballet technique, Tamiris gravitated toward the improvisational dance style pioneered by ISADORA DUNCAN in the 1920s. While studying at Duncan's studio, Tamiris made ends meet dancing at nightclubs. For six months, she also appeared in the *Music Box Revue,* sharing the stage with vaudeville legend FANNY BRICE.

In 1927 Tamiris abandoned these popular dance venues to organize her own modern dance concerts. In addition to performing as the lead dancer, she choreographed and designed the costumes for seven concerts held in New York and Europe. These early works were consciously provocative, stretching the limits of what modern dance could be. In *1927* (1927), Tamiris became one of the first dancers to perform to jazz. In *The Queen Walks in the Garden* (1927), she performed without musical accompaniment. And in *Subconscious* (1927), she dared to appear on stage in the nude.

Despite her innovations, Tamiris had less impact on modern dance than her contemporaries MARTHA GRAHAM and DORIS HUMPHREY, largely because Tamiris never developed a uniform technique. She instead encouraged her students to find their own natural style. In an era when modern dance purists held that dance should be abstract and free of content, Tamiris invited criticism for her insistence that movement be inspired by specific feelings and motivations. As Tamiris wrote in 1927, "The dance of today must . . . be vital, precise, spontaneous, free, normal, natural and human."

Tamiris was far more influential as a passionate promoter of modern dance. In 1930 and 1931, she was instrumental in organizing the Dance Repertory Theater, a week-long revue that showcased works of the day's leading choreographers. She also helped organize the Dance Association (later renamed the American Dance Association), an organization dedicated to looking out for dancers' financial interests.

After the establishment of the Works Progress Administration's Federal Theater Project, Tamiris was the leading force behind its Dance Project, which staged modern dance performances using federal funds. The Dance Project sponsored several of Tamiris's greatest works, including *How Long Brethren?* (1937), which won *Dance Magazine's* first annual award for choreography. Reflecting her long-time interest in social issues, *Brethren,* a commentary on the plight of American blacks, was performed to spirituals sung by an African-American choir. Although often branded as a communist sympathizer because of her politics, Tamiris contributed to the war effort by dancing in a show organized by the U.S. Department of Agriculture. She appeared as "Porterhouse Lucy" in a dance piece meant to caution Americans not to buy rationed goods on the black market.

Tamiris stopped performing in 1944 to devote herself to choreographing Broadway musical comedies. Although many choreographers resisted working in the popular theater, she embraced the chance to bring her style of dance to a larger audience. Often working with her former student Daniel Nagrin (whom she married in 1946), Tamiris choreographed 18 shows during the 1940s and 1950s. Among them were *Annie Get Your Gun* (1946) and *Touch and Go* (1949), for which she won a Tony Award.

In 1960 Tamiris and her husband formed the Tamiris-Nagrin Dance Company, which dissolved after the couple separated in 1964. Two years later, suffering from cancer, Helen Tamiris died on August 4 at the age of 63. In her will, she bequeathed a third of her estate to further the cause of American modern dance, a mission the Tamiris Foundation was subsequently founded to pursue.

Further Reading

Schlundt, Christena L. "Tamiris: A Chronicle of Her Dance Career, 1927–1955." *Studies in Dance History* 1 (fall-winter 1989): 65–154.

Tamiris, Helen. "Tamiris in Her Own Voice: Draft of an Autobiography." Edited by Daniel Nagrin. *Studies in Dance History* 1 (fall-winter 1989): 1–64.

❖ TANDY, JESSICA (Jessie Alice Tandy)
(1909–1994) *Actress*

In a career that spanned seven decades, Jessica Tandy emerged as one of the greatest actresses on the 20th-century American stage. A native of London, she was born Jessie Alice Tandy on June 7, 1909. Her mother, a teacher, encouraged in Jessie a love of the arts. At a young age, she steeped herself in literature, developing a special fondness for Shakespeare. Her growing fascination with the theater led her to the Ben Greet Academy of Acting, where she studied from 1924 to 1927.

At 18, Tandy made her London stage debut in *The Manderson Girls* (1927). A wide variety of roles followed, and by the 1930s, she was one of the leading young actresses in the English theater world. Her most notable triumphs included playing Ophelia in a 1934 production of *Hamlet* starring John Gielgud and Viola in a 1937 staging of *Twelfth Night* opposite Laurence Olivier and Alec Guinness. While working in London, she met and married fellow actor Jack Hawkins, with whom she had a daughter.

In late 1940, Tandy traveled to New York to appear on Broadway in *Jupiter Laughs.* Because of both the war in Europe and increasing tensions in her marriage, she decided to settle in the United States permanently. Tandy, however, soon became frustrated to learn that her success in London did little to win her parts on Broadway. She considered giving up acting, but her friend Hume Cronyn, who was also part of the *Jupiter Laughs* cast, persuaded her to stay with her first love. Tandy divorced Hawkins and married Cronyn in 1942.

Deciding she might have better luck in film, Tandy and Cronyn moved to Hollywood. She signed a contract with Twentieth Century-Fox, but her movie roles did little to showcase her talent. She was far better served by her part in a production of *Portrait of a Madonna,* a one-act play by Tennessee Williams directed in Los Angeles by Cronyn. Williams was so impressed by Tandy's work that he insisted she be given the lead role in his new Broadway play, *A Streetcar Named Desire*

(1947). Originating the role of fading southern beauty Blanche DuBois, Tandy at last achieved stardom in the United States. Although she won the Tony Award for best actress for her performance, she lost the role of Blanche in the movie adaptation to VIVIEN LEIGH. "I was disappointed and hurt," Tandy later told the press, "but I wasn't a film star. Vivien Leigh was."

Tandy parlayed her newfound fame into a long career on and off Broadway and in regional theater. She and Cronyn also became closely associated with Minneapolis's Guthrie Theater, which was founded by a friend of Tandy's from the London theater. Although Tandy often appeared in plays on her own, much of her finest work was in productions that also starred her husband. Tandy and Cronyn were particularly celebrated for their performances in Edward Albee's *A Delicate Balance* (1966) and D. L. Coburn's *The Gin Game* (1977). For her work in *The Gin Game* and in *Foxfire* (1982), Tandy won her second and third Tony Awards.

Finding the rigors of theater acting difficult as she aged, Tandy stopped performing on stage in the mid-1980s. She then returned to acting in films, including the popular comedy *Cocoon* (1985) and the Academy Award–winning *Driving Miss Daisy* (1989). In *Daisy,* Tandy was cast as a wealthy southern woman who develops a long-term friendship with her African-American chauffeur. Her sensitive portrayal won her the best actress Oscar. To new fans unfamiliar with her stage work, Tandy became an "overnight sensation" that had been more than 50 years in the making. Tandy continued to appear in films, most notably *Fried Green Tomatoes* (1991) and *Nobody's Fool* (1994), until her death from cancer on September 11, 1994.

Further Reading

Barranger, Milly S. *Jessica Tandy: A Bio-Bibliography.* New York: Greenwood Press, 1991.

Kalfatovic, Mary C. "Tandy, Jessica." In *American National Biography,* edited by John Arthur Garraty and Mark C. Carnes, vol. 21, pp. 294–296. New York: Oxford University Press, 1999.

Recommended Recorded and Videotaped Performances

Driving Miss Daisy (1989). Warner Home Video, DVD/VHS, 1997/2001.

Fried Green Tomatoes (1991). Universal, DVD/VHS, 2000.

Intimate Portrait: Jessica Tandy (1999). Unapix, VHS, 2000.

❖ TANGUAY, EVA
(1878–1947) *Singer, Actress*

Nicknamed the "I Don't Care Girl," Eva Tanguay became the highest-paid player in vaudeville during the early 20th century. She was born on August 1, 1878, in Marbleton, Quebec, but six years later her family resettled in Holyoke, Massachusetts. Soon after, her father died, leaving the Tanguays impoverished. After winning an amateur contest, eight-year-old Eva joined the Redding-Stanton theater company and became her family's breadwinner. She toured with the company for five years, then moved into adult roles in musical comedy.

In 1901 Tanguay had her first major brush with celebrity when she had an impromptu fistfight with a chorus girl during a production of *My Lady*. The resulting publicity helped her land a star vehicle, *The Chaperons,* in which she sang "My Sambo." Now a headliner, Tanguay fully established her stage persona in *The Blond in Black*. Exuberant and carefree, she won over audiences playing "the Sambo Girl." She was such a sensation that the show's producers soon renamed the show after her character.

Though now a leading star in theater, Tanguay moved into vaudeville in about 1906. Outrageous even offstage, her personality began to influence her stage performances more and more. She delighted in wearing scanty costumes, including one made entirely of dollar bills. Gyrating as she sang, she became famous for her rendition of "I Don't Care," a celebration of her lack of inhibition. The lyrics declared, "I don't care/What people say or do,/My voice, it may sound funny/But it's getting me the money,/So I don't care." In fact,

her voice did sound shrill, and it earned her as much as $3,500 a week. Theater owners blanched at Tanguay's risqué act, but her popularity was so great that they did little to censor her. Though described as "not beautiful, witty or graceful," she pleased audiences primarily through her disinterest in propriety. In addition to giving them a vicarious thrill, her attitude was a refreshing challenge to outmoded Victorian ideals.

Tanguay had far less success in her personal life. She wed twice; one marriage ended in divorce, the other in annulment. By the 1920s, her health began to fail, eventually to the point that she could no longer perform. Although she earned an estimated $2 million during her career, extravagant spending and the 1929 stock market crash left her with nothing. Desperate for money, Tanguay attempted a comeback in the early 1930s, but soon cataracts left her blind. Stage star SOPHIE TUCKER paid for an operation to restore her sight, but then Tanguay was stricken with paralyzing arthritis. She was forced to retire to her small home in Los Angeles. When she died on January 11, 1947, she was in the process of working on her memoirs, *Up and Down the Ladder*. She had tried to interest Hollywood in her story, but did not live to see *The I Don't Care Girl*, a 1952 musical starring Mitzi Gaynor as Tanguay.

Further Reading

Martin, Linda, and Kerry Seagrave. *Women in Comedy*. Secaucus, N.J.: Citadel Press, 1986.

Sochen, June. *From Mae to Madonna: Women Entertainers in Twentieth-Century America*. Lexington: University Press of Kentucky, 1999.

❖ TAYLOR, ELIZABETH
(1932–   ) *Actress*

Elizabeth Taylor remains perhaps the quintessential movie star, as legendary for her messy private life as for her glamorous screen performances. She was born in London, England, on February 27, 1932, to prosperous parents. Fleeing Europe during World War II, the Taylor family moved to Los

Angeles when Elizabeth was seven. Her mother, a former actress, then set about grooming her daughter for Hollywood. In 1941, Elizabeth was signed to Universal and cast in her first film, *There's One Born Every Minute* (1942). After appearing in *Lassie Come Home* (1943) opposite her lifelong friend Roddy McDowall, Elizabeth was given a contract with Metro-Goldwyn-Mayer, the studio best positioned to make her into a star.

At 12, Elizabeth Taylor fulfilled her early promise in *National Velvet* (1944), the story of a young girl's obsession with riding her horse in England's Grand National steeplechase. Initially, Taylor was considered too slight for the role, but after a four-month regime of exercise, she proved herself physically robust enough to take it on. On the set, she further showed her dedication by continuing to perform even after a throw from a horse left her with a serious back injury.

Emerging from *National Velvet* a star, Taylor was placed in a series of small ingenue roles, most successfully in *Little Women* (1949) and *Father of the Bride* (1950). By her 15th birthday, gossip columnist Hedda Hopper had declared that Taylor was the most beautiful woman in the world. Blessed with raven hair, violet eyes, and a heart-shaped face, the young Taylor established a standard of beauty for the 1950s.

In *A Place in the Sun* (1951), Taylor graduated to adult roles as a woman so desirable that a man is willing to kill to have her. Although thought of more as decoration than as a great talent, she slowly proved herself a skillful actress in such dramas as *Giant* (1956), *Suddenly Last Summer* (1959), and *Raintree County* (1957), for which she received her first Oscar nomination. Taylor had her greatest early success in *Cat on a Hot Tin Roof* (1958), the film version of Tennessee Williams's controversial play. Wearing a form-fitting white slip, she portrayed a woman seething with sexual frustration as her alcoholic husband (Paul Newman) draws away from her. The performance won her a second Academy Award nomination.

Throughout the 1950s, Taylor was as big a star in the gossip columns as she was onscreen. In just seven years, she married three famous men—hotelier Conrad "Nicky" Hilton (1950), actor Michael Wilding (1952), and producer Michael Todd (1957). Divorced from Hilton and Wilding, Taylor became a widow when Todd's plane, ironically named "the Lucky Liz," crashed in 1958. The great outpouring of public sympathy that ensued quickly dried up as Taylor became romantically involved with singer Eddie Fisher, who was still married to film star Debbie Reynolds. When Fisher left his wife and children to marry Taylor in 1959, she was condemned as the ultimate other woman. Her fans, though, again embraced Taylor after she fell ill from an almost-fatal case of pneumonia. Perhaps out of sympathy for her near-death experience, Academy voters awarded Taylor the best actress Oscar for *Butterfield 8* (1960).

Taylor's next role was as the title character in the four-hour extravaganza *Cleopatra* (1963). For her performance, she was paid a record-setting $1 million. The production itself cost $40 million, then the most ever spent on a film.

Cleopatra paired Taylor with British actor Richard Burton in the role of Marc Antony. Nearly from their meeting, rumors flew about a romance between the stars, who were both married at the time. Adding to the gossip, Taylor and Burton were prone to making scenes and having loud drunken arguments. An unapologetic hedonist, Taylor was denounced by members of Congress and condemned by the Vatican as "a woman of loose morals." Though *Cleopatra* was a box-office disaster, the public had a seemingly insatiable appetite for stories of Taylor and Burton's extravagant misbehavior. As Burton once observed, "For some reason, the world has always been amused by us two maniacs."

After their marriage in 1964, Taylor and Burton made nine more movies together. Most were forgettable, though two were among Taylor's best films. In *Who's Afraid of Virginia Woolf?* (1966) and *Taming of the Shrew* (1967), Taylor played two very different, yet equally difficult women, creating these characters out of intense, raw emotion. Her role as Martha in *Woolf* was especially impressive. Although only 34 at the time, Taylor was wholly

213

convincing as a decidedly unglamorous, middle-aged harridan. The part won Taylor her second Academy Award for best actress.

In the 1970s, Taylor's career began to decline as she appeared in a string of lackluster films. Her relationship with Burton fell apart as well. They were divorced in 1974 and remarried in 1975, though their second marriage lasted only four months. In 1978, Taylor wed for seventh time, becoming the wife of future U.S. senator John Warner.

Finding fewer appropriate roles in movies, Taylor moved to the stage in the early 1980s. She was nominated for a Tony Award for her theater debut in *The Little Foxes* (1981) but was slammed by critics for her performance in *Private Lives* (1983) opposite Burton. Taylor also began working in television in such films as *Poker Alice* (1987) and *Sweet Bird of Youth* (1989). In the 1990s, she made occasional guest appearances on situation comedies, most notably providing the voice for baby Maggie on an episode of the animated series *The Simpsons.*

Even when she was not performing, Taylor remained in the public eye, often through less-than-flattering gossip about her weight gain and problems with alcohol and painkillers. In 1983, she checked into Washington, D.C.'s Betty Ford Clinic, becoming the first high-profile celebrity to admit to her addictions. Returning to the clinic in 1988, she met construction worker Larry Fortensky. They were married in 1991 and divorced five years later.

While dealing with her own problems, Taylor began a new career as a crusader for AIDS awareness and research. In 1985 she cofounded the American Foundation for AIDS Research (AmFAR) and soon organized the first Hollywood gala fund-raiser for the cause. Also the founder of the Elizabeth Taylor Foundation for AIDS, she has helped raise more than $50 million for AIDS research. At the 1992 Academy Awards, she was given the Jean Hersholt Humanitarian Award for her charitable work.

Taylor added to her own bottom line with several perfume lines. Expertly marketed using her status as a cultural icon, her perfumes White Diamonds and Passion approached $200 million in annual sales by the early 1990s.

The mother of four children and grandmother of nine, Taylor has been plagued by health problems in recent years. During the late 1990s, she suffered from a broken back and a spinal fracture and had to have surgery for recurring hip problems and a benign brain tumor. As in the past, her personal difficulties have only seemed to add to her legend and endear her even more to her fans. In recognition of her charitable work and acting career, Taylor was named Dame—the female equivalent of knight—by Queen Elizabeth in 2000. The tribute seemed particularly fitting for the still glamorous Taylor, who had previously been dubbed by *People* magazine "the platinum grande dame of celebrities."

Further Reading

Amburn, Ellis. *The Most Beautiful Woman in the World: The Obsessions, Passions, and Courage of Elizabeth Taylor.* New York: Cliff Street Books, 2000.

Heymann, C. David. *Liz: An Intimate Biography of Elizabeth Taylor.* New York: Birch Lane Press, 1995.

Kelley, Kitty. *Elizabeth Taylor: The Last Star.* New York: Simon & Schuster, 1981.

Spoto, Donald. *A Passion for Life: The Biography of Elizabeth Taylor.* New York: HarperCollins, 1995.

Recommended Recorded and Videotaped Performances

Cat on a Hot Tin Roof (1958). Warner Home Video, DVD/VHS, 2000.

National Velvet (1945). Warner Home Video, DVD/VHS, 2001/2000.

A Place in the Sun (1951). Paramount, VHS, 1996.

Taming of the Shrew (1967). Columbia/Tristar, DVD/VHS, 1999/1998.

Who's Afraid of Virginia Woolf? (1966). Warner Home Video, DVD/VHS, 1998/2000.

❖ TEMPLE, SHIRLEY (Shirley Jane Temple Black)
(1928–)   *Actress, Singer, Dancer*

The most successful child performer in Hollywood history, Shirley Jane Temple was born in Santa Monica, California, on April 23, 1928. Deter-

Shirley Temple with Bill "Bojangles" Robinson in *The Little Colonel* (1935)
(Museum of Modern Art Film Stills Archive)

mined to make Shirley a star, her mother enrolled her in dance lessons when she was three. Two years later, Shirley was signed to a contract with a small movie studio, Educational Pictures. She sang and danced in two series of shorts, *Baby Burlesks* and *Frolics of Youth*. Temple later remembered how her mother, before each take, would yell "Sparkle!" as "a code word meaning concentrate."

Shirley's early efforts earned her contract with Fox paying $150 a week. In 1934, she was cast in *Carolina,* the first of eight features she would film that year. Among them was *Stand Up and Cheer,* in which she stole the picture singing and dancing to "Baby Takes a Bow." Its popularity led to *Little Miss Marker,* her first starring role. Also in 1934, she sang her signature song, "On the Good Ship Lollipop," in *Bright Eyes* and danced possibly her most famous routine with veteran tapper Bill "Bojangles" Robinson in *The Little Colonel.*

Filmgoers immediately embraced Shirley Temple as their favorite star. In the desperate years of the Great Depression, the cute and confident Temple became an icon, whose constant cheeriness inspired a comforting optimism that better times were ahead. In many of her films, her character's simple wisdom helped the adults around her deal with their problems. This formula earned Temple the nickname "Little Miss Fix-It" from movie industry insiders.

Temple's costars inevitably admired, however begrudgingly, her astounding professionalism. Though only five years old when she was thrust into movie stardom, she was able to master complex song-and-dance routines far faster than most of her adult partners. An amazingly quick study, she also memorized not only her own lines but all the other actors' as well. Actress Alice Faye once recalled, "She knew everyone's dialogue. If you forgot a line, she gave it to you. We all hated her for that."

Only a year after her feature debut, Temple won a special miniature-sized Oscar for her "outstanding contribution to screen entertainment." Her studio, which had merged with Twentieth Century, also appreciated her outstanding contribution to its bottom line. The $30 million Temple's pictures earned for Twentieth Century-Fox kept the fledgling studio afloat.

As the number-one box-office star between 1935 and 1938, Temple received a salary of $10,000 a week. She earned even more from a series of lucrative endorsements. Merchandise featuring her likeness became a significant industry. Nearly every little American girl in the late 1930s had a Shirley Temple doll or coloring book.

Wanting to cash in on the Shirley Temple phenomenon, Metro-Goldwyn-Mayer (MGM) tried to convince Twentieth Century-Fox to loan out its greatest star for MGM's musical extravaganza *The Wizard of Oz* (1939). When Temple's studio refused, MGM had to settle for the up-and-coming JUDY GARLAND instead. Few could see then that as Garland's star rose, Temple's would quickly fall. In 1940, she starred in her own musical fantasy, *The Blue Bird,* which proved to be her first substantial box-office failure.

As Temple moved into her teens, she tried to reconnect with her audience, who seemed to lose interest in her as she aged. She appeared in 15 films during the 1940s, but as a minor player rather than a star. Temple also struggled in her personal life. In 1945, she married John Agar, who subsequently became a film actor. They had one child, Susan, before his heavy drinking led them to divorce in 1950. The same year, Temple met and married California businessman Charles Black and retired from the movie business.

Now calling herself Shirley Temple Black, she moved with her husband to San Francisco, where they raised Susan and two children of their own, Charles and Lori. Black largely stayed out of the public eye until 1967 when she ran for Congress as a Republican. Although she was defeated in the primary, her political aspirations caught the attention of President Richard Nixon, who appointed her a United Nations representative. Widely respected for her intelligence, grace, and composure, Black later served as the ambassador to Ghana (1974–76) and Czechoslovakia (1989–92).

Despite her distinguished diplomatic career, Shirley Temple Black is still remembered by many as the smiling, curly-haired five-year-old beloved by millions of Americans during one of the country's darkest periods. Although she has not appeared on film for 50 years, she continues to receive hundreds of fan letters a week.

Further Reading

Black, Shirley Temple. *Child Star: An Autobiography.* New York: McGraw-Hill, 1988.

Edwards, Anne. *Shirley Temple: American Princess.* New York: William Morrow, 1988.

Hammontree, Patsy Guy. *Shirley Temple Black: A Bio-Bibliography.* Westport, Conn.: Greenwood Press, 1998.

Recommended Recorded and Videotaped Performances

The Little Colonel (1935). Twentieth Century-Fox, VHS, 1988.

Little Miss Marker (1934). Universal, VHS, 1996.

Stand Up and Cheer (1934). Twentieth Century-Fox, VHS, 1989.

❖ THARP, TWYLA
(1942–) *Dancer, Choreographer*

In the words of critic Arlene Croce, the innovative dancer and choreographer Twyla Tharp "swept away the ideological dividing line between 'classical' and 'modern' and 'pop.'" The eldest of four children, Twyla was born in rural Portland, Illinois, on July 1, 1942. Her mother, an aspiring concert pianist, gave her daughter her unusual name because she thought it would look good on a marquee.

When Twyla was eight, the Tharps moved to Rialto, California, where her father built and operated a drive-in theater. He also constructed the family home, which included a room equipped with a dance floor and ballet barre. Blessed with perfect pitch, Twyla started taking piano lessons from her mother before she was two. She later added classes in social dance, ballet, violin, drums, and baton. By negotiating a highly demanding schedule of lessons, she developed an impressive self-discipline that characterized her adult career.

After high school, Tharp entered Pomona College in California, intending to become a psychiatrist. Three semesters later, she transferred to New York City's Barnard College with the new goal of becoming a dancer. While majoring in art history at Barnard, Tharp studied ballet at the American Ballet Theater (ABT) and modern dance with MARTHA GRAHAM, Merce Cunningham, and Erick Hawkins. While in college, she married fellow student Peter Young. This marriage and a second one to artist Bob Huot ended in divorce. Jesse, her son by Huot, was born in 1971.

Graduating in 1963, Tharp joined the Paul Taylor Company, but her ambition and independence moved her to quit in order to form her own troupe the next year. Initially an all-woman company, the troupe appeared primarily in nontheater spaces, such as gyms, museums, and parks. In keeping with the avant-garde currents of the day, Tharp's dances tended toward minimalism in movement and in stage design. The pinnacle of her minimalist stage was *Fugue* (1970). The piece was performed without music, though its three dancers wore high-heeled boots equipped with micro-phones to create their own accompaniment.

Critics saw a new warmth and wit in Tharp's *Eight Jelly Rolls* (1971), during which her dancers wore backless tuxedos while moving to the music of early jazz great Jelly Roll Morton. Tharp also played with music in *The Bix Pieces* (1971). Though Tharp choreographed the work to Franz Joseph Haydn's Opus 76, it was performed to the jazz of Bix Beiderbecke.

Tharp's breakthrough work, *Deuce Coupe* (1973), was also a hallmark in modern dance history. Commissioned by the Joffrey Ballet, it was performed to 14 songs by the Beach Boys in front of a set painted anew before each performance by teenage graffiti artists. The choreography—an eclectic mix of movements from ballet, Graham technique, popular dances, tap, and jazz—was performed by dancers from the Joffrey and from Tharp's own company. One critic called it "a dialogue between American ballet and American Bandstand, which makes both seem more wonderful for the comparison."

The enormous success of *Deuce Coupe* made Tharp modern dance's most popular choreographer to "cross over," that is, to work in both classical and modern styles. She choreographed *As Time Goes By* (1973) for the Joffrey and then created five works for the ABT. There, she worked with dancer Mikhail Baryshnikov, with whom she developed a close professional and personal relationship. With him in mind, she choreographed *Push Comes to Shove* (1976), which dramatized the tensions between a ballet company and its star dancer. Other notable works by Tharp include *Brahms-Handel* (1984) for the New York City Ballet and *Rules of the Game* (1989) for the Paris Opera Ballet.

Always fascinated by film since working at her parents' drive-in, Tharp also welcomed movie and television projects. She choreographed dance sequences in three films directed by Milos Forman—*Hair* (1979), *Ragtime* (1980), and *Amadeus* (1984)—and created a dance number for Baryshnikov and tap dancer Gregory Hines in *White Nights* (1985). Tharp and her works have also been the sub-ject of several television specials, most notably *Making Television Dance* (1977), *Baryshnikov by Tharp* (1985), and *Twyla Tharp: Oppositions* (1996).

Tharp's interest in narrative has also led her to work on creating evening-long theater pieces. In both *When We Were Very Young* (1980) and *The Catherine Wheel* (1981), she told the story of chaotic, dysfunctional families. In 1985, on Broadway, she created choreography for *Singing in the Rain*—a stage adaptation of the classic 1952 movie musical *Singin' in the Rain*. The result was slammed by critics, though audience demand kept the show running for a year.

Stung by the bad reception of *Singing in the Rain,* Tharp's company lost some of its central members. This problem, combined with Tharp's weariness with continual fund-raising, led her to disband the group in 1988. The same year, she joined Baryshnikov at the ABT, where she served as an artistic associate. When Baryshnikov left the company a year later, Tharp followed suit.

Tharp has since toured frequently, putting together temporary troupes of talented young dancers. In addition to choreographing new works for the ABT, New York City Ballet, and the Boston Ballet, she wrote her autobiography, *Push Comes to Shove* (1992). For the new energy she brought to both classical ballet and modern dance, Tharp was awarded a MacArthur Foundation "genius" grant in 1992. In 1997, she was made an honorary member of the American Academy of Arts and Letters.

Throughout the 1990s, Tharp was in demand as a freelance choreographer. Among the companies she created dances for were the Paris Opera Ballet, the Royal Ballet, the Martha Graham Dance Company, and the American Ballet Theater. She formed a new company, the Twyla Tharp Dance company, in 2000 and began developing a dance school in Brooklyn, New York. In 2001, Tharp explained that she now wants to work with only "great" dancers, defining greatness as "ambition, sweetness, personableness . . . I mean there's something absolutely connected, a commitment that goes beyond sincerity. English does not supply the right descriptions for greatness—you just feel it."

Further Reading

Rogosin, Elinor. *The Dance Makers: Conversations with American Choreographers.* New York: Walker, 1980.

Tharp, Twyla. *Push Comes to Shove.* New York: Bantam, 1992.

Recommended Recorded and Videotaped Performances

Baryshnikov Dances Sinatra & More . . . (1984). Kultur Video, VHS, 1991.

The Catherine Wheel (1982). Elektra/Asylum, VHS, 1992.

Hair (1979). MGM Home Entertainment, DVD/VHS, 1999/2000.

❖ THORNTON, BIG MAMA (Willie Mae Thornton)
(1926–1984)   *Singer*

One of the last great traditional blues singers, Willie Mae Thornton was born on December 11, 1926, in Montgomery, Alabama, where her father was a minister. As a child, she began singing in his church and taught herself to play the harmonica and drums. With the death of her mother, Willie Mae at 14 went to work. While scrubbing floors in a saloon, she was drafted to fill in for the establishment's regular singer, and a performing career was born.

Thornton soon joined the Hot Harlem Revue, a traveling show that toured African-American communities in the Southeast. Because of her powerful voice, she was billed as "the new BESSIE SMITH." Other blues greats that influenced her style included GERTRUDE "MA" RAINEY and Memphis Minnie.

By 1948, Thornton was working clubs in Houston, Texas. She was signed to Peacock Records by owner Don Robey, who began helping her choose material and directing her onstage appearance. Thornton made her first record in 1951 and the next year she was recruited for the nationally known touring show led by Johnny Otis. With Otis, Thornton began playing venues in the North for the first time. Her full-throated style of country blues became one of the show's highlights. Six feet tall and nearly 300 pounds, Thornton earned the nickname "Big Mama" both for her imposing physical stature and her oversize personality.

In 1953, Thornton recorded her biggest hit, "Hound Dog." The song was credited to songwriters Jerry Lieber and Mike Stoller. According to Thornton, "[T]hey had this song written on the back of a brown paper bag. So I started to sing the words and put in some of my own." Characteristic of Thornton's work, the record features her growling and shouting sexually explicit lyrics about a no-good lover. Although it sold more than half a million copies in the urban African-American market, Thornton received a total of only $500 for her work. Even more galling, she saw absolutely no compensation when Elvis Presley's 1959 cover of "Hound Dog" became a sensation, rocketing Presley to stardom.

Thornton's success continued as Robey paired her with his other star, ballad singer Johnny Ace. They became a star attraction, called by some "the king and queen of the blues." Their partnership ended at a Christmas dance in 1954, when Ace accidentally killed himself during a game of Russian roulette. In the wake of the tragedy, Thornton's popularity began to wane. She stopped touring with Otis in 1955 and moved to San Francisco, California. Without a record contract, Thornton began playing small local clubs in the late 1950s.

After several lean years, a renewed interest in the blues by early rock artists brought Thornton back into the public eye. Following her appearance at the Monterey Jazz Festival in 1964, Thornton became a regular at jazz and blues festivals and at the best clubs in the United States and Europe. Her recording career was revived as well with a string of albums, including *Big Mama Thornton with the Chicago Blues Band* (1967), on which her band included musicians Muddy Waters, James Cotton, and Otis Spann. In the late 1960s, Thornton also became known as an inspiration to rock singer JANIS JOPLIN, who imitated Thornton's style and mannerisms on stage. One of Joplin's signature songs was her cover of Thornton's composition "Ball and Chain." For the second time, Thornton saw one of her songs help a white artist rise to international fame.

Always a heavy drinker, Thornton began to suffer from cirrhosis of the liver in the late 1970s and early 1980s. Even though the illness shrunk her body to less than 100 pounds, she continued to perform despite her physical frailty. On July 25, 1984, Big Mama Thornton died of a heart attack in a Los Angeles boardinghouse. A week later, friends and fans came together at a benefit concert organized by the Southern California Blues Society to pay for her funeral expenses.

Further Reading

Gart, Galen, and Roy C. Ames. *Duke/Peacock Records: An Illustrated History with Discography.* Milford, NH: Big Nickel Publications, 1990.

Shaw, Arnold. *Honkers and Shouters: The Golden Years of Rhythm and Blues.* New York: Macmillan, 1978.

Recommended Recorded and Videotaped Performances

The Complete Vanguard Recordings. Vanguard, CD, 2000.

❖   TOMLIN, LILY (Mary Jean Tomlin)
    (1939–   )   *Comic, Actress*

Renowned for her inventive comic characters, Lily Tomlin was born Mary Jean Tomlin on September 1, 1939. Growing up in Detroit, Michigan, she often accompanied her alcoholic father to bars, where she amused patrons by imitating their neighbors. Tomlin briefly attended Wayne State University as a premed student but quit after her performance in a campus play convinced her that she had a flair for comedy. For several years, she performed on local television and in coffeehouses.

To further her career, Tomlin moved to New York City in 1965. Engagements at such clubs as the Improv and Cafe Au Go Go led to a job performing on the nationally televised *Garry Moore Show* (1958–67). She left after three shows over arguments with the writing staff about the quality of her material.

In 1970, Tomlin returned to television as a regular on the comedy revue *Laugh-In* (1968–73). She became instantly famous for her monologues delivered in the voices of various characters. The most popular were Ernestine, a surly telephone operator, and Edith Ann, a five-and-a-half-year-old who was wise beyond her years. She showcased these and other characters on several successful comedy albums, including *This Is a Recording* (1971), for which she won a Grammy Award. While working her 1972 album *And That's the Truth,* she began writing with playwright Jane Wagner, who has remained a frequent collaborator.

A proud feminist, Tomlin refused to perform jokes on *Laugh-In* that she deemed sexist or racist. She also made news by walking off *The Dick Cavett Show,* a television talk show, when a fellow guest, actor Chad Everett, described his wife as his possession. In a 1981 interview, she replied to the question of how feminism had affected her career with, "If it hadn't been for the women's movement, people would call it my hobby."

After *Laugh-In,* Tomlin appeared in a series of television specials that challenged network censors. The most notorious was a one-hour variety show for CBS written by Tomlin and comic Richard Pryor. The network wanted to cut a sketch titled "Juke and Opal," in which Pryor portrayed a methadone addict. When Tomlin threatened to sue, CBS put the sketch at the end of the special and added an incongruous laugh track to detract viewers from the disturbing material. The special won an Emmy for its writing.

By the mid-1970s, Tomlin was also appearing in films. She made an auspicious debut in a dramatic role in *Nashville* (1975), in which she subtly portrayed the emotions of a mother of two deaf children drawn into a brief affair with a womanizing pop star. The performance won her a Oscar nomination for best supporting actress. After garnering good reviews in the modern-day noir *The Late Show* (1977), her film career almost ended with the critical and popular disaster *Moment by Moment* (1978), a romance costarring John Travolta and written by Wagner. Tomlin scored a much-needed hit two years later with the light office comedy *9 to 5* (1980), which also featured JANE FONDA and DOLLY PARTON. Most of her subsequent film work has been in supporting roles in fairly insubstantial comedies, including *Big*

Business (1988), *The Beverly Hillbillies* (1993), and *Disney's The Kid* (2000).

Tomlin has found much more success as a stage performer. After winning a special Tony Award for her show *Appearing Nitely* (1977), Tomlin received the best reviews of her career for *The Search for Signs of Intelligent Life in the Universe* (1986). This one-woman show, written and directed by Wagner, allowed Tomlin to create an array of unforgettable characters—from the bag lady Trudy to the miserable teen Agnes Angst to the caustic socialite Kate. Using virtually no props or scenery, she transformed from one to the next, employing just her voice and manner to indicate the character she had become. Tomlin and Wagner were hailed for daring to depict with affection characters who often bordered on the grotesque. Tomlin once explained, "I don't necessarily admire them, but I do them all with love."

Winning a Tony for its original run, Tomlin revived *Search* on Broadway in November 2000. Reviewers marveled at the energy Tomlin, at 61, still brought to the demanding show. "It's exhilarating," Tomlin told *USA Today,* adding, "It's such a joy to perform. . . . It's fun to play, you know?"

Further Reading

Kaplan, James. "The Search for Lily Tomlin." *US Weekly.* January 22, 2001, pp. 58–61.

Sorensen, Jeff. *Lily Tomlin: Woman of a Thousand Faces.* New York: St. Martin's Press, 1989.

Wagner, Jane. *Search for Signs of Intelligent Life in the Universe.* New York: Harper & Row, 1986.

Recommended Recorded and Videotaped Performances

Nashville (1975). Paramount, DVD/VHS, 2000/1991.

9 to 5 (1980). Twentieth Century-Fox, VHS, 1995.

The Search for Signs of Intelligent Life in the Universe (1992). Wolfe Video, VHS, 1995.

❖ TUCKER, SOPHIE (Sophie Abuza)
(1884–1966) *Singer*

For more than 60 years, Sophie Tucker was a dynamic live performer whose bold and sometimes racy singing style won her the title "Last of the Red Hot Mamas." On January 13, 1884, she was born Sophie Abuza in Russia. Her parents soon immigrated to the United States, first to Boston, then to Hartford, Connecticut, where they opened a restaurant. Sophie, hating working in the family business, was drawn to the performers from a local vaudeville theater who frequented her parents' establishment. As a girl, she often sang for their entertainment in exchange for a little pocket change. She decided show business was a much better way to earn a living than cooking meals and washing dishes.

In 1903 she married Louis Tuck and had a son, Albert. Though she later affectionately referred to Tuck as "a card and a wonderful dancer," she was disappointed by his inability to provide for the family. She soon left Albert with her family and took off for New York, hoping to carve out her own career as a singer.

Calling herself Sophie Tucker, she found work in cafes, beer halls, and movie houses, often singing as many as 100 songs a night. Moving into burlesque, she was initially forced to work in blackface, because theater managers, believing she was unattractive, wanted to hide her features. But when her luggage failed to arrive at one venue, she had to go on stage without makeup. She was such a hit with the audience that night that she refused to ever perform in blackface again.

In 1909, Tucker had become so successful that she was hired for the prestigious Ziegfeld Follies. She was quickly dismissed, however, when other female stars felt threatened by her show-stopping numbers. She then left for Chicago, where she appeared in several musical comedies and refined her vaudeville act. Tucker found great success belting out songs with suggestive lyrics, most notably the naughty "Nobody Loves a Fat Girl, But Oh How a Fat Girl Can Love." She also pleased crowds with sentimental ballads, including "M-O-T-H-E-R—A Name That Means the World to Me," a tear-jerking tribute to maternal love. Carefully crafting her act, Tucker learned to sing a variety of tunes to keep her audiences attentive. In her biography, titled *Some of These Days* after her signature song, she wrote, "I would start off with a lively rag, then would come a ballad, followed by a comedy song, and a novelty number . . . and finally, the hot song. In this way, I left the stage with the audience laughing their heads off." Tucker also excited her fans with her extravagant and ever-changing costumes, which cost many thousands of dollars each time she retooled her act.

By 1920, Tucker was a headlining star in New York. She achieved equal, if not greater, fame in England during her first tour there in 1922. Fitting well into the British music hall tradition, Tucker earned the adoration of English audiences on two more tours in 1925 and 1934. During the latter, she played a command performance for the royal family.

As vaudeville's popularity waned in the 1930s, Tucker began to work in films and radio, but neither medium made good use of her talents. She was always at her best with a live audience, and her act lost much of its punch when she had to clean up her language for a mass audience. (She once bemoaned what radio did to her routines, explaining, "I couldn't even say 'hell' or 'damn,' and nothing, honey, is more expressive than the way I say 'hell' or 'damn.'") Tucker felt much more at home in nightclubs, which she continued to play for the rest of her life. She also later appeared regularly on television, enjoying particular success as an early star of British TV.

In her personal life, Tucker, after her first husband's death in 1914, had two unsuccessful marriages to pianist Frank Westphal (1914–19) and personal manager Al Lackey (1928–33). She remained devoted to her family and used her fortune to make sure her parents lived well. Tucker was also extraordinarily generous to a wide variety of charities, which she supported with sizable donations and benefit performances. Founded from the proceeds from her autobiography, the Sophie Tucker Foundation established a chair for the theater arts at Brandeis University in 1955. According to the *New York Times,* Tucker donated an estimated $4 million to charity during her lifetime.

In 1965, Tucker collapsed onstage while performing in New York. She died four months later, February 9, 1966. A veritable institution of American entertainment, Tucker—with her brassy sound, comic sense, and intimate rapport with her audience—continued to find new generations of fans long after the vaudeville days that made her a star were all but forgotten.

Further Reading

Sochen, June. *From Mae to Madonna: Women Entertainers in Twentieth-Century America.* Lexington: University Press of Kentucky, 1999.

Tucker, Sophie. *Some of These Days: The Autobiography of Sophie Tucker.* Garden City, N.Y.: Doubleday, 1945.

Recommended Recorded and Videotaped Performances

Broadway Melody of 1938 (1937). MGM/UA, VHS, 1992.
Last of the Red Hot Mamas. Memoir Classics, CD, 1998.
Some of These Days. Pearl, CD, 1997.

❖ **TURNER, LANA (Julia Jean Mildred Frances Turner)**
(1920–1995) *Actress*

The epitome of the Hollywood glamour girl, Lana Turner was as famous for her melodramatic life as for her film performances. On February 8, 1920, she was born Julia Jean Mildred Frances Turner in Wallace, Idaho. Her family moved frequently as her father struggled to find work. When Julia was nine, he was murdered during a craps game. She and her mother subsequently moved first to San Francisco, then Los Angeles, where Julia attended Hollywood High School.

An unenthusiastic student, 15-year-old Julia attracted the attention of Billy Wilkerson, the editor of the *Hollywood Reporter,* while she was cutting class. (Legend has it that they met at the lunch counter at Schwab's drugstore, but some accounts cite other locations.) Wilkerson introduced her to Zeppo Marx of the Marx Brothers, who was then working as a casting director. Marx sent Turner to Warner Brothers producer Mervyn LeRoy. He was looking for a young actress who could project both sexiness and innocence. LeRoy placed her under contract and probably renamed her Lana, though Turner later claimed to have made up her stage name herself.

Turner's first film role was a small part in *They Won't Forget* (1937). While attending a screening with her mother, Turner was horrified when male audiences began to whistle when she appeared on screen wearing a tight sweater. Her appearance was so memorable that she became known as the "sweater girl."

After playing several more small roles, Turner followed LeRoy to Metro-Goldwyn-Mayer (MGM), She appeared in such films as *Love Finds Andy Hardy* (1938) and *Rich Man, Poor Girl* (1938) before winning her first starring role in *Dancing Coed* (1939). On the set, she met bandleader Artie Shaw, whom she wed on a whim in 1940. During their four-month marriage, Turner became pregnant, but had an illegal abortion under pressure by MGM. Shaw was the first of Turner's seven husbands. She also had many high-profile lovers, including Clark Gable, Tyrone Power, and Howard Hughes. Turner's reckless romantic life and her affection for the nightclub scene made her a regular feature in Hollywood gossip columns.

While emerging as a major MGM star, Turner married entrepreneur Stephen Crane in 1941. Soon after she learned she was again pregnant, she discovered that Crane had never divorced his first wife. At MGM's insistence, she married Crane after his divorce was finalized. She gave birth to a girl, Cheryl Crane, before dissolving the marriage.

In 1946, Turner played Cora Smith in *The Postman Always Rings Twice*. Wearing white in most scenes, she exuded a sinister sexuality while looking like the girl next door. The movie solidified her image as a femme fatale. It also helped to make her a favorite pinup during the war years.

Though popular with moviegoers, Turner was considered more of a beauty than an actress. Hoping to be taken more seriously, she effectively played a troubled starlet in the hit *The Bad and the Beautiful* (1953). Turner also won praise starring as

Lana Turner in *The Postman Always Rings Twice* (1946)
(Museum of Modern Art Film Stills Archive)

Constance MacKenzie in *Peyton Place* (1957). That performance earned Turner her only Academy Award nomination.

In 1958, Turner found herself at the center of a nationwide scandal. On April 4, her daughter, Cheryl, stabbed and killed Johnny Stompanato, a mobster who was dating Turner, at her Beverly Hills home. A sensational trial followed, during which Turner's explicit love letters to Stompanato were read as testimony. The stabbing was determined to be a justifiable homicide because Cheryl believed the abusive Stompanato was going to kill her mother. Still, the scandal tarnished Turner's reputation. Rumors spread that she herself had killed Stompanato, then forced Cheryl to take the rap.

While Hollywood insiders debated over whether Turner's career was over, she was asked to star in the melodrama *Imitation of Life* (1959) for Universal. Unsure about whether moviegoers were eager to see Turner, the studio required that she take a percentage of the profits rather than a salary up front. The deal was a boon to Turner, earning her $1 million when it became Universal's most profitable film ever.

Turner continued to act through the 1960s, though increasingly she was considered too old for the sexy roles she was best known for. She appeared in her final film, *Bittersweet Love,* in 1974. In her later years, Turner tried acting onstage, but was overwhelmed by fear when performing before a large audience. She also appeared on television periodically, most notably as a regular on the prime time soap opera *Falcon Crest* (1981–90). In 1983, Turner officially retired from show business.

After 1992, when Turner was diagnosed with throat cancer, she rarely left her Los Angeles home. Nevertheless, she was image-conscious to the end: she kept up a regime of facials, manicures, and hairstyling even as she was dying. On June 29, 1995, Turner died at the age of 75.

Further Reading

Crane, Cheryl, with Cliff Jahr. *Detour: A Hollywood Story.* New York: Arbor House, 1988.

Turner, Lana. *Lana: The Lady, the Legend, the Truth.* New York: Dutton, 1982.

Wayne, Jane Ellen. *Lana: The Life and Loves of Lana Turner.* New York: St. Martin's Press, 1995.

Recommended Recorded and Videotaped Performances

Peyton Place (1957). Twentieth Century-Fox, VHS, 1992.

Imitation of Life (1959). Universal, VHS, 1997.

The Postman Always Rings Twice (1946). Warner Home Video, VHS, 1996.

❖ **TURNER, TINA (Anna Mae Bullock, Little Anne)**

(1939–)   *Singer, Actress*

Overcoming an impoverished childhood and an abusive marriage, Tina Turner emerged as a rock superstar in the 1980s. Born Anna Mae Bullock on November 26, 1939, she was the daughter of a farm overseer in Nutbush, Tennessee. She later remembered that in her poor community "white people own[ed] the land and black people work[ed] the crops." She herself spent time picking cotton on the fields her father managed.

Anna Mae and her older sister, Alline, were shuttled from relative to relative during her parents' stormy marriage. After they divorced, her mother moved to St. Louis, Missouri, and sent for her daughters to join her in 1956. Both Bullock girls became intrigued by the city's rhythm-and-blues scene. Alline started dating the drummer of the Kings of Rhythm, a local band headed by Ike Turner. Anna Mae, billed as Little Anne, soon began singing with the group. She had a son, Craig, with the band's saxophone player before transferring her affections toward Turner. The relationship led to pregnancy, and Bullock had her second child, Ronald, in 1960. The same year, she and Ike, billed as Ike and Tina Turner, had their first hit single with "A Fool in Love."

Married in Mexico in 1962, the couple began performing as the Ike and Tina Turner Revue. While Ike managed the band, Tina sang lead vocals backed by three singers known as the Ikettes and an eight-piece band. Specializing in energetic rhythm and blues, the group released 15 albums in the 1960s. The Turners also perfected their stage act, which featured sexually charged dancing by Tina and her backup singers. Their biggest hit of the period was "River Deep, Mountain High" (1966). Though virtually ignored in the United States, it went to number three on the British charts, bringing the Turners to the attention of many influential English bands. The Rolling Stones were so impressed that they invited them to open their 1969 U.S. tour. Legend has it that Tina taught Rolling Stones frontman Mick Jagger how to dance in concert.

By the early 1970s, the Ike and Tina Turner Revue had achieved mainstream success in the United States. The group's first top 10 American hit, a cover of Creedence Clearwater Revival's

Tina Turner in concert in the 1970s
(© Neal Preston/CORBIS)

"Proud Mary" (1971), became their signature tune. Memorably, Tina growled on the song's introduction, "We never do anything nice and easy, we always do it nice—and rough." The record was awarded a Grammy in the rhythm and blues category in 1972. The Turners' other hits of the period included "I Want to Take You Higher" (1970) and "Nutbush City Limits" (1973), Tina's own composition about her hometown.

By the mid-1970s, the Turners career began to wane as their marriage fell apart. Fueled by a growing cocaine habit, Ike Turner mentally and physically abused Tina, who turned to Buddhism for relief. After recording several solo albums and appearing as the Acid Queen in the film musical *Tommy* (1976), she decided to shed herself of Ike once and for all. She left him in the middle of a 1976 tour, with only a gasoline credit card and 36 cents in her pocket. In 1978, they were divorced.

The same year, Tina Turner released the album *Rough* (1978), but it was virtually ignored by the critics and the public. Still popular in Europe, she spent the next few years touring there. She was given the break she needed to get her career on track in 1982, when the Rolling Stones asked her open their sold-out U.S. tour. She had a dance hit with a cover of Al Green's "Let Stay Together" (1983) before recording her comeback album, *Private Dancer* (1984). Aided by music videos that showcased her dynamic stage presence and shapely legs, the album was a worldwide sensation. The two biggest hits from *Private Dancer*—"What's Love Got to Do with It" and "Better Be Good to Me"—earned Turner three awards at the 1984 Grammys.

Turner followed *Private Dancer* with a second successful solo album, *Break Every Rule* (1986). She also appeared as Aunt Entity in the futuristic thriller *Mad Max: Beyond Thunderdome* (1985). Two songs from the soundtrack—"We Don't Need Another Hero" and "One of the Living"—scored as hits for Turner. The next year, she aired her life story in the best-selling autobiography *I, Tina*. It was made into the award-winning movie *What's Love Got to Do with It* (1993) starring Angela Bassett as Tina and Laurence Fishburne as Ike.

Turner was inducted in the Rock and Roll Hall of Fame in 1991. She spent much of the rest of the decade touring in the United States and in Europe, where she had moved in 1986 to be with her boyfriend, Erwin Bach, a German record executive. With lavish houses in France and Switzerland, Turner has embraced Europe as fondly as Europe has embraced her. As Turner has explained, "I am as big as MADONNA in Europe. I am as big, in some places, as the Rolling Stones."

In 2000, Turner released the album *Twenty-Four Seven* to coincide with her farewell tour. At 61 years old, she performed her last concert in Anaheim, California, in December of that year. Proud to be retiring from live concerts while still at the top of her game, she told *People* magazine, "What a way to go. I can step down and say, 'I did it, I enjoyed it, and I went out the right way.'"

Further Reading

Espinoza, Galina, and Fannie Weinstein. "Stage Flight." *People*. December 4, 2000, pp. 230+.

Ivory, Steve. *Tina!* New York: Putnam, 1985.

Turner, Tina, with Kurt Loder. *I, Tina: My Life Story*. New York: William Morrow, 1986.

Recommended Recorded and Videotaped Performances

The Best of Tina Turner: Celebrate! (2000). Image Entertainment, DVD/VHS, 2000.

The Collected Recordings. Capitol, CD set, 1994.

Tommy (1975). Columbia Tristar, DVD, 1999.

V

❖ **VAUGHAN, SARAH**
(1924–1990) *Singer*

Called by Frank Sinatra "one of the finest vocalists in the history of pop music," Sarah Lois Vaughan was born on March 27, 1924, in Newark, New Jersey. She began taking piano lessons at seven and by her teens had become a church organist. Vaughan dropped out of high school to work as a singer and pianist in local nightclubs.

On a dare, Vaughan entered a talent contest at the famed Apollo Theater in New York City in 1942. Performing "Body and Soul," she won not only first prize but also the attention of singer Billy Eckstine. Eckstine convinced Earl Hines to hire Vaughan as a singer for his big band, which then included bebop innovators Dizzy Gillespie and Charlie Parker. Two years later, Vaughan quit to join Eckstine's own band, where she worked with many other jazz greats, such as Miles Davis, Art Blakey, and Dexter Gordon.

Vaughan began performing as a solo act in 1945. The same year, she made her first important recording, "Lover Man." Among her other early hits were "If You Could See Me Now" (1946), "It's Magic" (1948), and "(I Love the Girl) I Love the Guy" (1950).

In 1946, Vaughan married trumpeter George Treadwell, whom she divorced 12 years later. She was subsequently married to and divorced from professional football player Clyde Atkins, restaurateur Marshall Fisher, and trumpeter Waymon Reed. With Atkins, she adopted a daughter, Deborah, who later became an actress working under the name Paris Vaughan.

Vaughan started recording with Mercury Records in 1954. The company encouraged her to sing both pop and jazz, releasing each genre on a different label. Although she generally preferred jazz, she recognized few differences between the two styles. "I just sing," Vaughan explained. "I sing whatever I can." Vaughan also became known for her phenomenal range. She maintained it was two and a half octaves, though her control over her voice allowed her to make it seemed even greater. In performance, especially, she displayed an enormous talent for improvising. Though Vaughan returned to the same standards throughout her career, she took pride in saying she never sang a song the same way twice.

For decades, Vaughan toured jazz venues in the United States and Europe backed by a trio of piano, bass, and drums. Beginning in 1954, she also became a fixture the Newport Jazz Festival. Later in her career, Vaughan frequently sang concerts with major city orchestras. Although some critics complained that Vaughan's sometimes showy vocal technique detracted from her ability to interpret a song, most lavished praise on her voice, which only became richer with time. Her fans included her contemporary ELLA FITZGER-ALD, who once claimed that "the greatest singing talent in the world today is Sarah Vaughan."

By the 1980s, Vaughan's talents were earning her awards and accolades worldwide. In 1981 she won a special Emmy Award for outstanding individual achievement for the television special "Rhapsody and Song: A Tribute to George Gershwin." Vaughan received her first Grammy Award two years later for best female jazz performance for her album *Gershwin Live!* Her second Grammy, a special lifetime achievement award, came in 1989.

Widely known by the nickname "The Divine One," Vaughan spent her final months recording songs for Quincy Jones's *Back on the Block.* The album included "Birdland," the only recorded duet between Vaughan and Fitzgerald. On April 4, 1990, the jazz world mourned when Vaughan died suddenly of lung cancer at her home in Los Angeles, California.

Further Reading

Brown, Denis. *Sarah Vaughn: A Bio-Bibliography.* New York: Greenwood, 1991.

Gourse, Leslie. *Sassy: The Life of Sarah Vaughan.* New York: Charles Scribner's Sons, 1993.

Recommended Recorded and Videotaped Performances

The Essential Sarah Vaughan. Mercury, CD, 1992.

Sarah Vaughan: The Divine One (1993). BMG Video, VHS, 1993.

Sarah Vaughan: Jazz Profile. EMD/Blue Note, CD, 1998.

❖ VERDON, GWEN (Gwyneth Evelyn Verdon)

(1925–2000) *Dancer, Actress, Singer, Choreographer*

The definitive Broadway dancer of the 20th century, Gwyneth Evelyn Verdon was born on January 13, 1925, in Culver City, California. A childhood case of rickets left her legs deformed. As therapy, her mother, a dancer with RUTH ST. DENIS's Denishawn troupe, enrolled her in dance classes when she was only two. Gwen studied a wide range of dance styles, including ballet, ballroom dancing, and tap. By age six, she was a professional dancer, often billed as "the fastest little tapper in the world." With flaming red hair and alabaster skin, her beauty won her the Miss California title when she was 14.

In 1941, Verdon eloped with James Henaghan, a *Hollywood Reporter* journalist. After five years, they divorced, and she resumed her dance career. They had one child, James.

Verdon won a spot as an assistant to Jack Cole, a noted Hollywood dance coach. Under his direction, she made her Broadway debut in 1950 in *Alive and Kicking,* but the musical was a commercial failure. While working with Cole, she became the leading interpreter of his expressive, sometimes erotic dance style. She appeared as a specialty dancer in several films, including *On the Riviera* (1951) and *Mississippi Gambler* (1953), in which she choreographed her own movements. She was also hired to teach stars such as MARILYN MONROE and BETTY GRABLE how to move seductively on screen.

Eager to get out from under Cole's thumb, Verdon accepted an invitation from choreographer Michael Kidd to audition for his Broadway show *Can-Can.* Cast as the second female lead, she stole the show during its tryouts. The show's jealous lead, the French actress Lilo, insisted Verdon's role be cut back. Verdon was so annoyed that she announced that she would soon be leaving the production.

The night *Can-Can* premiered on Broadway, however, Verdon became an instant star. After she performed her first number, she rushed to her dressing room for a costume change. She did not hear the audience chanting her name until a producer brought Verdon, wearing her bathrobe, back onstage for a curtain call. After winning her first Tony for *Can-Can,* Verdon became the hottest dancer in musical theater.

Her next show was *Damn Yankees,* the story of a baseball fan willing to sell his soul to see his favorite team win. Verdon appeared as Lola, the devil's helper, and performed a memorably seductive dance to the song "Whatever Lola Wants." The musical ran for more than 1,000 performances and won Verdon a second Tony Award. Verdon also starred in the film adaptation in 1958.

Damn Yankees marked the beginning of her collaboration with choreographer Bob Fosse. They worked together on *New Girl in Town* (1957) and *Redhead* (1959), for which Verdon was awarded two more Tonys. In 1960, she and Fosse were married.

After the birth of their daughter, Nicole, in 1963, Verdon briefly retired from show business. In 1966, she was lured back to star in *Sweet Charity,* a musical about a dance-hall girl that was directed and choreographed by her husband. Exhausted by its long run, Verdon surrendered the lead to Helen Gallagher before the show's close. Shirley MacLaine took over the part for the 1969 film version, though Verdon generously coached her for it.

In 1971, Verdon and Fosse were legally separated, though they never divorced. They continued their working relationship, most notably in Verdon's last musical, *Chicago* (1975). Verdon originated the role of Roxie Hart, a gold digger acquitted of shooting her lover. Audiences considered the show too dark and cynical in its first run, though it was revived to great acclaim in 1996.

Her dancing days over, Verdon began taking straight acting roles in the 1980s. She appeared in small parts in several films, among them *Cocoon* (1985) and *Marvin's Room* (1996). Verdon also was a guest on many television series including *Magnum, P.I.* and *Homicide.* Her television work won her three Emmy nominations.

After Fosse's death in 1987, Verdon emerged as a guardian of his artistic legacy. In 1999, she collaborated with dancer Ann Reinking—Fosse's former lover—on the dance revue *Fosse,* which was awarded a Tony for best musical. The following year, Gwen Verdon died on October 18 at her daughter's home in Woodstock, New York. That night, the lights of Broadway were dimmed in her memory.

Further Reading

Berkvist, Robert. "Gwen Verdon, Redhead Who High-Kicked Her Way to Stardom, Dies at 75." *The New York Times,* October 19, 2000, p. 21.

Grubb, Kevin Boyd. *Razzle Dazzle: The Life and Work of Bob Fosse.* New York: St. Martin's Press, 1989.

Recommended Recorded and Videotaped Performances

Damn Yankees (1958). Warner Home Video, VHS, 1991.

❖ **WARWICK, DIONNE** (Marie Dionne
Warrick, Dionne Warwicke)
(1940–) *Singer*

One of the first African-American recording artists
to cater to a mainstream audience, Dionne Warwick is best known for her collaborations with
songwriting team Burt Bacharach and Hal David.
Born Marie Dionne Warrick in East Orange, New
Jersey, on December 12, 1940, she began her
career as an occasional fill-in singer for the
Drinkard Singers, a gospel group managed by her
mother, Lee. As a teenager, she formed her own
group, the Gospelaires, with her sister Dee Dee
and two cousins.

On a scholarship, Warrick attended the University of Hartford in hopes of becoming a music
teacher. While at college, she worked as a backup
singer. Working with the Drifters on their song
"Mexican Divorce," she was introduced to the then-
unknown songwriter Burt Bacharach. He was
immediately struck by her talent and her presence.
As Bacharach later remembered, "Just the way she
carries herself, the way she works, her flow and feeling for the music—it was there when I first met her."

Bacharach and his writing partner, lyricist Hal
David, recruited Warrick to sing on a demo

recording of several of their songs. The demo won
her a contract with Spector Records. In 1962, she
had her first hit with "Don't Make Me Over," a
song penned by Bacharach and David. Her name
was printed as "Warwick" on the label, so Warrick
adopted the misspelling as her new stage name.

Through the 1960s, Warwick's collaboration
with Bacharach and David yielded dozens of top 10
hits. Among their charting songs were "Walk on By"
(1964), "I Say a Little Prayer," (1968), and "Alfie."
Warwick's recordings of "Do You Know the Way to
San Jose?" (1968) and "I'll Never Fall in Love"
(1970) also won Grammy Awards. Critics and the
public agreed that Warwick's polished and controlled
voice made her the perfect interpreter of Bacharach-
David's sophisticated pop songs.

In 1972, the team of Bacharach and David
broke up, with acrimony on both sides. Warwick,
who learned about split from a newspaper article,
later described the news as "devastating." Under
contract with Warner Brothers to deliver an album
of Bacharach-David songs, Warwick took her former friends to court for breach of contract. At the
same time, she was being sued for alimony by her
husband Billy Elliott, whom she had married in
1965. The couple had two sons, David and
Damon, before divorcing.

Creatively, the 1970s were difficult for Warwick. Although she toured constantly, she had only one hit, "Then Came You," a collaboration with the Spinners. On the advice of an astrologer and numerologist, she briefly added an *e* to the end of her last name, but the new billing did little to change her luck.

In 1979, Warwick finally received a career boost when she signed with Arista Records, which later became the label of her cousin, singer WHITNEY HOUSTON. Arista paired her with singer Barry Manilow as her producer. The resulting album, *Dionne* (1979), produced two Grammy-winning hits, "I'll Never Love This Way Again" and "Deja Vu." Warwick had less success as the host of *Solid Gold*, a television countdown of the music charts. Hired in July 1980, she was fired in less a year. Officially, the producers maintained they wanted a younger host, but rumors spread that Warwick had been deemed too difficult to work with.

Warwick had another hit album with *Heartbreaker* (1982), produced by Barry Gibb of the Bee Gees. But for the rest of the decade, she did her best work for charitable causes. In 1984, she sang with the all-star group USA for Africa on "We Are the World," whose proceeds were donated to African famine relief. Two years later, Warwick brought together Stevie Wonder, Gladys Knight, and Elton John to sing "That's What Friends Are For." Going to number one on the charts, the song earned $2 million for AIDS research. It also marked her public reconciliation with Burt Bacharach, who wrote the song with his wife, Carole Bayer Sager.

In the 1990s, Warwick became the spokeswoman for the Psychic Friends Network, a telephone psychic service advertised on a highly successful infomercial. She also continued to record, making some of the most adventurous albums of her career. Among them were *Aquarela do Brasil* (1994), a collection of Brazilian music, and *Friends Can Be Lovers* (1993), which included duets with Houston, Luther Vandross, and Lisa Stansfield. A revival of interest in her classic records of the 1960s inspired her to make *Dionne on Dionne* (1998). With her sons as backup singers, Warwick reinterpreted her earlier work on the album, which included a hip-hop version of "What the World Needs Now" and a salsa-flavored remake of "Do You Know the Way to San Jose?"

Further Reading

"Dionne Warwick." In *Contemporary Black Biography*. Detroit: Gale Research, 1998.
Ebert, Alan. "Dionne on Dionne." *Essence*. January 1992, pp. 62+.

Recommended Recorded and Videotaped Performances

Dionne Warwick: Her Classic Songs, Vol. 1. Curb, CD, 1997.
Dionne Warwick: Her Classic Songs, Vol. 2. Curb, CD, 1998.
Dionne Warwick: The Definitive Collection. Arista, CD, 1999.

❖ WASHINGTON, DINAH (Ruth Lee Jones) (1924–1962) *Singer, Musician*

Known as the "Queen of the Blues," Dinah Washington was the dominant female singer of rhythm and blues during the 1950s. She was born Ruth Lee Jones in Tuscaloosa, Alabama, in August 1924 (her exact birth date is debated). When she was three, her family moved to Chicago. Ruth received her first musical instruction at home, learning to sing and play the piano from her mother. By her teens, she was a well-known gospel singer at the St. Luke's Baptist Church.

After winning a talent contest, Jones started performing in local clubs. In 1940, she returned to religious music when gospel singer Sallie Martin hired her as her pianist. Two years later, Jones went back to the nightclub circuit, playing piano at the Three Deuces, a Chicago jazz club where her idol BILLIE HOLIDAY was performing. Soon, Jones herself was singing in the back room. There, she was spotted by bandleader Lionel Hampton, who hired her as his vocalist. Hampton later claimed that he gave Jones the stage name Dinah Washington.

While singing with Hampton's band, Washington began recording blues songs. In 1943, her "Evil Gal Blues" and "Salty Papa Blues" were hits with African-American audiences. Two years later, "Blowtop Blues"—the only song she recorded with Hampton—made her a star of rhythm and blues.

After going solo in 1945, Washington was signed by Mercury Records, which would remain her label for 15 years. While a Mercury artist, she recorded more than 400 songs for the burgeoning urban blues market. With records such as "Long John Blues" (1947) and "Trouble in Mind" (1952), she was considered by many to be the successor of blues great BESSIE SMITH. Washington, however, prided herself on being able to sing in any genre. She had great success with covers of Broadway show tunes and even had a country hit with a cover of Hank Williams's "Cold, Cold Heart" (1952).

Washington also developed a reputation as a jazz artist. On songs such as "Lover, Come Back to Me," she had a fruitful collaboration with pianist Wynton Kelly, which some compared to the working relationship between Holiday and Lester Young. Washington frequently performed at jazz clubs and festivals. Her triumphant appearance at the Newport Jazz Festival in 1958 was recorded in the concert film *Jazz on a Summer's Day* (1959). Washington also played the Palladium in London. With Elizabeth II in the audience, the Queen of the Blues announced, "There is but one heaven, one hell, and one queen, and your Elizabeth is an impostor."

For most of her recording career, Washington's music was sold nearly exclusively to African Americans. In 1959, however, she broke into the larger mainstream market with "What a Diff'rence a Day Makes." In addition to hitting the top 10 on the R&B charts, the record won a Grammy Award. The next year, Washington had three crossover hits. With fellow Mercury artist Brook Benton, she sang the duets "Baby, You've Got What it Takes" and "A Rockin' Good Way," while on her own she had a number-one hit with the mournful love song, "This Bitter Earth."

On- and offstage, she had a flair for the flamboyant. She loved tight dresses and mink coats and enjoyed shocking people with her rough language. Washington had at least eight husbands and two sons.

Late in her career, Washington became sensitive about her weight. Newly married to Detroit Lions football player Dick "Night Train" Lane, she went on a crash diet with fatal results. On December 14, 1963, Lane found Washington's body in their Detroit home. Only 39, Washington had died from an accidental overdose of alcohol, sedatives, and diet pills.

Further Reading

Barbera, André. "Washington, Dinah." In *American National Biography,* edited by John Arthur Garraty and Mark C. Carnes, vol. 22, pp. 757–758. New York: Oxford University Press, 1999.

Haskins, James. *Queen of the Blues: A Biography of Dinah Washington.* New York: William Morrow, 1987.

Recommended Recorded and Videotaped Performances

The Essential Dinah Washington: The Great Songs. Mercury, CD, 1992.

First Issue: The Dinah Washington Story. Polygram, CD set, 1993.

Jazz on a Summer's Day (1958). New Yorker Films, DVD/VHS, 2000.

❖ WATERS, ETHEL
(1896–1977) *Singer, Actress*

"Ethel Waters was the mother of us all," said LENA HORNE about Waters's influence as an interpreter of the American popular song. Born in Chester, Pennsylvania, on October 31, 1896, Waters was the result of the rape of her 12-year-old mother, who never fully recovered from the trauma. Unable to accept Ethel as her child, she sent the girl to live with her own mother. Though strong and devout, Ethel's grandmother, a live-in maid, had little time to instill her values in her granddaughter. Left largely on her own, Ethel essentially had to raise herself, becoming a leader in street gangs in her poor neighborhood. Her only experience with close adult supervision was two years spent in a Catholic school. The kindness of the nuns there made her a dedicated Christian throughout her life.

After a brief marriage when she was 13, Waters left school and began working as a hotel chambermaid. At night, she frequented black theaters and nightclubs, perfecting her skill at mimicking popular performers. Soon she began performing as a singer herself with the African-American vaudeville circuit around Baltimore. Billed as "Sweet Mama Stringbean" because of her tall, lanky frame, Waters became the first woman to sing W. C. Handy's "St. Louis Blues," a song that later became associated with BESSIE SMITH.

In 1921 Waters began making recordings, and in the next year she became one of the first African-Americans to sing on the radio. Her early hits included "Down Home Blues," "Dinah," and "Sweet Georgia Brown." Eventually recording more than 250 songs, Waters would be honored by the Popular Song Association in 1933 for introducing 50 hit songs to the American public.

Water's singing style was clear and natural, though her soft voice did not have the power of many of her contemporaries'. Her singing, however, was distinguished by her tendency to dramatize the lyrics. She once wrote that "A song is a story—that's how it is to me—and I sing it so it tells the story."

Throughout the 1920s, Waters performed in African-American clubs, but gradually also moved into the lucrative white vaudeville circuit. After appearing in the revue *Africana* (1927), she made it to Broadway in the all-black musicals *Blackbirds of 1930* and *Rhapsody in Black* (1931–32). Waters also broke into movies with her first feature, *On with the Show* (1929). The first full-color talkie, it featured Waters singing "Am I Blue," which became one of her many hit records. A year earlier, she had married Clyde Edward Matthews; the couple was divorced in 1934.

In 1933, Waters became the highest-paid performer ever to play New York City's famed Cotton Club. There, she was seen by composer Irving Berlin, who invited her to join his Broadway show *As Thousands Cheer* (1933). Her gift for impersonation was well-used in a song Berlin wrote especially for her, "Thief in the Night," which parodied the international sensation JOSEPHINE BAKER. Waters also delivered a dramatic rendition of "Supper Time," a dirgelike song that told of a black mother's sorrow over her husband's lynching. The only African American in an otherwise white cast, Waters challenged racial barriers when the show toured the segregated South.

After the success of *As Thousands Cheer* (1933), Waters appeared in another musical, *At Home Abroad* (1935), but longed to star in a drama. She appeared as a band vocalist for years, waiting for funding to come through for *Mamba's Daughter*, a play about an African-American family. In 1938 Water finally got her chance to play the hardworking, long-suffering grandmother in the piece, thereby becoming the first black actress to perform the lead role in a Broadway drama. Although the critical reception was mixed, audiences loved the play. On opening night, Waters received 17 curtain calls.

Thrilled with her acceptance as a dramatic actress, Waters denounced singing and looked for more plays to showcase her newly discovered talents. She found, however, that there were few roles in straight plays for African Americans. She instead settled for a part in *Cabin in the Sky* (1940), an all-black musical inspired by African-American folklore. Waters, however, insisted that her character be rewritten, making her into a respectable, pious woman instead of the passive victim of her husband's philanderings. The successful show became an equally successful film in 1943. Playing opposite such accomplished performers as Louis Armstrong and Lena Horne, Waters created one of the movie's most memorable moments in her performance of "Happiness Is Just a Thing Called Joe," a song written for her for the film adaptation.

Ethel Waters in 1946
(Library of Congress, neg. no. USZ62-111440)

In the late 1940s, Waters again had trouble finding dramatic work, but also discovered that, middle-aged and overweight, she was no longer in demand as a club singer. After several lean years, she made a comeback in the film *Pinky* (1949), in which she played the grandmother of a young African-American woman trying to pass as white. Her performance in the controversial film earned her an Academy Award nomination for best supporting actress.

With her renewed acclaim as a dramatic actress, Waters returned to the theater in Carson McCullers's play *The Member of the Wedding*. She had earlier turned down the part of Berenice, the wise housekeeper and caretaker of Frankie, a sensitive 12-year-old white girl. She took on the role only when McCullers agreed to rewrite the part, emphasizing Berenice's religious piety. Waters also insisted that she sing during the play "His Eye Is on the Sparrow," a song she remembered from her youth. (She later used its title for her 1951 best-selling autobiography.) In part because of Waters's changes, Berenice avoided the stereotypes associated with African-American "mammies," instead becoming a full character that, in the words of poet Langston Hughes, was "one of both dignity and gentleness."

In 1950 Waters became the first black performer to star in a television series, playing the title role in *Beulah*. Though the series was popular, some African Americans denounced her for playing a maid. The criticism offended Waters, who took it as an insult to her own grandmother. Waters herself was disenchanted with the television industry and left the show after only a year.

Once again, Waters had difficulty finding work, though she frequently appeared in revivals of *Wedding*. Weary of the entertainment industry, she took her career in a new direction after attending a crusade held by Baptist evangelist Billy Graham in 1957. She soon joined Graham's touring group, first as a member of the choir and later as a soloist. Waters continued to appear with Graham until 1976, when a host of health problems made it impossible for her to perform. She died the next year on September 1 at the age of 79.

Waters is remembered for her trailblazing work as both a singer and an actress. In music, she helped bridge the sounds of blues, jazz, and pop. On the stage and in films, she showed that African-American actors could attract audiences to serious drama.

Further Reading

Waters, Ethel, with Charles Samuels. *His Eye Is on the Sparrow.* 1951. Reprint, New York: Da Capo Press, 1992.
———. *To Me It's Wonderful.* New York: Harper & Row, 1972.

Recommended Recorded and Videotaped Performances

Cabin in the Sky (1943). Warner Home Video, VHS, 1999.
An Introduction to Ethel Waters: Her Best Recordings 1921–1940. Best of Jazz, CD, 1996.

Member of the Wedding (1953). Columbia/Tristar VHS, 1988.

Pinky (1949). Twentieth Century-Fox, VHS, 1994.

❖ WEST, MAE

(1893–1980) *Actress, Singer*

Clever and sultry, Mae West conquered both stage and screen, becoming America's favorite "sex goddess" of the 1920s and 1930s. Born in Brooklyn, New York, on August 17, 1893, West was the daughter of a former prizefighter and a model. Her mother encouraged her to enter amateur talent contests. Billed as "Baby Mae," she won her first contest at age eight with a song-and-dance act. Mae was soon in demand for child parts in stage shows. Almost immediately, she began rewriting her roles to better suit her talents, a habit she would practice throughout her performing career. By her teens, Mae was finding work in traveling shows. She briefly teamed up with Frank Wallace, whom she married in a secret ceremony in 1911. They soon separated, and they divorced in 1942.

At 18, West began appearing in musical revues in New York City. She also found success on the vaudeville circuit. Unlike most women in vaudeville, she usually performed as a solo act. Often dressed in satin and fur, she developed a sensual swagger while perfecting her comic gifts. West quickly emerged as a master of the double entendre. Even when she spoke a seemingly innocent line, her audience interpreted it as risqué. As West herself explained, "It wasn't what I said, but how I said it."

Disappointed with the roles she was offered, West decided to write her own. After penning three unproduced plays, she finally decided to produce her fourth herself. The play was provocatively titled *Sex* (1926) as a conscious bid for publicity. Broadsheet newspapers refused to run ads for the play, but the tabloids were plastered with stories about West and her production. She also sent boys all over New York with stickers featuring the play's title. West later wrote, "If you stopped for a minute when one walked by, why you got a sticker stuck clean across your back, with SEX printed on it."

The play was an enormous success. West starred as Margy Lamont, a former prostitute with a heart of gold. Far from ashamed of her past, Lamont is unrepentant over how she earned the money to pay for her mansion. She jeers at a snobbish socialite, "The only difference between us is that you could afford to give it away."

Despite its racy subject matter, the play ran without incident for 41 weeks, in part because New York's major was an admitted West fan. While the mayor was out of town, however, the vice mayor ordered a raid on the production. *Sex* was shut down, and West was arrested. In court, the city failed to prove that the play's text was obscene. West, though, was found guilty of "corrupting the morals of youth." Although she was fully clothed, her navel was said to move in an obscene manner during one of her dances. West was sentenced to 10 days in prison, though she was let out after eight for good behavior. She complained about the scratchy prison underwear but gleefully told the press that her jail experience had given her enough material for a dozen more plays.

West's next work, *The Drag* (1927), was among her most provocative. A comedic plea for tolerance of male homosexuality, it featured a great ball attended by drag queens. The play was produced in Paterson, New Jersey, but was deemed too controversial for Broadway.

The next year saw the play that would make her a legend, *Diamond Lil* (1928). Set in New York's Bowery, the play featured West as a singer hobnobbing with a variety of underworld figures. Showing an unerring instinct for how best to present herself on stage, West set *Diamond Lil* in the 1890s. Her full figure was too plump to dress in the slim, linear flapper style that defined 1920s sexuality. Her physique was ideal, however, for the low-cut, corseted look of Gay Nineties fashions.

The play also showcased West's own style of humor to its best advantage. As a critic in *The New Republic* wrote, "it uses every tried and trusted trick, hokum, motive and stage expectation, but always shrewdly." However old-fashioned the plot, the play offered West plenty of wisecracks. Her

Mae West with Cary Grant in *She Done Him Wrong* (1933)
(Museum of Modern Art Film Stills Archive)

favorite targets were sexual repression, hypocrisy, and romantic ideals. To West's Diamond Lil, sex was nothing but a pleasure to be enjoyed, and the only person a woman could depend on was herself.

After a raid shut down her next play, *The Pleasure Man* (1928), West went on tour with *Diamond Lil.* In 1932, she welcomed the chance to take on Hollywood, when her friend George Raft got her a small part as his girlfriend in *Night After Night.* West sparkled in her role, ad-libbing what became one of her most famous lines. After a coat-checker admires her jewelry with "Goodness, what beautiful diamonds," West replied, "Goodness had nothing to do with it." The line became the title of her 1959 autobiography.

Excited by its new star, Paramount Studios decided her next film would be an adaptation of *Diamond Lil.* The studio suggested calling it *He Done Her Wrong,* but West, offended by the passivity that title implied, insisted it be titled *She Done Him Wrong.* She also got her way in the selection of her costar—Cary Grant, a handsome actor 10 years her junior whom she spotted on the lot. The film broke box-office records, as did West's next movie, *I'm No Angel,* which teamed her again with Grant. These two films brought Grant to stardom, saved Paramount from bankruptcy, and made West the most powerful woman in Hollywood.

They also inspired Motion Picture Producers and Distributors of America to inaugurate a strict code of what could and could not been seen and heard on screen. West made seven more films during the 1930s and 1940s, but the strict rules of the production code increasingly reined in her risqué humor. She also wore out her welcome with audiences by playing over and over again variations on her Diamond Lil character. By the late 1930s, West had fallen so out of favor that she was considered box-office poison. She had a modest success with *My Little Chickadee* (1940), costarring W. C. Fields, but by 1943 she was forced to retire from films.

West returned to the stage, first with a misguided new play titled *Catherine Was Great* (1944), then with a touring revival of *Diamond Lil.* During the late 1950s, West, now in her 60s, developed a musical comedy revue, in which she shared the stage with a troupe of male bodybuilders. One of her troupe, Paul Novak, became West's companion for the last 25 years of her life.

West's brand of sexual humor found a new, young audience in the 1960s and 1970s. She tried to capitalize on the renewed interest in her movies by recording three record albums and appearing in two widely reviled films, *Myra Breckinridge* (1970) and *Sextette* (1978). At 87, West suffered a stroke. She died three months later, on November 22, 1980.

West's Diamond Lil has since emerged as iconic a film character as Charlie Chaplin's Little Tramp. Those who have never seen her movies are still familiar with her face, her voice, and her sashay. Even better known are West's bons mots—from "Come up sometime and see me" to "Peel me a grape"—making her perhaps the most quoted movie star of all time.

Further Reading

Curry, Ramona. *Too Much of a Good Thing: Mae West as Cultural Icon.* Minneapolis: University of Minnesota Press, 1996.

Leider, Emily Wortis. *Becoming Mae West.* New York: Farrar, Straus & Giroux, 1997.

West, Mae. *Goodness Had Nothing to Do With It.* Revised edition. New York: Macfadden-Bartell, 1970.

Recommended Recorded and Videotaped Performances

I'm No Angel (1933). Universal, VHS, 1993.
My Little Chickadee (1940). Universal, VHS, 1993.
She Done Him Wrong (1933). Universal, VHS, 1993.
Sextette (1979). Rhino, DVD/VHS, 2000/1997.

❖ WINFREY, OPRAH (Orpah Winfrey)
(1954–)   *Talk Show Host, Actress*

The phenomenal success of Oprah Winfrey's daytime talk show has made her the wealthiest and most powerful woman in the American entertainment industry. Born on January 29, 1954, she was raised in rural poverty in Kosciusko, Mississippi, on a pig farm owned by her maternal grandparents. Her parents never married. She was originally given the name Orpah from the biblical Book of Ruth, but when it proved to difficult to pronounce, her relatives rechristened her Oprah.

Oprah's grandmother taught her to read when she was only two and a half. By the time she was ready to enter kindergarten, she was literate enough to write a note convincing her teacher that she belonged in first grade. Despite her academic promise, Oprah's early childhood was otherwise grim. She later commented that "it was very lonely out in the country" and that her grandmother "could beat me for days and never get tired."

Oprah found little relief when at six she was sent to live with her mother, Vernita, at a rooming house in Milwaukee, Wisconsin. Vernita worked as a housecleaner and was rarely at home. Eager for her attention, Oprah became rebellious, especially after she was sexually abused by a teenage cousin when she was nine. Vernita had so little control over her daughter that she considered placing her in a detention center. Instead, she sent Oprah to live with her father, Vernon, in Nashville, Tennessee, when she was 14. Soon after arriving, Oprah confessed that she was pregnant, a condition she had managed to hide for seven months. She gave birth prematurely, and the baby died two weeks later.

A successful business owner and city council-man, Vernon imposed strict discipline on Oprah, which she later credited with putting her on the right path in life. She was inspired to meet his high expectations of her, particularly in her school work. Oprah became an excellent student and an enthusiastic member of her high school's drama and debate clubs. Her love of reading was also nurtured by her stepmother, Zelma. She took Oprah to the library every two weeks to pick out five books. Oprah was then expected to read them and write a report on each for her parents.

While still a teenager, Oprah began her broadcasting career. After being named Miss Fire Prevention, she impressed the management of WVOL radio with her poise and speaking ability. The station hired her as a part-time newscaster in 1971. The same year, while attending Tennessee State University, she won the titles Miss Black Nashville and Miss Black Tennessee. The exposure led to her first television job. At 19, she was hired as a news reporter and anchor for WTVF, Nashville's CBS affiliate.

Before graduating from college, Winfrey was lured to Baltimore, where she anchored the news at WJZ-TV. Her frequent on-air mispronunciations led to her firing, although the station gave her a second chance as the cohost of a morning talk show, *People Are Talking*. Winfrey has said that "the day I did that talk show, I felt like I'd come home." The audience embraced Winfrey with equal enthusiasm. Although she brought the show excellent ratings, the station continually criticized her appearance, particularly her weight. In their efforts to mold Winfrey's image, the management sent her to a New York City hair salon, where a botched permanent left her bald. The experience made her vow never to listen to image consultants again.

In 1984, Winfrey took a new job as the host of *AM Chicago* (soon retitled *The Oprah Winfrey Show*), which was then last in the ratings. Within four months, the show was leading in its time slot, besting even the show hosted by talk show pioneer Phil Donahue. One of her fans was composer Quincy Jones—a producer of the film adaptation of Alice Walker's novel *The Color Purple* (1985).

He invited Winfrey to audition for the role of Sofia, a powerful African-American woman whose spirit is broken by prejudice. Her acting debut earned her an Academy Award nomination.

In 1986, *The Oprah Winfrey Show* was syndicated nationally. Within five months, it became the number-one talk show, drawing more than 10 million viewers a day. Its success owed much to Winfrey's quick wit and empathy. As guests confessed their personal problems, Winfrey often held their hands and cried as they cried. She, too, made confessions. In 1991, on an episode about child abuse, Winfrey discussed the abuse she had suffered at the hands of male relatives.

Her audience also became involved in her continual struggle with her weight. In 1988, thousands of viewers went on the liquid diet that allowed her to lose 67 pounds. After regaining the weight, she again inspired her audience to exercise as she advocated a responsible diet and physical activity as the keys to weight control. Of equal fascination to her fans has been Oprah's romantic life. Since 1993, she has been engaged to Chicago businessman Steadman Graham. Her hesitancy to marry has fueled speculations that she is gay. In 1997, she answered the rumors with a public statement declaring that she is heterosexual.

As Winfrey's influence grew, so did her fortune. With her show owned by her own corporation—Harpo Productions (Oprah spelled backward), Winfrey was earning about $80 million a year by 1990. Her personal worth is estimated at more than $725 million.

Her finances secure, Winfrey began producing movies dealing with subjects of importance to her. In 1989, she produced and starred in the television film *The Women of Brewster Place,* a drama based on the 1982 novel by Gloria Naylor about seven African-American women living in a tenement. The movie spawned a short-lived television series, in which Winfrey also appeared. Harpo has also produced *There Are No Children Here* (1993), *Beloved* (1998), and *Tuesdays with Morrie* (1999).

On September 17, 1996, Winfrey announced on her show that she wanted "to get the country reading." She introduced viewers to Oprah's Book Club, a monthly feature during which an entire show would be devoted to discussing a book of Winfrey's choosing. Within a month after making her first selection, *Deep End of the Ocean* (1996), more than 750,000 copies of the novel were in print. Oprah's Book Club has since made bestsellers of dozens of titles and made Winfrey herself the most powerful book marketer in the United States.

After the 1997 death of Princess Diana, Winfrey reevaluated her life and career. As a result, she recast her show, calling it "change-your-life TV." By emphasizing self-help and advice, she tried to make the program "a catalyst for people beginning to think more insightfully about themselves." Among the show's new features was Oprah's Angel Network, a campaign for donations of spare change for college scholarships. In 1998, the charity collected more than $1 million from viewers, which Winfrey matched penny for penny. She has also made substantial donations to Morehouse College, the United Negro College Fund, and many other charities.

In anticipation of ending her talk show in 2002, Winfrey, in partnership with television executives Marcy Carsey and Geraldine Laybourne, formed Oxygen Media to create a female-oriented cable channel. In association with Hearst magazines, she also launched *O, The Oprah Magazine,* in April 2000. Targeted to women in their 30s, the glossy magazine features articles on family, health, spirituality, and books. The first issue was so successful that Hearst had to go back to press for 500,000 copies after the initial run of 1 million quickly sold out. Attesting to Winfrey's unending ability to attract an audience, Winfrey herself appears on the cover of each issue.

Further Reading

Mair, George. *Oprah Winfrey: The Real Story.* Revised edition. Secaucus, N.J.: Carol Publishing Group, 1998.

Pasternak, Judith Mahoney. *Oprah.* New York: Metro Books, 1999.

Recommended Recorded and Videotaped Performances

Beloved (1998). Buena Vista Home Entertainment, DVD, 1999.

The Color Purple (1985). Warner Home Video, DVD/VHS, 1997/1999.

The Women of Brewster Place (1989). Xenon, DVD/VHS, 2000/1998.

❖ WONG, ANNA MAY
(1907–1961) *Actress*

Most often cast as an "Oriental villainess," Chinese-American actress Anna May Wong was born in Los Angeles's Chinatown on January 3, 1907. Her parents ran a laundry where Anna May worked after school, though she much preferred spending her time at early movie theaters known as nickelodeons. Unbeknownst to her conservative parents, at 12 she first appeared as a film extra in *The Red Lantern* (1914). She continued her work in secret for two more years. She finally confessed about her new career to her father when she obtained her first real role in *Bits of Life* (1921).

Wong's high cheekbones and straight black bangs made her a striking presence on screen. But it was not until she compellingly played a Mongol slave girl in the 1924 extravaganza *The Thief of Bagdad* that she earned international fame. In the late 1920s, she was widely sought for roles in mystery films, many of which were then set in urban Chinatown districts. Although appreciating the work, Wong resented that these films generally presented Asians only as villains, employing the crudest of stereotypes.

By 1928, she was so disgusted by the roles she was offered that she abandoned Hollywood for Europe. As Wong later told a London interviewer, "Why should [Asian characters] always scheme, rob, kill? I got so weary of it all." In Europe, she found more satisfying parts in the German film *Song* (1928) and the English movie *Piccadilly* (1930). Wong also made her stage debut opposite Laurence Olivier in *The Circle of Chalk,* a play based on a Chinese legend that was written specif-

Anna May Wong in 1934
(Library of Congress, neg. no. USZ62-112059)

ically for Wong. As talkies replaced silents, Wong also learned to speak French and German fluently in order to keep her film career alive.

Wong's return to the United States in late 1930 ushered in the height of her film career. Although she had no problem finding film roles, the negative portrayals of Asian women continued to disturb her. Her greatest disappointment came with the casting of the film adaptation of Pearl Buck's novel *The Good Earth* (1937). Wong lobbied hard for the lead role as the selfless, stoic O-Lan. The part, however, was given to Luise Rainer, a German actress who won an Academy Award for her performance. Instead of the lead, Wong was offered the part of a scheming concubine. Insulted, she refused to appear in the film at all.

With the *Good Earth* fiasco fresh in her mind, Wong happily left the United States to visit China for the first time. Half hoping she could restart her career there, she was surprised to find herself vilified

by Chinese officials for the stereotyped Chinese characters she had played. When she explained these were the only parts available to her, she was able to fend off further criticisms. Yet, disheartened by the experience, Wong returned home after 10 months.

In Hollywood, she resumed her movie career, most notably playing a high-minded detective in the action film *Daughter of Shanghai* (1937). As the United States entered World War II, however, she found herself less in demand as an actress than as a consultant. As war movies came in vogue, producers were eager to hire her to teach Caucasian actors to act more convincingly Asian. Disgusted by this new indignity, Wong largely retired from film work. She only appeared in one more film and a few undistinguished television programs before her death of a heart attack on February 3, 1961.

Further Reading

"Anna May Wong." In *Notable Asian Americans.* Detroit: Gale Research, 1995.
Gee, Emma. "Wong, Anna May." In *Notable American Women: The Modern Period,* 744–745. Edited by Barbara Sicherman and Carol Hurd Green. Cambridge, Mass.: Belknap Press, 1980.

Recommended Recorded and Videotaped Performances

Shanghai Express (1932). Universal, VHS, 1993.
The Thief of Bagdad (1924). Image Entertainment, DVD, 1998.

❖ WOOD, NATALIE (Natasha Gurdin)
(1938–1981)   *Actress*

In a career that spanned almost 40 years, Natalie Wood succeeded in making the difficult transition from child star to ingenue to serious actress. On July 20, 1938, she was born Natasha Gurdin in San Francisco, California. Her parents were Russian immigrants who found work in the entertainment industry—her father as a set designer, her mother as a ballet dancer.

At five, Natasha made her film debut in *Happy Land* (1943). Her next movie had her playing opposite Orson Welles in *Tomorrow Is Forever* (1946). While working on the film, she was first dubbed Natalie Wood—"Natalie" as an Americanization of her given name and "Wood" as a tribute to the film director Sam Wood. Throughout the rest of her youth, Wood was in constant demand. Her winsome combination of intelligence and sweetness was most memorably captured in *Miracle on 34th Street,* in which she played a practical little girl who comes to believe in the magic of Christmas.

At 17, Wood re-created herself as a teen star in *Rebel Without a Cause* (1955). The film captured the anxieties of 1950s adolescents and made her an icon to her generation. Revealing a tender vulnerability, Wood won her first Academy Award nomination for the film.

Rebel also made Wood a star of the tabloids due to her romance with costar James Dean. She was linked with other rising celebrities, including singer Elvis Presley and actor Robert Wagner. Wood and Wagner were married in 1957 and starred in *All the Fine Young Cannibals* (1960). They were divorced in 1962.

In *Splendor in the Grass* (1961), which costarred Warren Beatty in his film debut, Wood made the jump to adult dramatic actress. Playing a young woman driven insane by sexual repression, she was nominated for her second Oscar. Wood also found success as a musical star, even though she could not sing or dance. She appeared (with her singing dubbed) as Maria in *West Side Story* (1961) and as GYPSY ROSE LEE in *Gypsy* (1962).

Throughout the 1960s, Wood played young women searching for their identity in a series of films. The most effective was *Love with the Proper Stranger* (1963), for which she received another Oscar nomination. At the end of the decade, she showed a newfound talent for comedy in *Bob & Carol & Ted & Alice* (1969), a satire of middle-class sexual mores.

In 1969, Wood married Robert Gregson, with whom she had a daughter, Natasha. After divorcing Gregson in 1972, she remarried her first husband, Robert Wagner. They had one child,

Courtney, and Wagner adopted Natasha, who would grow up to become a film actress.

In the 1970s, Wood teamed with Wagner for several television projects, including a production of Tennessee Williams's *Cat on a Hot Tin Roof* (1976). She had less success finding suitable film roles. Among her last movies were the disaster film *Meteor* (1979) and the science fiction thriller *Brainstorm* (1983). While still filming *Brainstorm,* Wood disappeared during a yachting vacation with Wagner and their guest, Wood's costar Christopher Walken. On November 29, 1981, her body was found off the coast of California's Santa Catalina Island. The victim of an accidental drowning, Natalie Wood died at the age of 43.

Further Reading

Finstad, Suzanne. *Natasha: The Biography of Natalie Wood.* New York: Crown, 2001.

Nickens, Christopher. *Natalie Wood: A Biography in Pictures.* Garden City, N.Y.: Doubleday, 1986.

Recommended Recorded and Videotaped Performances

Gypsy (1962). Warner Home Video, DVD/VHS, 2000.

Miracle on 34th Street (1947). Twentieth Century-Fox, DVD/VHS, 1999/1999.

West Side Story (1961). MGM/UA, DVD/VHS, 1998/1998.

❖ **WYNETTE, TAMMY (Virginia Wynette Pugh)**
(1942–1998) *Singer*

In the late 1960s, such hits as "Stand by Your Man" and "D-I-V-O-R-C-E" earned Tammy Wynette the title "First Lady of Country Music." On May 5, 1942, she was born Virginia Wynette Pugh in Itawamba County, Mississippi. When she was only nine months old, she experienced the first of many personal tragedies, the death of her father from a brain tumor. Five years later, Virginia's mother remarried. Because of tensions between Virginia and her stepfather, she spent much of her youth on her grandparents' farm, where she was often called upon to pick cotton.

Exhausted by farm work, she was determined "to get away as fast as I could," as Wynette later remembered. Just months shy of her high school graduation, she dropped out to marry Euple Byrd in 1959. For five years, they struggled to make ends meet while living in a shack with no electricity. When the couple separated in 1964, Virginia Pugh was pregnant with her third daughter. Soon after birth, the baby contracted spinal meningitis, leaving Pugh with $6,000 in medical bills.

Desperate to earn a decent living, Pugh moved to Birmingham, Alabama, where she worked as a beautician. At the same time, she harbored a grander ambition—to become a country singer. Pugh's first step was winning a regular spot on *The Country Boy Eddie Show,* a local television program. With the host's encouragement, Pugh moved her family to Nashville, Tennessee, to further her career.

Pugh went door to door, visiting every record company lining the city's Music Row, but no one seemed impressed by her. After a battery of rejections, she met Billy Sherrill at Epic Records. The young producer had been looking for a female soloist, then an oddity in country music. Sherrill signed Pugh to Epic and christened her "Tammy Wynette," taking her first name from the popular film *Tammy* (1965) starring Debbie Reynolds.

In 1966, Wynette's recording of the Johnny Paycheck song "Apartment No. 9" became her first hit. It was followed by a string of successful singles, including "D-I-V-O-R-C-E" and "I Don't Want to Play House," for which she won a Grammy Award in 1967. She received her second Grammy two years later for "Stand by Your Man," which, sold more than 6 million copies and became her signature song. The song drew criticism from feminists, who interpreted its lyrics as encouraging women to accept any type of treatment from their spouses, including physical abuse. Wynette was deeply offended by the suggestion, maintaining "the song doesn't say anything at all about being a doormat."

In fact, Wynette had her own difficulties standing by her man. In 1965, the year she divorced her first husband, she met Don Chapel, whom she married two years later. As her star rose, Wynette developed a close friendship with her childhood idol, country star George Jones. After Wynette's marriage to Chapel was annulled, she and Jones married in 1969.

The couple worked together on a series of recordings, including the classic duets "We're Going to Hold On" and "Near You." Many of their collaborations seemed to chronicle their own stormy romance, also a favorite subject of tabloids and music industry gossip. As Wynette later assessed, "I was naggin' and he was nippin'," referring to Jones's addiction to alcohol and cocaine. Wynette and Jones divorced in 1975, though they continued to record together for several more years. After a 44-day marriage to realtor Michael Tomlin and a brief affair with actor Burt Reynolds, Wynette finally settled down with George Richley, a singer-songwriter who became her manager. Married in 1978, the couple remained together until Wynette's death.

Beginning in the late 1970s, Wynette suffered a string of personal setbacks. In 1975, much of her house was destroyed by a fire. Three years later, she was kidnapped at a Nashville shopping mall and severely beaten. Her captor was never arrested. Wynette also found herself bankrupt in 1988 after investing her money in several unsuccessful real estate ventures in Florida.

Worst of all, Wynette suffered from serious health problems. Chronic inflammation of her bile ducts led to 17 operations. In constant pain, Wynette began abusing prescription painkillers. She eventually had to enter the Betty Ford Clinic in Washington, D.C., for treatment for her addiction.

Despite her ailments, Wynette continued to perform and record. In addition to recording duets with rock artists such as Sting and Elton John, she had a surprise international dance hit in 1992 with "Justified and Ancient," which she performed with the British synth-pop band KLF. The next year, Wynette joined fellow country legends LORETTA

LYNN and DOLLY PARTON on the successful album *Honky Tonk Angels*. She also reunited with Jones on the album *One* in 1995.

To the shock of her fans, Tammy Wynette died in her sleep on April 6, 1998, at the age of 55. A blood clot that reached her lungs was given as the cause of death, but three of her daughters in a lawsuit alleged that painkillers contributed to her demise. Just five months after her death, Wynette was inducted into the Country Music Hall of Fame.

Further Reading

Daly, Jackie, with Tom Carter. *Tammy Wynette: A Daughter Recalls Her Mother's Tragic Life and Death.* New York: Putnam, 2000.

Wynette, Tammy, with Joan Dew. *Stand By Your Man.* New York: Simon & Schuster, 1979.

Recommended Recorded and Videotaped Performances

Honky Tonk Angels. Sony/Columbia, CD, 1993.

Tammy Wynette in Concert (1986). Rhino, VHS, 1995.

Tears of Fire: The 25th Anniversary Collection. Sony/Columbia, CD set, 1992.

RECOMMENDED SOURCES ON AMERICAN WOMEN IN THE PERFORMING ARTS

Baehr, Helen, and Gillian Dyer, eds. *Boxed In: Women and Television.* New York: Pandora, 1987.

Barnes, Sally. *Dancing Women: Female Bodies on Stage.* New York: Routledge, 1998.

Bogle, Donald. *Brown Sugar: Eighty Years of America's Black Female Superstars.* New York: Da Capo Press, 1990.

Bufwack, Mary A., and Robert K. Oermann. *Finding Her Voice: The Saga of Women in Country Music.* New York: Crown Publishers, 1993.

Chinoy, Helen Krich, and Linda Walsh Jenkins, eds. *Women in American Theatre.* Revised edition. New York: Theatre Communications Group, 2000.

Cima, Gay Gibson. *Performing Women: Female Characters, Male Playwrights, and the Modern Stage.* Ithaca, N.Y.: Cornell University Press, 1993.

Cook, Pam, and Philip Dodd, eds. *Women and Film: A Sight and Sound Reader.* Philadelphia: Temple University Press, 1993.

Drew, William M. *At the Center of the Frame: Leading Ladies of the Twenties and Thirties.* Lanham, Md.: Vestal Press, 1999.

———. *Speaking of Silents: First Ladies of the Screen.* Vestal, N.Y.: Vestal Press, 1989.

Dudden, Faye E. *Women in the American Theater: Actress and Audiences, 1790–1870.* New Haven, Conn.: Yale University Press, 1994.

Ferris, Lesley. *Acting Women: Images of Women in Theatre.* New York: New York University Press, 1989.

Freeland, David. *Ladies of Soul.* Jackson: University of Mississippi Press, 2001.

Gaar, Gillian G. *She's a Rebel: The History of Women in Rock and Roll.* Seattle: Seal Press, 1992.

Glenn, Susan A. *Female Spectacle: The Theatrical Roots of Modern Feminism.* Cambridge, Mass.: Harvard University Press, 2000.

Hannsberry, Karen Burroughs. *Femme Noir: The Bad Girls of Film.* Jefferson, N.C.: McFarland, 1998.

Harris, Geraldine. *Staging Femininities: Performance and Performativity.* New York: Manchester University Press, 1999.

Harris, Roy, ed. *Eight Women of the American Stage: Talking About Acting.* Portsmouth, N.H.: Heinemann, 1997.

Harrison, Daphne Duval. *Black Pearls: Blues Queens of the 1920s.* New Brunswick, N.J.: Rutgers University Press, 1988.

Haskell, Molly. *From Reverence to Rape: The Treatment of Women in the Movies.* 2nd edition. Chicago: University of Chicago Press, 1987.

Hill, George, Lorraine Raglin, and Chas Floyd Johnson. *Black Women in Television: An Illustrated History and Bibliography.* New York: Garland Publishing, 1990.

Hirshey, Gerri. *Women Who Rock.* New York: Atlantic Monthly Press, 2000.

Horowitz, Susan. *Queens of Comedy: Lucille Ball, Phyllis Diller, Carol Burnett, Joan Rivers, and the New Generation of Funny Women.* Newark, N.J.: Gordon & Breach, 1997.

Kay, Karyn, and Gerald Peary, eds. *Women and the Cinema: A Critical Anthology.* New York: Dutton, 1977.

Kibler, M. Alison. *Rank Ladies: Gender and Cultural Hierarchy in American Vaudeville.* Chapel Hill: University of North Carolina Press, 1999.

Lasalle, Mick. *Complicated Women: Sex and Power in Pre-Code Hollywood.* New York: St. Martin's Press, 2000.

Lowe, Denise. *Women and American Television: An Encyclopedia.* Santa Barbara, Calif.: ABC-Clio, 1999.

Martin, Linda, and Kerry Segrave. *Women in Comedy.* Secaucus, N.J.: Citadel Press, 1986.

McLellan, Diana. *The Girls: Sappho Goes to Hollywood.* New York: St. Martin's Press, 2000.

Mellers, Wilfrid Howard. *Angels of the Night: Popular Female Singers of Our Time.* New York: B. Blackwell, 1986.

Mitchell, Caroline, ed. *Women and Radio.* New York: Routledge, 2001.

Nathan, David. *The Soulful Divas.* New York: Billboard Books, 1999.

O'Dair, Barbara, ed. *The Rolling Stone Book of Women in Rock.* New York: Random House, 1997.

O'Dell, Cary. *Women Pioneers in Television: Biographies of Fifteen Industry Leaders.* Jefferson, N.C.: McFarland, 1997.

Parish, James Robert, with Gregory W. Mank and Don E. Stanke. *The Hollywood Beauties.* New Rochelle, N.Y.: Arlington House, 1978.

Pendle, Karin, ed. *Women and Music: A History.* 2nd edition. Bloomington: Indiana University Press, 2000.

Robinson, Alice M., Vera Mowry Roberts, and Milly S. Barranger, eds. *Notable Women in the American Theater: A Biographical Dictionary.* New York: Greenwood Press, 1989.

Rosen, Marjorie. *Popcorn Venus.* New York: Coward, McCann & Geoghegan, 1973.

Schofield, Mary Anne, and Cecilia Macheski, eds. *Curtain Calls: British and American Women and the Theater, 1660–1820.* Athens: Ohio University Press, 1991.

Segrave, Kerry, and Linda Martin. *The Post-Feminist Hollywood Actress: Biographies and Filmographies of Stars Born After 1939.* Jefferson, N.C.: McFarland, 1990.

Silverman, Stephen M. *Funny Ladies.* New York: Harry N. Abrams, 1999.

Sochen, June. *From Mae to Madonna: Women Entertainers in Twentieth-Century America.* Lexington: University Press of Kentucky, 1999.

Tapert, Annette. *Power of Glamour: The Women Who Defined the Magic of Stardom.* New York: Crown Publishers, 1998.

Turner, Mary M. *Forgotten Leading Ladies of the American Theater.* Jefferson, N.C.: McFarland, 1990.

Unterbrink, Mary. *Funny Women: American Comediennes, 1860–1985.* Jefferson, N.C.: McFarland, 1987.

Whitall, Susan. *Women of Motown: An Oral History.* New York: Avon Books, 1998.

Wollstein, Hans J. *Vixens, Floozies and Molls: 28 Actresses of Late 1920s and 1930s Hollywood.* Jefferson, N.C: McFarland, 1999.

ENTRIES BY AREA OF ACTIVITY

Actress

Allen, Gracie
Arden, Eve
Arthur, Jean
Bacall, Lauren
Bailey, Pearl
Baker, Josephine
Ball, Lucille
Bankhead, Tallulah
Bara, Theda
Barrymore, Ethel
Berg, Gertrude
Bergen, Candace
Bergman, Ingrid
Bow, Clara
Brice, Fanny
Brooks, Louise
Burnett, Carol
Carroll, Diahann
Charisse, Cyd
Cher
Colbert, Claudette
Crawford, Joan
Cushman, Charlotte
Dandridge, Dorothy
Davis, Bette
Day, Doris
DeGeneres, Ellen
Del Rio, Dolores
Dietrich, Marlene

Diller, Phyllis
Fonda, Jane
Foster, Jodie
Garbo, Greta
Gardner, Ava
Garland, Judy
Gish, Dorothy
Gish, Lillian
Goldberg, Whoopi
Grable, Betty
Harlow, Jean
Hayes, Helen
Hayworth, Rita
Henie, Sonja
Hepburn, Audrey
Hepburn, Katharine
Horne, Lena
Houston, Whitney
Kelly, Grace
Kemble, Fanny
Leigh, Vivien
Lombard, Carole
Lupino, Ida
Mabley, Moms
McDaniel, Hattie
MacDonald, Jeanette
Madonna
Martin, Mary
Merman, Ethel
Midler, Bette

Minnelli, Liza
Miranda, Carmen
Monroe, Marilyn
Montez, Lola
Moore, Mary Tyler
Moreno, Rita
Normand, Mabel
Parton, Dolly
Pickford, Mary
Powell, Eleanor
Radner, Gilda
Rand, Sally
Roberts, Julia
Rogers, Ginger
Roseanne
Ross, Diana
Russell, Lillian
Russell, Rosalind
Sainte-Marie, Buffy
Sarandon, Susan
Shore, Dinah
Stanwyck, Barbara
Streep, Meryl
Streisand, Barbra
Swanson, Gloria
Talmadge, Norma
Tandy, Jessica
Tanguay, Eva
Taylor, Elizabeth
Temple, Shirley

Tomlin, Lily
Turner, Lana
Turner, Tina
Verdon, Gwen
Waters, Ethel
West, Mae
Winfrey, Oprah
Wong, Anna May
Wood, Natalie

Choreographer

De Mille, Agnes
Dunham, Katherine
Graham, Martha
Humphrey, Doris
Jamison, Judith
Monk, Meredith
Tamiris, Helen
Tharp, Twyla
Verdon, Gwen

Circus Performer

Leitzel, Lillian

Comic

Allen, Gracie
Brice, Fanny
DeGeneres, Ellen
Diller, Phyllis
Goldberg, Whoopi
Mabley, Moms
Pearl, Minnie
Radner, Gilda
Rivers, Joan
Roseanne
Tomlin, Lily

Dancer

Baker, Josephine
Castle, Irene
Charisse, Cyd
De Mille, Agnes

Duncan, Isadora
Dunham, Katherine
Farrell, Suzanne
Grable, Betty
Graham, Martha
Hayworth, Rita
Humphrey, Doris
Jamison, Judith
Madonna
Minnelli, Liza
Montez, Lola
Moreno, Rita
Powell, Eleanor
Rand, Sally
Rogers, Ginger
St. Denis, Ruth
Tallchief, Maria
Tamiris, Helen
Temple, Shirley
Tharp, Twyla
Verdon, Gwen

Director

De Mille, Agnes
Foster, Jodie
Gish, Lillian
Lupino, Ida
Streisand, Barbra

Musician

Baez, Joan
Carpenter, Karen
Carter, Maybelle
Leginska, Ethel
Mitchell, Joni
Powell, Maud
Price, Florence
Sainte-Marie, Buffy
Washington, Dinah

Performance Artist

Anderson, Laurie
Finley, Karen
Monk, Meredith

Singer

Anderson, Marian
Baez, Joan
Bailey, Pearl
Baker, Josephine
Burnett, Carol
Callas, Maria
Carpenter, Karen
Carroll, Diahann
Cher
Cline, Patsy
Day, Doris
Estefan, Gloria
Fitzgerald, Ella
Franklin, Aretha
Garland, Judy
Grable, Betty
Holiday, Billie
Horne, Lena
Houston, Whitney
Jackson, Mahalia
James, Etta
Joplin, Janis
Lynn, Loretta
McDaniel, Hattie
MacDonald, Jeanette
Madonna
Martin, Mary
Merman, Ethel
Midler, Bette
Mills, Florence
Minelli, Liza
Miranda, Carmen
Mitchell, Joni
Moreno, Rita
Norman, Jessye
Parton, Dolly
Powell, Eleanor
Price, Leontyne
Rainey, Ma
Rogers, Ginger
Ross, Diana
Russell, Lillian
Sainte-Marie, Buffy

Shore, Dinah
Sills, Beverly
Slick, Grace
Smith, Bessie
Smith, Patti
Streisand, Barbra
Tanguay, Eva
Temple, Shirley
Thornton, Big Mama
Tucker, Sophie
Turner, Tina
Vaughan, Sarah
Verdon, Gwen
Warwick, Dionne
Washington, Dinah
Waters, Ethel

West, Mae
Wynette, Tammy

Songwriter/Composer

Baez, Joan
Leginska, Ethel
Madonna
Mitchell, Joni
Monk, Meredith
Price, Florence
Sainte-Marie, Buffy
Slick, Grace

Stripper

Lee, Gypsy Rose

Talk Show Host

Bergen, Candace
Goldberg, Whoopi
Rivers, Joan
Roseanne
Shore, Dinah
Winfrey, Oprah

Wild West Show Performer

Oakley, Annie

ENTRIES BY YEAR OF BIRTH

1915–1919

Bailey, Pearl
Bergman, Ingrid
Diller, Phyllis
Fitzgerald, Ella
Grable, Betty
Hayworth, Rita
Holiday, Billie
Horne, Lena
Lee, Gypsy Rose
Lupino, Ida
Shore, Dinah

1920–1924

Bacall, Lauren
Callas, Maria
Charisse, Cyd
Dandridge, Dorothy
Day, Doris
Gardner, Ava
Garland, Judy
Turner, Lana
Vaughan, Sarah
Washington, Dinah

1925–1929

Hepburn, Audrey
Kelly, Grace
Monroe, Marilyn
Price, Leontyne
Sills, Beverly
Tallchief, Maria
Temple, Shirley
Thornton, Big Mama
Verdon, Gwen

1930–1934

Burnett, Carol
Cline, Patsy
Moreno, Rita
Rivers, Joan
Taylor, Elizabeth

1935–1939

Carroll, Diahann
Fonda, Jane
James, Etta
Lynn, Loretta
Moore, Mary Tyler
Slick, Grace
Tomlin, Lily
Turner, Tina
Wood, Natalie

1940–1944

Baez, Joan
Franklin, Aretha
Jamison, Judith
Joplin, Janis
Mitchell, Joni
Monk, Meredith
Ross, Diana
Sainte-Marie, Buffy
Streisand, Barbra
Tharp, Twyla
Warwick, Dionne
Wynette, Tammy

1945–1949

Anderson, Laurie
Bergen, Candace

Cher
Farrell, Suzanne
Midler, Bette
Minnelli, Liza
Norman, Jessye
Parton, Dolly
Radner, Gilda
Sarandon, Susan
Smith, Patti
Streep, Meryl

1950–1954

Carpenter, Karen
Roseanne
Winfrey, Oprah

1955–1959

Degeneres, Ellen
Estefan, Gloria
Finley, Karen
Goldberg, Whoopi
Madonna

1960–1964

Foster, Jodie
Houston, Whitney

1965–1969

Roberts, Julia

INDEX

Boldface numbers indicate entries. *Italic* numbers indicate illustrations.